THE SOUTH THROUGH TIME

A History of an American Region

Volume II

JOHN B. BOLES
Rice University

PEARSON
Prentice
Hall

Upper Saddle River, NJ 07458

Library of Congress Cataloging-in-Publication Data
Boles, John B.
    The South through time: a history of an American Region / John B. Boles.–3rd ed.
        p. cm.
    Includes bibliographical references and indexes.
    ISBN 0-13-183548-3 (v. 1) –ISBN 0-13-183549-1 (v. 2)
        1. Southern States–History. I. Title.

F209.B65 2004
975–dc21   2003052831

VP, Editorial Director: Charlyce Jones Owen
Senior Acquisitions Editor: Charles Cavaliere
Associate Editor: Emsal Hasan
Editorial Assistant: Shannon Corliss
Managing Editor: Joanne Riker
Production Liaison: Randy Pettit
Prepress and Manufacturing Buyer: Tricia Kenny
Director of Marketing: Beth Mejia
Art Director: Jayne Conte
Production Supervision and Composition: Preparé Inc.
Printer/Binder: RR Donnelley
Cover Printer: Phoenix

Dedicated to my teachers
at the public schools of Center, Texas, 1949–1961;
Rice University, 1961–1965;
University of Virginia, 1965–1969;
and, with love, to Nancy, David, and Matthew

Pearson Education Ltd.
Pearson Education Singapore Pte. Ltd.
Pearson Education Canada, Ltd.
Pearson Education—Japan

Pearson Education Australia Pty. Limited.
Pearson Education North Asia Ltd.
Pearson Educación de Mexico, S. A. de C.V.
Pearson Education Malaysia Pte. Ltd.

10   9   8   7   6   5   4   3   2   1
ISBN: 0-13-183549-1

Contents

Preface   xi

Acknowledgments   xiii

PART IV   THE COLONIAL SOUTH

Chapter 20
The Locus of Reconstruction   *373*

Lincolnian Reconstruction   373
Johnsonian Reconstruction   376
Congressional Reconstruction   382

Chapter 21
Getting on with Life   *386*

Reconstruction at the Local Level   386
Fiscal Reconstruction   393
The End of Political Reconstruction   396

Chapter 22
The Economic Tragedy of Reconstruction   *399*

Black Reconstruction   399
Black Sharecroppers   406
White Sharecroppers   413

Chapter 23
Old Verities Challenged   *418*

The First New South   418
Urban Growth   423
The Populist Challenge   429

Chapter 24
Change with a Southern Accent   *439*

Women in the Post–Civil War South   439
Progressivism, Southern Style   444
Industrializing the South   451

Chapter 25
Poverty and Race   *457*

Southern Farmers and the New Deal   457
The Nadir of Race Relations   466

Chapter 26
Cultural Riches in the Midst of Poverty   *477*

Emergence of a Southern Literary Tradition   477
Southern Music   486

Chapter 27
New Directions in Southern Politics   *492*

The Politics of Power   492
The Politics of Service   497

PART V   THE AMERICAN SOUTH

Chapter 28
The Dawning of a New South   *503*

The South and World War II   503
The Impact of Technology   509
Changes on the Face of the Land   512
Changes Down on the Farm   521
Emergence of the Sun Belt   526

Chapter 29
The Civil Rights Movement　　　　　　　　　　　　　　　*537*

Segregation Under Assault　　537
Civil Rights and Voting Rights　　555
The Solid Democratic South and Segregation　　562

Chapter 30
The Rise of the Republican Party　　　　　　　　　　　*566*

The Parties Switch on the Issue of Race　　566
The New Politics of Race　　570

Chapter 31
Southern Democrats and the Nation　　　　　　　　　*578*

The New Southern Democrats　　578
Democrats Discredited　　583
The End of Southern History?　　589

Chapter 32
Forever Southern　　　　　　　　　　　　　　　　　　*599*

The Search for Southern Identity　　599
Something Old, Something New　　604

A Guide to Further Reading　　　　　　　　　　　　　**610**
Index　　　　　　　　　　　　　　　　　　　　　　　**I-1**

VOLUME I

Contents

PART I   THE SOUTHERN COLONIES

Chapter 1
A Continent Invaded   *3*

The First South   3
The Old World Discovers the New   10
England Establishes a New World Colony   16

Chapter 2
A Tragedy in the Making   *27*

Maryland   27
Creating a Tobacco Economy in the Chesapeake Colonies   29
The Rise of Slavery in the Chesapeake Colonies   36

Chapter 3
Beyond the Chesapeake   *42*

Carolina: A Barbadian Colony on the Mainland   42
The Northern Portion of Carolina   48
The Latin South   51
The Founding of Georgia   55

Chapter 4
Colonial Societies   *62*

The Character of the Mid-Eighteenth-Century South   62
The Development of a Slave Culture   74
The Southern Backcountry   83

PART II   THE NATIONAL SOUTH

Chapter 5
International Entanglements   *91*

Virginia's First Quarrels with England   91
The French and Indian War and Its Consequences   93
British Imperial Adjustments to Victory   98

Chapter 6
An Uneasy Peace   *101*

The Social Context of Revolution   101
The Road to Revolution   107

Chapter 7
A War on Three Fronts   *119*

The Fight for Independence in the South   119
Slavery and the American Revolution   126
Indians and the American Revolution   128

Chapter 8
Southerners as Nation Builders   *132*

Creating the New Nation   132
The South and the Rise of Political Parties   143

Chapter 9
Land, Cotton, and Religion   *151*

The First West   151
The Old Southwest   155
The Rise of Cotton   159
The Great Revival in the South   163

Chapter 10
Nationalism Triumphant and Threatened   *170*

The Age of Jefferson   170
The War of 1812   176
The South Expands Westward   180
The Rise of Southern Self-Consciousness   182

PART III   THE SOUTHERN NATION

Chapter 11
An Agricultural Economy   *189*

The Rise of King Cotton   189
Cotton, Corn, and Commerce   199

Chapter 12
Diversity in the Old South   *206*

Southern White Society   206
Plantation Slavery in the Old South   213
Urban and Industrial Slavery and Free Blacks   231

Chapter 13
Beyond the White Patriarchy   *236*

White Women in the Old South   236
Slave Women   248
The Cherokee Tragedy   251

Chapter 14
The Southern Way of Life   *255*

The Distinctive South   255
Defending Slavery   261

Chapter 15
The Seeds of Conflict   266

The Beginning of Sectionalism   266
The Politics of Sectionalism   275
The Texas Question   277
The War with Mexico   281

Chapter 16
The Intractability of the Slavery Issue   283

Territorial Expansion, Conflict, and Compromise   283
The Compromise Breaks Down   287
The Kansas Affair   288
The Failure of Politics   297

Chapter 17
And the War Came   301

The Election of 1860   301
The Crisis of Secession   307
Fort Sumter   315

Chapter 18
War So Terrible   322

The War Begins   322
Antietam and the Emancipation Proclamation   332
A New Kind of War   336

Chapter 19
The Cause Lost   340

Gettysburg and Beyond   340
Confederate Defeat   345

A Guide to Further Reading   355

Index   I-1

Preface

For at least a half-century, southern history has been arguably the most robust field in the entire discipline of American history. The last twenty-five years have been especially fruitful, and a number of topics—slavery, women's history, the rise of sharecropping, the causes of Populism, and the impact of World War II, to name only a representative few—have undergone revisions in interpretation so fundamental that what was generally accepted just a generation ago is now rejected and replaced with a significantly different interpretation. This abundance of writing and the vigorous interpretative debates that have resulted have been exhilarating to professional historians, but much of the exciting new findings and viewpoints has been confined to scholarly articles and monographs, dissertations, and papers at academic meetings. The lay reader, the student, and the historian not specializing in the history of the South find it difficult to stay abreast of new writings.

Even specialists in the history of the South often discover that the amount of publications appearing in only a portion of the field, say slavery or the Civil War, is so extensive that it precludes keeping up with the entire field. And much of the most impressive new scholarship, methodologically innovative investigations of very narrow topics, is not fitted into the larger context of southern history. A reader must either remain content with, in effect, core samples of the new scholarship on the South or undergo a daunting regimen of reading in order to comprehend the larger contours of southern history. My purpose in planning this book was to be both inclusive and interpretative in my account. Perhaps having taught in Louisiana and Texas moved me away from seeing southern history as Virginia or Carolina writ large. My intended audience is the advanced undergraduate reader and the large public of lay historians—that plentiful group of well-read amateurs who are fascinated by the past. Of course, I hope that my academic colleagues approve of my distillation of a generation of scholarship and agree with my portrayal of the South's history, but even more do I hope that these pages whet the reading appetite of students and general readers. One of the real glories of American historical scholarship since World War II has been the field of southern history. I hope these pages reveal my debt to the work of two generations of diligent scholars and accurately represent their scholarship to a broad audience.

J.B.B.
1994

PREFACE TO THE SECOND EDITION

In response to the comments of faculty who have assigned this book in their classes, I have reformatted it into five parts and thirty-two chapters. I trust that will make it more compatible with course syllabi. The opportunity to revise also gave me the opportunity and incentive to read many of the new books and articles that have been published since I composed the original manuscript. As before, the riches of the writing in the broad field of southern history that I encountered were both inspiring and humbling. I hope that the resulting revisions, from the first chapter to the last, adequately indicate the methodological and analytical sophistication of this scholarship. I have added new material on women and gender, on race relations, on environmental history, on recent political developments, and on many other topics, trying to sharpen my interpretation and provide more illustrative examples. I believe the result is a more useful book. I hope that readers, especially students, will agree, and I look forward to their comments.

J.B.B.
1997

PREFACE TO THE THIRD EDITION

I have again corrected several errors, added new material based on additional reading and more recent scholarship, and tried to keep the book abreast of the exciting field of southern history. Southern history is such a dynamic enterprise that it is simply impossible for any one person to be fully aware of all the new scholarship, so I invite readers to send me suggestions for future revisions and to point out sections of the book that in their opinion need clarification or elaboration. Obviously I will use my own discretion with regard to such advice. My email address is *boles@rice.edu.*

J.B.B.
2003

Acknowledgments

I hardly know where to begin or end this section. For more than three decades, I have been reading in the field of southern history and attending the annual meetings of the Southern Historical Association. In addition, for a quarter-century I have had students, undergraduate and graduate, who have prepared papers, given in-class reports, asked probing questions, and often offered fresh ideas. I have benefited a great deal from the theses and dissertations of many graduate students. After two decades as managing editor of the *Journal of Southern History*, I have also read more than two thousand submitted manuscripts. From all of these sources I have learned. In addition, I have done specialized reading and research on topics that particularly intrigued me. However, in a book of synthesis such as this, I am most dependent on the scholarship of others. I hope that I have fairly, accurately, and succinctly borrowed from their work and sensibly related all the pieces to the whole.

My family aided me by putting up with my work habits and taking care of things I neglected, as did the wonderful staff of the *Journal of Southern History*—Evelyn Thomas Nolen, Patricia Dunn Burgess, Julia Cabanis Shivers, Patricia Bellis Bixel, Scott Marler, and Bethany L. Johnson. Allen J. Matusow, then dean of humanities at Rice University, and George E. Rupp, then president of the university, provided me with a year of released time during which a substantial portion of the original manuscript was written. A subsequent dean of humanities, Judith Brown, and the current president, Malcolm Gillis, provided me with another sabbatical during which revisions for the second edition were completed. Professors John C. Inscoe and Elizabeth Hayes Turner served as visiting managing editors of the *Journal of Southern History* during my absences, and their expertise and professionalism made the transition from editor to writer very pleasant indeed. My colleagues at Rice have created a very supportive research environment. Several graduate students assisted me in the final stages: Anya Jabour researched illustrations; Angela Boswell checked the bibliographical citations; Jennifer Payne corroborated obscure spellings; Jessica Cannon assisted with the index; and Melissa Kean helped with the proofreading. The dozen outside readers chosen by the press made valuable corrections and suggestions. Elizabeth Hayes Turner, Lynda Crist, Mary Dix, and Eric Walther read portions of the text and offered sound advice. The original text benefited from an extraordinarily careful reading by Evelyn Nolen, who saved me from many infelicitous phrases. I am particularly grateful for her assistance, both with this book and daily at the *Journal.* My younger son once asked me to dedicate this book to our family dog. I have resisted that well-intentioned request.

IMAGE CREDITS

Page 397, Alice Thiede; pages 403, 471, 557, Library of Congress; page 460, Walker Evans/Corbis Corporation; page 467, U.S. Information Agency; page 490, Elvis Presley Enterprises, Inc.; page 538, Elliott Erwitt/Magnum Photos, Inc.; page 582, Jimmy Carter Museum and Library

PART IV

The Colonial South

There are times in the life of a nation, as with some individuals, when tragedy seems to know no bounds. President Lincoln's death on April 15, 1865, from an assassin's bullet at Ford's Theatre was a bleak omen for a peace without rancor, and many southerners sensed that their last best hope for an easy reconciliation with the North died with Lincoln. That premonition proved to be correct, though no one at the time foresaw the curious twists events would take. Indeed, Andrew Johnson, the new president, could have been expected to direct a vengeful Reconstruction that would fundamentally transform class and racial relations in the South. But history seems to delight in upsetting expectations and confusing predictions, and contingency is more the rule than the exception. The decade or so following the end of the Civil War remains as difficult to decipher as it was important, and the South struggled with the unresolved problems of the era for more than a century. Probably no other period in southern history has been as insistently misunderstood. The general reading public has been slower to accept the conclusions of revisionist scholarship on Reconstruction than on any other topic in American history.

At the heart of Reconstruction was the continuing dilemma of working out the proper destiny of blacks within the nation. From the date of Lincoln's Emancipation Proclamation on, everyone understood that chattel slavery would be ended by northern victory, but few agreed on the role blacks should or could play in the restored nation. And how were the states of the defeated Confederacy actually to be brought back into the nation? What would be the political role of former Confederates? Were they to be punished for their actions, or nurtured back to support the Union? How would the South's war-ravaged countryside be restored and its economy be revived? What kinds of animosities between the regions, and between residents of the regions, might poison efforts at reconciliation? No one knew the answers to these questions in the spring of 1865, but the euphoria that warfare had finally ended was soon punctured by the pressing reality of insoluble problems. The era of Reconstruction is doubly tragic because solutions did not turn out well, and also—given the assumptions and passions of the age—no outcome that was possible would have been truly satisfactory in hindsight. The ultimate measure of that tragedy would be revealed in the history of the South over the next century.

For much of that time, the southern economy was mired in sharecropping and low-wage extractive industries, with most of the profits ultimately flowing northward. In many ways, the South was an economic colony of the North, and for two generations, it was politically impotent as well on the national stage. Poverty was rampant, racism harsh, politics irrational. This was the backward, colonial South, excoriated by northern critics and seemingly impervious to change or progress. Only at the end of the era, in the second quarter of the twentieth century, was there promise of a better tomorrow.

CHAPTER 20

The Locus of Reconstruction

LINCOLNIAN RECONSTRUCTION

By pedagogical convention, history courses and their accompanying textbooks divide the past into discrete units of time, but the flow of history is not as discontinuous as semester divisions imply. Slavery did not end, nor did the Old South, with Fort Sumter, or with the Emancipation Proclamation, or, to a very significant degree, even with Appomattox. Slavery did cease with the conclusion of the war, though the racial attitudes that underpinned bondage persisted, especially among white southerners, for generations more. Many of the values, economic assumptions, and mores associated with the Old South lingered for decades into the postwar period. And Reconstruction did not begin only after Appomattox. Instead, from the moment Union forces occupied regions of the South, the problems of Reconstruction were thrust upon the North even though no one had yet fully defined the nation's options or goals. Policy was makeshift, attitudes were in flux, and long-range social planning was overwhelmed by short-term military needs.

During the first summer of the Civil War, the U.S. House of Representatives had overwhelmingly passed the Crittenden Resolution, which specified that the purpose of the war was solely to defend the Constitution and to preserve the Union; the Senate had passed a similar resolution. But for Lincoln personally, and for the North collectively, the war aim gradually shifted, with the

Emancipation Proclamation evidence of that evolution. In the beginning, the status of the seceded states, not that of the slaves and freedpeople, was Lincoln's primary concern. After all, Lincoln accepted the Crittenden philosophy and was faced, as early as 1862, with the capture of significant portions of Louisiana, Tennessee, North Carolina, and South Carolina. Lincoln's attention at the time was focused on winning the war, not constructing an elaborate blueprint for remaking southern society.

Thus Lincoln's so-called Plan for Reconstruction never had the larger purpose of addressing the issues that came to bear so heavily on the nation after 1865. Rather, Lincoln wanted to weaken the Confederacy and strengthen the northern military effort, and he wanted to do so quickly and with a minimum of controversy. He also believed that there were significant numbers of former Whigs and reluctant secessionists in the South who might be wooed to the Union cause. Social engineering with regard to blacks was not only foreign to Lincoln's way of thinking in 1862, but it would also interfere with his war policy of attempting to attract influential white southerners to a Unionist position and thereby drain support from the Confederacy. He also realized that he risked alienating many in the North if he boldly redirected the war aim against slavery. So Lincoln's initial policy statements on occupied states should be seen in the light of winning the war, not reshaping the South.

By mid-1862, Lincoln had to establish some policy concerning the regions of Tennessee, Louisiana, and the Carolinas over which Union forces had control. He had long insisted that the southern states had no right to leave the Union, and, consistent with his theme of the inviolability of the Union, he sought to ease them back into a normal relationship with the Union as efficiently as possible. Thus, he appointed military governors in a stopgap measure to restore the captured states to the nation. Lincoln formalized this procedure on December 8, 1863, with the issuance of a Proclamation of Amnesty and Reconstruction, but again he was not attempting to solve all the outstanding questions regarding such matters as the rights of blacks, confiscated land, and Confederate debt that existed then and later loomed large as divisive issues. Lincoln was thinking pragmatically about the immediate problem of shortening the war when he offered a general amnesty to all white southerners who would take an oath pledging loyalty now and in the future to the Union, to the Constitution, and to the wartime proclamations (including emancipation) of the federal government. Lincoln assumed that most oath-takers would have in the recent past been supporters of the Confederate cause. Only high military and civil officers would be excluded from amnesty. All confiscated property except for slaves would be returned, and once the number of oath-takers equaled 10 percent of the number who had voted in the 1860 presidential election, that state would be allowed to draft a new constitution and elect state officials and members of Congress. There was, however, still the constitutional proviso that the U.S. Senate and

House ultimately had the privilege of judging the qualifications of their own members.

No further provisions were made for the freedpeople—for example, the right to vote and to equality before the law—although Lincoln expressed a hope that white southerners would pass laws guaranteeing permanent freedom and, perhaps for a few skilled, property-owning blacks, the right to vote. He issued a vague statement to the effect that he would not oppose southern legislation appropriate for a "laboring, landless, and homeless class." Southerners did not need instruction on devising laws to control the black population, as they showed in the infamous "Black Codes" at the conclusion of the war. Lincoln's, and the North's, opinion on the appropriate status of freed slaves proved to be in flux, but throughout the war, he occasionally mentioned colonization of free blacks as a solution to racial problems.

Arkansas, Louisiana, and Tennessee followed Lincoln's general prescription and in early 1864 formed loyal governments, only to have Congress reject their representatives and their electoral votes in the presidential election of 1864. Clearly Congress, unlike Lincoln, was acting on the assumption that the seceded states were still out of the Union, and Congress gave notice that it intended to be involved in any plan of restoration. The term Radical Republicans is more pejorative than descriptive, and the label covers a variety of viewpoints, but there was a loosely identifiable group of Republican Congressmen who fundamentally differed with Lincoln on how the conquered South should be treated. Vengeance was not their primary motive; rather, they intended to remold the South so a future secession would be impossible. They wanted to ensure that new leaders, who did not harbor secessionist sentiments and who were more in harmony with northern attitudes, would control the new state governments; and while they differed on exactly what guarantees and rights should be extended to blacks, they sincerely believed Lincoln had been too sanguine in his expectations of what white southerners might voluntarily do and too insensitive to the interests of the freedpeople themselves. A larger group of Moderate Republicans joined the Radicals in mid-1864 in an attempt to seize the Reconstruction initiative. On the Fourth of July, 1864, the Radical-Moderate coalition passed the Wade-Davis bill, co-sponsored by Senator Benjamin F. Wade of Ohio and Representative Henry Winter Davis of Maryland, outlining in some detail Congress's plan for dealing with the conquered South.

While Lincoln may have felt that whether the seceded states were really in or out of the Union was a "pernicious abstraction" that simply got in the way of restoring the Union proper, Congress operated on the assumption that the southern states in fact were out and should be treated by Congress as any other territory, whose admission or readmission to the Union was a matter of strictly Congressional jurisdiction. The Wade-Davis bill rejected Lincoln's lenient 10 percent plan and specified that a presidentially appointed provisional governor in each state should conduct a census. When a majority of the white males pledged loyalty to the Union, the governor should then call for an election of delegates to a new constitutional convention. Only those southerners who could swear that they had never been disloyal to the Union could vote for the constitutional delegates—a provision that obviously disenfranchised the overwhelming majority of all white southerners. Moreover, these new constitutions that were to be drafted would specifically have to abolish slavery, repudiate all Confederate and state debts, and take away the right to vote from former Confederate civil and military leaders. Then the national Congress would decide whether or not to accept these reconstructed states back into the family of the Union.

From the viewpoint of many northerners, who had seen the Union sundered by southern proslavery forces and who had suffered tens of thousands of deaths to restore the Union and end slavery, such an approach was merely sound policy to prevent a possible recurrence of the present difficulties—along with an understandable degree of repudiation and punishment meted out to the leaders who had precipitated the current unpleasantness. The Wade-Davis bill came in the midst of the 1864 presidential campaign, but Lincoln refused to let the Radical philosophy define either the party platform or his new policy. Disingenuously saying that the South could follow the Wade-Davis prescription if it wanted, but refusing to make it mandatory, Lincoln took advantage of the adjournment of Congress to kill the bill by use of a pocket veto, outraging the bill's authors.

Yet the Radicals had nowhere else to go that year, angry as they were, because they did not want to jeopardize Lincoln's election. After his reelection, they again pressed their claims, particularly to safeguard the results of the Emancipation Proclamation. Aware that the Constitution allowed slavery and that the Emancipation Proclamation was a war measure that could in theory be revoked when the war was over, Congress moved to change the Constitution by adopting the Thirteenth Amendment—abolishing slavery—in January 1865. It would eventually be ratified in December of that year by counting the votes of eight former Confederate states, accepted for the nonce as states for the purpose of ratifying the amendment. Consummate politician that he was, Lincoln sensed the ground shifting under him and seemed willing to compromise, to adjust, to experiment with Reconstruction in the Spring of 1865. But John Wilkes Booth's madness closed off that promising possibility.

JOHNSONIAN RECONSTRUCTION

Andrew Johnson became the seventeenth president of the United States following Lincoln's death. Like Lincoln, Johnson had been born in a border state and had been reared in poverty, but there the similarity ended. The school of adversity had taught Lincoln humility, humor, and flexibility; Johnson was tactless, unskilled in interpersonal relations, and stubbornly dogmatic. It is difficult to imagine a president faced with more intractable problems, or one less well equipped by temperament to handle those problems, than Andrew Johnson. Yet few anticipated his political clumsiness, especially those northerners who knew of his distaste for secession and his hatred of planter aristocrats. In the rough-and-tumble world of Tennessee politics, Johnson had risen to the Senate by galvanizing the yeomen of East Tennessee with his strictures against the cotton nabobs. But Johnson attacked the slaveholding aristocrats for reasons of class, not because he opposed slavery; in fact, he wished every white family had a slave or two to do their menial labor, and his attitudes toward blacks were conventionally racist. It was his antiplanter sentiment that made Johnson the only southern senator not to resign his seat after secession, and that dogged attachment to principle attracted Lincoln, who named Johnson military governor of Tennessee in March 1862 when Union forces captured part of the state. Johnson put Lincoln's moderate Reconstruction plans into action in Tennessee, and in 1864, even though he was a lifelong Democrat, the Republican party named Johnson to the ticket in a successful attempt to attract pro-war Democrats to the Republican camp. The strategy worked, Lincoln was reelected, and Johnson ascended to the presidency as a result of tragedy in 1865 with the South prostrate at his feet.

Johnson's abstract dedication to the idea of the indestructibility of the Union, which was why he felt secession was treason, also led him to disavow that the southern states had ever really been out of the Union; rather, they had been in an imperfect relationship to the Union, and they required only minor adjustments, as directed by the president, to restore them to the Union. Following that logic, and with little sensitivity to the interests of freedmen, Johnson moved swiftly to end the separation of the southern states. Within weeks, he recognized the governments that had been established in Arkansas, Louisiana, Tennessee, and Virginia under the terms of Lincoln's so-called 10 percent plan, then Johnson appointed military governors to the remaining seven states. On May 29, 1865, he issued a Proclamation of Amnesty offering a pardon to all white southerners who would now pledge present and future loyalty except for a minority of high-ranking military officers and civil officials and those persons who owned more than $20,000 worth of property—presumably the former slave-holding aristocracy who had perpetrated secession. These leaders of the Confederacy would have to receive individual pardons from the president himself.

The white population that received the general amnesty (no set percentage of the total population or 1860 vote was mandated) would elect delegates to constitutional conventions and draft new state constitutions that would expressly abolish slavery, revoke the ordinance of secession, ratify the Thirteenth Amendment, repudiate the state and Confederate war debts, and, when all this was done satisfactorily, elect a new state government and new members of Congress. The eleven ex-Confederate states, after some haggling, complied with Johnson's prescribed plan, and Johnson, pleased by the progress according to his terms, liberally handed out pardons to the erstwhile plantation elite with abandon, perhaps receiving some kind of psychological boost from the ability magisterially to dispense pardon to those he had formerly hated and to whom he had felt socially inferior. White southerners found Johnson surprisingly generous and seized the opportunity to regain control of their state governments and, it was reasonably assumed, the freedpeople. Dared they hope that the results of the defeat would not be as politically debilitating as they had at first feared? To the extent that Johnson fostered that sentiment among white southerners, he contributed mightily to his own fall and multiplied the tragedy of Reconstruction.

Many white southerners acted badly at this juncture of history, but our task is less to condemn them than to try to understand their motivations. Certainly most white men—the women we will address later—initially accepted the results of the war in the sense that they understood that slavery was now ended and that the South needed to get about the business of resuming normal life—planting crops, restoring commerce, reestablishing order, and solving immediate emergency situations of hunger and homelessness. As with any society facing crisis, white southerners turned to their putative leaders for guidance and authority, but they did so with a degree of discrimination. They largely recognized that secessionist firebrands were inappropriate for political office; in fact, such extremists now seemed culpable for the South's economic and political destitution. It was unthinkable to turn to nonleaders, to people so bereft of prewar or wartime respectability or prominence that they had not participated in any political or military capacity, for direction and leadership in such a momentous occasion as post–Civil War adjustment. Other prewar leaders were so clearly identified with the Unionist position that they in effect forfeited their right to govern afterwards. Elisha Marshall Pease of Texas, governor of the state from 1852 to 1857, was such a man. He had been a Unionist Democrat firmly opposed to secession, and he retired from public life rather than serve during the Confederacy. All was not forgotten after 1865, for he was rejected by postwar voters when he ran for the gubernatorial position again (although he later won military appointment as Republican governor in 1867).

But more moderate traditional leaders—men who before the Civil War had been Whigs and reluctant secessionists and who had sided with the Confederacy simply because they could not make war on their own state—were precisely the men southerners expected to help them deal pragmatically with the problems of defeat and restoration of normality. These neo-Whigs were exactly the people Lincoln and Johnson hoped would now rule the South, confident that their pledge of future loyalty would cement them to the cause of the restored Union. But to most northerners, the election of many former Confederates, even if they had been Johnny-come-lately-Rebs, looked suspiciously like southerners were trying to void the outcome of the war. How otherwise can the election of former Confederate vice-president Alexander H. Stephens as U.S. senator from Georgia be explained?

What strengthened this northern suspicion was even the moderate southerners' attitudes toward the freedpeople. As southern military fortunes had waned in the latter years of the war, influential Confederates had come to defend the idea of using slave troops who, by virtue of their military service, would earn their freedom, but beyond the press of felt necessity, few white southerners could imagine, much less countenance, a world in which blacks were the equals of whites. They might admit of individual exceptions here and there, and many of them came to advocate freeing slave men and drafting them into military service, but the mass of white southerners had so internalized a conception of black inferiority that they could not comprehend a world in which blacks were not disciplined and controlled by whites. They believed that blacks would not work, would not police themselves, and probably would not be able to survive physically without paternalistic (and not so paternalistic) white supervision. Blacks were deemed a permanently dependent class who by nature and justice should be subservient to whites. Antebellum hierarchical models of social relationships still obtained, with white males presumed to be rightly in authority of all blacks, their own wives, and their children—the family metaphor persisted from slavery days. Operating on these racist and hierarchical assumptions, whites saw as one of the first social priorities the development of governmental regulations regarding freedpeople that would replace planter authority with state authority.

The result, in 1865 and early 1866, was a series of Black Codes passed in one southern state after another. The freed blacks were guaranteed some rights that had not existed under slavery: the right to own property (except for a while they could not own land in Mississippi), sue and be sued in civil courts, have their marriages legally recognized, and testify in courts against whites in six states. But in no state could freedmen vote, hold political office, or legally bear arms. Freedom of assembly after dark was often limited. And most states severely restricted blacks leaving their jobs: Labor contracts bound them annually except under rare conditions. Vagrancy laws also allowed white officials to arrest blacks whom they judged to be insufficiently employed and, if the blacks were convicted, they could be bound over to work on chain gangs or contracted out to white planters. Through an apprenticeship system, black youths could be taken against their parents' wishes and assigned to labor for white planters. White southerners were moving only as far away from black slavery as they felt they had to, and northerners were quick to understand that the result was the wolf of slavery disguised by the sheepskin of vagrancy and apprenticeship laws.

The South's reaction to events is more difficult to explain than the North's. Even well-meaning, moderate southerners said and did things that seemed infuriatingly defiant to the North. Yet by their lights, the southerners had repudiated the secessionist extremists and turned, on the whole, to leaders who had been moderates in the past—men who had opposed secession. Again, in their view they had accepted the end of slavery and extended significant new rights to blacks, only holding back from full legal, economic, and social equality because to do so was absolutely unthinkable for the overwhelming majority of white southerners (and northerners, for that matter) in 1865. President Johnson neither requested nor demanded that they make further concessions, so most white southerners believed they had responded responsibly to the nation's mandate. To ask them to do more—either to repudiate all their wartime leaders or give up any more regulatory authority over the black population—white southerners saw as vengeful—trying to rub their noses in the stench of defeat. Defeated they were, and to some extent willing to accept modifications in their society, but they insisted on salvaging their honor. But it was precisely this southern unwillingness to acknowledge the dishonor of their late cause, to accept the moral right of northern victory and the moral wrong of slavery, that caused northerners to read in southern actions a streak of insolence that threatened to undo the results of the war. That the North would not countenance.

Congress met again in December 1865, and it had to face the Johnson-ordained southern state governments and the newly elected southern congressmen. Complicating the issue of the Confederate tinge to the fresh congressmen was that the South, now that slavery had ended and the three-fifths compromise was void, would have a larger congressional representation. Fearful that the fruits of victory were slipping away, the Radicals in Congress established a Joint Committee of Fifteen—six from the Senate, nine from the House—to review the credentials of the southern congressmen and to evaluate Johnson's Reconstruction policies and advise Congress on alternative policies. The committee quickly moved to change the direction of Reconstruction, first by refusing to seat the southern congressmen and secondly by moving to continue the Freedmen's Bureau, which had been established in March 1865 to protect the rights of and supply food and clothing to refugees and freed slaves. Johnson, who felt southern whites should be left alone to handle the freed-people, vetoed the bill; Johnson believed Reconstruction policy was wholly within the jurisdiction of the executive office. The Radicals, observing the harsh Black Codes, could well imagine what leaving the status of ex-slaves to southern whites meant, and their judgment that Johnson was inadequate to the task of truly reconstructing the South instantly hardened.

The bill to renew the Freedmen's Bureau had widened its authority to include the settling of labor disputes (intended to address the problem of the vagrancy laws but often working to the opposite effect, pressuring blacks to obey white labor contracts). On April 9, 1866, Congress passed a Civil Rights Act that bestowed citizenship upon blacks and granted them the same civil rights that whites enjoyed; again, a direct response to the extremes of the Black Codes. When Johnson vetoed this bill too, Moderate and Radical Republicans coalesced to override the veto and then repassed the Freedmen's Bureau bill. Realizing that these guarantees of the rights of freedpeople depended upon who controlled Congress and were hence potentially impermanent, the Joint Committee of Fifteen began work to put the guarantees in the Constitution, beyond the vagaries of congressional or court opinion. Violence in the South toward blacks gave impetus to the movement to amend the Constitution to protect the rights of all citizens.

A small race riot occurred in Norfolk in mid-April, 1866, but at the end of April and for several days in May, a full-scale race riot broke out in Memphis, and after almost a week of mindless violence forty-six blacks and two whites were dead, about eighty persons were injured, five black women were raped, and black churches, schools, and homes were torched. Southern whites pointed the finger at "uppity" blacks—black males in Union uniforms were especially irritating to former slaveholders—and felt force was justified to establish boundaries around acceptable black behavior; northern whites saw only intransigent former rebels determined to keep blacks down. Throughout the early spring, constitutional amendments were discussed, revised, and introduced to the Senate. In April, the Joint Committee of Fifteen drafted an amendment to protect the citizenship of blacks; debate was intensified by news of the violence in Norfolk and Memphis. On June 13, 1866, the Fourteenth Amendment passed Congress and three days later was submitted to the states, including the southern states, for ratification, which would not come for more than three long years. This amendment proved to be a turning point for Reconstruction.

The first section of the Fourteenth Amendment extended citizenship to all American-born blacks and said that no state could "abridge the privileges or immunities of citizens ... nor shall any State deprive any person of life, liberty, or property, without due process of law; nor deny to any person within its jurisdiction the equal protection of the laws." The intent of this section was to redress the Black Codes that so grossly deprived black individuals of "equal protection of the laws," though it later was applied to "legal persons" such as corporations. Section 2 did not require that states allow freedmen to vote, but it did mandate a proportionate reduction in the congressional representation of those states that did not allow all males the franchise. Actually, southern states would rather accept the congressional penalty than enfranchise their former slaves. Section 3 disallowed from federal or state political office, or from participation in the electoral college, any person who had once taken an oath of office to support the federal Constitution and then had supported the Confederacy. This disability, which affected practically all southern leaders, could be removed only by a two-thirds vote of both houses of Congress, not by individual presidential pardon. Section 4 specifically validated the federal debt and invalidated all Confederate debts, including claims for compensation for slaves.

The final section gave Congress the power "to enforce, by appropriate legislation" the provisions of the amendment.

The Fourteenth Amendment represented a series of compromises between the Moderate and Radical Republicans. It did not, for example, actually give the vote to black males, nor did it disenfranchise for years every person who had supported the Confederacy. Had the southern states ratified the amendment promptly, Congress would have seated their representatives, the states would in effect have been readmitted to the Union, and Reconstruction would have essentially been over. Tennessee, which had been captured early by Union forces, was the home of many Unionists. Led by strongly pro-Union governor W. G. "Parson" Brownlow, Tennessee promptly accepted the amendment. But every other former Confederate state found Section 3, which disfranchised most former Confederate leaders, an insurmountable stumbling block. Because many such leaders had been reluctant secessionists and now accepted the results of the war, albeit grudgingly, white southerners interpreted Section 3 as unnecessarily vindictive.

President Johnson, disputing Congress's role in Reconstruction, advised the southern states not to ratify the offending amendment, advice they were only too glad to accept. For most of the North, however, southern opposition seemed absolutely intolerable intransigence, and when, in the midst of the ratification debates, another bloody race riot occurred in New Orleans with over 150 casualties, northern public opinion turned solidly against the South. President Johnson knew that the fall congressional elections would determine his fate, so during the summer he and his friends organized a National Union Party in an effort to unite the handful of Conservative Republicans, northern Democrats, and southern whites. He then set out to campaign for his supporters in a number of key northern cities, but the more he traveled and talked the more intemperate he became. In the end, Johnson made a sorry spectacle of himself, discrediting his office and his cause. When the votes were tallied, the Republicans had veto-proof majorities in both houses of Congress. A new phase of Reconstruction was about to begin.

CONGRESSIONAL RECONSTRUCTION

Emboldened by their success in the fall elections, the Radicals in Congress decided to strike while the iron was hot. Even before the newly elected congressmen took office, the old Congress voted to move the convening of the new Congress up from December 1867 to March 4, 1867. Then, just two days before the old Congress expired, on March 2, 1867, it pushed through three measures that would determine subsequent events. Many Radicals wanted a thorough reshaping of the South—giving black males the right to vote, disenfranchising former Confederates for the foreseeable future, providing public education for blacks, and confiscating former rebel land and redistributing it to freedpeople. But Moderates were unwilling to go so far, restrained by racism, considerations for the rights of property ownership, and the basic commitment to majority rule in the various states. The resulting Military Reconstruction Act was a blend of constantly shifting Radical and Moderate elements, for neither group could control Congress on its own.

The Military Reconstruction Act declared that no legal state governments existed among the ten seceded states. (Tennessee had already accepted the Fourteenth Amendment and been readmitted to the Union.) While respecting the state boundaries, the act divided the South into five military districts, each under the control of a military commander backed by a small contingent of troops. The military commanders were authorized to use military tribunals in place of the civil courts (which were controlled by local whites) if necessary to maintain order and protect the "rights of persons and property." But the primary task of the district generals was to prepare the states under their authority for readmission to the Union. Several steps were required. First, the military commander would conduct a registration of voters, including all black adult males and white adult males who were not disqualified from officeholding by the terms of Section 3 of the Fourteenth Amendment. (About 10 percent of whites were so disenfranchised—perhaps another 25 percent did not vote for reasons of apathy or disgust with the whole political process.) The voters additionally had to take a complex loyalty oath to the Union. After this was done, the military commander was to call for the election of delegates to state conventions that would then draft new state constitutions, one provision of which had to be the extension of suffrage to black males. Once these constitutions were ratified by the registered loyal voters, then elections could be held for new state governments. If the new state legislatures accepted the Fourteenth Amendment, and if Congress accepted the new state constitutions, the states would be restored to the Union once the Fourteenth Amendment had been ratified by the mandatory three-fourths of all the states.

Quite obviously, Congress did not intend to leave the post–Civil War settlement up to ex-Confederates. But Congress's determination to thwart President Johnson and to guarantee that the South underwent at least minimal change was also revealed in two other acts passed on March 2, 1867. The Tenure of Office Act prevented the president from removing from office without the consent of Congress persons whose original appointment had required the consent of Congress. This act was intended to protect Secretary of War Edwin M. Stanton, the only member of Johnson's cabinet who favored congressional Reconstruction and supported protecting and expanding the rights of blacks. Congress also passed the Command of the Army Act, which required that all military orders issued by the president go through the commanding general of the army (Ulysses S. Grant), whose headquarters were restricted to Washington and who could not be removed from office or assigned elsewhere without Senate approval. This act was meant to prevent Johnson from subverting the intentions of the Military Reconstruction Act. These three acts were frontal assaults on the president's power to influence Reconstruction.

As some Radicals had predicted, several southern states chose not to act, preferring to remain under military rule rather than write new constitutions enfranchising the blacks on the often correct assumption that racist military officers would probably deal more favorably with southern whites than with freedpeople. The Military Reconstruction Act had no mainspring to push events forward, a failure that three supplementary acts passed later in 1867 were intended to correct. These additional acts required the military commanders to initiate the actions aimed toward the drafting of reform constitutions. By 1868, six of the seceded states—Arkansas, North Carolina, South Carolina, Louisiana, Alabama, and Florida—had met the prescribed procedures and were readmitted to the Union. And with the mandatory approval of the former Confederate states, the Fourteenth Amendment was declared ratified on July 28, 1868. The remaining four states—Mississippi, Virginia, Georgia, and Texas—were back in by 1870. By then Congress had passed and submitted to the states the Fifteenth Amendment, guaranteeing black men everywhere in the Union the right to vote; the last four states to be reconstructed had to accept the Fifteenth as well as the Fourteenth Amendment before they were readmitted to the Union.

By mid-1868, Johnson's ability to act as a roadblock to congressional Reconstruction had been eliminated. As early as 1867, Radicals had feared Johnson would willy-nilly turn control of the South and the freedpeople back to the former Confederates, and Radicals were suspicious that he would use the power of his office to delay, weaken, and destroy congressional plans for Reconstruction. And Johnson did replace several military governors who favored Radical policies with conservatives who predictably sided with white state leaders. On several occasions, half-baked charges and preliminary impeachment attempts were begun, but although Johnson clearly opposed the Radical version of Reconstruction, he was hardly guilty of "high crimes and misdemeanors," the Constitutional grounds for impeachment. Then in August 1867, Johnson rebuffed Congress by removing Secretary of War Stanton from office without congressional approval. Technically, because Stanton had been appointed by Lincoln, his position was not protected by the Tenure of Office Act, but in the superheated political atmosphere, Johnson seemed to be flagrantly defying the will of Congress. House Republicans, glad to have a pretext to attack the obstructionist Johnson, rushed through a resolution of impeachment.

The trial in the Senate elicited harsh attacks and bitter recriminations. There was no doubt that Johnson cared little about the plight of the freed slaves, vilified the Radicals, and undermined congressional Reconstruction at every opportunity, but by the Constitution's precise terms, he was not guilty of impeachable offenses. Johnson's lawyers clearly were superior to the Grand Old Party (GOP) impeachment managers when it came to the fine points of the law, but more important than technical arguments was the doctrine of separation of powers. Moderate Republicans might have been incensed at Johnson's recent policies, but they feared creating a precedent whereby a two-thirds majority of Congress could impeach any president with whom it disagreed on policy matters. The whole principle of the separation of powers, not just Johnson's plight, seemed to be at stake. Moderate members of the GOP made overtures to Johnson, seeking some sort of compromise. Johnson must have listened, because he conducted himself with uncharacteristic dignity thereafter and promised no longer to be obstructionist toward congressional Reconstruction policies. The implicit understanding worked. On May 16, 1868, enough Republican senators voted with the Democrats to prevent, by one vote, Johnson's conviction on impeachment charges, though there is evidence others were prepared to oppose his conviction if their vote was necessary.

Johnson was spared impeachment, but in his successful attempt to win support, he had agreed no longer to oppose congressional Reconstruction and had forwarded to Congress the newly written constitutions of Arkansas and South Carolina. After his ordeal in the Spring of 1868, Johnson ceased being a significant factor in Reconstruction. His own party rejected him as its nominee for the presidency later that year, while the Republicans, determined to win, nominated the popular war hero, Ulysses S. Grant, who had no known political ambitions or skills. The Republicans waved the bloody shirt to remind voters of the human costs of the late war, while Democratic candidate Horatio Seymour, courting western farmers who had agricultural debts, campaigned in favor of issuing cheap money—the so-called greenbacks. But the memories of the recent intersectional hostilities were stronger than the attraction of greenbackism, given Grant's martial fame and the Republican rhetoric about a Confederate resurgence. The Grand Old Party captured the White House in the fall of 1868 to go along with its control of Congress.

CHAPTER 21

Getting on with Life

RECONSTRUCTION AT THE LOCAL LEVEL

For the white South, however, the real issues were, and had always been, local. The devastation and demoralization of the war had embittered many white southerners, but most of them primarily wanted to put their lives together again after four years of conflict. Hardly a southern family stood untouched by death or injury in 1865, and slaveholders had lost their 2.5 billion-dollar investment in slavery, a severe economic loss despite the gain for humanity. The southern banking system was ruined, the South's railroads were almost beyond repair, and tens of thousands of homes, barns, bridges, public buildings, colleges, and churches were destroyed or badly damaged. Fences were gone, tools and wagons worn out, hundreds of thousands of head of livestock had been butchered to feed both invading and friendly armies. Land values plummeted too. But the economic losses were matched by the public despair. Gaunt Confederate veterans, thousands of them with missing limbs, returned home to find their farms in ruins, their cattle and hogs gone, and their wives utterly exhausted by the ordeal. Military defeat and economic devastation dealt a severe psychic blow to many white soldiers, demoralizing them and causing them to question their manliness because of traditional role models that portrayed fathers as protectors and providers—at both of which they had failed.

Often the women felt more frustrated than the returning Rebel soldiers, who at least had found the opportunity to express their feelings on the battlefield. Women without number had suffered loneliness, hunger, and endless toil trying to hold body and soul together while maintaining the family farm, supervising the slaves, and feeding their own children. Time and again, soldiers from both armies had marched through, taking whatever foodstuffs they needed despite the pleas of the distraught women. On many occasions, soldiers had treated southern women with respect and sensitivity; just as often, and especially so in the last years of the war and even more especially for those in the path of General William T. Sherman's march to the sea, Union soldiers had taken their anger for the horrors of the war out on southern women by cursing them; wantonly destroying crops, farm animals, and household larders; smashing household furnishings even to the extent of cutting portraits out of their frames; and purposely humiliating the women—whose smoldering anger Union troops rightfully translated as unrepenting support for the Confederacy—by scattering their clothes and undergarments. Little wonder that many postwar travelers commented on the unforgiving scorn southern white women often held for occupying Union troops.

Though the return of peace found the South in a state of shock, most white southerners recognized that there was much work to be done. Husbands and wives had to come to know one another again, a task complicated by the wrenching ordeal through which both had lived. Many women had lost their husbands and had to scramble to make a living by taking in boarders, teaching school, or becoming seamstresses or milliners. Farms had to be repaired, crops put in the ground, and livestock replenished. As a result of the armies having brought together thousands of horses (for transportation) and hogs (as a mobile food source) from across the South, several epidemic diseases—especially equine glanders and hog cholera—emerged and soon spread into farm animals, killing thousands of horses and pigs. Cattle fever also spread, again killing thousands of livestock. These animal epidemics severely impacted both farm income and the supply of meat for human consumption for a decade following the conclusion of the war. The economic and transportation infrastructure of the South also had to be rebuilt and marketing systems reestablished. How would blacks be controlled, disciplined, set to work, in the new age? How would whites get along without slaves to do much of the menial labor? How could demoralized white men be made to feel in command again, their habits of control renewed? No one had all the answers, but as the white South began to pull itself together, a consensus began to emerge. Some acceptance of the new political realities must be made. When first Lincoln and then Johnson outlined a process for restoring the seceded states within the nation, calling for men to pledge their present and future loyalty to the Union, moderate southerners accepted the call. Few were willing to repent for the past, to condemn their Confederate experience, but more, understanding that they had fought a good fight and had lost, were ready to accept the consequences of the war and follow the direction of the president. Grudgingly acknowledging that slavery had ended but unsure of how much equality had to be extended to freed people, southern whites after mid-1865 were ready to face the future on their own terms.

The southern white leaders elected according to the terms laid out by Lincoln and Johnson were not drawn from the tiny minority of wartime Unionists, but rather from the ranks of Confederate political and military officialdom, though few of them had been secession leaders. The great majority had been reluctant secessionists at best, and though they had served the Confederacy, they had joined the cause only after the election of Lincoln or after their states had actually seceded. These leaders, moderates in the southern universe, now sought to restore the southern economy. They understood the need for diversification away from a complete dependence on cotton. Consequently, they passed legislation to encourage banking, factories, and railroads. In fact, in their willingness to issue bonds to support railroad construction and in other ways promote industrialization, the moderate southern leaders of the Johnson governments acted almost identically to the later so-called Radical state governments, as well as the modernizing New South spokesmen who led the South after Reconstruction. The moderate ex-Confederate leaders were not diehard secessionist fanatics with their heads buried in the sands of the past. Their tragic flaw was that they could not conceive of a world in which blacks were allowed substantial control of their own lives. Nor could they repudiate in the abstract the principles of the Confederacy. The result was a public relations debacle, and the North felt justified in rejecting Johnsonian Reconstruction.

Once Reconstruction came under the control of Congress in the spring of 1867, many southern whites lost interest in state politics and turned their concerns inward, to devising plans to determine exclusively local politics and to managing their farms with free black laborers. Racism toward the freedpeople had increased significantly during the Civil War, and the animosity would be ratcheted up several notches in Reconstruction. While most antebellum whites had considered blacks a permanently inferior race, relations with their own slaves, and especially with certain favorites, whites had felt were quite cordial. Most slaves interpreted differently the merits of slavery, and when the opportunity offered itself during the war, they ran away by the thousands to join the Union liberating forces, sometimes threatening to overwhelm the logistical capacities of the army. Whites, who had convinced themselves that blacks were happy, natural slaves who felt affection at least toward their owners, were shocked by this turn of events. Rather than see it for what it was, evidence of slaves' hunger for freedom, many whites saw the slaves as ungrateful wretches, repaying whites for the care, food, and clothing provided during slavery times by running away to the Yankees the first chance they had. Disbelief was replaced with anger as again and again slaveholders saw their most favored slaves—the house servants, overseers, drivers, and artisans—leave the plantation in search of freedom. This anger escalated beyond general resentment to wrath toward black soldiers wearing the uniforms of the North. Military defeat, economic deprivation, and then the division of the postwar South into military districts turned the region into a pressure cooker of political racism.

Racism lay behind the writing of the infamous Black Codes, racism undergirded the southern opposition to the Fourteenth Amendment, racism made the Military Reconstruction Act of 1867, with its enfranchisement of black males and disenfranchisement of many whites, anathema even to most moderate southern whites. Many boycotted the elections mandated for the drafting of new state constitutions, and the constitutions were opposed more for their origin and authorship than for their content. In fact, these constitutions were in many ways the best the southern states had ever had; they modernized the systems of governance, outlawed imprisonment for debt, more fairly apportioned representation, made more offices elective, and provided for public education. But most southern whites never gave the new state governments a chance, for they were interpreted as the dictatorial results of a vindictive, race-mixing northern tyranny. Moderate northern hopes for a resurgence of prewar Whiggism were dashed by the southern opposition, giving credence to the Radical belief that black participation in southern politics, mandated and protected by Congress, was the only way to safeguard the fruits of victory in the South.

Of course there were anti-Confederate, consistently pro-Union whites in the South, predominantly in the mountainous regions, but their numbers alone were hardly sufficient to build a Republican party that could govern the region. Many of these loyal whites had been nonslaveholders, had opposed the political hegemony of the planters, and had even organized peace societies during the Civil War. To the white majority in the South, the loyalists seemed traitors to their native region. Few of these true Union loyalists had enjoyed political prestige or positions of leadership in their states, but after the war they were often joined as supporters of the Republican party by former lowcountry planters, native urban merchants, and political newcomers from the North. These groups have, in the mythology of southern Reconstruction, been consigned to the lowest level of hell. Native southern whites who joined the Republican cause were labeled "scalawags," a term originally referring to scrawny, inbred ponies on the Scottish island of Scalloway and later used to describe worthless, trash livestock in general, and the suggestion was that scalawags were shiftless ne'er-do-wells who opportunistically sold out their southern heritage for a mess of political porridge from the Republicans. Despite the prevalence of this image in American popular culture, it grossly misrepresents the social origins and political outlook of the native whites who cooperated with the Republicans.

During the middle decades of the antebellum period, the Whig party had competed equally with the Democrats for political control of the South. Primarily the party of the large planters and the numerically small urban merchant and banking class, the Whigs had been more reformist, more modernizing in general approach than the Democrats. With the national demise of the Whig party, southern Whigs became men in search of a party, and some had flirted with Know-Nothingism. In the secession crisis, most former Whigs had recommended caution, had favored the Constitutional Union movement, and only most reluctantly had supported the Confederacy after secession, Fort Sumter, and Lincoln's call for volunteers made fence-sitting politically impossible. From this prewar party of wealthy planters and urban commercial interests came the leadership of the scalawags. On the whole, these were hardheaded, practical men who understood that the postwar South's infrastructure had to be rebuilt, its economy and social conditions stabilized, its agricultural system reestablished. Their considered judgment was that cooperation with the Republicans, in part at least in order to control the mountain loyalists and the black masses, was necessary if the region were to regain prosperity. Moreover, they found the national Republican party position on economic matters compatible with their prewar Whig philosophy. A surprising number of former Confederate officers—including General James G. Longstreet, Lee's "Old War Horse"—eventually joined the southern Republican party. Lincoln and Johnson put much faith in a reemergent Whig movement to restore the South to order and the Union; they simply overestimated the numbers of former Whigs. As a group, the southern whites who became Republicans were neither vindictive nor unusually corrupt. They wanted the South—a reformed South—to rise again.

Another group of whites living in the South who became natural allies of the Republican governments were newcomers to the region. According to southern mythology, these interlopers were unprincipled opportunists who came south carrying all their worldly belongings in a cheap duffel bag made of carpet. These so-called carpetbaggers have been portrayed as economic vultures, flocking to buy up war-damaged plantations auctioned for nonpayment of taxes and conspiring with traitorous mountain Republicans and unscrupulous scalawags to use ignorant black voters to govern the defeated South for their private advantage. The stereotype fit some northern men who moved to the South, but it presents a glaringly distorted view of history. For one thing, the image often did not discriminate between men who had come before the war and those who came much later, and it misrepresented the motives of most who came in the immediate aftermath of the conflict.

Northern men had long come south because they saw the region as a land of opportunity. Many hoped to become cotton planters, while others brought their skills in commerce or merchandising or banking or industry to the South because they recognized those skills were in short supply there. In other words, for the same reasons people went west, they came south. The motive was the American dream of getting ahead. During the Civil War, several thousand northerners bought land in the South and set up farming, expecting northern work habits and Yankee thrift would reap them fortunes and, by the way, teach southern whites and blacks modern agricultural methods. Northern arrogance was often defeated by the vagaries of cotton growing, and southern workers of both races resisted Yankee industry, but southerners often welcomed the capital and job opportunities northern landowners provided. Southern cities and industries, such as the textile mills, had long been dependent upon northern marketing and technical know-how.

This northern migration to the South accelerated in the immediate aftermath of the war. For one thing, many former Union soldiers who had served in the region liked the climate; they saw firsthand the fertile soil, towering forests, evidence of rich deposits of coal and ore, and streams and rivers available both for water power and inexpensive transportation. They also understood that the region was capital-starved and short of people with entrepreneurial talent. A streak of northern arrogance was present—the South needed "northern" skill and direction to prosper. But the basic motive was traditionally American—to make money. Northern land purchasers, would-be cotton planters, merchant capitalists, and captains of industry came south in the spirit of the times to make money, not to crush, defraud, mongrelize, or humiliate the already defeated South. They recognized the Republican party, with its national business orientation, was more conducive to their interests, and they allied with loyal southern whites in support of the Reconstruction governments. Only when their economic ambitions faltered—northern agricultural experience did not guarantee success with cotton, and the animosity of local southern whites sometimes deprived carpetbaggers of business opportunity—did many northerners in the South, out of a sense of desperation, turn for their livelihood to political careers. Southern white Democrats called the result an attempt to impose alien rule on the poor, defeated South.

Republicans in Congress and loyalists in the South knew that without almost complete disenfranchisement of all former Confederates—a step some Radicals desired but most Republicans realized was counter to the basic American commitment to majority rule—there was no way white Republicans could maintain control of southern state governments. So the issue of black enfranchisement was as much one of Republican political expediency as high principle. There were a few moderate southerners who acknowledged that some blacks, educated and propertied, might indeed deserve the vote, and some Republicans had racist doubts about the propriety of blacks voting. But for most southern white Republicans, no matter how recent their conversion to the party, the black voter, disciplined and controlled by the party, was essential to the reforming of the South. Nothing else so infuriated the majority of southern whites as the spectacle of former slaves voting while former Confederate leaders were prevented from holding office; nothing else so poisoned race relations and made native whites absolutely determined to resist Republican rule with whatever means at their disposal. The result was a reign of violence unmatched in American history. White southerners conducted what can only be called a prolonged terrorist campaign against black voters. White men whose sense of command and authority had been defeated by military loss and economic collapse often relished the opportunity of disciplining and controlling blacks, finding thereby a means of reestablishing their persona of manly leadership and white supremacy.

The prevalence of black voting and its impact on southern politics was greatly exaggerated at the time, and inflated perceptions of "black rule" have been perpetuated by racist novels like Thomas W. Dixon's *The Clansman* (1905) and the movie it inspired, *Birth of a Nation* (1915). Popular history books with titles like *The Angry Scar* and the cinematic masterpiece *Gone with the Wind* have continued the stereotypical views. But nowhere did blacks rule the South; nowhere was a black elected governor (P. B. S. Pinchback served for five weeks [December 12, 1872 to January 13, 1873] as governor of Louisiana after the duly elected governor, Henry C. Warmoth, was impeached); nowhere did the number of black officeholders match their percentage of the population, nowhere did blacks control a state legislature, nowhere was legislation passed that flagrantly discriminated on behalf of blacks. During the entire course of Reconstruction, only fourteen blacks were elected to the U.S. House of Representatives, only two to the Senate—and both senators were distinguished and educated men.

Most of the approximately two thousand black officeholders served at the local level—sheriffs, justices of the peace, county tax collectors, members of city councils and boards of aldermen, and the like. The blacks elected to more elevated offices had disproportionally been free before the Civil War and had, as artisans, small businessmen, ministers, and teachers possessed demonstrable skills, including literacy, that prepared them to be credible officeholders. In the immediate aftermath of Reconstruction, blacks who had been free before the Civil War also dominated officeholding, particularly in states such as Virginia, South Carolina, and Louisiana where sizable free black communities had existed, but as political mobilization and organizing spread, former slaves gradually came to dominate local black officeholding, and they proved capable students of politics as well. Many of these freedmen had gained leadership ability through wartime service in the Union army or by working in some capacity for the Freedmen's Bureau as soon as the war was over.

Black voting did not unleash on the South a torrent of corrupt, ignorant, self-serving black politicians who rode roughshod over common decency, honesty, and fairness. Taken as a whole, black officeholders were overwhelmingly literate, and a very significant number either before the war as free blacks had been property holders, or after the war became so as freedmen. Most black politicians before they entered politics had careers that provided them with experience readily applicable to public service. The largest single prepolitical occupation was that of minister, with teacher second, followed by carpenter. Hundreds more had been storekeepers, merchants, editors, lawyers, barbers, blacksmiths, masons, and other artisanal trades. Still, most black officeholders represented very modest wealth, but nearly all represented the interests of their constituencies effectively, honestly, and with a concern not to flagrantly irritate conservative whites. But, of course, with black officeholders as with the Reconstruction constitutions, it was the mere principle of black participation that drove some southern whites almost to frenzy.

Many black officeholders—perhaps as many as 10 percent—were the victims of Reconstruction violence, and after the end of the era, some left the region. Harry M. Turner, a Methodist minister and member of the Georgia legislature until blacks were excluded in 1871, after his office-holding career ended began a lifelong campaign for blacks to migrate to Africa. Turner made four trips to Africa and lectured widely both in this country and in England on behalf of black nationalism and black culture. Other blacks moved North, or gave up politics entirely. Still others had to submerge their sentiments, only to emerge briefly during the Populist movement in the 1890s. Others regained their voices to protest the efforts to disenfranchise blacks at the end of the century. In several southern states—North Carolina and Texas, in particular—an influential smattering of black officeholders persisted until the very end of the century. Black participation in southern politics essentially ended by 1900. But especially for several years toward the end of the era of Reconstruction, hundreds of blacks served their region in politics, and although they were often disparaged by their contemporaries and forgotten by historians, they performed ably, without vengeance, and helped craft new state constitutions that were far better than the ones they replaced.

FISCAL RECONSTRUCTION

White southerners then and since have wanted to point accusing fingers at the so-called black-dominated Reconstruction governments for outrageous corruption. And, as is always the case in the course of human affairs, there were examples of moral and judgmental lapses. In the lower house of the South Carolina legislature, where for two years blacks were dominant, were found obvious cases of misrule, corruption, and extravagant misuse of public funds—two hundred porcelain spittoons purchased for the state house, for example. Louisiana also exhibited corruption, though of course, political chicanery and venality were as traditional in that colorful state, before Reconstruction and since, as a good roux. But Reconstruction-era corruption looks different when examined more closely. Corruption had existed in the all-white Johnson state governments; it was much worse in the Democratic urban political machines of the North, such as the notorious Tweed ring in New York City; and the southern Democrats, after they regained control of the South, exceeded the worst examples of Reconstruction corruption. Placed in historical context, in an era of loose political morality, the Reconstruction state governments were relatively clean. For example, the total cost of congressmen voting themselves stationery allowances that somehow paid for hams and champagne pales alongside the subsidies paid railroad companies for track never built, but in the latter case the malefactors were the rail magnates, not the Republican legislators. The magnates pocketed the profits and defrauded the states both before and after Republican Reconstruction. This was the baroque age of corporate corruption nationally, and it is manifestly unfair to single out southern Republicans or black officeholders for the failures of capitalism rampaging out of control.

Government expenditures went up significantly during Radical Reconstruction. However, this was evidence not of misgovernment but rather of attempting to meet the extraordinary needs of the times. Government buildings, bridges, and the like had to be rebuilt and enlarged. And the scope of government responsibility expanded, pushed in part by the black politicians, to provide needed hospitals, asylums, orphanages, and prisons for society. Eleemosynary institutions were also provided for the black populace, a flagrant misuse of funds in the eyes of most whites. But the most important reform of the Republican state governments was the development of systems of public education for all the children of the states. Southern whites were occasionally skeptical of public schools, even for their own children, but the idea of educating black children seemed hopelessly inappropriate. State governments floated bonds to raise the funds necessary to build the needed railroads and public works, and due to the unsettled economic situation, they had to offer northern creditors outrageous discounts, sometimes more than 50 percent of the face value of the bonds, to raise the required moneys. Any fair examination of state budgets of the South during the period will conclude that most of the expenditures were justified and indeed represented more responsible government than had existed in the antebellum era. That did not preclude southern white conservatives, looking for reasons to attack Republican rule and black participation, from attacking the regimes as extravagant examples of misrule that had to be ended.

Along with the justifiable increase in state expenditures came an increase in taxation. Again, given the real social needs of the region, these taxes were understandable. But southern whites, still suffering from the economic disruption of the war and struggling with reestablishing the profitability of their farms, considered the rise in taxes as but another example of Republican fraud, waste, and malfeasance. The majority of southern whites in the antebellum South had paid practically no taxes except for an inconsequential poll tax. The tax structure was not intentionally progressive, for most taxes were levied on property. However, the slave-holding minority owned most of the property in the form of the slaves, which meant that the majority, nonslaveholders, had a very light tax burden, and, given the lingering Republican ideology from the era of the American Revolution, they considered taxation a close cousin to tyranny. But the Thirteenth Amendment had ended slavery, forcing the tax burden to shift much more heavily toward land.

This meant, in effect, a significant increase in the tax liability of small farmers, most of whose property was land. To make matters seem worse, wartime destruction had resulted in a drastic lowering of the assessed value of southern farm lands, which in turn required that the tax rate increase. Small farmers—the overwhelming majority of the population—would have felt a double whammy even if there had been no need to increase total state revenues to meet the postwar exigencies. The justifiable expansion of government services exacerbated the tax bite the farmers felt, which likewise magnified the outrage directed toward the Reconstruction governments. Farmers not yet completely recovered from the war simply did not have the cash to pay their increased taxes, and the newspaper listings of farms being auctioned because of back taxes became a constant reminder to white Democrats of what they considered the injustice of Republican rule. The real rise in taxes also struck a devastating blow against the mountain Republicans, who never anticipated that the end of slavery and the provision of public schools would have so disproportionate an impact on them. The Republican state governments lost badly needed loyal white supporters because of taxation, many of whom felt somehow double-crossed. No one was really to blame; the times were simply out of joint.

The reality of higher taxes and black participation in the political process and the perception of unparalleled corruption and scandal in state government were a tragic combination that ultimately doomed Reconstruction. The white majority in the South determined to end Republican rule. In no state did a majority of the whites support the Reconstruction governments; only through the disenfranchisement of supporters of the Confederacy and the organization of black voters were the Republicans able to maintain tenuous control of state politics. In three states (Louisiana, Mississippi, and South Carolina), blacks were a majority of the population, and in several other states there were significant black minorities that—with the addition of relatively few white voters—could have controlled state elections. White Democrats saw that the path to regaining political hegemony lay through intimidating their opponents (especially the blacks) and reacquiring the right to vote. The latter came without bloodshed, both through presidential and congressional pardons. The basic national commitment to democracy meant that even the most radical in Congress had no stomach for depriving the majority of southern whites of a voice in their government. The pardoning process was substantially complete even before the Amnesty Act of 1872 restored political rights to the 150,000 or so ex-Confederates who remained unpardoned, leaving only several hundred outside the political system. In many regions of the South, political organizing by the white Democrats was sufficient to wrest political control away from the Republicans, especially after higher taxes caused leakage from GOP support.

THE END OF POLITICAL RECONSTRUCTION

Native whites also used violence, social ostracism, and economic pressure to persuade many so-called scalawags and carpetbaggers to withdraw from politics, change parties, or leave the region. Much of this political pressure was localized and ad hoc, but southern Democrats also developed racist organizations intended to terrorize Republican whites and especially black voters. The best known terrorist group was the Ku Klux Klan (KKK), first organized in Pulaski, Tennessee, in 1866, apparently as a social club. But its possibilities for harassing blacks after the beginning of Radical Reconstruction led to a transformation of the organization, and by 1867, provisions were made for various local dens, linked hierarchically from neighborhood to county to state to the entire South, with leaders bearing frightening titles like Grand Cyclops and Grand Wizard. Secret rituals, ceremonies, and the distinctive wearing of white sheets as ghost-like disguises contributed to the effect, and with a kind of mystical fervor, the KKK members roamed the South under cover of dark, disrupting Republican political rallies, threatening Republican officeholders, and intimidating black voters with torches and burning crosses, random beatings and killings, and several massacres.

A virtual guerrilla war erupted; hundreds of blacks were murdered for exercising the right of assembly or for voting. Other vigilante groups emerged, with euphemistic names like rifle clubs and the Red Shirts; their purpose was to drive the blacks out of politics. Grant, the Radicals in Congress, and even some decent people in the South were outraged by the lawlessness, and Congress in 1870 and 1871 passed a series of Enforcement Acts aimed to quell the KKK and similar organizations, such as the Knights of the White Camellia. Eventually, Grant declared nine counties in South Carolina to be under martial law in 1871, suspended habeas corpus, set up special courts, and sent in troops. This had some effect, but the KKK simply went underground and suspended its activities. The southern Democrats had essentially achieved their purpose and were able to ease up on their campaign of brutality, though the potential of violence remained to keep blacks in line after the federal presence was withdrawn. The North never had the willpower to smash southern violent opposition. To have done so would have required a commitment of troops and money less than a decade after the end of the Civil War, and would probably have been impossible without a suspension of Constitutional rights for the majority of southern whites.

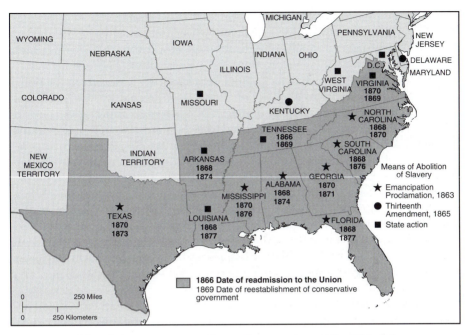

After the war: reconstruction and restoration. (Alice Thiede)

The North also had its own political and economic agenda to pursue, its public was tired of involvement with the South, and northern racism limited the willingness to interfere with southern racial mores—the North became morally exhausted and turned "the black problem" over to the South. In part, this followed from an ideological attachment to the idea that freedom alone should be sufficient to solve the freedpeople's dilemma. And, in part, northern business interests became disillusioned with the lack of progress in "reconstructing" the South and the continuing violence and disorder so disruptive to business investment. Powerful northern interests were willing to sacrifice the rights of the blacks in order to buy stability. Given the terrorism and the erosion of northern support, loyal southern whites wilted away from the Republican party, black political participation plummeted, and resurgent, pardoned southern white Democrats regained control of their state and local governments. Republican rule ended as early as 1870 in Virginia, North Carolina, and Georgia; in Texas, in 1873; in Alabama and Arkansas, in 1874; in Mississippi, in 1875; and in South Carolina, Louisiana, and Florida, in 1877.

Political Reconstruction ended that year in the resolution of the famous disputed presidential election of 1876. Samuel J. Tilden, the Democratic candidate, won 184 electoral votes, 1 vote short of victory, and Rutherford B. Hayes, the GOP candidate after scandal-plagued Grant had been refused the nomination, held 165 electoral votes. At stake, though, were the disputed 19 electoral votes of the last three states with Reconstruction governments, Florida, South Carolina, and Louisiana (and also one disputed electoral vote in Oregon, which Hayes had won and which involved a legal technicality). There is no way of knowing how many potential black voters were frightened away from the polls, but Tilden surely won the majority of the white vote that was cast. Because southern whites considered the elimination of black votes both normal and acceptable, they believed the Democrats had won the states fair and square. In the confusion and fraud that resulted, however, each state reported competing Democratic and Republican vote tallies. With but one additional vote, Tilden would become president and break the Republicans' sixteen-year hold on the White House. To settle the dispute, Congress established a special fifteen-member Election Commission consisting of five members from the House, five from the Senate, and five from the Supreme Court—eight Republicans and seven Democrats. Every issue was decided by the same eight-to-seven vote, with the result that when the dust had settled, Hayes had picked up all twenty votes and was declared the winner. So while the Democrats stole the original election, the Republicans stole the recount.

Yet the Democrats peacefully accepted the results, evidently because of additional bargaining that took place behind the scenes—in the Wormley House hotel, to be precise. Apparently, the Republicans promised that if Hayes were accepted, he "would deal justly and generously with the South," code language meaning he would remove the few remaining troops from the region and acquiesce in the Democratic takeover of the state governments of South Carolina and Louisiana. (Florida had been won by the Democrats several months earlier.) Moreover, Hayes or his agents promised that he would not use his patronage to defeat Democratic candidates in the region, would support federal appropriations for rebuilding much needed levees along the Mississippi River, and would support a southern route for a second intercontinental railroad. In return, Democrats pledged to recognize the basic rights of blacks as outlined by the Thirteenth, Fourteenth, and Fifteenth Amendments (the last of which gave black males the right to vote), to stop the quasi-warfare against southern Republicans, and to agree to Republican James A. Garfield as Speaker of the House. Neither side ultimately lived up to the complicated secret bargain, but with the troops removed and Democrats in control of all southern state governments, Reconstruction had really ended. Perhaps it hardly needs saying that southern Democrats also reneged on their promise to protect the constitutional rights of the blacks.

CHAPTER 22

The Economic Tragedy
of Reconstruction

BLACK RECONSTRUCTION

What had the South's 4 million blacks gained by the Civil War and Reconstruction? The easy answer is that slavery was destroyed, although neither the Emancipation Proclamation nor the Thirteenth Amendment ended bondage with the ease and finality of a magic wand. Slavery slowly disintegrated over the course of the Civil War, but vestiges of the institution lingered into Reconstruction and long afterward in sharecropping and racial segregation. Slavery began dying by degrees as soon as Union troops began moving into the South, and as soon as wartime mobilization drew planters away from the plantation to the battlefield. Union armies were the symbol of liberty, enticing slaves to risk escaping to freedom. The breakdown of plantation authority emboldened slaves, long schooled in caution, to dare to take that risk. The reality that slaves desired freedom and would act to gain it pressured the Lincoln administration to change its policies, leading to the Emancipation Proclamation.

An important part of slave culture had been learning ways to push at the boundaries of white discipline to gain advantages, but to do so in a manner that would minimize the chances of punishment. Slaves became masters of dissembling, hiding their real motives and feelings as they pushed and delayed, cajoled and played the childlike Sambo to persuade their master or mistress—or wear them down to the point of giving in—to make an accommodation. No one misunderstood that ultimate power stood with the whites, but every white, when honest, also understood that slaves carved out a degree of autonomy over their workplace that could be transgressed by the master only at the cost of trouble. Whites misread the slaves' accommodationist mien and their dissimulation as genuine contentment with their bondage. Whites would occasionally acknowledge that other planters' bondspeople were unhappy and might run away, but they seldom could see the same discontent in those they called their own people. Perhaps some ignorant field hands, they reasoned, duped by abolitionist propaganda, might run away; certainly the trusted mammy or the head driver would never do such a thing. Confederate mythology preserved a special place in its pantheon of heroes for the trusted slave who hid the family silver from the Yankees or stayed on the plantation to the very end, trying to void emancipation by pledging eternal loyalty to their sainted white owners.

Some slaves did show such faithfulness to the old order, or at least to their old owners, just enough to give some substance to the myth, and stories of the faithfulness of former slaves were especially treasured during Reconstruction when it seemed to white southerners that all the old verities of racial etiquette were being overturned by freedpeople. But many more slaves ran toward freedom when a good opportunity offered itself than stayed as the loyal retainers that supported the myth. Plantation discipline eroded with the planters off to war and with wives, younger sons, or elderly men left in control—few had the mark of authority the male head of household had exhibited, and slaves took advantage of the cracks in the command structure. Even so, slaves knew how important it was to be cautious, to avoid precipitate action that could result in capture and punishment. Armies moved forward and sometimes retreated. One had to be careful about running away to join the Union because if the Bluecoats retreated, one could be left stranded. As one elderly slave remarked to a conquering Union soldier in North Carolina in 1862, "We've long wished you well, but we daren't show it!"

Many slaves, sensing toward the later days of the war that the end was near, preferred to wait safely for Confederate defeat rather than make a possibly dangerous dash toward freedom. Yet despite all the experience that urged caution, tens of thousands of slaves left their plantations and fled to the Union armies. Long before Lincoln, Congress, or the army had developed a policy for dealing with refugee slaves, the slaves, by the press of their numbers, forced northern authorities to come to terms with their presence. Union armies very early in the war captured Confederate territory, and, especially in the sea islands of South Carolina, the wealthy white planters rushed to the interior leaving their slaves to the invading Union forces. Here, too, as with runaways, the Union had to come to grips with the basic question of Reconstruction: What was to be the proper role of blacks within the captured, and later defeated, South?

The Civil War was barely a month old when three slaves escaped to Union forces at Fort Monroe, Virginia, near where the first blacks had been introduced to Virginia in 1619. General Benjamin F. Butler, knowing the Confederates had been employing them as war laborers, accepted the runaways, called them contraband, and refused to return them as the normal operation of the fugitive slave laws provided. Yet Butler's ad hoc decision did not set national policy, and for months to come, commanders in the field were left to improvise. In June, General Henry W. Halleck decided to return fugitive slaves to their owners, but on July 9, the House resolved that it was not the duty of federal troops either to capture or to return them. A week later, General Winfield Scott requested permission to allow the owners of slave runaways to seek and recover their claimed property behind Union lines. The Crittenden Resolution of July 22, which stated that the war was not being waged for the purpose either "of overthrowing or interfering with the rights or established institutions" of the seceded states, seemed to confirm the Halleck-Scott position. Then on August 6, Congress passed the first Confiscation Act, authorizing the federal government to seize any property used to aid the rebellion and to free slaves employed either as soldiers or workers against the United States.

Neither the northern public nor Lincoln as president was ready to endorse emancipation as a war aim; Lincoln was restrained by his racism, conventional for the era, and by his concern that any emancipationist noises by the North might convince the skittish border states to lurch toward secession. But the realities of war made Lincoln's arm's-length stance toward slavery increasingly awkward. What was to be done with slaves who came to Union forces or were seized by the advance of Union troops? On August 30, 1861, General John C. Frémont declared Missouri to be under martial law and proclaimed that all the slaves belonging to persons resisting the Union were free. This clearly went beyond the Confiscation Act and threatened the fragile war consensus in the North, so Lincoln quickly ordered Frémont to observe the narrow emancipation parameters of the act.

Still, it did not seem right to turn away slaves seeking their freedom, and military officers became more aware of how the South's use of slave laborers in effect increased the number of white men ready for combat. Both military necessity and morality suggested that policy had to evolve. In October 1861, General Thomas W. Sherman was authorized to "employ fugitive slaves in such services as they may be fitted for," but the secretary of war made sure that the order not be construed as a general arming of slaves for military duty. And when, the following March, General David Hunter issued a proclamation freeing slaves in Georgia, Florida, and South Carolina, Lincoln promptly countermanded the proclamation. The legal demise of slavery would be as unplanned and evolutionary as its origins had been in the seventeenth century.

In May 1862, General Hunter, elaborating on the orders given General Sherman, began calling upon blacks to form what he called the First South Carolina Regiment, but again the idea of organizing black troops went beyond what Lincoln deemed possible, and he ordered the regiment disbanded. As emancipationist sentiment gained ground in the North, aided by the activities of prominent black abolitionists, and the number of slave runaways threatened in places to inundate Union forces, Lincoln and Congress were forced to experiment with policy. On March 13, 1862, Congress prohibited the use of military force to return runaways. With Lincoln's support, Congress on April 10 promised compensation to the former slave owners of any border state that developed a plan of gradual emancipation.

Less than a week later, slavery was abolished in Washington, D.C., and on May 20, the United States agreed to cooperate with England in suppressing the international slave trade. The pace accelerated; on June 19, 1862, Lincoln signed a bill abolishing slavery in the territories, and in less than a month, Congress passed a strengthened Confiscation Act that proclaimed free all those slaves belonging to disloyal masters who found themselves, either because the slaves had escaped to the Union lines or because the advancing army had occupied the region where they lived, within territory controlled by northern troops—whether the slaves were directly involved in the war effort or not. As the Union slowly began to capture and hold sections of the South, it created pockets of black freedom. For those geographical regions, Reconstruction began months and years before the end of the war.

It was in this context, within a week of the revised Confiscation Act, that Lincoln advised his cabinet that he intended, come January 1, 1863, to issue a general Emancipation Proclamation declaring free all the slaves within rebellious states, hence extending emancipation in the abstract far beyond the confines of conquered southern territory. His plan was publicly announced on September 22, 1862, after the abortive southern invasion of the North was squelched at Antietam. That announcement shifted the whole stated purpose of the war, eliminated any chances the South might have had of garnering significant British support, heartened northern abolitionists, and horrified white southerners even as it infused an almost millennial hope among the slaves. But after the announcement, it became impossible to continue the restraints against freedmen serving as military laborers and even soldiers, and the federal government had to begin making plans for solving the problem of what to do with freedpeople in the South.

During the autumn of 1862, Lincoln began to permit the enlistment on a limited basis of black troops. General Butler in New Orleans promptly mustered a troop composed of free men of color and ex-slaves; General Rufus Saxton reconstituted the South Carolina regiment that General Hunter had earlier formed only to have Lincoln dismiss. From the viewpoint of white southerners, nothing more symbolized the revolutionary—the horrendous—potential of defeat than the specter of armed black troops. White soldiers' response to their presence was nearly frenzied; a group of black Union soldiers, attempting to surrender, was massacred by Confederates at Fort Pillow, Tennessee, in 1864. When the Confederates defined black troops as slave insurrectionaries subject, if captured, to reenslavement or death, Lincoln responded that for every black sol-

After the Emancipation Proclamation freed slaves fled to the Union army. (Library of Congress)

dier so treated, a white rebel soldier would be executed. Whether it was Lincoln's threat or better judgment on the part of the Confederate government, southern troops as a matter of official policy never killed black soldiers in violation of the code of war. Even so, there were clearly incidents—Fort Pillow being the worst—where black soldiers were not allowed to surrender.

By late fall of 1862, the number of fugitives coming into Union lines increased as northern forces pushed deeper into the South. In November, General Ulysses S. Grant attempted to deal with the growing number of refugees in Tennessee by appointing Chaplain John Eaton, Jr., to be in charge of fugitives. A refugee camp was established at Grand Junction, and later moved to Memphis, where shelter, food, and a modicum of medical attention were supplied. Able-bodied freedpeople were hired out to loyal whites who had leased abandoned plantations. Henceforth, the emancipators were to deal with the refugee problem by adjusting the plantation system to the new realities of wage labor. This technique had been pioneered earlier in the vicinity of Port Royal, South Carolina, and the prospects of combining social control of the blacks with the profitable production of staple crops proved too enticing for northern reformers to resist. Seeing therein a way to teach newly freed slaves middle-class Yankee habits of self-discipline and industry, hardheaded military commanders and visionary reformers agreed on the utility of this gradual transformation of dependent slaves into independent farmers.

But Yankee notions of efficiency clashed with black notions of autonomy, and utopian dreams foundered as misunderstanding flourished. Freedpeople in general were never given the wherewithal to prosper—they had neither land, draft animals, tools, nor capital—and racism put limits on the patience of whites. In several locations, such as the Davis Bend, Mississippi, properties of Jefferson Davis and his brother Joseph, freedpeople were allotted land directly, planted food and cotton, and practiced virtual self-government under the watchful eye of army-appointed superintendents of Negro affairs. Despite localized success stories, most freedpeople who farmed behind Union lines did so as wage laborers on white-leased property.

At the very end of the war, on March 3, 1865, the Freedmen's Bureau (officially the Bureau of Refugees, Freedmen, and Abandoned Lands) was established, and it was primarily responsible for handing out emergency supplies to destitute freedpeople (and whites left impoverished by the war). But the disposition of abandoned lands was also one of the responsibilities of the Freedmen's Bureau, and during the final days of the war several thousand blacks were settled on land abandoned by southern planters, particularly in the coastal regions of South Carolina and Georgia, and throughout the South, the federal government had gained control of hundreds of thousands of acres of abandoned land. On a limited scale, in isolated regions, freedmen were granted ownership of small parcels of land. Partly because of this, and partly because of a much-discussed speech by Representative Thaddeus Stevens of Pennsylvania advocating that ex-slaves be given forty acres, the "forty acres and a mule" rumor swept across the South. However, there never was an explicit plan to confiscate and redistribute the property of wealthy planters—the respect for the Lockean right to property ownership prevented the federal government from seriously entertaining the idea of widespread land confiscation. Even the relatively small-scale efforts undertaken by the Freedmen's Bureau to provide land to freed slaves were aborted by President Johnson, who ordered all property returned to the Confederates, whom he pardoned with abundant generosity. Johnson's actions ended the best hope most freedpeople had for genuine financial independence.

So the return of peace in the late spring of 1865 found blacks betwixt and between slavery and real freedom. Legally they were slaves no longer, but they did not possess the necessary means to begin life anew as free farmers. They faced a southern white population more racist than ever and determined to regain through legal means—the infamous Black Codes—almost complete white control of the blacks in their midst. While blacks were soon introduced to political participation, they just as soon learned that their Republican friends did not have the power to protect them from southern whites' violence. In fact, for most blacks what was happening in Washington or in the state capitals was of less moment than immediately local events. Black men and women knew that by the fiat of law they were free, but precisely what that freedom meant in real-life terms was yet to be decided.

One of the first acts of many slave couples was to formalize their marriages. Whites supported such action because they believed it would limit so-called black promiscuity and support Christian morality. In fact, most blacks who as slaves had lived in what were essentially common-law marriages did settle down to one partner once they had a spouse. But freedpeople on their own seized upon formal, legal marriage as a way of cementing their marriage relationships, demonstrating their freedom, and strengthening their supervisory ties to their children. In time, the solidity of black households gave black parents a way successfully to protest in court the white practice of apprenticing black children who ostensibly were unsupervised.

The great majority of southern whites had experience dealing with blacks only as slaves, and most blacks had dealt with whites only in the unequal position of slave to master. A strict racial etiquette had placed firm boundaries around acceptable black behavior, and blacks had been socialized to observe those restraints. Whites still considered blacks to be a permanently dependent class and thus subject to white authority and direction. Blacks understood that freedom meant breaking down old barriers, but southern whites manned the barricades to prevent as much erosion of old habits as possible. Northern free black Robert G. Fitzgerald, teaching in North Carolina, saw freedmen going hungry because white storeowners refused them credit simply for voting Republican. Blacks wanted to experiment, to push at the old limits, but not to risk retribution any more than they had to. Yet what did freedom mean if it did not change the old ways of behavior? The ability to choose one's place of work seemed essential to freedom, but whites read such freedom of choice as detrimental to crop production and as evidence of black irresponsibility. The ability to travel, to move about, seemed to blacks at the heart of personal liberty, but again whites saw it as inefficient vagrancy.

Black Codes, with their labor contracts and antivagrancy provisions, struck against these simple manifestations of black freedom. Blacks did want to travel about, but the roaming was mostly neither random nor the result of laziness. Thousands of black families had been broken up and dislocated by the whites moving their workforces out of the way of invading Union armies, and many blacks were searching for loved ones from whom they had been separated. Blacks also desired to move to southern cities and towns, expecting to receive from the Freedmen's Bureau both provisions and protection from white violence. Action that seemed rational to blacks seemed to whites symptomatic of black irresponsibility, and what seemed proper and orderly to whites was to blacks an unaccceptable vestige of slavery. Whites expected to remain in control of black labor by use of antivagrancy laws and the apprenticing of black children. From the white viewpoint, agricultural recovery depended on blacks remaining steadily at work on farms from early spring planting through the final picking of cotton that occurred as late as December.

Early Reconstruction was a time of confusion, anger, and violence, but it was also a poignant time when whites and blacks were experimenting with how to act toward one another. How far could a black move away from earlier models of deferential behavior without being charged with uppity behavior that might bring retribution? How much equality in demeanor was a white required to accept? Such matters as terms of address, deciding on housing arrangements and crop choice, hiring and being hired, were fraught with problems even for cautious blacks and well-meaning whites. Who gave way on a crowded town sidewalk? How would plantation mistresses, never accustomed to the hard chores of cooking and washing, survive without easy access to black workers? Some mistresses kept up a brave front as they struggled to get the housework done, while others whined and cursed their fate. But for most blacks, as for most whites, the central problem was economic. The whites owned the land, the draft animals, and the tools, but what good were these without laborers? The freed slaves were propertyless, but their labor potential gave them some bargaining power. The crux of black-white relations during the first few years of Reconstruction was working out an acceptable arrangement for blacks to work on the land growing the self-same crops, but as people possessed of some degree of freedom. The ultimate result was the system of sharecropping that came to dominate the southern countryside for over half a century, involving in time the majority of white farmers as well as black.

BLACK SHARECROPPERS

In some ways, black emancipation was a mighty revolution, but in other ways, the more things changed, the more they stayed the same. The same actors were present, carrying many of their old attitudes with them, the climate and soil were unchanged, cotton still loomed as the great money crop, and the power relationships between blacks and whites remained unequal. With the war over and thoughts turning to making a living, people of both races primarily thought of the old staple-crop standbys: rice, sugar, tobacco, and especially cotton. Convinced that blacks would not work unless forced to, whites experimented with methods of exploiting them just short of slavery. Whites accepted with resentment that freedpeople now had to be paid wages in cash, but landowners expected the blacks to continue dwelling in the former slave quarters grouped together for ease of supervision near the big house and to continue working together in the fields in gangs under the direction of white overseers or foremen. Sometimes the wages were paid monthly (perhaps $10 per month for an adult male), but usually, at least half the wages were payable after the crops were harvested.

The system of cash wages proved unsatisfactory for everyone involved. Aware that without a stable workforce available through harvest, their prosperity was in jeopardy, whites required their farm laborers to sign contracts that severely limited their freedom of movement, often specifying the landowner's right to control the laborers' working hours and determine their chores and requiring strict obedience to the landowner. The contracts also contained limited guarantees of the rights of blacks, and for that reason—and because they shared the local whites' attitudes both toward blacks and toward the necessity of having workers in place throughout the crop year—Freedmen's Bureau agents often helped to persuade or force reluctant freedpeople to sign the agreements and keep their contractual obligations. Even some southern whites came to admit that the generally despised Freedmen's Bureau served the whites' own interests. Blacks obviously resented the heavy overtones of bondage associated with such labor contracts and work routines and resisted by shopping around for landowners who gave them marginally better terms.

In the midst of the postwar labor shortage, this limited ability of blacks to choose their employers gave them considerable leverage, and they used it to gain greater autonomy. After all, they understood too well how much the emerging system smacked of slavery, and they resisted precisely those arrangements that most affected personal freedom. Blacks pushed for the right to live apart from the old slave quarters, out from under the landowner's watchful eye. They wanted their houses on separate acreage, scattered around the landowner's property, so they could grow their crops as an independent family unit, not as members of work gangs laboring on common fields. Moreover, because landowners devised numerous methods of shortchanging illiterate blacks when payday came—even firing them a few days ahead on trumped-up charges and telling them they had thereby forfeited their wages—freedpeople preferred payment in the form of being allowed to keep a fractional share of the crop they produced. In a sense, blacks then felt they were paying a portion of their family agricultural output as rent rather than receiving a wage from the landowner. By receiving a specified percentage of their harvested crops, their skill and hard work would be rewarded.

Landowners, too, were quickly dissatisfied with the wage system that first evolved. Because it gave freedpeople no incentive to work hard, a great deal of costly, irksome supervision was required to maximize production. Occasionally, blacks departed in midseason, with or without their cash wages, leaving the landowner precariously short of manpower to harvest his crops at the most labor-intensive period of the year when temporary workers were impossible to hire. Primarily, however, white landowners—the former planters—desired a shift away from cash wages because there was a drastic shortage of money in the postwar South. Planters, even wealthy ones, were land poor and simply had no ready cash (and could not borrow any) with which to pay monthly wages. (There was a severe shortage of credit in the South, even for large landowners who needed money for wages. In the antebellum South banks had readily accepted slaves as collateral for loans because they were movable and there existed ready

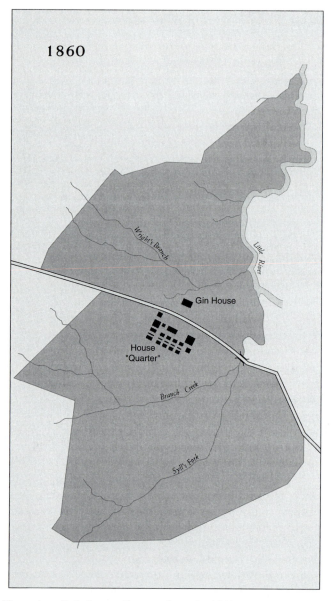

The Barrow Plantation, Oglethorpe County, Georgia, 1860 (approximately 2,000 acres). The maps on this page and the following, based on drawings from *Scribner's Monthly*, April 1881, show some of the changes brought by emancipation. In 1860, the plantation's entire black population lived in the communal slave quarters, next to the

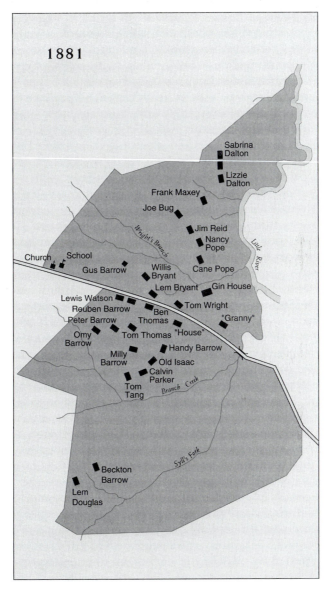

The Barrow Plantation, Oglethorpe County, Georgia, 1881.
white master's house. In 1881, black sharecropper and tenant families lived on individual plots, spread out across the land. The former slaves had also established their own school and church.

markets for them. But after the Civil War planters no longer owned blacks, and cautious bankers would not accept real estate as collateral—the National Banking System even prohibited loans backed by land. Hence cash-strapped landowners were stymied.) For that reason, they welcomed the development of a system of payment in crop shares, with settlement after harvest, for not only did it lessen their cash requirements, but it also placed an equal share of the crop risk on the freedpeople. Moreover, without really ever openly acknowledging it and despite all their expectations of black laziness and irresponsibility, whites discovered that blacks could and would work productively without substantial supervision when they and their families were allowed a measure of incentive. Ironically, what blacks desired and pressed for—the right as individual families to control their own labor on plots of land assigned to them—whites began to accept, too, as the best possible compromise. Sharecropping emerged as another form of mutual accommodation.

Most black families, without an opportunity to possess their own land in fee simple, came to see their assigned sharecropper's "farm" as the next best thing, for at least they had more control over their own work schedules and had privacy in their home life. The landowners' prewar unified plantation became, in effect, a collection of small farms cultivated (but not owned) by individual black families. In addition to their greater freedom, the ex-slaves in the years immediately after the war received more than twice as high a proportion of the agricultural output of the large agricultural units (an aggregate of many sharecroppers' plots, the new form of the old plantation) as they had in the days of slavery. In fact, considering the total standard of living, the basic material income of these blacks increased by about a third as a result of emancipation, though their plight may have later worsened as a consequence of the long-term decline in the price of cotton that occurred in the last decades of the nineteenth century. But what freedpeople valued more than their slight increase in income was their increased control over their own lives, over their patterns of consumption, over their leisure time.

On their individual agricultural units of from twenty to forty acres, black families could choose to maximize output by keeping the women and children in the fields as during slavery times, or they could accept a somewhat lower material standard of living by withholding a portion of the family members' labor. On the whole, black families preferred to withdraw the mother from the field except at periods of peak labor needs and let her perform more the role of mother and housewife than that of field hand. Similarly, children were exempted from some labor when public schooling was available. Because blacks chose, for cultural reasons, to withdraw some percentage of their labor force from the fields, at least for portions of the year, the total productivity of the black population—as compared with slavery times—decreased somewhat. From all accounts, blacks showed an intense interest in education, with children, their parents, and white-haired elders crowding the primitive classrooms hungry to learn to read. Robert G. Fitzgerald opened a Sunday School in Virginia in August 1866 in part to teach freedpeople to read, and he reported that "in a few days pupils were coming 5 or 6 miles to school. The 1st Sabbath I was here I had near 200 Sabbath scholars. They walk 10 miles some of them …. " Literacy was associated with freedom and getting ahead economically. Again Robert Fitzgerald observed that "they tell me before Mr. Lincoln made them free they had nothing to work for, to look up to, now they have everything, and will by God's help make the best of it." Southern whites condemned blacks' pursuit of learning as inappropriate for their station in life, an unnecessary government expense, and an impediment to maximum agricultural output. Blacks eventually learned the sad reality that in an impoverished, racist society, literacy alone did not promise progress. Blacks did, though, show great ingenuity and determination in augmenting their farm income: Men got occasional day labor for wages, women took in laundry, old folks and children contributed their mite. By such pooling of efforts, black households managed somehow to find money to support their schools, their churches, and other social organizations.

Sharecropping never became the exclusive system of agricultural organization in the postwar South, and in some areas the transition to it lasted for a decade or longer. A variety of systems existed: plain renting of land (tenant farmers), work for cash wages or wages paid in crop shares, and so on. The largest landowners would have some of their land cultivated by wage laborers, and perhaps a tenant farmer or two, in addition to several sharecroppers. Some blacks, utilizing the entrepreneurial or craft skills they had developed as slaves, combined hard work, skill, and luck to scrape together enough money to buy small parcels of land, and by 1880, about one-fifth of the black farmers in the South owned their land—a substantial achievement, even though the average size of the farms was less than half the size of those owned by whites. But for the majority of blacks, some variant of sharecropping was their lot. Those who owned their own mules, plows, and enough capital to provision themselves for the year needed a landowner to supply the actual land, a house, and usually firewood. In return, the blacks, called in this case share tenants, would pay the owner one-third of the corn and one-quarter of the cotton; this was called "working on thirds and fourths."

Most blacks, however, could offer only their labor. The landlord supplied everything else but food and clothing and for his efforts received one-half the cotton and grain production. For their essential food and clothing, the sharecroppers had to find a supplier who would extend them credit, the balance being due when the cotton was sold. Thousands of small country stores mushroomed across the cotton South in the years immediately following the war to perform this service, and many large landowners also began to offer their and their neighbors' sharecroppers store supplies on credit. These "furnishing merchants" cum planters charged the sharecroppers exorbitant "credit" prices that included interest rates averaging as high as 60 percent per annum on the provisions bought.

The stores were able to charge such rates because the sharecroppers often had no alternative supplier with lower credit prices. Stores were sparsely scattered across the rural South and transportation was primitive, so the stores had little competition. The merchants justified the charges by the high risk of offering credit to penniless farmers dependent upon an unreliable crop affected by the vagaries of the weather and the selling price. To make things worse, the large northern wholesale houses that supplied the local stores on credit routinely charged them enormously high interest rates because of the risks involved in their business. This point bears emphasis: the high credit prices charged sharecroppers were more a function of the huge risks involved than the venality of store owners (who themselves often went bankrupt). When sharecroppers had better access to more stores, that scarcely affected the rates they could obtain. Even well-disposed furnishing merchants had little choice but to pass the interest charged them on to their customers. Because of the inflated prices of necessary provisions, hundreds of thousands of sharecroppers found that their one-half of the cotton would not even cover their debt at the local store. So at the end of the year, at settling up time, the sharecroppers had no choice but to ask for credit for yet another year, in the futile hope that an extraordinary crop yield would finally boost them over their debt hurdle and allow them to buy a little patch of land. Another year's labor, another year's crop, usually left them deeper in debt. Even so, sharecroppers who gained a local reputation for hard work could often get slightly reduced prices—or credit when others were denied—so croppers had an incentive to stay with local stores and cultivate relationships of trust.

Merchants quite understandably wanted collateral from the sharecroppers for the credit extended them, but the landless farmers had no assets except the expectation of a crop. In the early postbellum years, the state legislatures passed crop-lien laws, which allowed merchants to require that the sharecroppers given credit sign a lien bond that legally bound the future crop to the merchant, and the merchants often stipulated that cotton be grown almost to the exclusion of grain crops. The lien laws had several effects. First, of course, the croppers were tied to the merchant by the legal promise of that year's harvest, and the merchant had first claim to the crop. If the sharecroppers' harvest did not cover what they owed the merchant, they ended the year further in debt. They had to get credit for the following year, often having to take a reduction in the amount loaned (and hence a cut in their already low standard of living), and by the lien that secured the credit were tied once more to cotton and farming on the shares. There simply was no escape; every year many slipped further behind, locked ever more firmly into an endless circle of cotton, credit, and economic catastrophe. Second, since the merchant demanded that they maximize cotton production because he expected to receive his payment from its sale, farmers on shares had to reduce the labor and land devoted to food crops and livestock, thus forcing them to buy more canned goods from the store, pushing them even deeper into debt. For hundreds of thousands of sharecroppers, black and white, King Cotton had become a tyrant from whose grasp there was no escape.

WHITE SHARECROPPERS

Sharecropping, in one guise or another, was never a phenomenon confined just to blacks. Before the Civil War, even stretching back to the colonial period, there had been thousands of landless white farmers who had worked as farm laborers for payment in kind. Yet the sharecropping system that developed after the Civil War became more firmly entrenched, and the marketing and provisioning system, secured by the lien laws, made it harder to escape. Changes in both local commerce and the international staple market also brought far more poor white farmers into the clasp of sharecropping and, by encouraging overproduction, produced lower prices and greater poverty. Sharecropping became more dominant in the post–Civil War South than the plantation had been in the antebellum South, and its social and political consequences were as great. The image of the poor benighted South largely owes its origin to the evils of sharecropping and the prevalence of essentially one-crop agriculture, and that image—alive even today—aptly characterized the South up to World War II. By the early twentieth century, a majority of white farmers had become landless sharecroppers, and they outnumbered black sharecroppers.

The large majority of southern whites had been landowners in 1860, and many who were not were children and relatives of landowners who could expect to inherit property in the near future. Small landholders, especially in the regions that because of terrain or inaccessibility to transportation were not dominated by staple-crop production, had practiced mixed farming, growing most of their foodstuffs along with some surplus or specialty goods they could either sell or barter—mules, hogs, corn, honey, apples, and barley. Often a few acres were devoted to cotton or tobacco to earn some cash, but these small farmers lived in a relatively cashless society, where goods or labor were bartered for supplies either with neighbors or with crossroad stores. The South as a whole before 1860 had been self-sufficient in terms of food production. Most of the household furnishings, clothing, and shoes were made in the home or by neighborhood craftsmen who exchanged them for a combination of cash and produce or labor. Slowly, almost imperceptibly at first, changes in the regional economy and transportation system after the Civil War disrupted this localized world of home consumption.

The great increase in property taxes, which had to be paid in money, and the fact that with the end of slavery the brunt of the tax assessment fell on land,

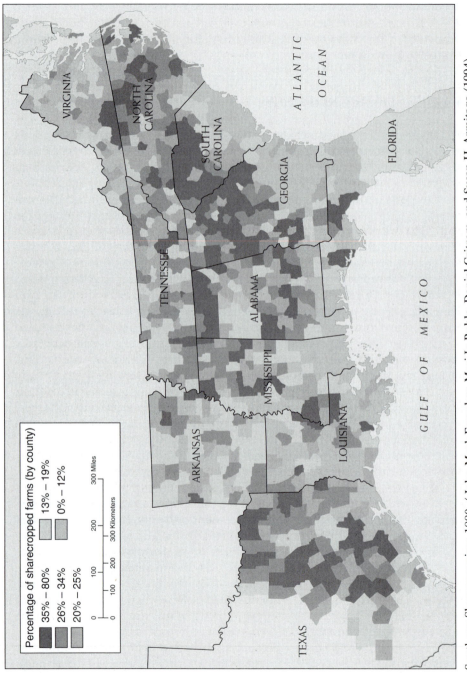

Southern Sharecropping, 1880. (John Mack Faragher, Mari Jo Buhle, Daniel Czitrom, and Susan H. Armitage (1994). *Out of Many: A History of the American People.* Upper Saddle River, New Jersey, Prentice Hall.)

Percentage of sharecropped farms (by county)

- 35% – 80%
- 26% – 34%
- 20% – 25%
- 13% – 19%
- 0% – 12%

meant that now small farmers had to be able to come up with more cash at one time than they had earlier been accustomed to handling, and this required that they exchange substantially more of their goods or services for money. In addition, the development of a railroad network allowed huge northern wholesale and merchandising houses to penetrate the rural southern countryside, both underselling local craftsmen and substituting a modern, commercial economy for the earlier, community-centered, barter or low-cash society. Sharecropping itself contributed to the proliferation of crossroad stores. In the southern plantation district during the antebellum period, the planter had not only sold all the cotton grown on his land but had done the central purchasing of goods, which he then distributed to his slaves; the planter's factor was his connection to the market in coastal port cities both to sell his crop and to purchase his goods (and those of his slaves) from wholesalers.

But with the rise of sharecropping, individual black families made their own purchases. This disaggregation of purchasing ended the dominance of the old-fashioned cotton factor, who was replaced with local furnishing merchants scattered throughout the countryside. The total value of their store assets was small—hence they represented a major risk to their suppliers—but they did offer aggressive northern wholesalers access to an expanding market. Highly competitive northern wholesale houses took advantage of this new marketing device and the penetration of the southern hinterland by railroads to spread the influence of modern commerce across the entire South. In the 1870s, railroad mileage expanded greatly, the number of country stores more than doubled, and the modern world of commerce swept beyond the old cotton-dominated black belt South to areas that before the Civil War had been characterized by mixed agriculture. This was not all bad, for it meant that isolated farmers now had easy access to goods—shoes, sewing needles, canned food, ready-made clothes, and commercial fertilizer—that had before been more expensive or hard to find.

But these goods had to be paid for in money. People came to prefer the new goods, and as local craftsmen found themselves undersold and quit their trades, people became dependent on store-bought goods paid for in money. Obviously, as the modern commercial system replaced the older system of self-reliance, barter, and cooperative labor, the cash nexus became supreme. Farmers who had previously been mostly self-sufficient now found that they needed a cash crop to be able to pay their infernal taxes and afford the goods available at crossroad stores. And in order to earn cash—or, more accurately, get credit from the stores—farmers had to shift away from production for home consumption to production of cotton for the cash market. No longer was the South self-sufficient in foodstuffs. In 1880, the region as a whole had to import more grain and livestock than it exported—a dramatic shift since 1860. Thus, across the South, white small farmers were sucked into the cotton trap. There was a world market for cotton, there was a pricing structure, there were agents who stood ready to purchase, gin, transport, and sell abroad even cotton grown in the remotest hinterland. No readily available market structure existed for other southern farm products, such as corn or barley, for example.

Cotton-buying agents used country stores to purchase the staple (thereby bringing even farmers in the interior into the realm of commercial agriculture), and improved transportation at first increased the price cotton growers received for their crop, further enticing them to shift acreage away from food crops to cotton. So countless thousands of small, landowning white farmers found themselves inexorably drawn into the commercial cultivation of cotton, resulting in a doubling of the acreage given over to cotton between 1859 and 1879. The number of bales produced went up accordingly as the relative self-sufficiency in foodstuffs plummeted. The tragedy was that the price of cotton soon fell to a fraction of its immediate postwar high, meaning that farmers grew ever more but got less and less in return.

Unfortunately, as the South produced more cotton, so did other regions of the world. The opening of the Suez Canal in 1869 shortened the distance from England to India by six thousand miles and made Indian cotton more competitive in price for the English mill owners, and vast cotton fields (sometimes managed by ex-southerners) also opened up in Egypt. At the same time that the worldwide supply was increasing, the global demand for cotton, which had risen almost uniformly for seven decades following 1790, flattened out in the postwar period. The result of worldwide overproduction was a constant decline in price. When individual southern sharecroppers and small farmers who had shifted to an emphasis on cotton production found out at settlement time that they had not broken even, they simply arranged another line of credit and did what to them seemed rational—they determined to work harder and plant more acres of cotton in hope that a bountiful harvest would allow them to pay out and escape their debt. But practically every cotton grower did the same, production increased accordingly, prices fell still further, and the poorest suffered the most. The crop lien tied the unfortunate sharecropper to cotton, and the merchant, who bought his goods on credit too from northern wholesalers and was thus also in debt to his suppliers, had to insist that his creditors plant the one sure money crop. The system could not be budged off center. And as the southern population grew—poor farmers had large families—simply more people cultivated more cotton.

Hundreds of thousands of white farmers, including many who began the postbellum era owning their land, were brought into the circuit of commercial agriculture, growing cotton for cash, and found themselves falling ever deeper into debt with the country store. First, they lost money, and then their land, to the clutches of the cotton market. They, too, by the hundreds of thousands, became landless sharecroppers, eventually outnumbering the freedpeople who never escaped from the grasp of the system. New white cotton farmers were primarily responsible for the significant increase in cotton acreage after the Civil War. Even had blacks during Reconstruction been given the fabled forty acres and a mule, chances are that they, too, having even less experience with money management and credit arrangements than the white farmers, would have backslid into sharecropping. Almost no one in southern agriculture, except perhaps some of the largest furnishing merchants, really prospered. The South's great lack of capital linked sharecropper to merchant to northern wholesaler, with enormous, though often hidden, interest rates extracted at each successive stage. Profits flowed to the North, poverty flourished in the South. By 1880, the per capita income of the southern states was about one-third that of the rest of the United States. The racism and political irrationality that marked so much of the South's history in the half-century following Reconstruction are inextricably linked to the region's poverty, as were the several efforts at significant political reform. But until the South escaped the paralysis of dependence on one crop, its economic and human potential was severely crippled.

CHAPTER 23

Old Verities Challenged

THE FIRST NEW SOUTH

Even during the antebellum period, the South had not been aggressively anti-industrial. Occasionally well-to-do planters had invested in factories, railroads, mining, and a variety of decidedly nonagricultural pursuits. Many of these industries, such as cottonseed oil plants, cotton compresses, jute bag (used to cover cotton bales) manufacturers, and so on, served agricultural interests. Sawmills, gristmills, ironworks, and saltworks also dotted the region. Southern industrialists like William Gregg worked tirelessly and with some success to plant textile mills across the region, and Joseph R. Anderson's Tredegar ironworks in Richmond pointed toward the later southern steel industry that would bloom in the vicinity of Birmingham, Alabama. Still, in 1860, the South produced only 15 percent of the nation's iron and about 25 percent of the textile goods. Southern banks and private individuals serving as lenders provided much of the credit and funds for investment, but the South remained overwhelmingly agricultural.

In part, this was due to the South's competitive advantage in growing certain marketable crops like cotton, tobacco, sugar, and rice. As long as these crops could be reasonably expected to provide a safe and profitable return, there was little incentive to risk money on alternative investments. A substantial portion of the southern population—the slaves—could not be avid consumers, and this lessened the market for locally produced goods. The southern transportation system in the antebellum era had been primarily designed to transport bulk agricultural products to port cities and as such was not conducive to facilitating the transportation of raw materials to industrial cities and the distribution of manufactured goods throughout the region. Moreover, the small-scale southern manufacturers were ill-equipped to compete either in the region or in the nation with larger, more efficient northern manufacturers. But the point is that there was a not insignificant industrial presence in the Old South. Many antebellum planters, merchants, and bankers were quick to respond to potentially profitable opportunities whether they were rich cotton lands or industrial schemes. Southern legislatures passed laws dealing with such matters as incorporation that, even if they did not unfairly favor manufacturing enterprises, did not discriminate against them, either. Shareholders in corporations were also extended the advantage of having limited liability. In South Carolina, the legislature in 1853 and 1854 exempted William Gregg's water-powered textile mills from having to allow river transportation through or around his dams on Horse Creek, thus privileging industrial interests over traditional navigation rights. In other words, the Old South was not intrinsically hostile to all industry.

During the course of the Civil War, the South's industrial potential was stretched beyond the breaking point, but in the process, the South underwent an almost miraculous temporary industrial transformation, developing munitions factories, ironworks, armories, shipbuilding facilities, and the like. The output was never enough to meet military and civilian needs, and in the end, shortages of nearly everything compounded the misery of death, disease, and emotional exhaustion that climaxed with Lee's surrender at Appomattox. The South did not undergo a permanent industrial revolution as a result of trying to meet wartime exigencies. But neither were southern leaders so hidebound in their infatuation with agriculture that they could not appreciate the importance of industrialization, which, along with crop diversification, promised to rescue the region from overdependence on one crop. The northern victory in itself showed how essential industry was not merely for military prowess but, by implication, for prosperity.

While southerners may have been slow to acknowledge the moral superiority of the North's cause in the first months after the war, they fully appreciated the success of the northern economy. J. D. B. De Bow, whose *De Bow's Review* in New Orleans had been the Old South's leading journal of political economy, led the chorus of voices calling for the recuperating South to purge itself of its addiction to cotton and strengthen itself through industrialization and crop diversification. The first post–Civil War state governments formed in the South in accordance with Andrew Johnson's directives made initial efforts to promote a more modern economic base in the region, but these efforts were soon swept aside by the torrents of Reconstruction politics. The issues of how to regulate the freedpeople and how to regain control of local politics were of paramount importance to white southerners, and their decisions on those matters—reasonable as they seemed to most white southerners themselves—suggested to national observers that the South had in mind repudiating the outcome of the war. The resulting political turmoil, which as we have seen soon descended to violence and fraud, obscured the South's initial efforts to modernize its economy.

During the periods of presidential and congressional Reconstruction, efforts were made to forward the industrialization of the region; Republican politicians, less wedded by tradition and experience to agriculture and more committed to commerce, industry, and the need for change in general, often advocated legislation that would benefit the South (and, in tune with the times, occasionally themselves). Legislatures passed bills and issued bonds to underwrite railroad construction, but southerners had done the same in the antebellum era and in the immediate aftermath of the Civil War. The underlying motive in each case was the stimulation of prosperity—seen as some industrialization along with an enhancement of commerce—with improved transportation. Some railroad enterprises went bankrupt, others swindled the taxpayers' money, and unscrupulous individuals on occasion lined their pockets, but all in the grand old American tradition of unregulated capitalism. Corruption was neither automatic to the process nor endemic among Republicans. Well-meaning Republicans from the North, ex-Confederates who wanted to put the past behind them and find prosperity for the region, and go-getters of all sorts saw in southern forests, mineral deposits, available cheap labor, and amenable climate the ingredients for economic growth. Nothing conspiratorial or anti-southern need be assumed in the emerging movement to modernize the South and renew its prosperity.

The rationales for development were many. For some advocates, there was a strong element of regional chauvinism, a desire to see the South share in national prosperity and be independent of northern manufactured goods. Other spokesmen, while not unaware of regional implications, were primarily local boosters who urged that their town garner the rail route or the new textile mill so as to keep up with the spirit of the times and perhaps a rival, upwardly mobile town. Would-be industrialists and capitalists were more than willing to prosper personally, and they justified the desire for economic gain both as getting in step with the rest of the nation and as a way to uplift the impoverished whites in their midst by providing manufacturing jobs. Suffice it to say that most of the jobs turned out to be low-skill, low-pay, dead-end work, and poor whites (and blacks) usually found themselves simply exchanging rural poverty and back-breaking labor for long, monotonous hours of environmentally hazardous work in factories or mines with little or no improvement in living standard.

The managerial and industrial elite of the postwar South evolved from the antebellum planter class, but the evolution required less of a break with the past than sometimes recognized. While most prosperous planters liked to imagine themselves as paternalistic agriculturists who treated all their dependents—white and black—in benevolent fashion, they on the whole made hardheaded business decisions about crops, land and slave purchases, and even relocations to other sections of the South with a keen eye on profits and what they called getting ahead. When times and conditions changed, as they surely did in the 1860s, able planters changed with the times. Even the fictional Scarlett O'Hara, surely a plantation stereotype, became a sawmill operator when the need and the opportunity presented themselves.

In the real world, too, countless planters and sons of planters (and occasionally daughters) reassessed the opportunities facing them in the 1870s and determined to cultivate industrial prospects rather than agricultural crops. They expected at least to maintain and hoped to improve their social position. They expected to control cheap labor with a paternalistic rationale that shielded them from facing their exploitation of their employees, but their flexibility on matters of occupation and regional economy did not extend to matters of race and politics. Much had changed, but much remained unchanged. The shift from antebellum planter to postbellum industrialist required a change in investment strategies, but it neither required nor produced a fundamental change in ethos. Younger sons of prewar planters, with one foot still in the soil, eagerly stepped with the other foot toward industrialization and the siren song of modern prosperity. Without ever repudiating the past, they lunged for new ways of advancing both themselves and their local community. And just as the prewar planter class had been open to able young men on the make (either through hard work and good luck or advantageous marriage), the southern planter-cum-industrial class welcomed northern investors and promoters who promised to enhance profits and maintain the racial and class status quo. The business and industrial elite fully intended, in cooperation with the agricultural elite, to control politics for their mutual benefit. Both wanted low taxes, a docile labor force, and "stability" in order to attract northern investments.

In truth, industrial activity substantially increased in the South in the two decades following Reconstruction. Railroad mileage grew fourfold between 1865 and 1890, and there was an even greater increase in the number of cotton spindles as at last the textile mills, seeking cheap labor and reduced transportation costs from the cotton fields, began relocating with a vengeance from New England to the cotton-producing states. By 1900, the South was the nation's leading producer of textiles. Lumber production multiplied, an iron industry developed in the vicinity of Birmingham, Alabama, and new deposits of coal began to be exploited. However, the real southern attractions were cheap labor and raw materials; a handful of owners and managers (many northern) prospered, but the laboring masses toiled with little hope of ever achieving a satisfactory standard of living.

If the growth in investment in southern industry or the value of southern manufactured goods is compared with the rest of the nation, then the industrial

boom in the South seems more a bust, for after more than two decades of activity, the South's share of the national output remained constant. But when one
remembers that this was a period of phenomenal industrial growth nationwide,
then the South's ability to stay in the same relative position meant that the
South was industrializing at a brisk rate. A comparison not with the nation but
with southern output in 1860 or 1865 reveals the dimension of that growth.
This economic revitalization of the South was in part the result of a concerted
policy of a number of southern businessmen, would-be industrialists, promoters, and publicists who advocated the development of a so-called New South of
progress and prosperity to replace the lamented and admittedly irrecoverable
Old South of slavery and defeat.

A number of newspaper and magazine editors took the lead in this effort, and at first it seemed a rational, matter-of-fact analysis of the present
state of the regional economy and an evaluation of the South's human and
natural resources, with an eye to attracting substantial northern investment
both of money and know-how. Editors such as Henry W. Grady of the *Atlanta
Constitution*, aided by staff writer Joel Chandler Harris, who collected Uncle
Remus tales for pleasure but wrote promotional editorials at work, Francis
W. Dawson of the *Charleston News and Courier*, and Henry Watterson of the
Louisville Courier-Journal, tirelessly promoted the advantages of crop diversification, industrialization, and the wider acceptance of Yankee-like, get-ahead
attitudes. Richard H. Edmonds of Baltimore published in his *Manufacturer's
Record* an unending paean to factories and investment, and his pages parad-
ed seemingly every broom factory and wagon shop established from Maryland
to Texas, with each opening memorialized as a step toward progress and prosperity. Talk of steel mills in Anniston or the discovery of coal deposits in Tennessee led to rhapsodic discussion of how that region was the coming Ruhr
of the United States, Birmingham the next Pittsburgh. According to the
Manufacturer's Record, every mountain city had a healthful climate to go along
with its sparkling prospects.

Within a decade of the end of Reconstruction, this New South journalism
had ceased being exhortatory and had begun being congratulatory. The New
South spokesmen subtly convinced themselves that the South had become what
the spokesmen had so ardently called for. One notices a shift in the tone of
the editorials; by the 1880s, articles on new factories or plans for a new town
were offered as proof that the South had become prosperous, the industrial
heartland of the nation. Was this really only an effort to persuade northern investors to invest their dollars in a stable, progressive region, or did that intention evolve from conscious strategy to unconscious myth? The evidence seems
to suggest the latter, wish being father to belief. The best-known spokesman
became Henry W. Grady, who in a famous address in 1886 to the New England
Society of New York at Delmonico's Restaurant in New York City captured the
mythical essence of the finished New South message.

Following William Tecumseh Sherman, the scourge of Georgia, on the program, Grady artfully gained the favor of his audience by stating that while once there had been "a South of slavery and secession—that South is dead. There is a South of union and freedom—that South, thank God, is living, breathing, growing every hour." He went on to assure his northern listeners that southerners had "sowed towns and cities in the place of theories, and put business above politics.... We have fallen in love with work." Reaching out for capital, he insisted that "we have smoothed the path to Southward, wiped out where the Mason and Dixon's line used to be, and hung out our latchstring to you and yours." Thundering applause sealed his audience's approval of his sentiments, and Grady and like-minded New South promoters seemed convinced that a new age of prosperity and racial and class harmony had arrived. Those northerners who had wanted to remake the South in the image of the North in the aftermath of the Civil War could believe that Grady and others were doing just that. But the New South spokesmen implicitly assumed that a business-industry-planter oligarchy would rule southern politics, with taxes and government services kept low and wages dampened. Blacks would be held "in their place," performing the most menial or distasteful jobs, and all would supposedly work together in harmony and efficiency to create a truly New South with the same elite as always in control. With the North safely assured that the South had accepted northern attitudes, the federal government could relax its concern about the plight of the freedpeople in the South, a message most northern whites were only too willing to believe. The shadow of the Old South lay over the New South, and prosperity proved as illusory in the 1880s and 1890s as Confederate success had proven in the 1860s.

URBAN GROWTH

One of the most striking features of the Old South had been its relative lack of urbanization. In 1860 only 7.1 percent of the region's population had lived in urban areas (defined as twenty-five hundred people or more), roughly one-third the percentage for the North. New Orleans was the only large city in the Confederacy, and it ranked only sixth in size among the nation's cities. New Orleans was more than four times as populous as Charleston, the second-largest southern city. Moreover, the ten major southern urban areas were all river or seaport cities. Since 1840, the urban share of the South's total population had been declining, but that decline was halted immediately after the Civil War, in large part because of a very significant migration of rural blacks to the region's cities both to seek the protection of the Freedmen's Bureau officials and to seek improved job opportunities. The nationally depressed economy of the 1870s, along with the South's peculiar cotton depression, slowed urban growth in that decade, but the 1880s saw a renewed acceleration of the growth of cities.

This development would continue into the twentieth century, resulting in a doubling of the proportion of the South's population that were urban dwellers, to 15.2 percent in 1900. Despite this marked growth, the South lagged even further behind the nation as a whole that year—New Orleans, for example, had slipped to fifteenth among America's largest cities. But the truly remarkable urbanization of the nation as a whole should not be allowed to obscure the rise of an urban South during this period.

Several aspects of this postwar southern urbanization are noteworthy. It came about less because of the rapid growth of older cities than as a result of a new generation of cities located in the interior of the South and to the west. While the sons of pre–Civil War commercial and planter interests tended to dominate the leadership of the older, slower-growing cities, the new cities were led by a newer class of southerners, less tied by kinship and viewpoint to the past. Family name counted for less in the emerging cities than skill, hard work, and drive. By 1890, the list of ten largest southern cities included such new marketing and manufacturing centers as Nashville, Atlanta, Dallas, and San Antonio, with Houston and Birmingham on the rise. These cities, and dozens not so large in the region, grew not as the result of immigration from Europe but mainly from internal southern migration. The depressed agricultural economy gave an added attraction to southern cities, dreary though they might have been. Blacks, young men on the make, widows, and single women saw towns and cities as places of opportunity. With the exception of Birmingham, most of these urban seats were closely related to the region's cotton economy.

Typically, small marketing towns would have cotton gins and a handful of stores; slightly larger towns would have, along with their rail depot, cotton compresses, where the cotton bales were reduced in size for ease of transport, and cottonseed oil mills that extracted oil by crushing the seeds that were a by-product of ginning. The oil was marketed for illumination and lubricating purposes. Still larger towns, small cities, would combine these functions and also collect the compressed bales from a wide hinterland and ship them, by water or rail, to manufacturing centers in the South, the North, or England. In return, linked by rail to northern or regional wholesale houses, the marketing cities would initiate the distribution of manufactured consumer goods, usually from the North, back down the trade network to agents and storekeepers in towns and ultimately to small stores at the village crossroads. Commerce and agricultural services, not manufacturing, were the chief functions of southern urban places.

No particular city had a special advantage over another, or a way to increase significantly the size of either its cotton servicing or consumer-goods market. Consequently, although a number of southern towns grew into small cities, with the largest of them having populations ranging from 40,000 to 100,000, none of them came close to rivaling the really large cities that were emerging in the North. Dozens of marketing towns of 5,000 to 10,000 people came to dot the South, and while many of the towns were ambitious and the town promoters active, few ever grew into real cities. Nevertheless, much that was progressive in the South centered in the urban areas. Waxahachie, for example, in Ellis County southeast of Dallas, Texas, enjoyed a spectacular cotton boom after 1879 when railroads reached the county with its rich blackland prairie soil. By the early twentieth century Ellis County led the nation in cotton production, and the newfound prosperity for some—even here two-thirds of the farmers were tenants in 1900—built a handsome red sandstone courthouse, nine stories tall in ornate Richardsonian Romanesque style; attractive stone buildings around the courthouse square and many large homes in the town; and an octagonal Chautauqua Auditorium (1902) that seated more than a thousand people who gathered to hear the likes of William Jennings Bryan. In middling-sized towns such as Waxahachie (population of 3,701 in 1890; 4,215 in 1900; 6,205 in 1910) across the South congregated southerners of talent, of entrepreneurial ability, with a desire to change the region for the better. Here were most of the region's lawyers, doctors, and other professionals. "Boosterism" was the word of the day, and business enterprise was assumed to be the magic key to growth, progress, and prosperity. The economic development that occurred—whether the appearance of textile mills or steel mills, or the attracting of a new railroad line—usually came because the urban business class advocated it. The results might have seemed puny to a visitor from New York City or Chicago, but for the son or daughter of a small farmer, the commerce and ambition of a regional marketing city symbolized the first step out of lethargy and poverty. Business progress, women's civic reform efforts, black middle-class prosperity, all originated in the South's postwar cities.

Because the railroad was the necessary link to the markets of the North, often the largest and grandest building in a city on the make was the train station.

THE CONFEDERATE SOUTH'S TEN LARGEST CITIES, 1860 AND 1890

1860		*1890*	
New Orleans	168,675	New Orleans	242,039
Charleston	40,519	Richmond	81,388
Richmond	37,910	Nashville	76,168
Mobile	29,258	Atlanta	65,533
Memphis	22,623	Memphis	64,495
Savannah	22,292	Charleston	54,955
Petersburg	18,266	Savannah	43,189
Nashville	16,988	Dallas	38,067
Norfolk	14,620	San Antonio	37,673
Alexandria	12,652	Norfolk	34,871

Sources: Richard C. Wade, *Slavery in the Cities: The South, 1820–1860* (New York, 1964), 325–27; Donald B. Dodd and Wynelle S. Dodd, *Historical Statistics of the South, 1790–1970* (University, Ala., 1973), 74–76.

In antebellum cities, church steeples had been the tallest symbol of a city's pride, but now the cathedrals to rail commerce were what inhabitants proudly pointed to. Soon showcase government and civic buildings followed in their wake. The office and storefront buildings were still low—two to four stories. Not until the 1890s did the first skyscrapers begin to appear in the very largest southern cities, Atlanta leading the way in 1892 with the Equitable Building. Cities touted their hotels, especially their one grand hotel, and most managed to have an opulent opera house, both assumed to be sure symbols of a progressive city with a get-ahead attitude. These cities, for all their hunger for growth and modernity, were by present-day standards amazingly backward at the beginning of the 1880s. Most of the roads were unpaved, almost no modern sewer systems existed, pure city water was a thing of the future, police forces were unprofessionalized and crime was rampant, and fire protection was primitive. Practically every city had at least one disastrous fire during the period, with scores of homes and businesses destroyed. There were almost no public parks and few public schools, and the provisions for black education were shockingly inadequate.

Cities like New Orleans and Memphis, in particular, were regularly plagued with horrendous epidemics of yellow fever or cholera, with deaths mounting into the thousands. The Memphis yellow fever scourge of 1878 to 1879 alone took almost six thousand lives. On several occasions, the entire city had to be quarantined, bringing commerce to almost a complete halt. The infant mortality rates were high, especially for blacks, but all races and classes suffered from a broad range of illnesses. Cities were a public health nightmare, with privies and sewers emptying onto the open ground or streets, along with tons of horse manure and urine (the pollution of horse-drawn transportation) with little thought given to the location of water wells. Urban dwellers often kept chickens, hogs, milk cows, and horses penned behind their homes or in stables, contributing to the rural look and smell of late nineteenth-century cities.

It was not until the 1890s that cities began systematically to build sewer systems, construct modern water works to replace private wells and cisterns, and pave more than just a few blocks of streets in the heart of the cities. By the 1870s, most southern cities had horse-drawn streetcars linking the outskirts to the central business district, and by the late 1880s, southern cities actually outpaced their northern counterparts in pioneering the development of all-electric trolley systems. This improved transportation began to make possible a spatial rearrangement of the class and racial structure of the cities, with those of higher income now able to move out and commute in to work. The first so-called streetcar suburbs then developed in Atlanta, Birmingham, Houston, and other cities. Also, by the 1890s, electric lights became the sine qua non of the self-consciously progressive cities, and hundreds of municipalities developed their own public power plants. Telephones were not far behind, with local telephone companies providing the miracle of modern communication to small networks of subscribers. The South was somewhat slower in becoming integrated into the larger Bell networks than was the North because the region's commitment to localism retarded the process. Population growth as measured by the decennial national census was taken as a promise of better things to come by town boosters, and cities often annexed adjacent areas simply to augment their census numbers, not to provide better urban services to the neighboring regions.

Some of the stories of urban growth and development were remarkable. Birmingham had been founded in a cornfield in north-central Alabama in 1871, near iron ore and coal deposits. Promoters like the Louisville and Nashville Railroad quickly linked it by rail to Atlanta and points northward. The investors came both from the North and from the region—Henry De Bardeleben, who had married one of the daughters of Old South textile manufacturer Daniel Pratt, was a local entrepreneur who pushed the manufacturing and successful marketing of Birmingham steel, despite fighting freight rates and pricing strategies imposed from without that penalized southern production. The population of Birmingham swelled from 3,086 in 1880 to 26,178 in 1890, 38,414 in 1900, and an incredible 132,685 in 1910. No other southern city could claim such meteoric growth, but Birmingham was not the only beneficiary of development schemes. A concerted campaign to build cotton mills along the route of the Southern Railroad in North and South Carolina resulted not only in the rapid rise of small cities like Charlotte, Greenville, and Spartanburg, but in the South's overtaking of New England as the nation's textile center by 1900. Railroad connections also led to the rapid expansion of Atlanta, Dallas, and Houston, and made possible the burgeoning growth of the port of Norfolk.

For no group of southerners did the cities produce greater change than for blacks. While many arrived in early Reconstruction to escape the violence of the countryside, blacks quickly came to associate urban areas with enhanced opportunity and freedom. The older southern cities, whose residential neighborhoods had been integrated before the Civil War, retained that pattern, although by the end of the century, totally black neighborhoods had developed. The newer cities that were springing up in the South's interior tended much more quickly to segregate the races, a process accentuated by the exploding black urban population. By 1890, 15 percent of the South's blacks had moved to cities and towns, where they represented fully one-third of the region's total urban population and a remarkable 70 percent of the nation's urban black population. Whites seemed both resentful of and frustrated by the growing black numbers, and spatial separation by race became far more pronounced and rigid. Blacks now were often excluded from theaters, restaurants, and railroad station waiting rooms. Blacks were not excluded from the streetcars, though efforts at the end of the period to require them to sit in backseats (or give up their seats to whites) occasionally caused blacks to boycott the transportation systems, with some success. As a result, urban streetcar systems tended to be less segregated than other aspects of city life.

Before the Civil War, blacks had often dominated certain skilled trades, such as carpentry and masonry, and they were well represented in many others. In the harsher racial environment of the New South, and particularly so in the newer cities, white craftsmen and artisans pushed black males out of most traditional skilled trades and did not allow them to find employment in new occupations like plumbing and electrical work. The result was a very significant de-skilling of the black male work force, with black men increasingly concentrated in low-skill, low-pay jobs. Many whites, frightened by the competition with the growing number of urban blacks and worried that the countryside would soon have a shortage of black agricultural laborers, strongly advocated that the proper place for blacks was in the cotton fields. As a result of the de-skilling of black male job opportunities in the cities, many males did have to leave their wives and families and seek at least temporary work elsewhere—on railroad construction crews, in lumber camps, and as temporary harvest laborers. Black women could usually find urban employment as domestics, beginning the phenomenon of female-headed families in the cities. By 1890, as many as 25 percent of urban black households had only the mother present.

The growth of the black population in the towns and cities, and their increasing segregation, brought about the rise of a separate black economy. Most cities saw the rise of black business districts featuring black-owned stores, cafés, undertaking establishments, and shops and services of every sort that catered to the black population. Whites often rejected black customers or treated them poorly, which only drove blacks to prefer their own establishments. An indigenous professional class of black lawyers, teachers, doctors, dentists, and pharmacists began to emerge, the result either of blacks going north for education or graduating from the black colleges and medical schools established across the region during the era of Reconstruction—institutions such as Howard University, Hampton Institute, Fisk University, Atlanta University, and Meharry Medical College. These black business and professional people had an all-black clientele, and while many blacks were proud to be able to confine their business to fellow blacks, the black entrepreneurs and professionals often prospered. This black elite largely adopted the Victorian manners and the ideology of thrift, hard work, and education that whites accepted, but the achievements and success of the upwardly mobile blacks, rather than earn the respect of whites, frightened them. Whites feared the economic competition of prosperous blacks, found their success threatening to white racial theories, and responded with increasingly harsh and vindictive laws and ordinances.

As a result of white prejudice and black opportunism, a black elite began to develop in the cities. Many of these well-to-do blacks possessed not only skill and business acumen but a strong sense of obligation toward their people, and this felt responsibility was strengthened by the growth of white discrimination. Such black leaders often pioneered a number of organizations that nurtured and served the black community. Blacks founded and managed their own hospitals, schools, and other institutions; during the antebellum period blacks had often been actively excluded from such facilities. Separate, segregated facilities were seen in the post–Civil War era by blacks as an improvement of their situation, and whites preferred the growing degree of racial separation in the cities. Excluded from white organizations, black men formed clubs and fraternal organizations like the Colored Masons, the Colored Odd Fellows, and the Knights of Pythias. Black women likewise found community and performed service in the United Daughters of Ham, the Ladies' Benevolent Society, and Order of the Eastern Star. Blacks established teacher-training institutes, raised funds for schools, and developed a wide range of social service clubs and agencies. Black savings banks, burial societies, and insurance companies were organized to benefit both urban and rural blacks, often filling a void that white businesses ignored. In all the cities, black community and social life often revolved around the churches, and ministers were vital social and often political leaders in the black community. Black women were extremely important to the churches, helping broaden their mission from the purely spiritual to the full spectrum of human needs. The intensification of racism and separatism in the era affected blacks every day of their lives, but the simultaneous growth of manifold community institutions, especially the churches, helped the black population survive. The black professional class would, in coming decades, discover new ways to minister to their people in a Jim Crow age and ultimately begin to chip away at the entire racist edifice. But before the region saw the color code recede, race relations would grow still worse.

THE POPULIST CHALLENGE

Despite all the New South rhetoric about industrialization, agriculture was still the backbone of the southern economy, and all was not well down on the farms. Sharecroppers and tenant farmers, white and black, seldom prospered, but neither did most small landowners. Dependence upon one crop—though the crop varied from region to region—made the entire South hostage to the vagaries of the climate and the international market. The biggest black-belt planters and their business and industrial allies controlled state and local politics, and the interests of the poor hardly concerned the New South politicos. Low wages, low taxes, and minimal government services were what the development crowd wanted and got, and the sharecroppers and small farmers had little say in the affairs of state. Hard times were endemic, but poor white men—

perhaps accustomed by their Civil War military experience to follow the command of their leaders—were afraid to risk upsetting the Democratic party's control of racial matters by protesting economic policies strenuously, and of course the blacks had practically no influence on such matters.

Several times in the 1870s and 1880s, discontent from the lower orders bubbled up, with real political impact in the case of the Readjuster movement in Virginia. Money was dear, taxes on farm land relatively high, schools and most social services woefully inadequate, and the conservative Democrats blithely unresponsive to the people's needs. In this situation, a gifted politician and former Confederate general, William Mahone, led a reform movement that burned brightly for several years on either side of 1880. Before the Conservative Democrats were able to mount an effective counterattack by raising the specter of a Republican comeback and black rule, the Readjusters—so-called because one of their major causes was scaling back or readjusting the state debt—politically dominated the state and revised the tax system, increased funding for education, reformed aspects of the penal system, and in general tried to make government more responsive to the needs of a broader spectrum of the populace. But the Democrats put an end to "Mahoneism" by the mid-1880s.

The Virginia situation was unique in terms of the success of the reformers; yet most southern states had flurries of political protest in the 1870s and 1880s. Greenbackism flourished in many areas, and it spoke to farmers' desires for inflationary monetary policies to ease their burden of debt. Local reform movements aimed to end the domination of courthouse gangs who ruled county politics for the aggrandizement of the few at the expense of the masses. Protests over such things as high taxes or unfair valuation, exorbitant railroad rates, and outrages in the convict lease system were common but produced no general remedies. Agricultural reform was a perennial cause, and farmers supported first the Grange then a variety of organizations like the Agricultural Wheel that blended community-building social functions with the dispensing of useful economic and scientific advice. Ideas associated with reform movements that originated outside the South, such as the Knights of Labor and the Single Tax crusade of Henry George and Edward Bellamy's Nationalist movements (which arose as an outgrowth of the popularity of his futuristic reform novel, *Looking Backward* [1881]), also filtered southward and gained scattered adherents. For example, Ernest B. Gaston, a newspaperman from Iowa outraged by the excesses of Gilded Age industrialism that produced great wealth for some and great poverty for many, led a group of fellow believers from the Midwest to the eastern shore of Mobile Bay and established in 1894 the communitarian settlement of Fairhope. There the principles of Henry George were put into practice, and the Fairhope Industrial Association—later the Fairhope Single Tax Corporation, which still exists—owned the land and developed town amenities for all the inhabitants. A remarkably progressive school was also established. High ideals and good intentions motivated the community and its leaders, but Fairhope had no appreciable effect on the South as a whole. Still the plight of the plain folk seemed to worsen, and, what made it more painful, who noticed or understood or cared? A number of mostly short-lived utopian movements, religious and secular, sprang up in this age of dissatisfaction. Many southerners also became disillusioned with mainstream religious denominations and either found comfort in a world-denying holiness movement in Methodism or joined new sects that sought to reject this world and pursue spiritual perfectionism. From these impulses, the Pentecostal movement evolved, which in the twentieth century became the fastest growing branch of Christianity in the world. Pentecostal religions in a variety of forms offered hard-pressed southerners of both races a participatory faith that created a strong sense of community, a vivid encounter with what was understood to be the Holy Spirit, and a contentment and purpose in life that helped to counter hopelessness and frustration.

As this range of responses suggests, the farmers' sad condition, real and perceived, was not narrowly economic. Farmers felt unappreciated, forgotten, and condescended to by the shapers of national opinion. Their own political leaders neglected their needs and governed to please northern investors and southern businessmen-industrialists. Farmers in the more isolated, fringe regions of the South felt particularly abandoned. Their hard work earned them little money and no respect from the larger world. They were ridiculed as hayseeds and country bumpkins while well-dressed financiers whose hands never toiled to produce anything real dictated the laws and reaped the profits. It did not seem right that hard-working, God-fearing tillers of the soil should suffer while eastern and urban philistines prospered. The farm protesters shared with industrial laborers a commitment to producerism, an old idea that stretched back to the republicanism of Thomas Jefferson and beyond. According to producerism, the actual producer (a farmer, artisan, or industrial worker) deserved the fruit of his or her labor. Groups with special privileges—monopolists, railroad interests, and purchasing cartels—should not interfere with the natural, legitimate, and, the farmers would say, God-given right of the producer to benefit fully and fairly from his or her labors.

As railroads and ready-made goods penetrated the countryside and undercut traditional crafts—making obsolete old habits of barter and the sharing of skills and labor, and putting everything on a cash basis determined by unseen wholesale houses—an entire way of life was threatened with destruction. The price fetched by the primary money crop, cotton, was determined not by a farmer's skill but by the vagaries of an impersonal international market. New phosphate fertilizers became available for purchase because of railroads and country stores, and although the chemical fertilizers improved crop yields and hence were almost mandatory to buy and apply, they also increased farmers' costs (debts) and the corresponding risks of failure. Southern farmers in the generation after Reconstruction lived in times of wrenching change, and the political establishment failed to understand and address the pain and cognitive dissonance many farmers felt. Tens of thousands of white farmers sank deeper and deeper into debt, bankruptcy, then loss of their land. Black farmers, and sharecroppers, already living at the very edge of desperation, found their plight worsening still. The result was a long season of despair that led to a period of unprecedented political protest.

In a profound sense, the farmers were responding to modernity, which from their perspective victimized them and the ethos of their local communities. There were objective reasons for farmers' discontent—the prices for staple crops fell in the 1880s and early 1890s, for example—but in some inchoate way, the farmers felt their decline in social status and the constant slights to their dignity more than the pinch in their pocketbooks. This acute sense of loss, economic and cultural, first began to reveal itself on the farming frontier of northwestern Texas, in Lampasas County, where obscure farm clubs began to organize in the mid-1870s into a fledgling Texas Farmers' Alliance. Charles W. Macune, a self-taught practitioner of pharmacy, medicine, and law, and organizer par excellence, emerged as head of the group in 1886. Meanwhile similar farmers' organizations—the Arkansas Wheel and the Louisiana Farmers' Union—had arisen, and Macune persuaded the sister groups to merge themselves with the Texas Farmers' Alliance to form the National Farmers' Alliance and Cooperative Union. Macune was an enormously skilled leader and educator whose speeches and editorials shaped the thinking of increasing numbers of southern farmers because he so accurately captured their mood and prescribed remedies that seemed both to tame the impersonalism and greed of modern capitalism and harken back to a cooperative world of the past.

If Macune had an equal in appealing to the farmers' sense of discontent in order to mobilize them for change, it was Leonidas Lafayette Polk of North Carolina. With a military and political career spanning from the Civil War era and a commitment to agricultural reform beginning in 1877, when he was named North Carolina's first commissioner of agriculture, Polk knew his state and its farmers' problems intimately. In 1886, he had founded the magazine *Progressive Farmer* to urge scientific agricultural practices, and when the Farmers' Alliance appeared the following year in North Carolina, Polk quickly saw its promise and rose to its leadership. By 1888, Polk and Macune had, through effective advocacy and personal charisma, helped fold all the southern farm organizations, from Texas to the seaboard, into the Southern Farmers' Alliance (called the Southern Alliance), with headquarters in Washington, D.C. (There was a roughly parallel organization of black farmers, called the Colored National Farmers' Alliance and Cooperative Union, which the Southern Alliance now and again reached out to and timidly cooperated with.) Macune was the first president of the Southern Alliance, but soon Polk succeeded him as president, and Macune served as the pithy, shrewd editor of the association's primary educational organ, the *National Economist.*

The Southern Alliance sponsored traveling speakers, a variety of local newspapers, and a steady procession of state conventions and local picnics and rallies that had much of the look and feel of a religious camp meeting. Both men and women were charter members of the fledgling Southern Alliance. The women were often more radicalized than the men were, for no one suffered longer or harder from the numbing poverty and bone-aching exhaustion of farm labor than did the womenfolk. The result was an intense period of what we call today consciousness-raising. Farmers found a new sense of community and purpose through meeting with others and reading and hearing about their plight and their social and moral worth. It was always somehow comforting to know that one was not alone in misery. The Southern Alliance became a movement of over a million farmers, men and women, and their evolving prescription of what should be done represented a radical challenge to the New South advocates of limited government and unchecked capitalism. The Alliance developed the most sustained mass critique of unrestrained free-market capitalism in American history, and it was by far the most far-reaching and radical protest political movement in the South from Reconstruction to the 1960s. The heart of the Populist movement, the incubator of its most profound challenge to modern capitalist America, lay in the South.

The Southern Alliance was simultaneously backward looking and uncannily modern in its program. Its myriad local social gatherings attempted to rekindle the sense of community and belonging that many farmers, especially the more geographically isolated ones, longed for. In an era of dog-eat-dog competition and laissez-faire economics, the Alliance spokesmen called for harmony and cooperation in society. In a period when local politics were often controlled by courthouse gangs and efforts were already beginning to limit the franchise, the Alliance promoted an increase in participatory democracy. Faced with distant monopolies that set policies and prices and rates with callous indifference to how they affected small farmers, the Alliance called for government price and rate controls. Aware that overproduction pushed prices down, the Alliance called for government limitation of crop acreage. Beset with high costs and exorbitant charges for services, they formed cooperative grain elevators, cotton gins, stores, and factories to make farm implements. Battered by interest rates and monetary deflation, the Alliance demanded government intervention both to bring down the cost of borrowing money and to increase the money supply. At the mercy of crop prices when harvest times bloated the immediate supplies, the Alliance—and in all these suggested remedies Macune was the primary inspiration—advocated a series of government warehouses called subtreasuries that would store nonperishable crops until the prices went up, and in the meantime would give farmers negotiable subtreasury notes worth 80 percent of the local market value of the warehoused crop.

In sum, the Southern Alliance represented a frontal assault against the governing principles of the regnant big planter-businessman-industrialist class, who, not unexpectedly, responded to the Alliance as though it were the bubonic plague. Even so, across the South between 1887 and 1890, the Alliance, finding here and there seemingly cooperative Democrats, elected six governors and gained control of eight state legislatures. But the Alliance supporters were soon disappointed by the so-called friends of the farmers they elected. Most Democratic politicians were more interested in gaining the Alliance vote than enacting their program after they were elected.

Agrarian discontent and reform were not limited to the South; farmers in the Midwest, from the Dakotas though Kansas, had been devastated by crop failures and price collapses, and the Northern Alliance that developed there— its way prepared by the organizing and teaching efforts of the Southern Alliance—mirrored the growth of the farmers' rebellion in the South. Farmers had been lulled by several years of atypically bountiful rainfall and wildly optimistic promotional literature—some of which argued that rainfall followed the plow—into moving onto the high plains and adapting agricultural practices there not really suited to the climate. When the rainy years ended, farmers found themselves bankrupt, often hungry, and with absolutely no resources left. False promises of prosperity were replaced by terrible hardship. In the northern prairie states, the Republican party was entrenched, and finding it as unresponsive to their needs as southern Alliance members found the Democrats, northern farmers pioneered the formation of a third party to carry their banner. The issue of a third party was extremely controversial in the South, where the memory of Reconstruction still made any threat to the Democratic party practically unthinkable to most southern whites. Hard-pressed Kansas farmers actually first organized a third party with the name the People's party, soon called the Populist party, and third-partyism spread across the central plains, initially provoking anguish and argument among Southern Alliance members in Texas and elsewhere in the South.

By 1890, the People's party had begun to incorporate into its membership all sorts of disillusioned farmers and reformers—old Grange members, former Greenbackers, and current Alliance spokesmen. The Populists represented a broad synthesis of protest attitudes: some were advocates of producerism, a view reminiscent of an earlier age; others shared much with modern capitalist America and simply wanted a quick economic fix, the monetization of silver; still others were strongly antimonopolistic and supported a communal, noncompetitive society. All were gathered under the broad tent of Populism, and this breadth of opinion often led to division within the ranks. Still, the communal/ producer ethos represented the cultural center of gravity of the Populist movement in the South. By 1891, the People's party was planning a national convention to be held the following year that would represent the aggregate of all these reform ideas—many of which were more relevant to farmers on the northern prairies than to those in the creek bottoms and among the red clay hills of the South. The formal organization of the People's party as a nationwide institution occurred in St. Louis in February 1892, and a presidential nominating convention was scheduled that July to meet in Omaha, Nebraska.

Although the Southern Alliance officially supported the transformation of the farmers' movement into a political party, many southern Alliance members, such as Charles Macune himself, bitterly opposed the formation of a third party. Another leader, Leonidas L. Polk, suddenly died, and with him died the Populists' best chance of bridging the sectional and ideological divisions that existed within the movement. The Southern Alliance was splintered by the controversy over entering partisan politics, and many sincere friends of reform could never bring themselves to leave the Democratic party, especially after the Senate Republicans in 1890 and 1891 had tried to pass a so-called Force Bill that would give the federal government supervisory control of elections, raising again in southerners' minds the bugaboo of a revival of Reconstruction. Other Alliance members, convinced that only a third party could deliver the needed changes, made the break. The Populist presidential candidate was James B. Weaver of Iowa, and the party platform, though it did endorse Macune's idea of a subtreasury plan, was more attuned to the needs of midwestern prairie farmers. Consequently the Populists won slightly more than a million votes nationwide, and even elected governors in Colorado, Kansas, and North Dakota, but most southern voters remained loyal to the Democratic party. Still, no third party had ever done so well in its initial presidential campaign. When in the following year the nation plunged into the worst depression in its history and the administration of Grover Cleveland, the recently elected Democratic president, seemed paralyzed over how to respond, agrarian reformers and third-party advocates felt vindicated and emboldened.

In the mid-term elections of 1894, the People's party did surprisingly well in the South, particularly in Alabama, North Carolina, and Georgia, and in a number of regions Populist leaders began cautiously to explore both cooperation with black voters and the idea of combining or "fusion" with southern Republicans. The aim was to break the Democratic stranglehold on southern politics. In North Carolina a coalition of Populists and Republicans actually gained control of the general assembly, and Texas Populists were forthright about the need to put aside meaningless racism and work together with blacks to improve everyone's economic condition. A superbly skilled black orator, John B. Rayner, was employed to speak to Texas whites in an attempt to defuse their fear of blacks' participating in politics and to speak to blacks about their need to support Populist candidates. But the Democrats proved a wary foe, both adopting some of the reforms of the Populists—again, especially in Texas and North Carolina—and employing fraud and brutality to maintain their political dominance. The stakes were high, and the presidential election of 1896 loomed as an epochal battle that might well determine the future of southern politics and the southern economy.

The nation itself approached the election with foreboding. Depression, bloody industrial strikes, and agricultural unrest had marked Cleveland's term, and while no one really knew the solution to the myriad problems facing the nation, one chimerical idea had emerged. The Silver Purchase Act of 1890, which had in effect monetized silver through the issuance of treasury notes, had been repealed in 1893 at the urging of Cleveland. The resulting deflation had exaggerated the hard times of many farmers. Western mining interests had pushed the idea that the remonetizing of silver would, by effectively expanding the money supply, bring inflation that would benefit farmers who suffered under a heavy burden of debt. The national Republican party tried to evade the issue, but at the insistence of eastern banking and commercial interests, it came out against silver and in support of the gold standard as the only basis of a sound economy. In preparation for the 1896 presidential election, Republican political operators hand-picked William McKinley of Ohio to run a front-porch campaign that kept him away from reporters and controversial statements, and the party used its ample financial resources and its influence over urban factory workers to either buy or command votes.

The conservative Democrats wanted to run Cleveland again on a strict gold standard platform, but reform Democrats had had enough. Persuaded almost against their good sense that the monetization of silver would be a panacea for the nation's problems, they succeeded in nominating a Nebraska agrarian reformer and silverite, young William Jennings Bryan, for the presidency after he had electrified the Democratic convention with a soaring oration against the evils of gold-based deflation and in favor of the "producing masses of this nation"—a phrase that farmers particularly felt described them as opposed to the evil money changers in faraway big city banks. In one deft stroke, the reform Democrats had skewered the Populists, for if they put forward their own candidate (who most certainly would have to be a silverite, too, to attract the western votes) the Populists would divide the prosilver vote and hand the election to the Republicans.

But when the Democrats, with a strong platform plank calling for the unlimited coinage of silver at the rate of sixteen ounces of silver to one ounce of gold, opportunistically reached out to the eastern Democratic goldbugs and nominated conservative Maine banker Arthur Sewall for the vice-presidency, it was more political inconsistency than the Populists could stomach. The national Populist convention went along with the Democrats and also nominated Bryan as its presidential candidate, but repudiating Sewall, the Populists nominated a true southern radical, Thomas E. Watson of Georgia, as their vice-presidential candidate. So William Jennings Bryan was saddled with two vice-presidential nominees who represented opposite visions of America. Bryan's response was to barnstorm the nation, preaching old-time virtues and the redemption of the body politic through silver. Populists in the prairie states could in good conscience urge a fusion with the Democrats because the party in local control was the Republican; for many southern Populists, faced with the memory of several years of conflict with the locally dominant Democrats—who had used fraud and violence to steal elections from the Populists in 1894—the idea of fusion with the Democrats was ideologically bankrupt.

Populist purists in the South disparaged the idea of cooperating with their erstwhile enemy, and in a number of states, Populist leaders urged the faithful to fuse with the Republicans instead. The fight was especially bitter in Texas, where Populist leaders tried to convince their followers to put aside Reconstruction memories and racial fears and combine with blacks to throw the Democrats out for the sake of Populist orthodoxy. But racism proved stronger than reform, and the Democrats had learned too well in the aftermath of Reconstruction how to steal an election. Democratic demagogues stirred up old fears with farfetched warnings of black domination. Populist efforts at fusion and at building biracial coalitions failed, and Democratic-Populist voters nationwide were confused by the opposing vice presidents that were linked to Bryan. When push came to shove, too many southerners were hesitant to break with the entrenched Democratic party and its essentially conservative political leaders they supported as much out of a habit of deference as for fear of racial change. Perhaps more important nationally, the Republicans had superior organizational skills and money galore, and their power over industrial workers allowed them often to dictate their vote. The result was a resounding victory for McKinley, a devastating defeat for the Democrats, and a movement-ending debacle for the Populists.

Southern Populists in particular were crushed. The Democrats responded in two ways. One was to perfect several schemes already underway to limit the participation of blacks in politics. The ill-fated Populist effort to form biracial coalitions in support of political reform frightened Democrats and in their minds justified their use of shocking electoral fraud in 1896. The solution to fraud, argued the Democrats, was to remove the possibility of black voting, and some disillusioned Populists like Tom Watson now agreed. (Watson in fact soon repudiated most of the liberal causes he had fought for previously and took a vicious right turn politically, becoming a fanatical racist who spewed forth venomous attacks on Jews, Catholics, and blacks. Fortunately he did not carry all his Populist supporters with him, but he sowed seeds of hatred that would in coming decades produce a shameful harvest of inhumanity in the South. Watson legitimated a kind of group paranoia whereby otherwise reasonable people could justify horrendous actions against perceived enemies.) The majority of Populists continued to advocate the widest possible franchise and the truest possible democracy, but the conservative, racist forces in the larger white population carried the day. In state after state, ingenious methods of disenfranchising blacks were enacted, and new requirements that voters be literate and be able to interpret the state constitution, pay a poll tax, and have grandfathers who had been eligible to vote were transparent attempts to hide the raw anti-black motives of the election "reformers." The result, by 1900, was the almost complete disenfranchisement of southern blacks and—not completely unintentionally—a substantial reduction in the number of rural poor whites who could vote. (Democratic elites had over the previous two decades already limited voting by propertyless urban whites whose potential political power they feared.) The conservative Democrats had devised a sure method of maintaining themselves in firm control of southern politics.

The other way Democrats shored up their control was, once blacks were safely excluded from the franchise along with the poorest and potentially most radical whites, to open up the Democratic party to popular participation. Party rules were liberalized, United States senators were directly elected by the people rather than by the state legislatures, and statewide primaries, in which only whites were permitted to vote, were developed to give voters a voice in the selection of party candidates. Now that the threat of voter rebellion was no more, the Democrats approved making elections more honest, with rules about regularizing polling places and ballots, outlawing bribes, and even accepting the secret ballot. Many old Populist reformers were both too tired and too disheartened to protest much any more. Restrictions on voting drastically shrank the number of people participating in elections, and in several states there emerged Democrats of modest reform intentions, such as Governor James S. Hogg of Texas, who adopted some Populist reform ideas. With this combination of opening up politics to safe white voters and depriving blacks of the right to vote, seasoned with a sprinkling of reform, southern Democrats had learned the recipe for control; they ruled the region almost unchallenged for the next half-century. This was the era of the Solid South.

CHAPTER 24

Change with
a Southern Accent

WOMEN IN THE POST–CIVIL WAR SOUTH

The Confederate South was forced by wartime necessity to undergo remarkable changes—its cities grew, its industrial base expanded, and its central government strengthened and sought to control aspects of life southerners had always thought beyond the law. But these revolutionary changes were temporary. White women, too, found their lives only momentarily changed in some ways, while in other respects their lives were transformed. At the heart of the transformation was the demise of slavery. White women living on plantations, who were a small minority of southern women, suddenly found themselves without maids, cooks, washerwomen, and the like. For wives of yeoman with few or no slaves, the prospect of making do without black labor was less daunting; such women had always worked long and hard to keep their families' tables set and their husband and children in clothes. For plantation mistresses, emancipation meant they had to garden, cook, wash, mend, and keep house themselves, and many found such unending and often monotonous labor a disheartening postscript to Confederate defeat. Many held up bravely and professed to being glad they were free of the responsibility of disciplining and caring for slaves, but most missed the luxury of having others perform the humdrum chores of everyday life. Some at first took their anger and frustration out on any Yankees they happened to meet. Time did not heal these wounds, but plantation mistresses came to terms with their changed world and learned to make do.

Of course, many erstwhile plantation mistresses still had husbands who were landowners, or were landowners themselves, and over time, and through such arrangements as sharecropping, many southern white women in short order again had the wherewithal to have black women, now free but still poor and powerless, back in their houses cooking and washing and caring for the babies. White women had also, during the course of the war, learned they had skills and money-earning capacities they had never before had to use; with husbands dead or lame, and with low cotton prices putting financial pressure on even the owners of many acres, women found ways to augment the family income. Sometimes they did sewing, became postmistresses, took in boarders, taught school, sold eggs and butter to merchants in local towns, or found any number of ways to supplement what the crops brought in. Probably, in most cases, women used the money they earned to pay for their families' necessities, but certainly such income augmentation also helped on occasion to pay for the black woman who daily had first to care for the white family before she could care for her own.

Freedwomen had minimally more freedom than before the war, and they along with their husbands had the benefit of a slightly larger portion of their agricultural output. The sharecropping system—despite the hard work, poverty, and constant moving from farm to farm—meant a greater control over their lives than they had enjoyed as slaves. Black families were more intact in freedom than in slavery, and black mothers did not have to fear losing their husband or children through sale. Still, most black women could look forward to lives filled with back-breaking toil, long hours, and extremely limited upward mobility. Yet poverty was far better than slavery.

For many white women, the net economic result of the Civil War was a fall in their standard of living. The price of cotton fell, state and local taxes increased, and many of their husbands and sons either did not return from battle or came home missing a leg or an arm and found their productive capacity lessened. White women, particularly the increased number of war widows, were often forced to find employment, but even when they had to earn money, their domestic duties did not lessen. They still had hungry mouths at home to feed and the laundry to do. Women's lives were no longer confined to the home, but their lives were enriched little by their gainful employment. One of the common justifications for attracting textile mills to the South was that they would provide badly needed job opportunities for women and children; factory work, however, meant long hours, boredom, danger, bad pay, and little or no upward mobility. Perhaps one of the reasons southern white males so glorified the image of southern womanhood was because they somehow understood how dreary and unrewarding the reality of life was for their mothers and wives. And perhaps one of the reasons most southern white women continued to accept hierarchical conceptions of family life that elevated the husband's authority is because they sought to mend the wounded morale of menfolk defeated on both the military and economic battlefields. Women returning to traditional roles, like the rise of the Lost Cause movement that practically sacralized the Confederate effort even as it accepted defeat, was a response to the attenuation of traditional male roles in the decades after the Civil War.

From a modern perspective, farm women of both races had a very confining existence. Most days and early evenings were filled with the unending chores associated with running a household in days before modern conveniences (which, it later has turned out, are not as liberating as futurists had once hoped). All the food had to be homegrown or at least processed at home. All the water used in a household had to be drawn from a well or spring and carried to the home. The cooking was done on woodstoves, and of course wood had to be cut, brought into the house, loaded in the stoves, the fires tended, the ashes taken out. Washing and ironing clothes required arduous labor, with clothes agitated in a huge pot over a low fire using a stick, complemented with hand-rubbing the wet clothes over a corrugated "rub board." The clothes were wrung by hand, then hung on lines or fences or obliging tree limbs to dry. Those that were to be ironed had to have starch added, and the irons were heavy "iron" devices that were heated on the stove or fireplace and had to be held with a rag. The whole enterprise was hot, tiring labor that was especially hard on the back, making many women stooped at an early age.

Childrearing in an age before paper diapers or diaper service, pre-processed baby food, or supplemental infant formula was equally arduous. Women performed these duties without ceasing, having seen their mothers so burdened, and expected little relief in the future. Economically better-off white women turned, as we have seen, to black women for help; but most white women could not afford paid assistance, and black women often had to do double duty, for they had responsibilities at their own home. Older children, as a matter of course, were involved in the work of childrearing and running a household.

Rural farm women's lives revolved around their domestic duties. There was no money or leisure time for extensive traveling or the kind of drawing room culture associated with upper-middle-class women in northeastern cities. What few diaries exist reveal preoccupation with the affairs of everyday life: comments about when the peas will be ready to be picked, the setting hen about to hatch, a neighbor's child sick with the croup, and the number of jars of jelly and jam put up. This represented a body of concerns separate from men's, and to that degree, a separate women's culture existed, but it was more matter of fact than self-conscious, and little theorizing was devoted to it. Even in music there seems to have been some gender differentiation, with women usually singing ballads and sentimental parlor songs in domestic situations, while men occasionally sang humorous and bawdy songs outside the home. It was also usually the men who played the fiddle or banjo. But certainly when families sat around on long evenings and sang for their own entertainment, both men and women (and children, also) knew, loved, and sang together most of the common repertoire. Women especially were involved in the church, and not just as hearers of the word but as doers too. On average, they made up at least two-thirds of church membership. They taught Sunday School classes, organized themselves into societies to visit the sick and raise money for various church needs, and planned days to beautify the graveyard. By some form of alchemy, women combined their courage, grit, and love for family members to produce an often surprising zest for living. Such women discovered hope, purpose, and joy in their mundane endeavors. In their church participation, through songs and tales, by the comforting ties of kinship and friendship, and by means of simple forms of folk recreation, ranging from camp meetings to quilting parties, they found a way partially to overcome the dreary vicissitudes of poverty and unceasing labor. These were not women without spunk, and they often overcame in spirit what they lacked in worldly wealth.

Even while women in the late nineteenth century could not vote and were presumed to have no expertise in politics, they were at least as aware as their husbands were of their family's economic plight in days of falling cotton prices. Women as well as men understood that the economic system was not working well when a season of hard work left them further in debt at the country store. The Grange movement had offered farm women an opportunity to visit and commiserate with neighboring women, and the Farmer's Alliance meetings were often family affairs. Farm women read the Alliance and later Populist newspapers, occasionally wrote pungent letters to both, and emboldened their husbands to work for reform. The economic injustice associated with sharecropping in an age of agricultural surplus, high interest rates, and both restricted markets and sources of credit served to bend rigid gender roles. But while farm women were morally outraged at injustice, advocated economic change, stiffened their husbands' reform backbones, and sometimes wished wistfully for the vote themselves, an aggressive women's rights movement did not develop among southern farm women. One Texas woman, after an especially pithy letter in 1878 to the *Southern Mercury*, the Texas Populist newspaper, felt constrained to add apologetically that "this is written in rather coarse language for the ladies department, but my very soul is stirred and prompts me to say what I have said."

Urbanization in the South lagged far behind that of the Northeast and Midwest, but there was a proliferation of marketing towns in the South after the Civil War and gradual growth of the old port, river, and railroad cities. Southern women in towns and small cities had many more opportunities to interact with other women and organize themselves as various interest groups. There had long been women's societies attached to churches and benevolent societies of various kinds, including temperance societies. The Woman's Christian Temperance Union (WCTU), the best known of these, first began in the North in the mid-1870s, and by the early 1880s, WCTU clubs began organizing across the South. Even earlier, women in several northeastern cities had formed women's clubs of various names, but aimed less at societal ills than at the self-improvement of their individual members. By the final two decades of the nineteenth century, the women's club movement had spread to the South, and every small town soon had an organization of women seeking self-education in literature, music, new developments in science, and the like. Black women had separate but similar clubs for self-improvement. In an age when there were few opportunities for women to get post-secondary education, these women's clubs answered to a strong hunger for learning, a sense of community outside the household and more inclusive than the members' own church, and a seldom articulated discontent with the limits placed on women's lives by social habit.

State federations of women's clubs were soon organized, and after 1890, state federations in the South affiliated with the General Federation of Women's Clubs, a national association. To some degree, this national tie broadened the agendas of the southern clubs, but primarily their purposes evolved in relation to local concerns. The appeal of these clubs to informed, energetic, upper-middle-class women was in direct response to the limits they found elsewhere in society. By the turn of the century, the club women sought ways to inject their values into the larger society. They held to traditional women's values in that their concerns dealt with matters of health, aesthetics, education, cleanliness—attitudes normally associated with women's nurturing responsibilities in the household. But with their increasing self-confidence in these values, women broadened their concept of the household, recognizing that good health, good morals, good education, and "higher" values should not be confined to the home.

Women began seeking ways to extend their nurturing skills to the community around them, and as such, their clubs evolved in purpose from self-culture to community service. By 1900, women's clubs in the South were advocating health reforms in the schools, clean water fountains in towns, playgrounds, city beautification projects, and cleanliness standards for dairies and city markets. They worked with male politicians, pressuring them through increasing public awareness of their aims and raising funds to begin pilot projects that they then shamed the men into taking over as public responsibilities. Long before they won the right to vote, southern white women worked for civic improvement, and both helped usher in the Progressive movement in the South and represented the ethos of the movement. Black club women were also avid promoters of efforts to benefit their race. They could not, of course, appeal to their disenfranchised husbands for overt political support, but black women had long experience with using their social and civic clubs, their churches, and their inexhaustible determination to address the needs of the black population. Black women were often politically invisible but they were not without influence, and they helped secure a modicum of Progressive-era services for black communities across the South.

Historians have long been aware that the churches offered an important arena for women's activity in the South. Even in the antebellum era, southern white women through their churches had organized for benevolent purposes, raising money for charity, for funding Sunday Schools, and for supporting church programs of many sorts. In the postbellum period, church women expanded these activities, and in many cities, female leaders in evangelical churches progressed from efforts on behalf of their local churches to broader denominational activities to work ultimately on behalf of such interdenominational movements as the Woman's Christian Temperance Union and general programs focused on community uplift and social betterment. Frustration engendered by the discrepancy between such women's community-improvement agendas and their political disenfranchisement often led to support for woman suffrage.

Yet clearly the progression was not always thus from evangelical churches to the campaign to vote. Research on women's reform activities in Galveston, Texas, for example, suggests that at least in older, more established southern urban regions, elite white women from Episcopal and Presbyterian churches first responded to the social problems associated with urban growth. These women organized a variety of church-based associations that addressed a range of urban ills. In the case of Galveston, the great hurricane of 1900, in effect, wiped the slate clean, and in the face of that unprecedented challenge, elite women with strong connections to the male political establishment pioneered a broad range of responses that prefigured, promoted, and institutionalized what historians have labeled Progressivism. Such white-gloved elite women identified urban community ills, diagnosed solutions, and worked to achieve both short-term and permanent reforms and regulatory agencies. Ultimately, many of these women from the social and economic elite became effective proponents of their right to vote. Women's involvement in politics, reform, and suffrage was both varied and complex, but women were heard, and they learned how to be effective.

PROGRESSIVISM, SOUTHERN STYLE

The election "reforms" devised by the various southern states in the final decade of the nineteenth century had been rationalized as precursors to honest politics by removing the possibility of black votes being bought or stolen to promote one party or another. We have already seen how devastating these new election procedures—poll taxes, registration requirements, literacy or grandfather clauses, and the like—were on black participation in politics. Not incidentally, hundreds of thousands of white voters, too—the very ones who had been most apt to support political radicalism—were also eliminated from voting. Soon most states completed the process by developing white Democratic primaries. In one sense, the primary was more democratic than the old procedure of having a caucus of party bigwigs pick party candidates, and initially primaries were used only on a local or county level. South Carolina first began the procedure on a statewide basis in 1896, but the development rapidly spread throughout the South.

Because the majority of southern voters were Democrats, and blacks had been largely eliminated from voting, the white primary effectively became *the* election that counted in most of the South. Most counties did not even have an active Republican party organization or, if one existed, it was an empty shell of a party that continued mainly as a way to get patronage jobs (at the post office, for example) from Republican presidents. Hence, the winner of the Democratic primary was a shoo-in in the official election and, in fact, all the competition, hoopla, and enthusiasm associated with politics revolved around the primary. The official election was anticlimactic, with the turnout only a tiny percentage even of the reduced vote of the primary.

With blacks effectively eliminated as voters and the Republican party uncompetitive almost everywhere and practically nonexistent in most places, the locus of political conflict shifted to the Democratic white primary. In fact, by doing away with party caucuses, the primary opened up white politics to influence by organized pressure groups, and by disenfranchising blacks and most dispossessed whites (especially propertyless urban whites), politics was rendered safe enough to allow spirited debate among competing factions of white Democrats. The result, in every southern state, was the emergence of a bifactional politics that pitted a variety of reform forces against the forces of status quo. The South was a region of one-party politics, but under the umbrella of that one party there was significant protest, competition, and pressure for change. Yet the most effective promoters of change, aware of the bitter controversies of the Reconstruction and Populist eras, tried to throttle radicalism and modulate the call for reform by appealing to southern tradition. The perceived necessity to work safely within the confines of the possible often cast a conservative shadow even over the most significant reform efforts of the period, particularly with regard to race. To an unfortunate degree, Progressivism in the early twentieth-century South was mostly for whites.

Yet there were some restraints on reform everywhere in the nation, and the social drag of racism and tradition in the South did not completely thwart the reform impulse. There was a notable Progressive movement in the South— a recognition that the region had severe problems and needed an effort to solve them. Every historical event has antecedents, and Progressivism was obviously related to its rural predecessor, Populism. Yet the relationship between the two was not always obvious, and the sources of support, even the desired social outcomes, were often quite different. Populism at its most radical sought to repudiate the competitive basis of modern capitalism and return society to an earlier model of political economy founded on cooperation and face-to-face relationships. The stinging and demoralizing defeat of 1896, accompanied by fraud, violence, and broken promises, caused many Populist supporters simply to withdraw from politics, more disillusioned than ever with the modern market economy. But then cotton prices improved slightly in the two decades following 1896, taking even more of the edge off political protest. Muted prosperity associated with urban growth, an increase in manufacturing—particularly textiles in the Southeast, iron and steel in Alabama, and the beginning of the oil industry in Texas, Louisiana, and Oklahoma—and the gradual rise of an urban-commercial-professional-industrial middle class in the South created new support for change.

All the problems of farmers had by no means been solved, and a significant portion of the Populist agenda was taken up by the new breed of reformers, especially the call to regulate railroad rates in many states and to control monopolistic purchasing practices for certain crops, such as the effort to end the domination of the tobacco trust in the Black Patch tobacco region of Kentucky in the early twentieth century. But there was a different tone, a different vision of the future, among Progressive reformers. In large part because of where they lived and how they made their living, the urban middle-class reformers were not at war with modernity. They accepted the idea of competition, large-scale industry, and the market economy; they simply wanted the system to work more fairly, more efficiently, and to the maximum benefit of the majority. In other words, the Progressives believed in what at the time was called good government.

This concern with the commonweal had several origins. The genuine excesses of unregulated capitalism—brutalization of employees, vicious competition, environmental destruction, exploitation of child laborers, and nightmarish unconcern with cleanliness in food processing—produced a counterreaction in the South as well as in the nation, and national magazines and published exposés fueled indigenous anticorporation sentiment among many southerners. Humanitarianism burgeoned, and many comparatively well-off urban dwellers became sensitive to the poverty and injustice surrounding them but not actually impinging on their own lives. This growth in moral consciousness came in part from the moral outrage that had often marked Populist reformers in the recent past and in part from a handful of urban ministers and denominational leaders and publicists who developed a new social consciousness that represented a mild regional variant of the Social Gospel. And, almost phoenix-like, the old ideology of southern progress first articulated in the New South movement of the 1880s reemerged, chastened of its easy optimism and now recommending a series of reforms necessary to facilitate prosperity and progress. This new ideology of progress emphasized the aspects of southern life that had to be improved if the South were to enjoy abundance and partake of the American dream.

The result of these various and often complementary sources of reform was a cornucopia of efforts, large and small, to remake the South. Farmers should diversify their crops and practice scientific agriculture, hence the promotion of agricultural colleges and the development of model farms and the farm extension service. Education was seen to be a prerequisite to economic growth, so many efforts arose to improve schools, train better teachers, and enforce school attendance. Diseases such as hookworm and pellagra were slowly recognized to be sapping southerners of both races of the energy necessary to be efficient workers or students, so agencies arose to promote cleanliness, sanitary toilets and water supplies, and uncontaminated meat and dairy products. Evidence available today suggests that because of poverty and malnutrition, southerners on average were shorter, slighter, and more prone to debilitating diseases than were their northern contemporaries, conditions that obviously had economic consequences. Urban experts were called upon to make cities cleaner, provide the rudiments of a public health system, and develop efficient governing mechanisms for urban areas—the commission form of city government, for example, developed in Galveston in 1900 after the great hurricane had almost destroyed the city and forced its leaders boldly to consider new ways of meeting unprecedented problems. Staunton, Virginia, in 1908, pioneered the use of the city manager system of municipal governance. While Progressive-era reform is usually associated with whites, blacks also identified only-too-real social problems, advocated ameliorative actions, and learned to pry benefits from unfriendly government agencies. Black women appeared less threatening to white male officials than did black males; consequently, organized black women were often an effective voice for their people. Black women reached out creatively to form alliances with white women reformers, and although the whites found it almost impossible to submerge their racism, a degree of interracial cooperation did occur, bringing some social services to blacks and creating tiny cracks in the massive wall of segregation that paralyzed southern political and social life.

The reform message, usually argued with the benefit of scientific and sociological data and advocated both for economic and humanitarian reasons, covered a broad range of activities. Farmers were taught new techniques and new crops; housewives learned improved ways of preserving and canning food; towns and cities developed sewage and water works and attempted to control the indiscriminate spitting of tobacco juice and the use of a common dipper at water fountains. Prostitution, drunkenness, abandoned children, victims of disease and industrial accident—all forms of evil and misfortune—found groups and agencies armed to combat them. Prohibition was a particularly divisive cause. The movement had begun in earnest in the 1880s with local option laws; supported strongly by women, rural voters, and evangelical Protestants, in the early twentieth century, the movement began to focus on statewide prohibition. Georgia was the first state (in 1907) to become legally dry, and thereafter states were often in turmoil over the issue, with some states reversing their positions in subsequent elections. However, by 1919, when the Eighteenth Amendment passed with overwhelming southern support, every former state of the Confederacy except Louisiana had adopted state prohibition. Of course, no one should think that the drinking of alcoholic beverages ceased in the region. As always, many southerners had a casual or selective attitude toward the law, and some saw prohibition more as a way to restrict drinking by blacks than by respectable citizens such as themselves.

Businessmen addressed ways to improve the efficiency of their workers and, with an educated, healthy work force, attract additional northern investment. Religious leaders dispensed charity to the destitute and battled such enemies of moral behavior as the whiskey distillers, though unlike northern Social Gospel ministers, they seldom constructed a theological critique of the social institutions that produced or allowed poverty and injustice. Women organized first in church societies or in culture clubs came to expand their conception of their proper nurturing role to include not just their homes but their communities. The result was an effective phalanx of female reformers who both pointed out social problems—in schools and food processing plants, for example—and worked for solutions. Most of these southern reformers were white, and most of them were blind to racial injustice and the special needs of the blacks, but despite their limitations, the southern Progressives produced a significant body of reform. Working cautiously and with an eye always on the politically possible, blacks—especially black women—succeeded in preventing Progressivism from being a completely white-only movement. That they were able to do so in an era of heightened racial tensions speaks to both their skill and their determination.

Reform proposals, of course, required changes in the social policies of industries, institutions, and individuals, so in the end, reform led to politics. Reform meant pressure to change, meant regulation, meant developing standards and seeing that they were met. So whether the source of Progressive ideas was religion, general humanitarianism, the ethos of scientific efficiency, organized women's groups, or the lingering influence of Populism, the result came to express itself in the political arena. And the peculiar, changed politics of the post-Populist era—a shrunken plebiscite and the procedures of the white primary—contributed ironically to an effervescence of political debate and reform. Beginning on the local and state levels, southern Progressivism eventually partook of the national movement, eventually playing an essential role in Woodrow Wilson's congressional efforts to enact reform legislation. For the first time in over fifty years, southern legislators, whose seniority gave them disproportionate power in Congress, played a positive role in national policy.

The conservative Democrats and disillusioned Populists who had supported restricting the right to vote had been more interested in removing blacks from politics and preventing a recurrence of popular reform than in cleaning up politics—as the ostensible rationale had it—so whites could freely discuss the real issues facing their region. But once more, history had a way of producing unexpected results. As discussed before, the development of the party primary and the abolition of the party caucus in fact made the Democratic party responsive to issue-oriented groups, as long as they were white. And the Progressive era generated many groups who had strong concerns about the ills of southern society, men and women who were motivated, informed, and willing to unite to effect change. Politics became the arena in which the issues of the day were debated, coalitions formed, and policies proposed to correct whatever various groups identified as societal problems. Southern political contests were hard-fought because the stakes were high—or so they seemed to highly motivated and committed reformers at every level of society. The Democratic party in local and state elections witnessed a new level of issue-oriented politics in the early twentieth century and a new kind of political leader.

A significant number of Progressive mayors, governors, and legislative leaders represented the southern genteel tradition, except that now they tended to be from urban areas. Educated, moderate, they calmly, almost scientifically, studied southern problems and advocated cautious, rational solutions. They established boards to evaluate the conditions of various aspects of society and called upon experts to suggest proper action. Boards of health were one result, and commissions were formed to study and make recommendations. Urban Progressives—governors such as Andrew J. Montague of Virginia, Hoke Smith of Georgia, and Braxton B. Comer of Alabama—were genuinely motivated by a sense of *noblesse oblige* to serve the people of their state and thereby usher in progress and prosperity, and they intended by doing so to prevent potentially more radical change—the specter of a Populist revolt run rampant.

Such governors, in fact, did push through far-reaching legislation that improved the public schools and the public health, expanded the range of governmental services, and prevented the worst excesses of exploitative capitalism. Several states passed child labor laws and rules to regulate working hours and safety conditions in coal mines and textile mills. But perhaps even more important than the legislation passed were the boards and commissions that resulted, agencies that attempted to regulate railroads, insurance companies, and public utilities. Regulatory commissions often failed to meet expectations because commission members frequently were too close to the interests they were supposed to regulate, but the commissions usually prevented the worst abuses. Local civic organizations and state-funded agencies also did everything from providing agricultural extension services and demonstration farms to home economics instruction to hookworm eradication programs. Government on the state and local level gained a new importance and became far more pervasive in its influence for the public good. Government was, in the eyes of the urban Progressives, society's helpmate, not its enemy. But another type of Progressive politician emerged too, one whose roots clearly went back to Populism and whose appeal was more visceral and less dependent upon experts.

Like some effervescence from the agrarian radicalism of the past, in several southern states, popular leaders arose who used an emotional appeal to the interests of the common people to win political office and push through legislation that was narrowly progressive. In fact, in programs that they advanced, these more rough-hewn leaders differed little from their more genteel urban counterparts who used expert opinion to promote their causes, but the often outrageous stump behavior of these popular leaders has frequently obscured their genuine and substantial reform efforts. With flamboyant rhetoric and resort to a politics of symbols, these skilled mass politicians, dismissively called southern demagogues, used their ability to win popular support to push against the obstacles to change. Conservative political leaders and institutions resistant to reform saw these politicians as unprincipled manipulators of the unwashed, and in truth, occasionally these so-called demagogues blurred the line between truth and propaganda, honesty and corruption, public service and self-aggrandizement, but no more so than the opponents of reform did. In the rough-and-tumble world of southern politics, reformers did not always play by Sunday-School rules, and neither did their opponents. We should look more at results than process, but the demagogues were often so colorful that their antics deserve description.

Mississippi produced two popular leaders who revolted aristocratic planters. The first was James K. Vardaman, a tall, dramatic-looking man with his long black hair hanging to his shoulders, wearing a trademark white Prince Albert coat, a big black hat, and riding to rural political gatherings aboard an eight-wheeled log wagon pulled by twenty yoke of oxen. From the speaker's stand he held his audiences spellbound, his powerful oratory rolling out over the crowd and, by turn, inspiring them, angering them, and empowering them to believe they amounted to something. With the persuasive tools of the country revivalist, Vardaman—the Great White Chief, he was called—employed stark racism and class divisiveness to battle the establishment and push forward a remarkably progressive program for whites only. "He looked like a top-notch medicine man," Delta aristocrat William Alexander Percy said in derision, but Vardaman was governor of Mississippi from 1904 to 1908 and in 1911 rose to the U.S. Senate.

One of Vardaman's protégés, Theodore G. Bilbo, after a short interlude followed the White Chief to the governor's office. Bilbo was a small, feisty, ratterrier of a man, whose ability to employ invective and scurrilous sarcasm at his opponents' expense recalls John Randolph of Roanoke back in the Age of Jefferson. William Alexander Percy might call Bilbo a "pert little monster, glib and shameless, with that sort of cunning common to criminals which passes for intelligence," but Bilbo was the hero of the backcountry rednecks with whom he cultivated an identity. Less an overt racist than Vardaman, Bilbo, too, shepherded modest progressive reforms through the Mississippi legislature.

The campaign style of Vardaman and Bilbo helped popularize the stereotype of the southern demagogue as a stock character in American political culture, but to the extent that the stereotype presents a one-dimensional portrait of the demagogue as simply a racist, it is false. Racist they were, as indeed was the society in which they thrived, but the so-called demagogues often understood the needs of the common man, even sometimes the blacks, and practicing politics as the art of the possible, they used Negro-baiting and verbal pyrotechnics to budge the status quo. The Mississippi pair, of course, were not the only such practitioners of mass politics.

In state after state, masters of political harangue arose who understood the common people and often articulated their needs and fears. Not all these so-called demagogues who became governors ever developed a program of progressive legislation. Some, like South Carolina's Pitchfork Ben Tillman, divided class against class mainly to get control of the Democratic party, but others were like Tillman's successor, Coleman Blease, who used his power to sway the textile workers to advocate changes that benefited the poor. Jeff Davis of Arkansas espoused radical reforms on behalf of the common folk and wore a Confederate-gray frock coat to complete the symbolism suggested by his name, but he was ultimately ineffective in the state legislature. And Georgia's Tom Watson had been a heroic figure battling the establishment in the heyday of the Populist revolt, but in the early twentieth century, the meaner angel of his personality became dominant and he became a bitter, racist, Jew-baiting, anti-Catholic professional hater.

There were also significant reform politicians such as Governor John M. Parker of Louisiana, who hailed from the planter class (he was a prominent New Orleans cotton buyer as well) and showed that the Progressive impulse ranged from hillbilly radicals to planters and urban patricians. All in all, in the early twentieth-century South, Progressivism was a multifaceted movement that lent Woodrow Wilson support on the national level. Yet, in the final analysis, the Progressive reforms that were enacted and the innumerable agencies and institutions that developed on the state and local level made only incremental progress in solving the deep-rooted economic and racial problems of the South. Even Franklin D. Roosevelt's more thoroughgoing New Deal found the impoverished South a daunting project.

INDUSTRIALIZING THE SOUTH

For most readers, any discussion of so-called southern demagogues and southern poverty in the early twentieth century produces ready images of woebegone sharecroppers and mountain hillbillies living in unkempt shacks amid eroded cotton fields or beyond the forks of the creek. The South was still poor and still primarily agricultural into the 1930s, but that stereotype of rural destitution insufficiently recognizes the degree to which industrialization had begun to change the economic landscape of the region. Cotton textile mills had, of course, begun to develop in the late antebellum era, but by the closing decades of the nineteenth century, the textile mill village had become commonplace along the Piedmont of Virginia, the Carolinas, Georgia, and into Alabama. Powered by water, made profitable by cheap labor—much of it supplied by women and children—and often controlled by autocratic, if paternalistic, owners, textile mills provided dead-end jobs for almost 100,000 southerners in 1900, roughly one-third of the nation's textile workers. The pay was low, the hours long, the air filled with lint, and the employment precarious, but for many poor whites, the prospects in the factory seemed brighter than in the cotton or tobacco fields.

Town leaders and investors saw cotton mills as a visible symbol of modernity and an object of civic pride even as they hoped to profit; occasionally, advocates of mills actually believed that providing factory jobs was a species of philanthropy. Yet, too often, poor whites merely traded agricultural poverty for mill poverty, and even though community support structures emerged in both the mills themselves and in the mill villages, they were seldom as strong and complete as those in rural agricultural settings. Textile mill workers' low salaries made them weak consumers, and the resulting low tax base hindered the development of such basic institutions as adequate schools. Agricultural poverty had similar results. The point is that a significant increase in industrial employment in much of the South should not be automatically equated with emergent prosperity.

Since colonial days, many southerners had worked in the mines and the forests, but not until the end of the nineteenth century did the South engage in both extractive industries in truly large-scale fashion. Both northern and southern military engineers and topographers noticed evidence of significant coal reserves during the Civil War, but many of the best sources were too remote to be economically feasible. Only when railroads began to penetrate the Appalachian mountains in western Maryland, West Virginia, western North Carolina, and eastern Kentucky and Tennessee did southern coal find ready access to fuel northern industrial growth. One of the profound ironies of southern history is that about the same time that the national press discovered Appalachia and portrayed it as a region suspended in time—a sort of cultural fossil where our "contemporary ancestors" lived as they might have lived centuries ago—the region was being delivered to the industrial interests of the North.

Coal agents traveled through Appalachia buying mineral rights for a pittance, rails snaked up river valleys into the innermost recesses of the region, and ill-paid miners began their dangerous borings into the hearts of the mountains to cart out the fuel that fed the blast furnaces and factories of the nation. Even the small-scale efforts of the 1880s and 1890s had environmental consequences, but as the equipment and demands of the new century grew in size, mountains were literally devoured. The cost in both human and ecological terms was catastrophic. Grimy company coal towns dotted the region; miners died from cave-ins and noxious gases; and violence met workers' efforts to earn more than starvation wages. Some fortunes were made, but few of the fortunate lived permanently in the South. Cheap coal, low wages, and intimidated or sold-out governing officials made much of Appalachia an angry wound—hardly the romantic land of folk ballads and primitive customs described in travel and local-color literature. Bitter labor strikes, such as the one in the 1930s that caused Harlan County, Kentucky, to become known as "Bloody Harlan," finally brought to much of the nation's attention the complicated and often tragic results of untrammeled modernization and exploitation of a fragile human and natural ecosystem.

In the late nineteenth and early twentieth centuries, southern workers, especially in mining, iron and steel production, and lumbering, had occasionally attempted to unionize for better wages and safer working conditions. Companies used violence and employed strikebreakers to defeat these efforts. Many of these union activities were surprisingly biracial—workers black and white often toiled side by side and understood their common economic needs. However, relations outside the work site (company picnics, for example) that involved women and children were strictly segregated. Companies were quick to fan the embers of racism when they saw its divisive possibilities. Some of the anti-union violence, like the so-called Louisiana-Texas lumber war of 1911 to 1913, was shockingly brutal, and it succeeded in crushing union organizing activities. Not until the New Deal and afterward were unions moderately successful in the South.

Like mining, the lumber industry had existed in the South since colonial days. But also like mining, the scale and ecological effects of lumbering changed dramatically between 1880 and 1920. Of course, the people of the South had long made their houses and barns and fences of wood, burned it for fuel, and laid ties under the rails that increasingly bound the region into a nationwide economy. But in the final two decades of the nineteenth century, as northern urban growth mushroomed even as the forest reserves of the Northeast and Midwest dwindled, the demand for southern hardwoods in particular boomed. By the early twentieth century, giant national lumber companies were buying huge tracts of southern timberland and transforming the scale of the lumber industry.

Earlier log cutting had been almost a family activity, performed by fathers and sons and brothers when agricultural tasks allowed. Increased markets began to change the industry; in the Piedmont and coastal South, logs were cut and hauled to railheads or rivers by ox-drawn wagons. In the mountains of Appalachia, logs were cut and floated down streams and rivers; sometimes when the water level was too low, loggers waited for spring rains or even built dams to stockpile water for scheduled releases. In these cases, the rampaging logs gouged out the banks and damaged the natural water courses, but few involved in the lumber trade had strong environmental scruples. Agents for giant lumber companies roamed the South, buying timber rights. Much of the South's virgin forest still stood in 1880, with mighty hardwood trees of four to eight feet in diameter soaring 150 feet or more in the sky. In early logging days, only

Part IV

the tallest, straightest trees were cut, trimmed, then pulled out by mules or oxen to the streams or wagons. But after 1900, train tracks increasingly reached out from huge hardwood and long-leaf pine mills into the surrounding forest. Steam-powered skidders replaced animals to pull the logs to waiting railcars, and improved band saws sped the process of felling logs. In 1900, about one-fifth of the southern industrial workers were employed in some aspect of the timber industry. In 1910, Louisiana was the second-largest producer of lumber in the nation. By 2000 the South alone produced more lumber than any other country in the world, about 16 percent of the world's total.

Clear-cutting techniques left the land denuded, producing problems of erosion. From Appalachia to East Texas, gigantic hardwood mills entered a region, reached their rail tentacles out, quickly cut the forests, then closed the mill and took up the rails and moved on. Almost a century later, embankments in second-growth forest are often a mute reminder of rail lines that once served a lumbering boom of giant proportions. On the eve of World War I, southern lumber mills turned out billions of board feet annually. By the 1930s, with national demand at low levels and the great forests cut over, southern lumber production plummeted. Now, primarily second-growth trees were available, and on cotton-exhausted lands, scrub yellow pine was a pale reflection of the forest that once swept almost unbroken from Maryland past East Texas.

On the very eve of the depression, chemist Dr. Charles H. Herty, working for the U.S. Forest Service, perfected a process to produce pulp and newsprint from southern yellow pine. A prototype paper mill—appropriately named Southland Paper Mill, Inc.—was constructed in Lufkin, Texas, in 1939, with production beginning in 1940, and a new southern forest industry was launched. (Before, most newsprint was imported from Canada.) Entrepreneur Ernest Kurth spearheaded construction of the mill, assisted by funding from the federal government, and skilled paper workers were imported from Canada. Yellow pine was plentiful now in the region. The majestic long-leaf pines that had three centuries earlier dominated southern forests had been decimated by generations of logging, slashing for turpentine production, and even the grazing of herds of feral hogs that acquired a place in southern legend as "piney wood rooters." Smaller yellow pine was in the twentieth century the most ubiquitous of southern trees; it grew rapidly on poor, worn-out soil—often abandoned cotton fields—and the paper mills required small, short logs easily lifted by hand onto inexpensive bobtail trucks. With cotton production dying because of the boll weevil and many former sharecroppers underemployed because of farm mechanization (the tractor and the mechanical cotton picker), thousands of rural men supplemented their income cutting pulpwood in off-season, hauling it in old trucks over the network of farm-to-market paved roads being built in the South. The pulpwood truck became as much a symbol of the post–World War II South as had the cotton wagon earlier, and by mid-century the South was producing more than half the nation's basic pulp paper stock. In more recent decades thousands of acres have been devoted to pine-tree farms, producing not only pulpwood but also logs once again for the lumber industry. More than a billion pine trees are now planted annually in the South, but the results are not natural forests—with abundant birds and small animal life—but relatively sterile monocultural "crops" of pines planted row by row.

In 1861, everyone considered Texas a part of the South; a century later its regional identification was debatable, while Texans themselves often claimed with what had become typical braggadocio that Texas was a world unto itself. What made all the difference was oil—black gold—an unctuous combustible liquid that brought untold wealth to the state and transformed its economy and cities. As early as the mid-sixteenth century, a remnant of Hernando de Soto's men, wrecked ashore eastern Texas, had used a gooey petroleum substance found floating in the water to caulk their boats. Later observers noted traces of oil and tar balls in the gulf waters, and on occasion, oil seepage ruined water wells. Perhaps the first oil found on purpose was discovered in a shallow well near Nacogdoches, Texas, in 1866, but there was little or no market for the substance—neither as lubricant nor as the basis of various patent medicines. The first real production came in Corsicana, Texas, in 1894 as an incidental result of a well drilled to provide artesian water for the town. Within several years, the local glut of oil proved a minor environmental disaster; town leaders even attracted J. S. Cullinan from Pennsylvania in 1897 to develop the state's first commercial refinery, but still the economic viability of the petroleum was problematical. Slowly markets developed, with, for example, trains switching from coal to oil-fired boilers, but before the automobile with its gas-guzzling internal combustion engine, oil seemed a natural resource of minor significance.

The twentieth century would come to be known as the age of the automobile, and, auspiciously enough, the century had barely opened when the modern petroleum era began in southeast Texas. Captain A. F. Lucas, a military engineer who had worked in the salt domes of Louisiana, reasoned that great reservoirs of oil might be found trapped beneath the giant salt domes west of Beaumont, and with money raised from a variety of sources, including the Mellon fortune in Pittsburgh, he hired a small drilling company from Corsicana to bring their new rotary rig to a salt dome known locally as Spindletop. On January 10, 1901, the bit dug through the surface and hit the oil that was contained under great pressure in a cavernous chamber. The pressure blew the bit and rig out of the hole and a mighty geyser of oil spurted more than a hundred feet into the air. For more than a week 70,000 to 100,000 barrels of oil gushed forth each day, capturing the nation's attention. In the resulting oil rush, drillers and investors swarmed to southeast Texas, with roughnecks, roustabouts, and wildcatters adding new terminology to the vocabulary of southern occupations. Hundreds of oil companies were incorporated within several years, including the predecessors of Mobil, Gulf, Exxon, Texaco—the industry behemoths. By 1902, Texas oil production totaled 21 million barrels, refineries sprang up across the region, along with the firms that provided oil tools, drilling mud, and technical expertise. Discoveries in the next decade added names like Sour Lake, Humble, and Goose Creek to the roll call of oil fields. The modern petroleum industry had been born; by 1930, huge oil deposits had also been found in Oklahoma and Louisiana, state legislation provided for a modicum of control of runaway production, pipeline laws made access to refineries open to small producers as well as the established giants, and the South produced two-thirds of the nation's oil.

Oil fueled the growth of Houston, which came from practically nowhere in 1900 to become the South's largest city in 1950. Houston was one-sixth the size of New Orleans in 1900, and Galveston was the center of Texas commerce and ocean shipping. Then in September 1900, a hurricane devastated the island city, killing six thousand people—the greatest natural disaster in American history—and Galveston was still suffering from this catastrophe when, barely four months later, oil was discovered at Spindletop. Galveston was in no position to respond to this new opportunity, so Houston investors seized the moment. Since its founding in 1836, Houston had had an inadequate link to the sea via a crooked, shallow, tree-overhung Buffalo Bayou, but years of lobbying finally paid off. In 1914, President Woodrow Wilson pushed a button in Washington, thereby firing a cannon that officially opened the Houston Ship Channel, a straightened, widened, deepened version of the bayou with a basin near downtown where oceangoing ships could be turned by tugs. At last Houston had direct access to the Gulf of Mexico. With both oil and shipping, Houston began a prolonged boom that would not slow until the mid-1980s, and then only temporarily. It became not only the South's largest city, but the national and international center of oil production, technology, refining, and petrochemicals—and it was the nation's third-ranked port as well. Houston was the most spectacular example, but in similar fashion, oil reshaped much of the region from Baton Rouge to Midland.

CHAPTER 25

Poverty and Race

SOUTHERN FARMERS AND THE NEW DEAL

By the early decades of the twentieth century, the South had achieved what a generation ago was called the take-off point for industrialization, but low-wage jobs in textile mills and extractive industries like coal mining and lumbering did not work an economic transformation on the region. Oil brought more wealth, but to a tiny minority in a limited subregion. Despite the economic changes, the growth of new industries and new cities, the South before World War II remained—as it had been for almost a century—the nation's poorest section. The South was still largely dependent upon the production of several staple crops, mainly cotton, rice, and tobacco; its farms were still far smaller than the national average; and the majority of its farmers were impoverished, possessed little equipment or machinery, were poorly educated, and worked as landless tenant farmers or sharecroppers. The major railroads, mining and petroleum companies, and lumbering interests had northern owners, and while the low wages remained in the South, the corporate profits flowed northward. Three generations after the Civil War, the South was an economic colony of the North, a source of cheap labor and raw products, dominated by an inefficient agricultural system that seemingly could not be budged off center. When Franklin D. Roosevelt called the South "the Nation's No. 1 economic problem" in 1938, the description would have been accurate for practically any date since 1865.

And at the heart of the problem was an antiquated agricultural economy that had trapped millions of southerners, white and black, in abject poverty for generations. Simply too many people were trying to eke out a living on too little—and overused—land. There seemed to be no escape from the vagaries of the fluctuating prices that agricultural crops fetched, farmers' debts, occasional drought and boll weevil infestation, and small, underequipped farms that offered no chance for profitability. The impoverished South of 1938 bore an unmistakable resemblance to the South of 1870.

It is important to remember, however, that not all rural southerners were sharecroppers. Many were small farmers who owned their land, and these were decidedly *family* farms. Farm wives certainly did field labor, especially chopping cotton and harvesting various crops. Women were often in charge of the gardens and the poultry, and—if their families had a cow—the dairy. Older children also contributed their labor. The chores were unending—tending the crops, drawing and hauling water, cutting firewood, preparing food for the table when practically everything had to be grown, gathered, and processed at home. Farm wives were laborers and producers as well as wives and mothers, and many showed remarkable skill and ingenuity at providing for their families. There was nothing romantic about farm life in the South for most families, but many were proud to say that despite their poverty and hard work, they "never went hungry." They were poor but proud, with admirable traits.

In the aftermath of the Populist debacle of the 1890s, various spokespeople addressed the problems of southern agriculture. Reformers advocated crop diversification in the pages of farm journals and magazines and at agricultural fairs. Large, prosperous farmers in state after state experimented with improved breeds of livestock, crop rotation and diversification, and improved plows for deeper plowing and better cultivation techniques, but despite their demonstrations of the undeniable benefits that would result when their practices were followed, most small farmers were in no position to emulate their successes. The United States Department of Agriculture (USDA) similarly advocated improved farming techniques, and agricultural scientist Seaman H. Knapp of the USDA, using demonstration farms, proved to small numbers of agriculturists the merits of reform. State experiment stations, colleges of agriculture, extension services, and editors like Clarence H. Poe of the *Progressive Farmer* all worked in vain to transform southern farming practices. The Smith-Lever Act of 1914 institutionalized, along with the Federal Extension Service, the kind of educational efforts Knapp had promoted, and the Smith-Hughes Act of 1917 provided federal grants-in-aid to support agricultural education in the region's high schools. Land-grant universities developed major agricultural research programs as well.

None of these well-intentioned efforts had significant success for the simple reason that the farmers who most needed to reform did not have the economic wherewithal to change their practices. Almost half of the farms had less than fifty total acres, and the improved acreage was even smaller. In 1920, for example, the average farm in North Carolina harvested only twenty-one acres, the average farm in Mississippi twenty-three acres. Most farmers had only one mule, practically no modern implements, a handful of chickens, perhaps a half-dozen pigs, and many had a cow or two, although fully a quarter of the farms did not have a source of milk. How could such a farmer selectively breed his livestock? Which land could be removed from planting in the money crop to facilitate crop rotation or the cultivation of food crops?

Even had the acreage allowed, the landowner and the country store insisted that the farmers maximize cotton (or tobacco) production in order to pay off the sharecropper's debt for goods purchased on credit throughout the year. Certainly the worn-out soils needed more chemical fertilizers, but how was this to be paid for? How could a farmer dependent upon the credit of the local store for his very sustenance opt out of the cotton system and instead experiment with another crop? To make matters worse, no marketing mechanisms existed for other potential crops. Sure, too much cotton was grown, but tobacco, rice, and indigo had severe geographic limits on where they could be cultivated successfully. The South's abundant spring rainfall and acidic soils meant that such crops as grains, grasses, and legumes could not be grown competitively with states in more temperate zones. Moreover, a species of cholera and animal parasites killed hogs and significantly reduced the weight gain and milk production of cattle. Even for those small farmers who learned about alternative agricultural techniques and understood the benefits to be gained, such knowledge lay in the realm of impossible theory; nature seemed to conspire against the region, and there was insufficient economic freedom to experiment with improvement. Few, if any, small farmers, and no tenants or sharecroppers, could ever hope to save up enough money to buy and equip a dairy farm, for example.

Moreover, improved efficiency, deeper plowing, and increased use of fertilizer promised bigger crops, but that was as much problem as solution. Farmers were always plagued by overproduction that reduced the prices the crops brought. World War I temporarily stimulated the markets for all the South's agricultural products, and the year or two following the war promised unprecedented farm prosperity, but the prosperity proved dishearteningly short-lived. Cotton prices shot up, farmers calculated their profits and planned expanding their acres, then overproduction ushered in years of falling prices, bankruptcy, and debilitating poverty. Plagued at the end of the year with being unable to pay up at the store, farmers determined the following year to work harder and plant still more acres, with the result that prices fell further. Like ants in a doodlebug hole, climbing out of their economic trap was impossible for small-scale southern farmers. Slowly farm organizations and state politicians began to advocate voluntary acreage reduction, but no workable, region-wide enforcement mechanism was ever devised by the states. Effective crop reduction required that all states and all farmers participate.

Louisiana governor Huey Long proposed a Cotton Holiday for a year, but when Texas refused to go along, the experiment failed. And if some farmers reduced their cotton acreage but others did not, the uncooperative farmers would benefit doubly. Even southern politicians, who had been suspicious of the national government for a century, began to understand that the problem of overproduction had only a national solution.

The South's agricultural dilemma was exacerbated by the stock market collapse of 1929 and by a prolonged drought that began in late 1929 and lasted through the following year. The region's crops were devastated by the most severe shortage of rainfall in the nation's climatological history. Output fell by more than half in many states, but even worse than the decline in cash crops was the loss in feed and food crops. The severity of southern poverty, even hardship and hunger, shocked outside observers. Insensitive novels, such as Erskine Caldwell's *Tobacco Road* (published in 1932), portrayed white sharecroppers as

Sharecropper family, by Walker Evans, 1939. This photograph of the Bud and Ivy Woods family was first published in the 1941 book *Let Us Now Praise Famous Men*, with text by James Agee. Evans's spare, direct pictures revealed his subjects to be not merely victims but strong and complex individuals as well. (Corbis Corporation)

ignorant, physically and morally deformed, socially irredeemable trash, and this image was seared in the American imagination, but more thoughtful persons recognized the human tragedy in the region. The South's land, plowed for generations and subject to the summers' normal assault of thunderstorms that washed away the topsoil, was depleted of nutrients; nature was now sending a drought, but earlier, in the 1890s, the boll weevil had invaded south Texas from Mexico and, year after year, had marched slowly but inexorably northward and eastward across the South, a kind of insect version of General Sherman, devastating all the cotton fields in its wake. Chronic overproduction, parching drought, inefficiently scaled farms, capital-starved farmers, boll-weevil-ravaged crops—was there no end to southern agricultural misery?

The South had long voted overwhelmingly Democratic, and when Franklin D. Roosevelt ran in 1932, the voters of Dixie gave the New York patrician their strong support. Roosevelt understood that the whole nation was in the midst of an economic crisis, and he was of an experimentalist temperament, willing to try practically anything to effect change. Most of his concerns and most of his advisers were northern, but southern congressional delegations, powerfully placed because of the seniority system, helped push southern issues onto the New Deal agenda. The major response was the Agricultural Adjustment Act (AAA), signed into law on May 12, 1933. The aim of the AAA was to eliminate overproduction by curtailing the cultivation of certain enumerated crops (including cotton, rice, and tobacco) and to prop up the prices of these enumerated crops to match the average purchasing power of the nation's farmers during the relatively prosperous years of 1909 to 1914 (for tobacco alone, the base years were 1919 to 1929). The so-called parity prices and the reduced production would, it was hoped, begin to restore if not prosperity, at least survival. To persuade farmers to reduce their acreage, the AAA provided that in exchange for voluntarily reducing the size of their crops, cooperating farmers would be paid directly, and the funds for doing so would be derived from levies placed on the processors of the various farm products. Moreover, to help relieve the credit crunch that habitually crippled farmers, the AAA also established the Federal Land Banks.

Farmers had their cotton planted by the spring the AAA became law, and even though many farmers had previously felt there was something unnatural, almost irreverent, about plowing under crops, by the summer of 1933, they were desperate enough to try anything. The mules, however, long trained to walk between the rows avoiding the plants, were less flexible, and farmers reported great difficulty in persuading the stubborn draft animals to cast aside training and perhaps conviction and plow up the cotton plants. Nevertheless, almost 10.5 million acres of cotton were removed from cultivation in 1933, farmers received 116 million dollars in direct payments, and—true to the forecasts—the price of cotton increased.

But the AAA was unable to save the small cotton farmers and bring relief to the hundreds of thousands of sharecroppers before it was declared unconstitutional in 1936. For small landowners, the benefit payments (ranging roughly from seven dollars to twenty dollars per acre), even with the slight increase in prices, did not spell the difference between poverty and prosperity. But for the large landowners whose acres were worked by tenants and sharecroppers, the AAA proved a bonanza. They could cut back on the cotton they planted, receive the AAA benefits, and evict croppers from the land because their labor was no longer needed. The landowners took the money and the landless laborers were left homeless. In theory, some of the money should have gotten to the sharecroppers, and landowners were not supposed to reduce their number of workers, but the law provided no effective means of enforcement. Some argued that the benefits should only be paid to the small farmers, but the real purpose of the AAA was to reduce crop production, and that could only happen if the largest producers were involved. By the mid-1930s New Deal planners had devised the Federal Emergency Relief Administration and the Resettlement Administration, among other agencies, and although some farmers did get loans and were helped to acquire their own farms, the dimensions of the South's agricultural illness completely swamped the planners' tentative efforts to throw the sinking farmers a governmental lifeline. The intentions were good, but the immediate despair of the South's farmers was largely unsolved by the New Deal's direct relief programs.

Yet, in other ways, the New Deal helped set into motion a number of forces that would eventually help lift the South out of its economic mire. And other developments, incidental to New Deal policies, that helped reshape the South's economy and demography were going on apace. Imperceptible at first, the foundations for change began to be set in place during the 1930s that would make the decade of the 1940s a true watershed in the region's history. The point here is that New Deal programs, many of which were not directed specifically at the South, nevertheless helped transform the land of cotton.

Congress established the Soil Erosion Service in 1933, later renamed the Soil Conservation Service. This agency had no special southern agenda, but its services were especially needed in the region. The hilly farm lands, planted unremittingly in cotton and subject to the harsh downpours of summer thunderstorms, were badly eroded and leached of their nutrients—the South had more acres of badly eroded soil than all the rest of the nation combined. The Soil Erosion Service taught farmers the importance of contour plowing and terracing the hillsides, and provided funds for doing so. Crop rotation schemes were developed, with legumes and pasturage replenishing the exhausted soils. After World War II, thousands of southern farmers improved their livestock-raising facilities by removing scrub timber from pastures and digging stock ponds, and the cost of these improvements to the farmers was reduced by subsidies from the Soil Conservation Service. By 1950, cattle had replaced cotton on many acres in the Southeast. The Soil Conservation Service also engaged in a major and very successful effort to reforest the South, concentrating on planting hardy pines on abandoned cotton fields. The development of the pulp-paper industry beginning in the late 1930s proved the economic wisdom of reforestation and provided employment and supplemental income to many small farmers who learned to cut and haul pulpwood after crops were laid by.

Another grandiose government scheme was the Tennessee Valley Authority (TVA), which Congress established in 1933 to address the human and ecological problems of a large portion of the southern heartland. The purposes of TVA were flood control, soil conservation, reforestation, recreation, improvement of agricultural practices, and the generation of cheap electricity. Government studies of small mountain communities that were moved in order to avoid inundation by the system of TVA lakes produced a valuable by-product: sociological, economic, and demographic analyses of the southern poor. Begun with a spirit of idealism, TVA aroused much controversy from conservatives who feared government planning and involvement with local life. And, in truth, the economic payoff to the region did not really occur until after World War II. But TVA was one of the nation's first coordinated efforts to improve the socioeconomic well-being of the people of a large region. It exemplified the expansion of the accepted role of government.

The TVA was not the federal government's only effort with electricity. Of far greater importance was the Rural Electrification Administration (REA), written into law in 1935. Utilizing cooperatives whereby the rural recipients of electrical service also belonged to and supported the local electrical co-ops, REA brought low-cost electricity to rural areas where private enterprise had been hesitant to enter. Perhaps nothing since the development at the beginning of the century of Rural Free Delivery of the mail so changed southern life. Now farms could have electric lights, refrigerators, radios (broadcasting stations proliferated in the region after the mid-1920s, filling the airwaves with the sounds of local singers and musicians as well as preachers), water pumps, and indoor plumbing. Refrigeration made possible better food in the winter months, lessening the prevalence of niacin- and protein-deficiency diseases like pellagra. By the mid-1930s the majority of southern farmers also had access to telephones, usually by so-called "party lines" with as many as eight families sharing the same lines, each household identified by the number of rings. Rural mail delivery, telephones, radios, phonographs, and the good roads movement—which had begun in the first decade of the century, received a powerful stimulus in 1916 with the Federal Highways Act, and proliferated in part because of state aid in the 1920s and 1930s—took hundreds of thousands of farmers out of the mud and rural isolation and helped them enter the American mainstream. Often the states utilized the labor of convicts to build the roads, an effort whose purpose was captured in the phrase "bad men make good roads." In truth, conditions in the road gangs were commonly brutal, and the workers were disproportionately black, but many Progressives believed such labor could be socially rehabilitative for the men at the same time that it improved the roads.

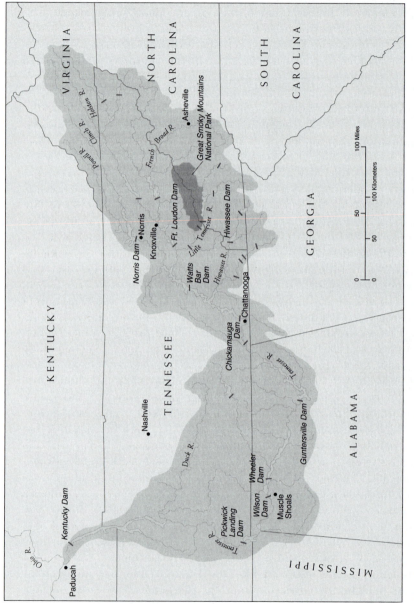

The Tennessee Valley Authority built five dams and improved twenty others along the Tennessee River. It brought electricity to rural areas, sold cheap fertilizer to farmers, engaged in flood control and soil conservation projects, and improved river navigation. (John Mack Faragher, Mari Jo Buhle, Daniel Czitrom, and Susan H. Armitage (1994). *Out of Many: A History of the American People.* Upper Saddle River, New Jersey, Prentice Hall.)

Better roads also meant that farmers could have part-time jobs in small towns and commute to and from their farm, thereby augmenting their income. Farmers could also sell their truck crops in neighboring towns more easily via paved roads, often accurately called farm-to-market roads, and growing truck crops helped many small farmers cope with the collapse of the cotton crop. As the boll weevil, crop reduction programs, and, later, farm mechanization reduced the number of full-time farm laborers needed, improved and especially paved roads often meant the difference between deprivation and a modicum of well-being for farm families.

The New Deal also produced a variety of relief agencies that provided many southerners with either a low-paying job or direct relief benefits. The great Mississippi River flood of 1927 followed by the unprecedented drought of 1930 had attracted national Red Cross attention. Relief payments then prevented widespread starvation and helped significant numbers of the poorest southerners come to accept the idea of relief. The Federal Emergency Relief Administration spent hundreds of millions of dollars in the South, but only scraped the surface of poverty there. The Civilian Conservation Corps with its Tree Army, the Works Progress Administration, and the National Youth Administration not only performed very worthwhile public services—building parks, lakes, recreation buildings, and so on that still benefit the region—but provided absolutely essential wages that literally saw many families through the nadir of the Great Depression. For the first time, millions of southerners came to see the federal government as a friend indeed. A hyper-energetic young Texas administrator, Lyndon B. Johnson, made that state's National Youth Administration a model agency, and he learned in the process powerful lessons about how the government could transform for the better the lives and hopes of distressed people.

Meanwhile, far-reaching changes were underway in the agricultural economy. The citrus industry began to prosper in the Florida peninsula and in the Rio Grande Valley region of Texas. Farmers forced away from cotton by the boll weevil and the AAA shifted to peaches, peanuts, soybeans, cattle and—increasingly after the 1930s—large-scale broiler production. Flue-cured tobacco was slow to mechanize and impervious to the boll weevil, and, in part because the market was controlled by several large tobacco companies, that industry managed its 1930s crop reductions better than cotton growers did. Tobacco farmers suffered in the Great Depression, but not to the extent that cotton farmers did. Cotton was already beginning to shift west to the drier soils of West Texas and later New Mexico, Arizona, and California. Boll weevil infestation was minimal there, and the huge, level, irrigated fields were more accommodating to mechanization. As a result, the center of the cotton industry shifted away from Dixie to the New Southwest, but the full effects of this movement became visible only after World War II. Between 1900 and 1920, rice cultivation had also shifted west, away from the tidal areas of South Carolina and Georgia to the prairies of southwestern Louisiana, southeastern Texas, and the delta regions of Mississippi and Arkansas. Pioneered in this region by midwestern farmers who adapted reapers and giant tractors to rice cultivation, rice plantations were truly factories in the field. Well capitalized, organized by producers' groups, and amenable to AAA reduction plans, the southwestern rice industry managed to survive the Great Depression relatively intact.

Cotton, which had long dominated the South, was more traumatically affected by the forces of change in the 1930s than any other major agricultural industry. The boll weevil and AAA acreage restrictions proved a double whammy, and the result was a halving of the cotton acreage between 1930 and 1940. The source of agricultural poverty in the cotton regions of the South had been too many laborers and farms that were too small to be profitable. The shattering poverty of the depression years, combined with the expectation of jobs in the North (occasioned in part by post–World War I laws that increased the restrictions on foreign immigration), pushed and pulled the southern farm poor toward northern destinations. Southern blacks had the added incentive of escaping the virulent racism of Dixie. The result, over the whole first half of the twentieth century, was the largest internal mass migration in American history. Between 1900 and 1950 almost 10 million southerners (equally divided between the two races) fled the region.

Black and poor white ghettoes developed in every northern city and in cities such as Bakersfield, California. The "Okie" phenomenon was much more widespread, in terms of both origins and destinations, than the powerful depression-era novel *The Grapes of Wrath* (1939) suggests. Southern culture, white and black, gained outposts far beyond the confines of the former Confederate States where cotton had once been king. While owners of larger, more prosperous southern farms had begun to purchase tractors in the 1930s, and, after years of experimentation, a workable mechanical cotton picker was finally developed at the very end of the 1930s, significant farm mechanization came only after World War II and was more a result of sharecropper migration than a cause of it. In fact, the vaunted mechanical cotton picker really depended upon new strains (hybrids) of cotton plants on which bolls grew higher up on the stalk and opened more evenly and upon chemical defoliants that caused the leaves to fall off so they would not contaminate the lint sucked into the trailers. Modern pesticides, huge tractors, and high-tech cotton farming really prospered on the giant agribusiness farms of the Texas plains and further west in the 1960s, not on the exhausted soil of the suffering South in the 1930s.

THE NADIR OF RACE RELATIONS

In agricultural practices, the South of 1930 or so seemed almost indistinguishable from the South of 1900 or 1870. Poor black and white farmers walked behind mules in dusty cotton fields; lived in small, unpainted shacks made simply of planks nailed to a frame, without inner walls or ceilings; and stayed in hock to the furnishing merchant—almost powerless to change their lives for the better. The southern journalist, Walter Hines Page, returned to his homeland in 1902 after an absence of two decades and found life and labor practically unchanged; "pickled" was his phrase. "Southern rural society," he wrote, "has remained stationary longer than English-speaking people have remained stationary anywhere else in the world." But in one area there was change, and in large measure for the worse. Perhaps it should be no surprise that in an era of increasing agricultural poverty and the disillusionment following the Populist collapse, white racism increased. Blacks became the scapegoats for the frustration, poverty, and bitterness of poor whites, and the white establishment harnessed this displaced anger to thwart threats to its power. Blacks' hard-earned economic successes, limited though they were, by implication threatened whites' image of superiority, and the specter of black political influence in the wake of the Populist revolt unleashed white hate. White politicians played the race card to push down blacks and created a rape hysteria to weld together a cross-class coalition of white support. The poorest class of white women was elevated by political rhetoric to the sacred ranks of southern ladyhood in order to win the support of their husbands at the polls—white economic interests was trumped by social fears. This was the nadir of race relations in post-slavery America.

Scene from a lynching. (U.S. Information Agency)

Blacks were almost completely disenfranchised by the end of the century, but disenfranchisement is only one index of the dilemma. Lynching had long been a weapon of vigilantes in the South. Well into the 1880s, it was frequently used against whites, but the race of its victims changed. In 1885, for example, of the 184 lynchings in the nation (almost all of which were in the South), 110 of the victims were white, 74 black. By 1900, the ratio had drastically reversed; of 115 total lynchings, 9 were of whites, and 106 victims were black. Two blacks a week were lynched in the South. The number of lynchings decreased in the next three decades, but the overwhelming majority of victims remained black—53 blacks and 5 whites in 1920; 20 blacks and 1 white in 1930. In addition, many southern trials were simply domesticated forms of lynching, with evidence ignored and innocent blacks—like the nine so-called Scottsboro boys in Alabama in 1931—victimized by what were, in effect, kangaroo courts. It has been suggested that southern white men who had largely lost their ability to provide for their families sought in compensation to enhance their manly self-images by casting black males as beasts—as an enemy within—from whom their white families had to be protected.

Prominent white southerners also, men and women, publicly and privately defended the lynching of blacks as necessary to defend Western civilization, the sanctity of womanhood, and the southern way of life. In fact, a distinct minority of lynching victims were accused of raping white women, yet in the rhetoric used to defend the heinous practice of lynching, rape was almost always the alleged crime being punished or being prevented. The climate of hate and suspicion, fanned by such spokespersons as Tom Watson, the former Georgia Populist leader, and Senator Furnifold Simmons of North Carolina, created an environment where almost unbelievable prejudice and violence became socially acceptable. Even a white person who seemed foreign or insufficiently supportive of southern customs could be shunned, beaten, or killed. Leo Frank, for example, a mild-mannered, well-educated, but Brooklyn-reared Jewish factory manager in Atlanta, was accused in 1913 of raping and killing a thirteen-year-old white girl, Mary Phagan, who worked in his factory. The evidence was scanty, but the jury, whose members hated and feared people of the Jewish "race," convicted Frank and sentenced him to die. When the governor, after an investigation, commuted Frank's sentence to life imprisonment, an outraged mob on August 17, 1915, seized Frank from his jail cell in Marietta and lynched him. What happened to Frank—which became a cause célèbre across the nation—happened to hundreds of blacks throughout the South.

Many lynchings were not secret affairs, conducted surreptitiously under cover of darkness or sheets. On the contrary, lynchings often became public spectacles, with huge crowds, voluntary participation, refreshments served, innocent blacks terrified, law enforcement officials averting their eyes. At some of the more outrageous events, any interested party could shoot, stab, hit, burn, or otherwise brutalize the victim. A particularly brutal fate befell Sam Hose, a black from a rural Georgia community who allegedly killed his white employee, raped his wife, and robbed them as well. Hose was apprehended and lynched on April 23, 1899, with special trains bringing spectators from Atlanta to witness the Sunday event. After the lynching, Hose was burned, his body cut open, and cooked slices of his heart and liver sold as prize souvenirs; his knuckles were later displayed in the window of an Atlanta grocery store. In the largest sense, the respectable white society condoned such barbarities while members of the lower order did most of the dirty work. In 1898, Rebecca Latimer Felton of Georgia, a leading Methodist layperson, journalist, prohibitionist, feminist, and the first woman appointed to the U.S. Senate, exhorted white men that "if it takes lynching to protect woman's dearest possession from drunken, ravening human beasts, then I say lynch a thousand a week if it becomes necessary."

Popular stereotypes and literary depictions of blacks revealed the heightened racial animosities during the 1890s and thereafter. The iconography of blacks degenerated. Children's books, cartoons, face mugs, miniature statues for lawns, knick-knacks, and advertising all exaggerated the black phenotype. Every black male had grossly oversized lips, bulging eyes, and awkward posture; every black woman was rotund, with a shiny black face and a turban; every black child seemed to cavort unharmed with jungle animals and eat watermelon and appear not fully human. Often these images were not consciously vicious, although on occasion black males were depicted with razor in hand as though a quick slice was as natural as a handshake. Blacks were shown as decidedly comical or dangerous or ridiculous, never as mature, thinking, self-possessed adults; even the images that whites insisted were lovable—like Little Black Sambo— were inherently demeaning to blacks.

Popular literature and film expressed identical images, as did vernacular humor. One of the more vicious literary portrayals occurred in Thomas Dixon, Jr.'s lurid bestsellers, *The Leopard's Spots: A Romance of the White Man's Burden, 1865–1900* (1902) and *The Clansman: An Historical Romance of the Ku Klux Klan* (1905). These two novels represented the darkest interpretation of Reconstruction, a vengeful period in American history when evil outside forces attempted to destroy southern white Christian civilization and mongrelize the population. Every imaginable stereotype was given memorable form: opportunistic, corrupt carpetbaggers hoping to enrich themselves; mousy scalawags bent on humiliating former planters; ignorant, smelly, barbarous blacks whose votes were manipulated by the carpetbaggers; beautiful white women, pious and genteel, subject to the animalistic desires of black beasts; and heroic southern white men fighting against all odds for civilization. The obvious stereotypes ring hollow today, but such images seemed to many white southerners at the turn of the century to capture essential truths about the last generation. Blacks were the foulest villains: no longer smiling, shuffling Sambos, but evil beasts. Such images lay behind the white defenses of disenfranchisement and lynching. *The Clansman* was loosely adapted as the story line for the 1915 movie *Birth of a Nation*, breathtakingly innovative cinematographically but reactionary in message. When Woodrow Wilson first saw this film with its stark portrayal of Reconstruction, he is said to have commented that this was history written with lightning. The racist portrayals of blacks, larger than life on the silver screen, were seared into the southern white psyche.

It is difficult for readers today to grasp how rigid and far-reaching segregation became in the South during the two generations after 1900. Blacks went to separate schools and churches, lived in separate parts of town (often called "nigger town" or "nigger quarters"), used separate water fountains and restrooms, and had separate waiting rooms; they were often prohibited from parks, playgrounds, and music halls; and they could not sit in a restaurant and order a meal—perhaps they could enter through a back door and eat in the kitchen with the cooks. Blacks had to sit at the rear of trolleys and in special train cars; they often could not try on clothes in department stores; they could not stay at "white" hotels but had to try to find black relatives or an obliging black family to stay with when traveling across the South—a dangerous trip even when not inconvenient. Curfews were enforced in some cities—Mobile in 1909, for example, required blacks to be off the streets by 10:00 P.M. In every personal interaction with a white, blacks had to be careful to be properly deferential, to "know their place."

The retribution for being "uppity" could be both economic and physical, and, if a white woman was involved, a black male even rumored to have breached in the slightest regard the racial etiquette was very likely to be severely beaten, castrated, or killed. Several southern cities—Wilmington, North Carolina, in 1898, New Orleans in 1900, Atlanta in 1906, for example—suffered terrible race riots: In Atlanta as many as ten thousand whites went on a rampage against blacks, killing or beating every black they encountered. When the violence finally subsided after hours of lawless assaults, 25 blacks were dead, 150 wounded, and hundreds left the city for good. Over a thousand black Wilmingtonians fled that city never to return. Black prison inmates were also victimized by the cruel system of leasing them out to private employers, and when that was reformed and replaced by the chain gang—building and repairing roads for the state—the violence was only moderated, not stopped. Violence toward blacks was the reverse side of southern gentility. Blacks often had no practical recourse but to grin and bear it or to flee the region; and millions fled. In 1910, fifty years after the Civil War, nine out of ten American blacks still lived in the South; by 1960, only six out of ten blacks lived in Dixie. In that half-century, 4,473,300 blacks migrated from the South to the North and the West.

Blacks in the South constituted a society within a society. Blacks lived in segregated sections of cities, and black-owned businesses and a black professional class arose to serve their needs. Black leadership came disproportionately from this business and professional class, especially from ministers. Following the organization of the National Association for the Advancement of Colored People (NAACP) in 1910, black leaders joined the NAACP in hopes of advancing their race. Efforts in the South had to be cautious, gradual, and piecemeal. For most American whites, and probably most southern blacks, the preeminent black leader was educator Booker T. Washington.

Washington had been born a slave in Virginia in 1856, and after the Civil War, his family labored in the salt works and coal mines of West Virginia. Eventually, through drive and ambition, Washington graduated from Hampton Institute, and although he briefly considered other careers, a stint teaching at Hampton convinced him that education was to be his mission in life. In 1881, following the Hampton example, he founded Tuskegee Normal and Industrial Institute in Macon County, Alabama. All the staff at Tuskegee were black, and Washington promoted the college and his conception of a black self-help philosophy throughout the nation with great success. Undervaluing courses in

Booker T. Washington. (Library of Congress)

the arts and humanities, Washington advocated a practical curriculum, essentially vocational. He believed that learning a trade and habits of self-discipline were the avenue to prosperity for blacks, and this prosperity, based upon their economic utility to the larger white community, he believed would eventually earn blacks the respect and support of whites.

In a famous speech in Atlanta in 1895 at the Cotton States International Exposition, Washington galvanized his audience with his vivid image of blacks and whites working together for common economic prosperity but remaining separate in social matters. Washington tacitly accepted social segregation and political disenfranchisement in return for white acceptance of limited black economic opportunity. This was precisely the message that whites wanted to hear (Washington's 1901 autobiography, *Up From Slavery*, became an instant classic in the up-by-the-boot-strap tradition begun by Benjamin Franklin's autobiography at the end of the eighteenth century), and Washington became the leading spokesman for blacks. Consequently, Washington became also the most powerful black man in the nation, and he used his power craftily and ruthlessly to maintain his position vis-á-vis the white establishment by undermining potential black rivals and opponents. Privately and secretly, Washington was more critical of segregation and worked to effect change in a wide variety of ways, but he accurately gauged the temper of racial sentiment in the white South and judged that a frontal assault on racism would be counterproductive.

New Englander William E. B. Du Bois, who was the first black to earn a Ph.D. at Harvard (1895), disdained such temporizing and argued that a talented minority of blacks should work for enhanced opportunities in matters cultural and social as well as economic. Du Bois argued that Washington insufficiently appreciated black culture and history and was too deferential toward the regnant ideas of business capitalism. Du Bois's eloquent book of essays, *The Souls of Black Folk* (1903), a kind of antidote to *Up From Slavery*, also became a classic and was particularly venerated by black intellectuals. The black community itself was divided on the proper response to segregation, but maneuvering room for southern blacks was extremely limited.

In the early twentieth century, as in slavery times, some blacks did learn ways to carve out more autonomy and freedom of action than the system seemed to allow. Black ingenuity, creativity, and an inextinguishable desire to maximize control of their own lives resulted in a limited degree of black progress, prosperity, and cultural expression in a desperately racist society. (One white Freedmen's Bureau official, J. W. Alvord, had recognized the blacks' potential even in the depths of Reconstruction. "This people is destined to rise," he wrote. "They have within themselves an instinct which anticipates this: a vitality of hope, coupled with patience and willingness to struggle, which foreshadows with certainty their higher condition as a people in the coming time ....") Black businessmen in certain trades, especially those with an all-black clientele, occasionally prospered, and the National Negro Business League by 1915 had dozens of chapters across the South. Throughout the region there were prosperous black stores, pharmacies, and funeral homes. Black banks, though usually small and prone to failure because of their depositors' weak resources, nonetheless sprouted across the South. Several black-owned and -operated insurance companies were founded, the largest of which was the North Carolina Mutual Life Insurance Company of Durham, established in 1899 by John Merrick.

Black churches grew rapidly in size and influence in the decades after Reconstruction, and frequently they were the largest religious institutions in southern cities. The churches ministered to a broad spectrum of human needs—social, educational, economic, cultural, and recreational—not just spiritual. Black women, especially, found in the churches an opportunity for service and growth, although the male ministers were often authoritarian. Black fraternal organizations and social clubs offered additional ways for finding an arena for self-expression and community service. A typically impressive self-help community organization was the Neighborhood League, founded in 1908 in Atlanta by Mrs. Lugenia Hope, the wife of Atlanta University president John Hope. The Neighborhood Union successfully advocated street, sanitation, and educational improvements in the city's black neighborhoods. In other states and other cities, talented black women—like Charlotte Hawkins Brown in North Carolina—organized clubs, civic leagues, and even interracial initiatives with white women reformers to offer home demonstration courses, sewing classes, and health clinics. No matter how bad conditions got, many black women maintained their dignity and dedicated heroic amounts of time and effort to "raise their race." But while it is important to recognize black victories over the system, one should never minimize the prejudice, poverty, injustice, and violence that afflicted southern blacks in the midst of what was ironically labeled the Progressive Era.

During the course of World War I, approximately fifty thousand American blacks, most of them from the South, served in the military. Most of them had auxiliary duties, but some were combatants and, because of their bravery and ferocious fighting, they suffered casualties out of proportion to their numbers. When black soldiers returned home after the war, they found racism just as entrenched as before. The war might have been intended to make the world safe for democracy, but democracy was for whites only in the American South. Black soldiers were less willing after their military experience to turn the other cheek to repeated insults and injury. The result, in response usually to unprovoked assaults by whites, was a series of deadly race riots in Longview and Houston, Texas; in Knoxville, Tennessee; in Elaine, Arkansas; and in Tulsa, Oklahoma. The North, too, was wracked with a string of bloody confrontations, and a newly emergent Ku Klux Klan found as strong an acceptance in the North and West as in the South. Catholics, immigrants, and outsiders in general, not just blacks, were the victims of the resurgent KKK of the 1920s.

Southern rural blacks in particular, though, were pummeled with repeated blows of hateful racism, random violence, and a cotton economy ravaged
by boll weevils and overproduction. Blacks were hardly in a position to withstand
the collapse of the sharecropping system. When, during the Great Depression,
planters reduced their crop acreage and kept the government reimbursements
to themselves, blacks had no means to defend their interests. When white government officials disbursed welfare payments and severely discriminated against
blacks, no effective black challenge could be mounted. Whites, often ravaged
by the depression themselves, could rarely find within themselves the moral
resources to be magnanimous toward the poor blacks in their midst. In this
context, the effort of the NAACP to chip away legally at the monolith of segregation is a tale of heroism and persistence.

One of the first efforts of the NAACP was through research and publication to reveal the extent of lynching in the South. A study was issued in 1919,
but had little effect, and in 1929, Walter White, executive secretary of the
NAACP, published *Rope and Faggot: A Biography of Judge Lynch.* The NAACP, with
the help of northern liberals, tried to push federal antilynching legislation
through Congress. Southern congressmen fought these efforts hard and successfully. Although Eleanor Roosevelt encouraged her husband to propose
racial reform, Franklin D. Roosevelt thought his New Deal programs too dependent on southern Democratic support to risk alienating southern congressmen on the lynching issue. The concern of southern whites—especially the
Association of Southern Women for the Prevention of Lynching, organized in
1930 by Jessie Daniel Ames from Texas—over the damage to the South's reputation caused by lynching gradually limited the evil. By the late 1930s, the
number of blacks lynched annually fell to eight, then six, then two, in 1939.

The NAACP attacked discrimination in voting and higher education. A
series of cases mounted in Texas in the 1930s culminated in 1944 in a Supreme
Court decision, *Smith v. Allwright*, that outlawed the white primary. And in Maryland, Thurgood Marshall, a black attorney on the staff of the NAACP, successfully challenged state laws that prevented an otherwise-qualified black applicant,
Donald Gaines Murray, from attending the University of Maryland's law school.
A Baltimore municipal court in 1935 and the state supreme court the following year agreed with Marshall's logic, and the law school was desegregated. A
similar case originated in Missouri with the application of Lloyd Gaines to the
all-white University of Missouri law school. Marshall ultimately won this case in
the U.S. Supreme Court in 1938. These two cases dealt only with postgraduate
education, but Marshall and the NAACP were encouraged to hope that careful legal argument carried all the way to the highest court of the land would
eventually be the key to desegregating the nation's entire educational system.

As storm clouds of war rose over Europe at the end of the decade, few observers of the South fully understood the significance of the changes underway.
Blacks were leaving the South in record numbers, propelled by crushing rural

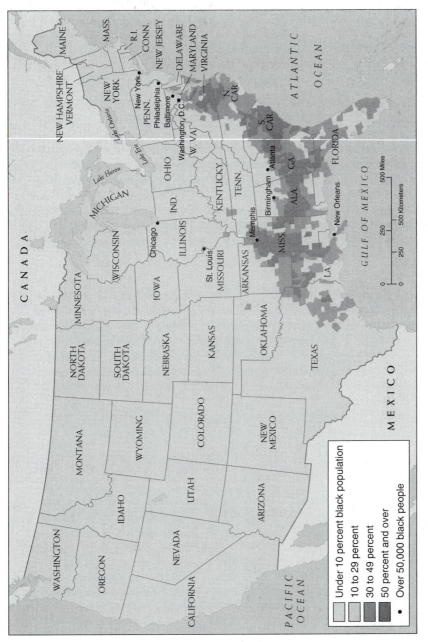

Black Population, 1920

The former states of the Confederacy still remained the center of the African-American population in 1920, but the "Great Migration" would soon transform the demographics of northern urban areas. (John Mack Faragher, Mari Jo Buhle, Daniel Czitrom, and Susan H. Armitage (1994). *Out of Many: A History of the American People.* Upper Saddle River, New Jersey, Prentice Hall.)

Legend (map key):
- Under 10 percent black population
- 10 to 29 percent
- 30 to 49 percent
- 50 percent and over
- • Over 50,000 black people

poverty, the constant threat of violence, and continuing racial discrimination. The boll weevil, crop limitation policies, and the bare hint of farm mechanization suggested that real agricultural change was imminent. The courts seemed to reformers to be the mechanism to break the nearly fatal hold of legal segregation. But taken as a whole, the South still seemed to be pickled in time, as Walter Hines Page had described it, rather than a region on the edge of transformation. W. J. Cash, a North Carolina journalist who had a morbid fascination with the South and a penchant for overripe prose, summed up his critical evaluation of the South's entire history and—in *The Mind of the South,* published in 1941, a mediation on the meaning of the South now universally considered a classic—deemed the region's history tragically marked by continuity with the past. But he was writing of the South he had known. Even so probing an analyst as Cash could not foresee as the decade of the 1930s closed that the South was nearing the end of an era. Events in the next decade and a half would reconstruct the South more completely than had the Civil War and Reconstruction fourscore years earlier.

CHAPTER 26

Cultural Riches in the Midst of Poverty

EMERGENCE OF A SOUTHERN LITERARY TRADITION

Southern blacks hardly dared hope throughout much of the first four decades of the twentieth century that their condition would improve; for them, change usually meant a decline. And most southern whites, given the rigidity of their intellectual and religious worldviews, could not imagine a South significantly different from what they had experienced. For complex reasons, the South was a world apart from the rest of the nation during this period, aggressively resistant to outside criticism and with an underdeveloped tradition of self-criticism. In the North, Protestant theologians in the several decades following 1880 developed a penetrating religious critique of the social institutions that produced poverty and injustice, but such analysis was almost completely absent among southern Protestants. Most of the historical and memoir writing that followed the Civil War defended the Confederacy and its leaders and, even when the end of slavery was accepted as ultimately beneficial to the South, the institution was remembered, by whites at least, as benevolent on the whole. In the words (1929) of the first great historian of slavery, Georgia-born but Yale-teaching Ulrich B. Phillips, "their [planter] despotism, so far as it might properly be called, was benevolent in intent and on the whole beneficial in effect."

The imaginative literature of the generation following the war consisted mostly of sentimental, romantic fiction about plantation life, with happy darkies and gentle planters. Thomas Nelson Page perfected this genre of writing, and through such stories as "Marse Chan," published in *Century* magazine in 1884, he perpetuated the memories of white southerners of a lost utopia and catered to a growing acceptance by white northerners of the southern idyll both as an implicit criticism of northern industrialism and urbanization and as a reflection of their belief that southern whites knew best how to handle the race problem. In several novels and many stories, the best of which were collected as *In Ole Virginia* (1897), Page portrayed the blacks of the Old South as dependent Sambos who revered their masters and mistresses. Joel Chandler Harris, on the other hand, in his Uncle Remus stories that retold in dialect black folklore and folktales, presented, along with a panoply of stereotypical images of plantation blacks, a counterimage of blacks who often possessed a sensitivity, an ability to care for others, and a depth of folk wisdom that made them seem more authentically human than the hegemonic whites.

Yet another popular genre of southern belles lettres was local color, a form that was enormously successful. Despite the popularity of many of these writers, a surprising number of whom were women, this literature is little known today and even less read. But authors such as Frances Courtenay Baylor, Sarah Barnwell Elliott, James Lane Allen, Mary Murfee, Sherwood Bonner, and Augusta Evans Wilson (with her spectacularly best-selling *St. Elmo* [1866]) dominated southern reading habits during the generation following the Civil War. These local-color writers emphasized story, narrative, description, and character sketch. Seldom were their works experimental, psychologically probing, or critical of the region, the society, or middle-class values.

George W. Cable was one of the few exceptions to the conservatism of the local color school, for his depictions of Creole life in antebellum Louisiana (*Old Creole Days* [1879] and *The Grandissimes* [1880]) contained subtle criticisms of Creole racial mores, and his later essays on civil rights, *The Silent South* (1885) and *The Negro Question* (1890), were pointed in their critique of southern racial attitudes. Cable predictably became a persona non grata in New Orleans, and left the region. Another Louisianian, Kate Chopin, used the local-color medium to explore more boldly the contradictions of multiracial sexual mores in *The Awakening* (1899), the story of a woman who, dissatisfied with her marriage to a businessman, had an extramarital affair. Public outrage at such frankness practically made her a recluse, and she had difficulty publishing subsequent work.

Not until the very end of the nineteenth century did writing critical of the South, its racial views, its stultifying political establishment, and its continuing economic backwardness come to appear with some degree of regularity. Walter Hines Page, a native North Carolinian, with safe editorial and publishing positions in Boston and New York City, led this appraisal of the South. By virtue of his editorship of such prominent national journals as *Forum* and *Atlantic Monthly*, he published his own essays and those by fellow southerners, like Edgar

Garner Murphy, Edwin Alderman, William P. Trent, and John Spencer Bassett, that criticized aspects of southern life. Page, later in his life a prominent diplomat and U.S. ambassador to Great Britain, was actually quite restrained, even diplomatic, in his censure of southern ways, and he hoped, by pointing out errors, promoting regional education, and prodding gently, to lead the South away from the errors of its ways. William P. Trent, who taught at the University of the South in Sewanee, Tennessee, was more blunt. His scholarly biography of William Gilmore Simms, the antebellum Charleston novelist, was scathing in its portrayal of the Charleston aristocracy and its arrested intellectual life. Trent founded the *Sewanee Review* in 1892 as a forum for open-minded, critical analysis of southern life and letters. Trent left Sewanee for Columbia University in 1900, but the journal he founded there is extant.

In 1902, another young southern academic, John Spencer Bassett, founded an even more South-focused journal, the *South Atlantic Quarterly*, at Trinity College, the predecessor of Duke University. In those pages, Bassett forthrightly rebuked the South for its racial attitudes, its intolerance, its absence of a critical spirit, and its politics of reaction. A storm of criticism arose over Bassett's essays, with demands that he be fired from Trinity College. The college boldly and successfully stood up for academic freedom, but Bassett understood the intellectual climate of the state. In 1906, he resigned and moved to Smith College, in Massachusetts. While some southerners were able to see the faults of their region and were courageous enough to publish their views, the region at large had no tolerance for criticism.

The South's unreceptivity to censure was vividly illustrated by the hostility many citizens of Waco, Texas, exhibited toward W. C. Brann, a vituperative journalist whose monthly publication, *Brann's Iconoclast*, reached an international circulation of over ninety thousand in the late 1890s. Brann, inconsistently reformist, was primarily critical of what he viewed as social sham and religious hyprocrisy (Waco had a district for legal prostitution on one side and Baylor, a Baptist university, on the other.) Brann, who once called himself a redbug on the body politic, sometimes attacked political mossbacks and often advanced radical economic ideas; he also savagely attacked blacks and opposed expanding the rights of women. But he aimed his most acerbic diatribes at the local Baptists and Baylor University. Although faculty members rescued him in 1897 from being hanged by students, less than a year later he was fatally shot in the back by the father of a Baylor coed who may have felt Brann's charges that the college was merely a "manufactory of ministers and Magdalenes"—and that worldly men considered it "worse than a harem"—were simply beyond the bounds of acceptable journalism. Brann's wildly intemperate attacks against the dominant Protestant denomination would have made him enemies almost anywhere, but in central Texas in 1898 his words cost him his life.

It was precisely that touchiness about criticism that made the South extraordinarily sensitive to the national coverage, in 1925, of the trial in Dayton,

Tennessee, of a young school teacher charged with teaching biological evolution in defiance of a state law that forbade teaching "any theory that denies the story of the Divine Creation of man as taught in the Bible, and to teach instead that man has descended from a lower order of animals." Actually the act that made teaching evolution illegal had little support, but few legislators, clergymen, and educated laypersons cared to attract the antipathy of single-issue fanatics by criticizing a law they expected to be more honored in the breach than in the observance. Then the American Civil Liberties Union advertised that it would provide free legal services to the first person charged with breaking the anti-evolution statute. John Thomas Scopes, science teacher and football coach, believed that evolution and the Bible were reconcilable, and because he used the state-adopted textbook that discussed evolution, he anticipated no problem with the law. In fact, there is little evidence he really taught scientific evolution as opposed to biblical creation. But town leaders, egged on by a northern engineer who managed a large mining operation locally, and hoping to put Dayton on the map, decided to protest the state law and convinced Scopes to take up the challenge. The case exploded into a major national press extravaganza.

Clarence Darrow, the great Chicago courtroom orator and self-professed agnostic, came to defend the right to teach evolution (and only incidentally to defend Scopes), and William Jennings Bryan, the aging three-time candidate for the presidency and defender of old-time religion, headed the prosecution team. H. L. Mencken, the outrageously iconoclastic columnist for the *Baltimore Sun* and coeditor of *Smart Set* magazine, led the flock of journalists who came to Dayton to cover what was soon described as the great war between the forces of modernity (Darrow) and blind fundamentalism (Bryan).

When the trial opened, movie cameras were there to record the spectacle, and radio station WGN of Chicago broadcast live the epic battle. With Mencken labeling the case the "Monkey Trial," reporters from around the world rushed to describe, sensationalize, and ridicule the courtroom drama. Bryan willingly accepted the role of defender of the faith, although he, like most southerners, was not a fundamentalist in the modern sense of the word but rather was simply a biblical literalist. For Bryan, however, at issue was the true faith, especially when the antagonist, Clarence Darrow, was modern unbelief personified. Bryan was hardly a sophisticated Bible scholar, and was clearly past his prime; nevertheless, he let Darrow put him on the witness stand.

Darrow had no equal at interrogation and he annihilated Bryan by catching him in contradictions and forcing him to admit that there were parts of the Bible that even Bryan himself did not take literally—neither did most other southern literalists, who were conservative Christians, not fundamentalists, a northern-based strain of Christianity that did not really penetrate the South until after World War II. Though Bryan was made to look ridiculous and died several days later—a sure sign, thought the secularists, that modern views were correct—Scopes himself, practically forgotten by the mighty contenders and the press, was convicted and fined $100. The *Baltimore Sun* promptly paid his fines, Scopes was never sentenced to jail, and shortly the state supreme court overturned the verdict on a technicality. But the outcome of the case was less important than how the national and international press, following Mencken's lead, had used the Scopes trial to portray the town of Dayton, the state of Tennessee, and the South at large as the land of ignorance, prejudice, and reaction. Even more so than Darrow, Mencken was the master of ridicule, and with his acid pen he created and disseminated a devastatingly negative portrait of the South.

Mencken's diatribe against the South had begun in 1917, when he published a scathing essay entitled "The Sahara of the Bozart" in the *New York Evening Mail*, reprinted with access to a far broader audience in his book *Prejudices: Second Series* (1920). With hyperbole and acerbic wit the Baltimore critic surveyed the state of the mind in the South: "Down there," he wrote, "a poet is now almost as rare as an oboe-player, a drypoint etcher or a metaphysician." But worse yet, as for "critics, musical composers, painters, sculptors, architects… there is not even a bad one between the Potomac mud-flats and the Gulf. Nor an historian…sociologist…philosopher…theologian…scientist. In all these fields the South is an awe-inspiring blank." Warming up to his subject, Mencken concluded that "In all that gargantuan paradise of the fourth-rate there is not a single picture gallery worth going into, or a single orchestra capable of playing the nine symphonies of Beethoven, or a single opera-house, or a single theater devoted to decent plays, or a single public monument (built since the war) that is worth looking at, or a single workshop devoted to the making of beautiful things."

Given Mencken's attitude, the Scopes "Monkey Trial," with all its attendant excesses, provided him with abundant ammunition to fire at the backward, provincial South, and fire away he did. But southerners far removed in geography and sophistication from the townsfolk of Dayton, Tennessee, read Mencken's dispatches, and as they did, anger and determination arose defensively in their breasts. None reacted more effectively than a group of poets, writers, literary critics, and historians loosely associated with Vanderbilt University. Several of them, including John Crowe Ransom, Donald Davidson, Allen Tate, and Robert Penn Warren, had begun meeting in 1920 to read and critique each other's poetry, and in the process, they developed a methodology that later became known as the New Criticism. Between 1922 and 1925, they published some nineteen issues of an enormously influential little magazine, the *Fugitive*, and the writers themselves became known as the fugitives. The attitudes, styles, and talent of the group varied and evolved, but most of them, joined by other southern academics of similar spirit and men of letters, responded vitriolically to Mencken's regional put-down.

Led by Tate, Ransom, and Davidson, and joined by others—historian Frank L. Owsley, political scientist H. C. Nixon, and novelist Andrew Lytle—these self-styled Agrarians defended the South, its people, character, religious traditions, and folk culture from the likes of Mencken by portraying the region as a humane, people-centered folk culture as compared to the cold, urban-industrialized modern culture that had, sadly, they felt, emerged in the North. Caroline Gordon, writing from the Agrarian perspective, depicted the destruction of the family as a result of the economic dissolution of the traditional agrarian order in *None Shall Look Back* (1937). Twelve Agrarian authors published as their manifesto in 1930 a powerful book of essays, *I'll Take My Stand*, but this volume was more a heartfelt defense of the traditional South than a prescription of how that South might be nurtured and, God forbid, follow the path of the North. Yet the book was partially successful in trying to turn the South's localism and sense of family and place into sources of strength and pride, not symptoms of social pathology. The South should not become an undifferentiated part of the American urban-industrial behemoth. Barely beneath the surface of the debate was the reality of change. The forces of modernity, of shifting attitudes about race and economics and gender and politics—as well as literature—were beginning to tug and pull at a South stuck in the mud of poverty, racism, and religious and political conservatism. Some, like Mencken, wanted to throw out both the past and the present South and jerk the region into the future; others, like the Agrarians, understood some of the present problems, feared an all-new future, and desperately tried to mediate between the two. Yet another group of southerners were willing to usher in the future South with comparative alacrity.

If Nashville was the center of the orbit of the Agrarians, then the Regionalists revolved about Chapel Hill. The movement began in 1920, when Howard W. Odom came to the University of North Carolina as head of the Department of Sociology and the School of Public Welfare. Odom developed these academic divisions into centers for applying the methods of modern social science to the life and problems of the South, all with the intention of reforming, improving, and modernizing Dixie. Soon joined by an equally able colleague, Rupert B. Vance, Odom and co-author published a series of influential books—*Human Factors in Cotton Culture* (1929), *An American Epoch: Southern Portraiture in the National Picture* (1930), *Human Geography of the South* (1932), and *Southern Regions of the United States* (1936)—that helped define what was called the Regionalist position. Sectionalism smacked of conflict and carried the aroma of the Civil War; Regionalism, on the other hand, suggested diversity within a cooperative context.

Odom founded the *Journal of Social Forces* and the Institute for Research in Social Science, both of which put the University of North Carolina in the national forefront of such studies and generated a powerful impulse for southern reform. Actually, both Vance and Odom liked more aspects of the traditional South than they were willing to admit even to themselves, but their work called for southern industrialization and urbanization, improved schools, public health measures, and rational politics. One of Odom's associates, W. T. Couch, editor of the University of North Carolina Press, edited in 1934 a volume entitled *Culture in the South* that, while it tended to refute H. L. Mencken, tended also to combine the Agrarian and Regionalist viewpoints, even to the point of containing essays by several Agrarians.

H. L. Mencken could hardly have imagined in 1917, when he first published "Sahara of the Bozart," or in 1920, when it was reprinted in *Prejudices,* or in 1925 when he covered the Scopes trial, that, partly in response to his writings, two such movements as Agrarianism and Regionalism would have resulted. But had he recognized yet another development, Mencken would have been alert to the irony that at almost the very moment he was attacking the literary output of the South, a magnificent outpouring of southern literature was just beginning. That movement in general has gained the sobriquet of "the southern renascence."

Nobel Prize–winning novelist William Faulkner (born William Falkner in 1897) came to symbolize the rich tradition of southern literature that effloresced in the decades after 1925. Faulkner employed a dense, convoluted, hauntingly beautiful prose style to probe the human tragedy in "Yoknapatawpha," a fictional county in Mississippi. Not all his novels and stories were set in that imaginative distillation of Mississippi geography and history, but Faulkner cultivated the South's history and racial complexities to create out of local materials plots and characters involving universal dilemmas. The southern past, present, and future at times seemed to intermingle and war with one another in Faulkner's writing, and during the decade following 1929, he produced single-handedly a bookshelf of distinguished novels: *The Sound and the Fury* (1929), *As I Lay Dying* (1930), *Sanctuary* (1931), *Light in August* (1932), and *Absalom, Absalom!* (1936). Yet Faulkner had gained comparatively little fame or profit from his novels until Malcolm Cowley's *The Portable Faulkner* in 1946 introduced his complex fiction to a broader audience. And then the Nobel Prize for Literature in 1950 ensured Faulkner's fame. Before his death in 1962, he was universally recognized as one of the world's greatest literary artists.

But Faulkner was not alone. Thomas Wolfe in North Carolina in 1929 published *Look Homeward, Angel,* beginning a torrent of words that exemplified his intense love-hate relationship with his native region. Richmond, Virginia, had its own mini-renascence, beginning with Ellen Glasgow, two of whose later books, *Barren Ground* (1922) and *The Sheltered Life* (1932), were masterpieces in their own right. More exotic was James Branch Cabell, whose *Jurgen* (1919) was the only book Mencken had excepted from his attack on the aridity of southern literature. Erskine Caldwell wrote blisteringly critical portrayals of poor white culture, while Stark Young and Marjorie Kinnan Rawlings wrote more sympathetically.

Black writers, too, participated in the southern literary outpouring, with Langston Hughes, Jean Toomer, Countee Cullen, James Weldon Johnson, and perhaps especially Zora Neale Hurston with her *Their Eyes Were Watching God*

(1937) making particularly noteworthy contributions; each of these authors used the black experience in the South as material for their artistic achievements. The outstanding black writer of the time, Richard Wright, published his most famous books just as the era was ending. Born, like Faulkner, in Mississippi, the child of sharecroppers whose father abandoned the family, Wright spent most of his youth in Elaine, Arkansas; Jackson, Mississippi; and Memphis, Tennessee, living with relatives. His first book appeared in 1938, but it was *Native Son* (1940) that gained him instant acclaim. The major protagonist of the novel, Bigger Thomas, is one of the most memorable characters in all of American literature. Though the novel is set entirely in the North, it is a scathing portrayal of the racial tragedy of pre–World War II America. Five years later, Wright's semi-autobiographical *Black Boy* presented a searing depiction of the violent racism he had encountered growing up in the urban South. Wright's South and the racial dilemma it represented haunted all his best books. In 1946, Wright and his wife and daughter moved to Paris, France, and, sadly, his subsequent writing, cut off from its sources, suffered.

All these authors—from Faulkner and Wolfe to Wright—were serious writers, the kind whose life and oeuvre constitute courses in university English departments. But the blockbuster novel of the 1930s has only recently been raised to the category of even semi-serious literature. On June 30, 1936, *Gone with the Wind* was published with an unheard of initial printing of one hundred thousand copies, yet the demand far outpaced the supply. Within six months, 1 million copies had been sold, and the book continues to sell tens of thousands of copies annually more than a half-century later. On December 15, 1939, the movie version by David O. Selznick premiered to enormous acclaim in Atlanta. The movie has been the most popular movie in the history of the media. No other novel/movie has so entered the national and regional imagination, becoming the central image in popular culture of the Old South, the Civil War, and Reconstruction. This stunningly successful work of fiction, a bulky novel of 1,035 pages, was written by a one-time Atlanta newspaper woman, Margaret Mitchell, in part for self-amusement as she recuperated from a lengthy illness. Little could she know that the long manuscript she had practically completed by 1930—and the only book she ever wrote—would transform her life.

On one level, the secret of *Gone with the Wind's* success was its story line, a fascinating and engagingly told tale of war and tragedy and love and courage peopled with memorably sketched characters, all of whom quickly became part of American folklore: Scarlett O'Hara, Rhett Butler, Ashley Wilkes, Melanie Hamilton, Mammie, and Gerald and Ellen O'Hara. Even the plantation house, Tara, has become as much a part of American folk memory as Mount Vernon or Monticello. At the popular level *GWTW*, as it came to be called, was marvelous escapism for a South and nation mired in the Great Depression, with Scarlett's indomitable will to overcome the post–Civil War poverty and destruction a metaphor for contemporary impoverished readers striving to pull themselves up from destitution.

Yet, at another level, Margaret Mitchell had written a novel that represented the inner struggle for the soul of the South that had been going on for several decades. Even as early as the propaganda of New South spokesmen like Henry Grady in the 1880s, there had been an implicit conflict between reverence for the Old South and a recognition of the need for industrial development. In different ways, both the Agrarians and the Regionalists of the 1930s addressed this issue. The South was undeniably the least economically advanced region of the nation, with a particularly distressed agricultural economy. How could prosperity and urbanization—modernization, in short—be brought to the region without a loss of certain older values and without acceptance of the imagined crassness and impersonalism of the industrial North? This inner tension that played itself out in the works of Edwin Mims and Howard W. Odom provided the deeper mainspring to the story that Margaret Mitchell spun. *Gone with the Wind* depicted less a moonlight-and-magnolia romance of the Old South than a hard-fought conflict between modern and traditional values in the post–Civil War South, and that fictional controversy that mirrored historical experience elevated the novel above being simply escapist literature.

The characters of Margaret Mitchell's book were representations of images and aspects of the South: Ashley Wilkes was the idealistic but impractical Old South; Melanie the sentimentalized southern belle cum plantation mistress; Rhett Butler the hardheaded critic of the antebellum South's fire-eating arrogance, who nevertheless ultimately could not accept the New South's modernizing trends; Scarlett O'Hara, in her willingness to cast aside the ruffles and pretensions of aristocracy and do whatever was necessary to regain prosperity—including running a sawmill and hiring and firing employees in decidedly "unladylike" fashion—to a degree personified what the New South had to do to escape its past of backwardness and poverty. And yet Scarlett longed for the love of Ashley, and when, finally, she recognized that Rhett was her true love, he had already rejected her and the new ways she represented and returned to the myth of the older South. So the novel does not end with the two lovers living happily ever after—nor had the South quieted the war within. But that is not *GWTW*'s only departure from pedestrian historical romances. Scarlett O'Hara is ultimately depicted as a strong, take-charge woman, no wilting southern belle. She takes her life and her situation in her own strong hands and creates her own destiny. As such, Scarlett takes the southern woman off the pedestal and puts her in the middle of history. The movie version is far more traditional, stereotypical, and romantic in its portrayal of changing southern ways than Margaret Mitchell's book, and she was justifiably upset by the liberties movie producer Selznick took with her creation. The book *Gone with the Wind* is a pioneering work of fiction that deserves more than popular success.

SOUTHERN MUSIC

Southern writers in both the high and popular art forms—from William Faulkner to Margaret Mitchell—gained readers and admirers in the North and throughout Europe. The South as a historical place and as an imaginary construct became familiar to readers outside the region. Yet the South thus understood did not always bear close resemblance to reality. Even more problematical was the movie version of the South. Most of the early film portrayals of Dixie were unrelentingly romantic—*Hearts in Dixie* (1929), *So Red the Rose* (1934), *Steamboat 'Round the Bend* (1935), and *The Littlest Rebel* (1935) starring Shirley Temple—escapism for Depression-era viewers with blacks presented as loving, comically simpleminded, deferential Sambos skilled at little beyond soft-shoe. Perhaps this was some improvement over the vicious imagery of *Birth of a Nation*, and it gave employment to some gifted black actors and actresses, but it indicated that neither southern nor northern audiences, nor the movie moguls behind the productions, had a very sophisticated historical understanding of the South, past or present. And the movies, even while they reflected sentimental southern white attitudes about the region, were Hollywood productions, not genuine southern cultural artifacts. Through the cinema, the North and the world got a secondhand version of the South that seldom provided a glimpse of the real folk and folkways of Dixie.

However, one quintessential southern folk art found its way beyond the region and came to have an enormous worldwide impact. Southern literature found audiences above the Mason-Dixon line and across the seas, but southern music has proved even more universal. The first southern style of music to move beyond the region and become part of American popular culture was ragtime, a highly rhythmic, syncopated style of music whose origins lay on the old plantations. The fiddle and the banjo, complemented with foot stomping and hand clapping, had been an energetic, joyful kind of dance music, and in the latter part of the nineteenth century, as the piano became increasingly popular, innovative black musicians adapted the form to the keyboard. With a new instrument and an old musical style, so-called ragtime music was especially popular in the barrelhouses of lumber camps, in bawdy houses, in saloons, and in honky-tonks.

Scott Joplin, a classically trained black musician and composer from Texarkana, Texas, heard the music and incorporated it into short compositions called piano rags. His most famous piece was the 1899 composition "Maple Leaf Rag," named after a club in Sedalia, Missouri, where he occasionally performed. The sheet music version became a best-seller, the first of many ragtime compositions that proved profitable to publishing houses. (Many people today know Joplin only through the music in the movie *The Sting*, although the Houston Grand Opera's 1970s version of his folk opera *Treemonisha* was seen on public television nationally and toured several U.S. and European cities to great critical acclaim.) By way of published sheet music, ragtime piano compositions entered homes across America, and a variety of composers, many white, absorbed the style and began writing popular pieces, one of the most famous of which was the national hit, "Alexander's Ragtime Band," by Irving Berlin. Other black writers and musicians, such as Eubie Blake, kept ragtime alive for audiences of both races, rural and urban, throughout the nation. At first, proper white audiences were scandalized by ragtime, but it soon became sanitized, domesticated, and harmless, though in such popular form it was a far remove from its bawdy-house roots.

Black blues, too, spread beyond its southern black roots in the field hollers, work shouts, and spirituals of the slave community, but it never moved as far from its origins as jazz did. Blues songs were secular, individual rather than group performances the way slave spirituals had been, and they usually spoke of personal despair, racial injustice, crushing poverty. But when the individual blues singer performed, his or her listeners could identify with the singer's plight and feel the desperation, anger, and sense of release. Often the solo performer accompanied himself with a guitar, with the instrument—sometimes its sound transformed by sliding a bottle or pocket knife along the strings—used almost as a second voice to accentuate the singer's words or answer them. Such blues arose almost simultaneously in the Mississippi Delta and in East Texas, and in Texas the style was influenced by cowboy, German, Czech, Cajun, Mexican, and other styles. The rural blues was almost always a solo male singer accompanying himself on the guitar.

Singers such as John Hurt in Mississippi and Blind Lemon Jefferson in Texas were extremely influential, but it was another trained black musician who, like Scott Joplin with ragtime, really broadened the appeal of the blues. William C. Handy's band was playing in the Mississippi Delta when he first became aware of the power of rural blues, and, absorbing the raw style, he began to write music for his largely brass band that incorporated the new music. Handy soon moved to Memphis and found employment in the clubs and brothels associated with Beale Street, and the rural blues, moved to an urban context and adapted to a wider range of instruments, found a popular audience among the blacks who had crowded to the cities for jobs. Handy's most famous composition was "St. Louis Blues," and others began to write urban, band-backed versions of the once-rural blues, with singers male and female singing lyrics that touched black listeners.

In 1920, a young black woman from Ohio, Mamie Smith, recorded two songs, and the record proved enormously popular with southern blacks. Then, when Columbia Records in 1923 began recording Bessie Smith, usually accompanied with a brass-dominated band (once including a young trumpet player named Louis Armstrong), the blues found its first superstar and one whose extraordinary popularity with black audiences nationwide awoke the recording industry to the size of the black market. Bessie Smith, originally from Chattanooga, Tennessee, became a blues singer known around the world.

If the roots of ragtime and blues were rural and black, the origins of jazz were urban and more ethnically complex. Jazz represented a creative blending of music of many types and from many peoples: African, Caribbean, and European; religious music, secular music; minstrelsy, ragtime, blues, and brass marching bands. This heady mixture most often occurred in cities, and most often of all in New Orleans, and it was primarily instrumental music. While the instruments were mainly of European derivation, and the occasion for playing was often to accompany social dancing, which had become a national pastime at the turn of the century, the black urban musicians, in particular, drew upon African-American traditions to create a new blend of music that was characterized by syncopation, antiphony, polyrhythm, blues notes, and especially virtuoso instrumental improvisation. Perhaps the first to perfect a recognizably distinct sound that came to be called jazz was the black New Orleans trumpeter Charles "Buddy" Bolden in the period from 1895 to 1907. But almost simultaneously, musicians, black and white, in New Orleans, Memphis, St. Louis, and other river towns connected by the Mississippi River and its showboat bands, contributed to and helped develop the style.

This infectious, individualistic, and improvisational style of music spread through several white bands to Chicago and thence to New York. First spelled jass and considered lascivious because of its association with bawdy houses, the music was domesticated, popularized, had its spelling standardized to jazz, and became a national vogue soon after records began to be pressed in 1917. Hence, Americans in general first came to know essentially white "Dixieland" jazz that was one step removed from the music as it originated in New Orleans. It was not until five years later that the initial recordings of black jazz musicians were made, with Joseph "King" Oliver and Louis Armstrong leading the way. The music took the nation by storm, hailed by many as a fresh, energetic, liberating art form and attacked by others as indecent and undisciplined. But for many people, George Gershwin's adaptation of the form in 1924 with his "Rhapsody in Blue" represented the legitimating of a powerful, distinctly American style of music. Louis Armstrong in particular became practically a national icon, and his trumpet playing and scat singing (nonsense syllables) made him world famous. Today jazz is played, listened to, and loved around the globe, from Russia to Japan, and it has continued to evolve, absorbing still newer influences.

Recording had first been the medium whereby southern folk musical expression reached a large public, but it was the development of commercial radio broadcasting that created a national awareness, then a market for the broadest form of southern music, variously called hillbilly or country music. Southern radio stations began broadcasting in 1922, and, eager to fill their programming hours (there being no syndicated shows then), they sought local entertainers. When local singers and instrumentalists began to perform, local listeners immediately responded, and this response led to more entertainers, more recordings, more broadcasts, and the proliferation of the musical form.

Commercial record producers often incorrectly portrayed the music and the performers as the product of either the southern mountains or western ranches, and the performers just as often accepted the commercial image, even adopting appropriate costumes and stage names untrue to their origins. This was true for the music of all areas of the South.

This was also truly the music of the white folk, with voices and styles influenced by a broad catholicity of traditions. It was the kind of music that families sang in their parlors or to friends; it was heard at house parties and at barn dances; it represented the values, the ethos, the pains and joys, of the plain folk of the rural South. This music did not arise in a vacuum but rather it grew out of sentimental parlor songs, variations upon ballads and dance music from the British and European past, and every new kind of music with which the folk came into contact— jazz, Tin Pan Alley, minstrel melodies, brass bands on steamboats plying the southern rivers, Hawaiian music, blues, and Mexican and Cajun music. White southerners had always been eclectic about music; they simply accepted music they liked from whatever source and made it their own. They little cared, for example, that "Dixie" was the composition of an Ohio-born minstrel singer, or that "Carry Me Back to Old Virginia" had been written by a Long Island black songwriter. The lyrics themselves are an index to the complex concerns of the folk: conflicting opinions toward modern ways and modern inventions; expressions of wanderlust and carousing and love for home and dear old mom; protests about working conditions and irreligion and a lost way of life; and unrequited love and love casually offered. Country music lyrics represented a wide range of political viewpoints too, from praise of new inventions, such as Mr. Ford's Model A, to conservative opposition to change to radical protests of economic injustice, bad working conditions, and environmental destruction. The voices were seldom polished; rather, in raw, unaffected ways this was the authentic expression of the plain white people of the South, who, though mostly rural, even when they had moved to the towns and cities retained the outlook of the countryside. In the music of the Carter family, of Jimmie Rodgers, and myriad others, southern families in the 1920s and 1930s found spending evenings by the side of the radio to be not only entertainment but also a means of achieving self-awareness.

Programs such as the "Grand Old Opry" and the "Louisiana Hayride," and various barn dances, created an industry in response to the folk music of the white South, and entertainers and songs entered the mainstream. The music evolved and grew, from the simple mountain music of Appalachia to Bob Wills's Western Swing, with its broad range of instruments, and its use of jazz and the big band swing sound. In the south of Texas, Mexican influences produced "Tex-Mex music"; in Louisiana, a distinct Cajun form of music developed; as a result of the increasing use of electrical amplification in the noisy beer joints of the Texas oil fields, loud, often rambunctious "honky-tonk" music emerged. In 1934, a gifted singer from Tioga, Texas, named Gene Autry, made the first of the singing cowboy movies, creating a popular new form of cinema and reinforcing the western image of what would soon be known as "country and western" music. Americans everywhere came to know this wide range of music, and like jazz, it affected popular music of all styles in this nation and spread throughout the world.

Closely related to so-called country music, if not a subset of it, was gospel music, a genuine expression of the folk piety of the region. A variety of influences created gospel music, and black composers and singers made major contributions. Songbook publishers had traveling quartets that introduced new songs, peddled the newest song books, and absorbed the newest musical trends. Radio programs, all-day singings, and singing schools conducted by the itinerant song masters were other means of promoting gospel music, and many young people who learned to sing in their church quartet—like Elvis Presley, who was

Elvis Presley on stage, c. 1955. Presley's music owed a great deal to African-American rhythm and blues. (Elvis Presley Enterprises, Inc.)

born in Tupelo, Mississippi, in 1935—later moved to blues, country, and, in the 1950s, rock. The influence was two-way, with the gospel sound identifiable in much secular music and vice versa. The piano-banging secular singers and hell-raisers Jerry Lee Lewis and Mickey Gilley are cousins of piano-banging religious singer and Pentecostal revivalist Jimmy Swaggart. The music spanned the spectrum. As in the other forms of southern music, gospel has entered the American mainstream, with songs like Thomas A. Dorsey's "Precious Lord, Take My Hand" and "Peace in the Valley" and Albert E. Brumley's "I'll Fly Away" becoming special favorites. Dorsey was black, Brumley white, but listeners of both races loved their songs and seldom knew the racial background of the composers. Elvis Presley, in particular, became an international star, popularizing a blues-gospel-rock-influenced style of southern music that blended black and white inspirations and gained a world-wide following. Presley died in 1977, but since that time, his appeal has taken on the trappings of a religion. Hundreds of thousands of people annually visit Graceland, his mansion in Memphis, as though on a spiritual pilgrimage.

One of the greatest cultural productions of the South, indeed the nation during the first four decades of the twentieth century, was its varieties of folk music. In the same way that Mencken, in his "Sahara of the Bozart" diatribe of 1917 and in later writings, had not foreseen the literary outpouring now known as the Southern literary renascence, his snide comments about music showed no awareness of the richness of the folk music traditions. In fact, Mencken had in mind when he bemoaned the state of culture in the South the institutionalized high culture of museums, symphony orchestras, and grand opera. Yet their relative absence in the South of 1920 or so was not an indication of congenital southern backwardness, but rather was a symptom of the poverty and rurality of the South. Museums, symphonies, and opera companies require the wealth and numbers of supporters that only big cities can offer, and the South of 1920 had no big cities other than New Orleans. The Crescent City had the size, but Mardi Gras absorbed the money and leisure that elsewhere flowed into high art. So Mencken's observation about the absence of a certain kind of high art was accurate, but his analysis of why was wrong. In more individualistic, less expensive art forms—a writer writing, a singer singing—the South's creativity blossomed. Only later, after World War II, would rapid urbanization and greater wealth lead to major southern museums, orchestras, and opera companies. But in its literary productions and in the music of its folk, the South left its impress on the world.

CHAPTER 27

New Directions in Southern Politics

THE POLITICS OF POWER

When Walter Hines Page wrote in 1902 that southern life had been "pickled" for decades, by which he meant that it seemed impervious to change, politics was one of the key factors he identified that kept the South stuck in the ways of the past. It is easy to accept the general features of such an argument. Southern politicians had had little national influence and a scant national role since 1861—the Wilson presidency being an exception—and with the largest arena closed to them, it was only natural that politicians tried to identify and promote provincial interests. No candidate running from the South had sought the presidency since 1860. What did it benefit a leader to advocate a national agenda if in so doing he risked losing his office? In a region with only one viable party, how did one differentiate oneself and gain public support? An often accepted way was to use rhetorical excess to gain attention, a ploy that worked especially well if the oratory attacked safe enemies and promoted policies that promised to help the economically depressed masses.

Here was a situation primed to allow a proliferation of demagoguery, and leaders skilled in invective and empty promises arose in plenty. Certainly some politicians were serious and tried to deliver on their promises, but on occasion promises were more a means to gain political office than to help the needy. Racism was always the convenient means to galvanize political supporters. As blacks were increasingly disenfranchised, anti-black political rhetoric intensified. Now no potential black votes were to be lost, and anti-black sentiment could be counted on either to keep supporters in line or to threaten and destroy political enemies.

Too often, all a politician had to do to gain and stay in office was rant about blacks, recall for his listeners the threat of northern domination and Republican rule, and hoodwink the poor white voters at the same time that the entrenched business interests were surreptitiously served. The losers were the white majority, all the blacks, and ultimately the South as a whole. Despite not inconsiderable Progressive-era reforms, most of the region's people were left untouched by the policies of good government advocates. Often the business environment was more improved than the quality of life of the average person, and Progressive reforms were far more evident in the large marketing towns and cities than in the countryside, where most southerners lived.

It is difficult for modern readers to comprehend the quality of life that obtained for most southern folk practically down to World War II. Imagine a region whose per capita income was less than half the rest of the nation; a region where the average white child attended school for fewer than three months annually, and the black child even less; where modern medical care was unavailable; and where the incidence of disease, tooth decay, illiteracy, infant mortality, murder, and practically all other bad social indices were significantly higher than elsewhere in the nation.

The typical farmer, white or black, was a sharecropper, living in a shotgun shack two or three rooms deep. Many such farmers did not even have an outdoor privy. Shallow water wells, unscreened windows, and incomplete acceptance of the idea of using soap helped the spread of microorganisms. The typical shack was a wooden frame building, sitting off the ground on sections of tree stumps; the exterior walls were wide boards nailed to the frame, with narrow slats nailed over the cracks—tongue-and-groove planks were too expensive to use. Most such houses had neither a ceiling nor interior walls. Sometimes newspapers tacked or glued to the walls served as makeshift wallpaper to help keep out the wind. In cold weather, the family huddled around a wood heater or stove for warmth and slept crowded together in bed. Drafts of cold air defeated even the hottest stoves, and through the cracks in the floor one could see the chickens and dogs and feel the chill wind blow.

The families living together in such uncomfortable homes, accustomed to hard work and little reward, often found succor in their religion, their love for one another, and their music and stories. They did not wallow in self-pity and through their folk art and culture persevered with their basic humanity surprisingly intact. But their poverty, their limited political and cultural vision, the degree to which they were trapped in their station in life, all contributed to a sense of quiet desperation. Yet hope for a better existence was never completely extinguished. It was that yearning, and that desperation, that both fueled racist demagoguery and occasional reformist crusades. And it was out of that milieu that three politicians arose who would represent the transformation of the region from the post–Civil War colonial South of poverty and prejudice to the post–World War II South of relative prosperity and racial moderation. Huey P. Long, Lyndon B. Johnson, and James Earl (Jimmy) Carter both led and symbolized the emergence of the American South in the last half of the twentieth century.

Huey Pierce Long was born in 1893—in the midst of the deepest economic depression of the century—in Winn Parish, Louisiana, a county in the north-central portion of the state that had been a stronghold of Unionist sentiment in 1861 and that gave the Populists the highest percentage of votes of any county in the South in 1896; a county, moreover, that on the eve of World War I saw a socialist slate of candidates elected in the county seat of Winnfield. This tradition of dissent has often been suggested as somehow influential in the gestation of Huey Long as a political leader, but that is far too deterministic. Long was, to continue the biological metaphor, a sport. He was, in his own words, *sui generis*, and it would be a mistake to see him as a twentieth-century version of the Populist revolt. But Long did understand how the poor people of Louisiana suffered, how the political establishment cared more about staying in power through serving the interests of the wealthy and powerful than addressing the serious economic and racial maladies of the state. Long understood the folk, knew how to harness their frustration, could ignite their hope for a better life and use it to promote his policies the way no one else could, and he was an absolute genius at speaking their language and gaining their vote. Whether he truly believed in their cause is problematical; what is certain is that he believed in his cause.

Even as a child, Long impressed everyone with his energy, his brains, his sass, and his desire to be in the limelight. His rebelliousness kept him from being allowed to graduate from high school, but after a quick succession of salesman positions and several months of reading law at Tulane University, he was able to pass the state bar exam. As a lawyer, his personality traits soon made him successful, but it was his race to become a member of the state railroad commission that first really indicated that he would be a force to be reckoned with. Barnstorming across the multicounty district in a secondhand Oldsmobile at a time when a car still attracted attention, Long drew upon his sales experience (and his phenomenal ability seemingly to remember every face and name he had ever known) to win a spirited runoff campaign. And once in office, Long began attacking Standard Oil and other big corporations and promoting the welfare of the common farmers. He quickly showed a flair for winning publicity, deflating his enemies with colorful nicknames, skewering them with pithy invective. He successfully presented himself as the selfless protector of the poor, doing battle against the powerful forces of Wall Street. Although he lost his first campaign for the governor's office in 1924, his ruthlessly efficient political machine was being perfected, and four years later, he won the gubernatorial race. Baton Rouge had never seen anything like Huey Long before, nor had the nation, and the state would never be the same again.

Long took over the governor's office and the huge state bureaucracy like a man possessed. He would stop at nothing to get his programs through. If that required taking over the assembly with a combination of bluster, bribery, bullying, wily parliamentary maneuvering, and ruthless hardball politics, then so be it. Huey Long was not concerned with civics-class politics. He took Louisiana government by the neck and wrung out of it the results he wanted. His first priority was political power—staying in office—and Long understood that that was best achieved in a state accustomed to corruption, misrule, and poverty by catering to the palpable needs of the voting masses. Long correctly identified the interests of the people and capitalized on the pent-up desire for government help to solidify his position. The delivery of services was the means, through the agency of democracy, for Huey Long to rule Louisiana with the iron-like grip of a tyrant.

For the people, the cost of preserving Long's power often seemed a bargain. The governor provided entertaining rhetoric, got in good licks against the traditional enemies of the poor—"pour it on, Huey" was a common refrain at his political rallies—and delivered real benefits: several thousand miles of paved roads, bridges across the state's numerous rivers, free textbooks for school children, and hospitals financed largely by increased taxes on the large corporations that were headquartered elsewhere but extracting Louisiana's mineral wealth. But the larger cost was in the principles of fair play, honesty, the rule of law. Long's political machine extorted huge sums of money ("deducts," short for deductions) by requiring that state employees give a certain set percentage of their wage as a mandatory contribution. Opponents, even principled ones, were crushed. Long manipulated the assembly with an utter disdain for rules and orderly procedures; he had contempt for anyone who stood in his way.

Long was not above using racist charges and innuendoes when it served his political purpose. Unlike some earlier southern demagogues, ugly race politics was not Long's primary method, perhaps because he knew how to use other issues so effectively. But neither was Long very interested in providing significant government benefits to blacks, in part, because they could not vote. We should not expect Long to have been anything other than a person of his times; however, his outrageous political corruption and ruthlessness have been excused because he supposedly did not use race-baiting and saw to it that blacks benefited from his programs. When they did so, it was only incidentally. In balance, Long was more concerned with maintaining his power than benefiting the poor, white or black. He was a populist by political strategy, an autocrat by temperament.

But Long did control the state the way no governor ever had, anywhere else in the nation. Even after being elected to the U.S. Senate in 1930, he spent an inordinate amount of time in Baton Rouge and thoroughly controlled his hand-picked successor, O. K. Allen. Long withstood an impeachment attempt, the concerted opposition of all "good government" types, and in essence was a Dixie dictator. "I'm the Kingfish," Long said, referring to the character on the popular "Amos and Andy" radio show. In the Senate, Long continued to gain press attention by extravagant antics. He soon broke with Franklin D. Roosevelt, proposed more radical solutions to the Great Depression with his redistributive scheme called "Every Man a King," and caused Roosevelt to call him one of the two most dangerous men in America (the other was Douglas MacArthur). Partly in response to Long's perceived threat, Roosevelt's New Deal policies shifted slightly leftward to preempt some of the Kingfish's appeal.

But Long's great self-described trajectory to become president came crashing down in a quick, bloody encounter in the corridors of his new capitol building in Baton Rouge one muggy September evening. Long had long been at odds with Judge B. Henry Pavy of St. Landry Parish, who remained a steadfast opponent of the Long political machine. During 1935, Long had apparently threatened the judge that if he did not prove more cooperative, Long would spread an old rumor (dating from an earlier scurrilous opponent of Pavy's in 1910) that Pavy had "coffee blood"—a Louisiana euphemism for saying that some black blood coursed through Pavy's veins. A young Baton Rouge surgeon, Dr. Carl Austin Weiss, had married Pavy's daughter Yvonne. Somehow Dr. Weiss heard of the threatened smear both to his father-in-law and, by implication, to Weiss's wife.

On Sunday evening, September 8, 1935, shortly after tucking their infant in bed, Dr. Weiss told his wife he had to go out to see a patient. Slipping a cheap .32 automatic pistol into his coat pocket, he drove toward the spire of the thirty-two story capitol, parked his car, walked inconspicuously into the building, and stood behind a column. Shortly, Huey Long came walking briskly down the hallway, accompanied by his retinue of bodyguards. Suddenly Dr. Weiss stepped forward with his hand outreached. Just as he fired a bodyguard slapped his hand, causing the bullet to enter Long's abdomen. A barrage of bullets from the guards then slammed into Weiss, and apparently a ricochet from that attack hit Long in the lower spine. In seconds it was all over—Dr. Weiss, his corpse riddled, lay dead in a pool of blood; Long was fatally wounded and died some thirty hours later. An inglorious era in Louisiana politics had come to an inglorious end.

For decades after Long's assassination, the state's politics largely consisted of Long and anti-Long factions. The roads remained, the bridges stood, the children had textbooks. But the state's tolerance of political corruption still set it apart. Class and racial conflict marred the political process; Long had not promoted the idea that the purpose of government was to solve problems and to deliver services because people had a right to them. Rather, Long suggested that it was he personally who provided necessary services. Long did not attempt to persuade the citizens of Louisiana that the federal government had a legitimate role to play in their lives. In a sense, Long did not routinize government; instead, governing for him was the means to personal power for no greater end. It would be another southern politician, equally energetic, equally concerned with power, who would promote the idea in the South that the purpose of government (and the purpose of power) was to improve the lives of constituents. Lyndon B. Johnson appreciated the positive role of the federal government, but despite the surface similarities to Long, LBJ was a very different kind of politician.

THE POLITICS OF SERVICE

In 1908, Lyndon Baines Johnson, the first child of Sam and Rebekah Johnson, was born in Gillespie County, Texas, just west of Austin, the state capital, in a semi-arid region of rolling hills, springtime bluebonnets, outcroppings of limestone, and stark beauty. For his whole life, Johnson had great affection for the county and its inhabitants, later purchasing a ranch there on the Pedernales River and turning it into his Texas White House. Sam Johnson, LBJ's father, was a tall, lanky, compassionate man, given to great outbursts of anger but possessing enormous personal charm. A farmer early in his life, Sam was, by 1904, a Populist-minded state legislator who traveled to Austin to represent his rural neighbors. But after marrying Rebekah Baines in 1907, Sam reluctantly did not run for reelection in 1908; instead, he had to support his wife and then their baby boy. Rebekah was an impressive person in her own right. She was smart, determined to make something of herself and her children, strong willed, and an unusually nurturing mother. Much of Lyndon's genuine compassion for the plain folk of his region, state, and nation and his fascination with politics came from his parents.

In 1918, Sam again became a state legislator, and he often proudly brought Lyndon with him to Austin. Little Lyndon, just ten years old, roamed the state capitol, listening to speeches and absorbing the bustle, the bombast, the camaraderie, and intrigue of Texas politics. When Sam went out on the hustings to seek votes, Lyndon was in his glory. If ever a child grew up in politics, it was Lyndon B. Johnson. He discovered how empowering it was to feel one was doing important things, to solicit and win public approval, to be a person of influence. Politics, to him, was the noblest profession, and from his parents he learned that the purpose of the political process was to serve constituents, to use government to improve the lives of the decent hill country farmers eking out a hard-scrabble existence on the rugged landscape. And Lyndon learned that to be effective one had to be noticed, had to be heard.

Everyone who knew Lyndon as a child remembered him for being a show-off. He was always wilder, or louder, or dressed flashier than anyone else, and in every classroom, he did whatever it took to stand apart. Such behavior did not win everyone's favor, but everyone did sense that Lyndon was also, to use Huey Long's phrase about himself, *sui generis.* By the time he graduated from high school and entered Southwest State Teachers College in nearby San Marcos, certain of Lyndon's lifelong characteristics were well formed: He was a consummate political animal, he could persuade almost anyone to do what he wanted by talking right into their face, at times charming and beguiling and at times pleading and angry, and then again logical and impressive with factual analysis. When Lyndon got involved in campus politics, he was like a man among boys. He even had the highest school administrators on his side, and his political opponents felt that they had been both steam-rolled and snookered.

Leaving behind him a trail of devoted friends and smoldering enemies, Lyndon graduated in 1930 with his political calluses well formed.

Lyndon had barely been able to scrape together enough money to attend college, and he borrowed money, worked odd jobs at the college, and had to drop out in 1927 to 1928 to teach school in the tiny town of Cotulla, near the Mexican border. There he taught in a segregated elementary school for Mexican children, and their poverty touched Lyndon's heart. He threw himself into the task with the kind of Johnsonian energy that later became legendary. He came to love the children and abhor their situation; he determined to enhance their self-image, inspire them to study, and motivate them to change their lives. He drove himself, the other teachers, and the students, but the children and their families loved him for his obvious devotion to them.

After graduating from Southwest Texas State, Lyndon began teaching speech and debate at Sam Houston High School in Houston. Again he completely threw himself into the task; he inspired, cajoled, pushed the students to excel and win debate tournaments. He became their coach, their father figure, their champion. And again, Lyndon found his heart going out to the children from poor families. He fervently came to believe that the government had a responsibility to its citizens; government should be a friend, a helpmate, not a distant, impersonal force. With his earlier political instinct and his experience teaching, Lyndon Johnson saw government as the means to an important end—improving constituents' lives. But of course one had to be in politics and win elections to help achieve that purpose.

In the fall of his second year of teaching, Lyndon's opportunity came. The newly elected congressman from his home district, Richard Kleburg, a member of the wealthy King Ranch family, was only nominally interested in the legislative, political aspects of his new position, and when an adviser suggested that old Sam Johnson's boy—an energetic political whiz kid—be appointed his secretary, Kleberg sent word to Lyndon to meet him in Corpus Christi. So excited he could hardly function, Lyndon came to the interview, got the job, secured a leave of absence from Sam Houston High School, and arranged to move to the U.S. capital. On December 2, 1931, Lyndon Johnson was Washington bound, to a city he essentially never left again.

In everything but name, Lyndon Johnson became a congressman in 1932. He was the hardest working, most driven, most compulsive congressional secretary and aide anyone had ever seen. He had an unquenchable hunger to know how the institution worked; he practically worked to death the office staff, but no one worked as long and hard and with as much intensity as he did. Kleberg let Johnson make decisions and handle constituent matters and intervene with various government agencies far beyond what his age and title suggested was appropriate, but Johnson was up to the task. He learned whom to contact to get a constituent's problem solved; he learned which congressman's office was effective; he asked questions and talked and absolutely mastered the art of congressional politics. Lyndon quickly impressed the power wielders in the capital, especially Sam Rayburn and eventually President Roosevelt. When Roosevelt pushed through the National Youth Administration (NYA) in 1935 to alleviate the problems of the youthful poor, Johnson used all his connections to win appointment as head of the NYA in Texas.

Once he became Texas director of the NYA, Lyndon poured his almost superhuman energy into the agency, determined to do all that was possible to improve the lives of young Texans. He seemed consumed both by the immensity of the job to be done and by the potential for good of targeted, compassionate, government action. Individuals, families, communities, and eventually the entire state, region, and nation would be the beneficiaries. At a time when most southerners were still suspicious of the federal government, Johnson understood the role it could play in addressing the ills of an impoverished region. Johnson's ambition for political power—for his own inner needs and for what he could do for the people—would not long be satisfied by the NYA, however, and when he saw an opportunity to run for a seat in Congress in 1937 after the incumbent congressman died, he threw himself into the campaign with the all-consuming energy with which he now seemed to approach every task he considered important. Cloaking himself with the support of Franklin D. Roosevelt and promoting the successes and connections he had gained through the NYA, young Lyndon won the election.

No sooner was he in Washington than Johnson showed he understood how political power was wielded. He quickly became a friend of such influential congressmen as Carl Vinson of Georgia and Sam Rayburn of Texas, majority leader of the House. The no-holds-barred political practices of Texas were second nature to Johnson, and he campaigned with the compulsive zeal that was his trademark. In his first and most famous Senate race in 1948, he campaigned by helicopter, still a novelty and a sure attractor of crowds in small-town Texas. Politics in the Lone State were hard-fought and often corrupt, and Johnson followed conventional political ethics in winning his Senate runoff election by the landslide margin of eighty-seven votes. But Johnson, once firmly in power, used the federal government as a tool to advance the interests of his district and state. He never lost sight of the political implications of any act, but he pursued power for a purpose larger than himself. Johnson was perhaps the first modern southern politician to understand that the South had to change its attitude toward the federal government if it wanted economic redemption. For Johnson, a growing federal government meant the potential for good for the whole South, not something to be feared because it might interfere with southern institutions (i.e., segregation). In a very fundamental way, the central government in the years following 1941 remade the South more completely than either the Civil War or the first Reconstruction did. Lyndon B. Johnson represented a new, forward-looking generation of southern politicians who understood that some changes had to come gradually, some could be pushed forthrightly, but that the lives of whites and blacks in the South would be improved as the whole economic pie enlarged. Johnson intended to profit, too, and he surely did, but he never lost sight of the raison d'etre of national political power. As such, he was the first modern southern politician.

But Lyndon Johnson had won the presidency with the identity of a Washington insider and a bigger-than-life Texan, not exactly as a southerner. And Woodrow Wilson had successfully run for the presidency in 1912 as the able reform governor of New Jersey and former president of Princeton University. The honor of being the first clearly identifiable southern post–Civil War president would ultimately fall to a young Georgian who only came of age at the end of World War II. But as a child in the 1930s, Jimmy Carter learned the lesson that the federal government could bring benefits. His father, like Johnson's, was an avid politico who often took his son Jimmy to hear campaign speeches. From his father and from family stories he heard about his maternal grandfather, Jim Jack Gordy, who supposedly had first suggested the idea of Rural Free Delivery of the mail, Jimmy Carter, too, learned that government could and should be a helpmate to its citizens. He remembered how, when he was thirteen years of age, the New Deal–sponsored Rural Electrification Agency (REA) brought electricity to the Georgia countryside. But the change was not merely in running water and electric lights. As he wrote in his campaign autobiography, *Why Not the Best?* (1975), "Farmers began to have county and regional meetings to discuss the changes that were taking place in their lives, to elect REA directors, to discuss national legislation, to determine rate structures, to bargain with the Georgia Power Company on electricity supplies, and to determine which new areas would be covered next by the electric power line. In general our families' horizons were expanded greatly."

The perverse localism of the rural South was being changed; southerners came to understand that there was more to politics than race-baiting. But World War II was to bring even more of a transformation, both in economics and race, and Carter himself, a generation later as governor of Georgia (1971–1975), would announce to his state that it was time to put an end to discrimination. He symbolically hung a portrait of civil rights leader Martin Luther King, Jr., in the Georgia statehouse. A new age in the history of the South had begun. The era of World War II would be a major watershed in the history of the South, making possible, at last, a New South. The election of Carter in 1976, and even more so of William Jefferson Clinton as president and Albert Gore, Jr., as vice president in 1992, represented for liberal southerners the coming of age of the American South. But that proved to be a short-lived dream. Conservative Republicanism triumphed in 2000, as it had in 1980, and the one term of Carter and the two terms of Clinton look in 2003 more like anomalies than trends.

PART V

The American South

Hundreds of millions of television viewers around the world sat nervously watching their screens on July 20, 1969, listening with incredulous attention to radio transmissions of the conversation of three American astronauts as two of them, inside an ungainly lunar module, prepared to land on the moon's surface. The crackling radio communications described the lunar module's uncoupling from the command module, then its gradual, almost science-fiction-like descent to the moon's cold surface, blowing up lunar dust before the final touchdown. The first word uttered from the moon was "Houston," followed by "the eagle has landed." Who would have anticipated, two generations earlier, when H. L. Mencken made the South a byword for scientific ignorance and backwardness, that a southern city would one day be associated around the world with the greatest high-tech adventure to date in human history?

Who could have imagined, in the midst of the Depression-era South, that less than a half-century hence Atlanta would be identified worldwide with Cable News Network, the most advanced communication network in the world? Or who, aware of those haggard faces in the 1930s Works Progress Administration documentary photographs of southern sharecroppers, could have foreseen that little more than a generation later, the South would be associated with the gleaming skyscrapers of Atlanta, Dallas, and Houston? Who, appalled by the spectacle of public lynchings in the 1920s and 1930s, could have anticipated a South two generations later with more elected black public officials than any other region of the country, several of its largest cities having black mayors, and Virginia having a black governor—the grandson of a slave? The ugliest race riots in recent times have occurred in Los Angeles, Detroit, and Washington, not New Orleans or Charlotte.

Clearly to even the most casual observer of the American scene, the South of the 1990s was profoundly different from the South of the 1930s and before. In fact, southerners of 1930 would have felt more at home in the South of the 1830s than in the South of 1970 and later. It might reasonably be argued that the era of World War II initiated more far-reaching change in the South than did the Civil War. How had Dixie been transformed in the generation after 1940, and which aspects, if any, of that older, distinctive South remained in the so-called Sun Belt South of the 1990s? Was there anything still identifiably southern about the genuine New South that had evolved over the past half-century? Or had the region finally reached the end of its peculiar history? The making of the American South represents the coming full circle of the story.

CHAPTER 28

The Dawning of a New South

THE SOUTH AND WORLD WAR II

In retrospect, the New Deal was more of a transition period than most contemporaries could understand. From the Tennessee Valley Authority to the Soil
Conservation Service, the federal government had acknowledged a responsibility for addressing the economic, agricultural, environmental, and human
problems of the poorest region in the nation. Slowly a new breed of southern
politicians, such as Lyndon B. Johnson, began to see the national government
not as the enemy of the South but as a legitimate helpmate. President Franklin
D. Roosevelt was careful to protect his political flanks in the region, because he
knew that he needed Solid South Democratic support for his programs—
consequently he never actively campaigned for federal antilynching legislation
and he cooperated with entrenched Democratic machines. But he did convene
a national conference in 1938 that identified the South as the nation's premier
economic problem.

Roosevelt and other New Dealers understood that poverty lay at the root of
many southern maladies, including persistent racism, and they also saw that the
South's low wages exacerbated the problem. Much of the southern political and
business establishment supported the concept of lower southern wages, arguing
that low wages were the South's most telling competitive advantage in trying to
attract northern investment and industry. Moreover, most southern business and

industry leaders profited in the short run by paying their employees wages as much as 40 percent lower than those paid for comparable jobs outside the South. They often justified their policies by pointing out that southern workers, especially blacks, were unskilled and lacking in motivation. New Deal economic planners saw the relationship between southern poverty and unskilled laborers, on the one hand, and substandard wages on the other. Better wages would begin to break the back of poverty, and, of course, better wages also meant that wage earners became consumers who could purchase goods and pay taxes that could improve schools and infrastructure. Wages earned would be spent locally, and each additional dollar in a given community turned over several times, multiplying the effect. Over the opposition of local interests, Washington pushed for uniform national wages in government-related programs and, although some compromises to southern political stubbornness were necessary, the New Deal began the process that ultimately raised southern wages above the poverty level. The southern worker and the region were the beneficiaries.

Southern state governments also slowly realized that the regional economy had to change if prosperity were ever to return to the region. Reliance on the old standbys of cotton cultivation and extractive industries (such as lumber production) did not seem to herald good times, especially because most of the South's first growth of timber had been cut by 1930 and cotton had been devastated initially by the boll weevil and then by overproduction and reduced acreage. Mississippi, a state peculiarly lacking in natural resources, possessing no major port, and correctly seeing that future cotton prosperity was a chimera, led the way in seeking new economic development. In 1936, Governor Hugh L. White pushed through the Mississippi legislature the Balance Agriculture With Industry Act (BAWI). Through this act, communities would use local government bonds to construct factories to be leased at a cut rate to industries that would in turn commit to hiring a requisite number of employees for a prescribed number of years. Other tax benefits and promotions were also devised to persuade industry to locate in Mississippi. Before World War II, a dozen plants had been attracted to the state, and after the war the BAWI program was renewed and strengthened.

Soon states across the region were competing with one another as well as with northern states to increase industrial investment and manufacturing jobs. Within a generation, every southern state had commissions and was sending representatives around the globe promoting industrial development. Unfortunately, the only comparative advantages that much of the South had to dangle in front of prospective investors were comparatively low wages, low taxes, nonunion labor, and lax pollution laws. As a consequence, many of the jobs that were created produced minimum income, scant tax receipts, environmental problems, and continued regional poverty. Manufacturing, states like North Carolina came to realize, did not automatically mean middle-class prosperity for its industrial workers.

But, far more than state industrial agencies and New Deal wage equal-
ization programs, World War II–related investments began to create a new
South. The South's climate—relatively mild winters and long growing seasons—
had earlier contributed to the South's staple crop production, and after 1941,
its climate played an important role in defense expenditures. It obviously made
military sense not to have all essential war materiel plants in the Northeast or
Midwest, and military training bases would be more efficient if located in all-
season locations. On both counts, the South stood to gain. The result, helped
along by southern congressional seniority, was a proliferation of defense-relat-
ed industries and a huge expansion of military bases. The Marines had long
trained at Parris Island in South Carolina, but now from Virginia to Texas, the
South gained more than its share of military expenditures. In addition to the
meager salaries of the military personnel, every base generated construction
jobs, clerical and support staff employment, and the related growth of stores,
schools, and churches. For tens of thousands of southerners who had always
been dependent upon agriculture or extractive industry for jobs, military bases
meant steady, indoor, and relatively high-paying work. Tens of thousands of
rural or small town migrants moved to southern cities or near bases for wartime
employment. Many of the cities experienced very serious housing shortages, and
seldom could public services keep pace with the wartime population booms. As
formerly rural whites and blacks crowded into cities, racial tensions often became inflamed. This clearly was a time of transition for the region.

Across the South—Newport News, Charleston, Pascagoula, New Orleans,
and Houston—the government supported shipbuilding activities, and in each
case, the initial construction investment, the new wages for southern skilled
workers (such as welders and pipe fitters), and salaries for thousands of auxiliary workers brought pockets of prosperity to the region. B-24 bombers were
built in Fort Worth, B-29s in Marietta, Georgia, bringing defense plant jobs to
the southern interior also. Many southern women for the first time found paid
work outside the home and off the farm in munitions plants and defense factories. Spin-off employment again multiplied the effect on local economies of
defense expenditures for equipment and salaries. In all, the federal government spent more than 4 billion dollars on actual military facilities in the South,
and another 4 billion dollars in contracts was awarded to privately owned military construction firms.

The southern industrial contribution to the Allied war effort was significant. Two-thirds of the nation's supply of toluene, a petroleum-based compo-
nent of the explosive TNT, was produced at the Baytown Ordinance Works,
near Houston. Half of the Allied bombs dropped on Axis targets were made possible by this Texas toluene. Most of the nation's synthetic rubber, called Buna-
S and used primarily for tires, also was manufactured in a series of giant plants
near Houston that used petroleum as their essential raw material. And most of
the nation's need for high-octane aviation gasoline was supplied by a number

of newly modified and enlarged refineries in Houston and along the upper Texas coast. Moreover, much of the industrial North and Northeast was fueled by natural gas and oil shipped by two massive pipeline systems, the "Big Inch" and the "Little Big Inch," each more than a thousand miles long, that linked the producing fields of Texas to the factories and homes of the northern states.

Suddenly, the South began producing entrepreneurs like Andrew Jackson Higgins in New Orleans. With military support, he transformed his small boat-building firm into a giant, modern, efficient producer of Liberty ships, eventually employing twenty thousand workers at eight plants in and near New Orleans. Higgins cooperated with unions, paid his black employees the same as white, and loved to stroll through his shipyards shouting encouragement to his workers with a bullhorn. His employees loved him, and the federal government appreciated his managerial acumen. In 1942, he won a huge contract to build over a thousand cargo planes in a gigantic factory that he built in Michoud, just east of New Orleans. A generation later, the Michoud Plant was chosen by the National Aeronautics and Space Administration (NASA) as the assembly site for the Apollo rockets in another spree of government-related expenditures that would promote high-tech employment in the South from Cape Canaveral to Huntsville to Houston.

A similar story unfolded in Houston with the construction firm headed by George and Herman Brown. (The original co-founder, Dan Root, had died in 1929, but his name was retained by the company.) An early supporter of Lyndon B. Johnson, George R. Brown utilized his political contacts to win a large contract in June 1940 to construct the Corpus Christi Naval Station. America's entry into World War II required enlargements to the facility, which quadrupled the value of the contract to Brown and Root. With this major success under its belt, the firm soon won a series of contracts to build destroyer escorts and landing crafts at a newly formed subsidiary, Brown Shipbuilding Company, near Houston. This company eventually employed 25,000 workers, built 354 combat ships, and acquired total government contracts of about 1 billion dollars. Brown and Root remained major supporters of Johnson, and in 1961, when he was Vice President, Houston was chosen as the site for NASA's Manned Spacecraft Center (later renamed the Johnson Space Center). Not surprisingly, Brown and Root won the construction contract. In the decades after 1961, NASA programs would pour additional billions of federal funds into the South.

During the course of World War II, more than 4 million southerners served in the armed forces. This often involved training at a variety of sites, occasionally outside the South, and training introduced young southern men to skills, techniques, managerial practices, and worldviews far removed from what they had known on the farms and in the small towns of Dixie. After training, most southern enlistees served throughout the United States and abroad, further introducing them to ideas, technologies, and attitudes greatly at variance with their prewar experience. Thousands of men were introduced to college life and the larger world of academia through such military training projects as the Navy's V-12 program. After the war, these veterans wanted to return to the classroom. Much of the actual wartime experience was unpleasant: boring, tiring, lonely, confusing, dangerous, even deadly. But many southern soldiers had, through the military, their first introduction to a larger, potentially more exciting, liberating, and lucrative world.

They returned home after the war with, figuratively speaking, money in their pockets, newfound skills under their belts, confidence in their nation and their own ability, and broader horizons beckoning. Their worldview had changed; they were now less provincial, less fatalistic, and more comfortable with large-scale enterprise and centralized authority. Few would have been able to put their fingers on precisely how they had been transformed by involvement in a world war, but perhaps a shorthand expression would be to say that millions of southerners, white and black, had been modernized to some degree by the events of the last four years. The G.I. Bill subsidized the collegiate education of tens of thousands of veterans (though mostly whites benefited from this program), which proved to be a boom to the southern economy. Returning GIs wanted honest elections, responsible local government, and enhanced economic opportunities. In many towns and cities, they led good-government revolts and worked to improve education, attract industry, and clean up politics. Blacks, in particular, came to understand their own experience differently as a result of their participation in the war effort. Serving in a war for justice and liberty and in opposition to Nazi theories of racial superiority highlighted for blacks their second-class citizenship in the nation, particularly in the South. The discrepancy between stated ideals and lived reality became more obvious to many whites, too. The military was in advance of other American institutions in breaking down the color line, and southerners of both races came to appreciate that change might be not only possible, but possibly salutary. That membership in the

INCREASE IN UNIVERSITY ENROLLMENT, 1940–1950

	1940		1950	
	Students	Faculty	Students	Faculty
Baylor University	2,477	129	6,083	237
University of Georgia	3,688	205	6,974	398
University of Texas	11,627	636	18,535	1,165
Vanderbilt University	1,831	460	3,484	375
Louisiana State University	8,426	450	11,760	670
University of North Carolina	3,842	316	7,419	603
Virginia Polytechnic Institute	3,119	219	4,857	333
University of Tennessee	3,728	238	11,171	1,422
University of Mississippi	1,482	95	3,884	294
University of South Carolina	2,051	110	3,806	245

Source: *World Almanacs* for 1941 and 1951.

National Association for the Advancement of Colored People increased from 50,000 in 1940 to 450,000 in 1946 suggested the change in outlook—even a new militancy—that was underway and heralded a legal transformation in racial practices in less than a decade.

By every index of measurement, the South's economy took off during World War II. The value added from industry tripled, personal income more than doubled, and the number of industrial workers grew by better than 50 percent. The South even narrowed the gap between its per capita income and the national average. With soldiers returning home no longer content to return to a sharecroppers' existence, the economic future was unclear. But what had happened in the previous five years was exactly what the region had needed. The tremendous infusion of capital, managerial talent, and industrial skills primed the South for sustained industrial growth. During the decade and a half of depression and war, more than 2 million southerners, many of them former agricultural workers, had left the region. In fact, it was largely in response to that wartime and immediate postwar shortage of agricultural workers that southern landowners had begun the rapid shift to farm mechanization that ended the regional identification with sharecropping.

The end of the war brought a downsizing of the military forces, but the almost simultaneous outbreak of the Cold War soon guaranteed the continued advantage for the South of huge military expenditures. The presumed threat of Russian missile attack gave further credence to the practice of scattering defense plants and military training installations across the nation, and the South prospered disproportionately from such practices. The former bomber factory at Marietta, Georgia, for example, was reopened by Lockheed in 1951 and ultimately became the biggest industrial employer in the Southeast. Other prominent players in what was soon called the military-industrial complex— companies such as McDonnell-Douglas, General Dynamics, and Rockwell International—opened and operated large plants in the South, at such places as Fort Worth. San Antonio was ringed with Air Force bases; Columbus, Georgia, and Fort Hood, Texas, were temporary homes to tens of thousands of Army draftees. Well-placed southern congressmen used their seniority to gain military benefits for Virginia, North Carolina, and such cities as Charleston and Savannah, in particular, whose powerful congressmen won one Pentagon plum after another for their district. The Tennessee Valley Authority, which had begun in the New Deal with utopian visions of providing good jobs and bucolic family recreation for the people of southern Appalachia, had by the 1950s almost become an arm of the military as a cheap source for the enormous electrical needs of aluminum production for airplanes and nuclear materials for bombs at the Atomic Energy Commission at nearby Oak Ridge, in eastern Tennessee.

National companies, seeking comparatively low wages and docile (nonunion), semiskilled workers, now flocked to the South. Textile manufacturing boomed in North and South Carolina; plywood, lumber, and paper production prospered on second-growth timber; and tourism produced plentiful but low-salaried jobs, particularly in Florida. The modern petrochemical industry grew by leaps and bounds in Texas and Louisiana, fueled by the long American love affair with the personal automobile. Improved economic conditions and bountiful paved roads caused a remarkable expansion in car ownership in the South. During the Eisenhower administration, another huge government project, the federal interstate highway system—justified for reasons of national defense—generated billions of dollars of construction jobs in the region and for the first time created a modern, efficient transportation system linking the South internally and to national markets. Trucking replaced the railroads as the major transporter of goods, and northern tourists and would-be manufacturers found Dixie more accessible as a result of multilane, divided superhighways.

THE IMPACT OF TECHNOLOGY

A technological breakthrough also made the southern climate more bearable in the summertime. As early as the nineteenth century, inventive southerners had experimented with fans blowing air across ice and various Rube-Goldberg contraptions to cool the hot, humid air. The modern air conditioner is a marvel of efficiency and reliability, but it requires a complex combination of electrical motors, thermostats, and leak-proof tubes filled with an inert gas called freon. The first skyscraper to be air-conditioned was the Milam Building in San Antonio in 1928, but the cooling system was too large, cumbersome, and costly to be practical. In 1939, Willis Carrier, a pioneer in the field, developed the system of pushing cooled air with powerful fans through small ducts to the various rooms of a building, and the first buildings so air-conditioned were the Bankers Life Building in Macon, Georgia, the Durham Life Building in Raleigh, North Carolina, and the United Carbon Building in Charleston, West Virginia. This system, essentially the same as in use today, was soon common in the newest office buildings throughout the South. By the 1950s, hospitals, banks, and movie theaters became some of the first public facilities to offer climate-controlled comfort. Motels springing up along the interstate highways advertised that they were air-conditioned, a luxury that was expected to gain them appreciative customers. Many older southerners can remember what a treat it was on a sweltering summer evening fifty years ago to go to a theater and enjoy the cool air as much as the color movie on the screen.

Almost no private homes were air-conditioned before World War II, and in the immediate postwar years, home units were still too bulky and expensive to be common. In 1951, small window units were perfected, and the air-conditioned house became the realizable dream of the upwardly mobile southern middle class. By 1960, almost one-fifth of the homes in the South were air-conditioned, and by 1980, almost four-fifths were. Domestic architecture changed in response to air conditioning: tall ceilings, large windows that could be raised, and generous porches became less common. No one appreciated the new comfort possible more than old-time southerners; electric lights, screened windows to keep out the tiny insects that were attracted to the lights, and now refreshingly cool and dehumidified air—southern summers could be quite pleasant after all. It is difficult to imagine the large-scale migration of northerners to southern cities and retirement communities had modern air-conditioning not been available. By the mid-1950s, "factory air" was available in automobiles too. In fact, it soon became impossible to buy a non–air-conditioned car in deep South cities unless it was specially ordered from the factory. The American South is now the most air-conditioned society in the world. Public schools, universities, grocery stores, city buses, sports stadiums (in 1965, the Astrodome in Houston showed that it was possible to cool an entire playing field—and the spectators), gymnasiums, outdoor queues at amusement parks, everything is cooled artificially. City skyscrapers are linked by air-conditioned tunnels or over-the-road glassed-in walkways. Except for a quick dash from one's car to the door, one can now completely escape the long, hot summers in Dixie. Electrical usage has gone up as room temperatures have gone down—summer electrical usage per customer in Houston, for example, is the highest in the world. The air conditioner may not have been as truly important as Eli Whitney's cotton gin was in 1793, but it certainly brought more comfort.

The changes brought by air-conditioning are obvious and well documented, but far less appreciated are the contributions to comfort offered by the availability of two forms of liquefied petroleum gas (LPG): butane and propane. Both these colorless, flammable gases are by-products of the refining of oil to produce gasoline, a process called cracking. Butane and propane were discovered shortly before World War I, although their manufacture did not become commercially feasible until the 1930s. In 1935 safe, practical heaters for domestic use were developed, but military needs during World War II slowed the growth of the domestic market. Peacetime saw an astronomical increase in the production and domestic use of LPG. Both butane and propane become liquid under pressure at normal temperatures. In liquid form, they are easily transported in trucks and can be stored under pressure in metal tanks in sizes adaptable to home use. Here was an inexpensive, portable source of heating fuel for isolated farm homes. No longer was it necessary for an expensive, lengthy system of pipes to bring a heating gas from central storage tanks to individual homes—practical only for urban areas. A small butane tank in the backyard, filled occasionally by a visiting tank truck, could, with a minimum of plumbing, provide a safe fuel for cooking and heating.

At first, many farm families used butane or propane for their cooking ranges, lifting a heavy burden from farm wives and mothers. Gone forever was the necessity, first thing each morning, of starting the fire in the kitchen stove, with all the attendant trouble of bringing in the wood and kindling and regularly cleaning out the ashes. The appliance that usually first followed the gas range was the gas water heater. Electric pumps could effortlessly bring water into the home; the water heater just as effortlessly warmed the water for bathing or washing dishes. At this point, the modern bathroom could become a reality in farm houses, and it is difficult for modern urban readers to comprehend the manifold improvement in southern rural life this small room affected. Both these applications—gas range and water heater—were often followed, very quickly, by the space heater, which replaced the wood heater and fireplace for warming dwelling rooms. Portable butane and propane released southern farmers from the enormous annual chore of cutting, splitting, and hauling small mountains of firewood. For every southern family who lived through the transition from firewood to LPG, the change seemed almost miraculous. A cleaner, safer, easier way to cook and heat brought an unforgettable improvement in quality of life. For many rural southerners LPG—because of its labor-saving and comfort-providing qualities—was an even greater advance than air-conditioning. Even the mobile home—or house trailer, as it was originally called—represented for many lower-income southerners a dwelling that was easier to cool and heat, more comfortable, and significantly more modern than anything they had ever before been able to afford. Mobile homes quickly sprung up along country roads throughout the region; by the 1990s, the South possessed over half of all mobile homes in America.

The South's sense of isolation from the American mainstream was significantly removed by television, which, beginning in the early 1950s, began to be accessible throughout most of the region. At first, television reception was possible only in the largest cities, and rural homes had to erect tall outside antennas, sometimes as high as one hundred feet and supported by guy wires, in order to receive the flickering black-and-white pictures often afflicted by what was called snow. For some in the deep South, this was the only snow they ever saw. But southerners of every income level and race shared the national fascination with television, and southerners now heard a bland, accentless English being spoken, saw immediately the newest fashions in clothes and hairstyles, heard the same music the rest of the nation listened to, and had brought into their living rooms and dens white and black entertainers performing together.

Critics argued that reading was being replaced by passive TV viewing, while others lamented the loss of the colorful conversation and storytelling that had once graced southern porches and backyards. But most southerners, certainly rural ones, now that they had electricity, television, and soon room air conditioners, were only too glad to join the television generation. In fact, southern musical traditions and life styles, occasionally caricatured but often presented sympathetically, began to be beamed across the nation by the TV networks. From Elvis Presley to "The Andy Griffith Show" and finally "The Waltons," the South was winning a place in the national entertainment supermarket. The region seemed more creative, more wholesome, than the stereotypes presented by H. L. Mencken and Erskine Caldwell in the 1920s and 1930s. The South may not yet have been culturally redeemed in the eyes of the nation by the 1970s, but it seemed far less pathological.

CHANGES ON THE FACE OF THE LAND

For most southerners, the development of air conditioning and the availability of propane gas, which allows them to control the ambient temperature of their homes and work places, are the most obvious and important ways of changing their environment. But long before careful applications of engineering and science made possible these modifications for the sake of comfort, southerners had been both inadvertently and purposefully shaping the regional environment. The introduction of Old World microorganisms in the sixteenth and seventeenth centuries took a heavy toll on the indigenous Indian population, but neither Europeans nor American Indians at the time understood the cause of the diseases that wreaked such havoc on the native peoples. European ships also inadvertently introduced the black rat and the common house mouse to the New World, and southern farmers for the next four centuries would seek ways to limit the loss of grains and other harvested products to the voracious appetites of these small creatures. The cockroach was also imported into the New World, probably carried in the holds of ships. The Hessian fly, yet another import, would, in its larvae form, later ravage southern wheat crops. Of course, not all early nonhuman immigrants were destructive: The honeybee, brought from Europe, provided a plentiful source of honey and also improved certain plant and crop yields by aiding pollination. Every significant food and fiber crop associated with the South—corn, potatoes, sweet potatoes, peanuts, beans, squash, rice, wheat, okra, sugar cane, cotton, hemp—was introduced from outside, as was every domesticated animal (except the dog): cows, pigs, horses, goats, sheep, mules, chickens. European and African population growth in the South depended on the successful transplantation of these useful plants and animals in the region. The peanut, for example, widely used for food for both slaves and livestock and later in the nineteenth century—thanks to black scientist George Washington Carver—used for hundreds of purposes, was native to Bolivia. It was taken by Spanish explorers back to Europe in the mid-sixteenth century. From there it spread to Africa, where it became a major food source and was a common provision on slave ships. Slaves brought to the New World introduced the peanut to the American South in the mid-eighteenth century. Today the peanut seems as American as baseball, and in the form of peanut butter it has become an iconic snack food, but its U.S. origins lie in the trans-Atlantic slave trade.

The growing population of the colonial and nineteenth-century South also had a devastating effect on several indigenous fauna. By 1800, buffalo were almost entirely gone from the Southeast, and elk and even white-tailed deer were scarce. Within another generation, once-common animals like beavers, mink, bobcats, panthers, bears, and wolves (of which early Europeans were irrationally terrified) were nearly eliminated from the South, except for small numbers of animals in isolated mountain and swamp regions. In the colonial period and early nineteenth century, several billion passenger pigeons migrated across the Southeast each fall; their numbers were so great that when they flew they darkened the sky, and when they lighted their numbers broke tree limbs. The manure following a night's roost was so thick, it killed the grass underneath the trees. But hunters and poachers killed them by the thousands in great orgies of hunting, and by the late eighteenth century, their numbers decreased noticeably. By the 1880s, they had become rare and actually became extinct in 1932. The brightly colored and almost unnaturally tame Carolina parakeet had also once been present in prodigious profusion. Unfortunately, their sociability made them too easy a target for hunters; total extinction of the parakeets was the result.

The point is that the fauna of a region can be altered by human interaction and natural invasion, and this process is ongoing. Several of the plants and animals that today are so associated with the South as to practically be a part of the self-identity of the region are the result of recent biological importations or migrations, and the speed of such migrations is often astonishing. The armadillo, for example, has in recent years become so popular a "folk critter" in Texas that its image has become ubiquitous. Actually, the armadillo is a mammal that evolved over 65 million years ago and, though a hog-sized species roamed parts of the South eons past, it became extinct long before human habitation. The modern species, the small nine-banded armadillo, migrated northward from Mexico, crossing the Rio Grande about 1840. Before 1880, it was found only south of Corpus Christi, but by World War II, it had spread into east Texas. By the 1970s, the armadillo was found all the way to Florida and South Carolina and into Missouri. As much as the longhorn, it has become a symbol of Texas, and moves were made (unsuccessfully) to have the armadillo named the state mammal. Much less affection has been showered upon another migrant from Mexico, the cotton boll weevil, which crossed over near Brownsville, Texas, in 1892 and by the 1920s had devastated cotton crops throughout the South. Modern chemicals have finally controlled boll weevil infestation.

In more recent times, fire ants have invaded the South. They were initially reported in Mobile, Alabama, in 1929, where presumably they first arrived in ship ballast about 1918. Fire ants build foot-high mounds—as many as one hundred per acre—have very aggressive stinging behavior, and possess enormous reproductive capacity. They apparently spread by means of nursery plants and quickly moved beyond Mobile. By 1953, they had established toeholds in every southern state from North Carolina to Texas. Within three decades, they heavily infected almost every county in a huge sweep from coastal North Carolina to central Texas and were the most detested pest in the entire region (although Marshall, Texas, hosts a Fire Ant Festival each fall). So far, climate has restricted their spread to the deep South. Far less painful has been the rapid spread of kudzu, a climbing vine native to Asia, which can grow at the astounding rate of one foot per day. It apparently was first introduced to the South at the Japanese pavilion of the 1884 to 1886 New Orleans Exposition, and it quickly was praised as a shade plant for arbors and porch trellises. For a while, farmers even experimented with kudzu as a hay crop for cattle, and then in 1935 the U.S. Soil Conservation Service promoted it for erosion control along road embankments. As the saying goes, the rest is history. In the southern climate, kudzu grew beyond anyone's expectations, covering up telephone poles, strangling trees, threatening, it seemed, to smother everything that did not move out of its way. Southerners reacted with a mixture of annoyance and affection, and kudzu in the Southeast, like the armadillo in Texas, became the topic of jokes, the name of musical groups, clubs, festivals, and a comic strip, and an organic symbol for Dixie. It is now estimated to cover more than 7 million acres of the southern landscape, an area approximately the size of Massachusetts.

Almost no one has found very endearing another import, the nutria, a large aquatic rodent with a hairless tail and large orange teeth. This native of South America and the Caribbean can grow as large as twenty pounds, and it was introduced into south Louisiana in the 1930s because of the market value of its fur. Several early importers and growers of nutria purposely loosed them into the wild in an attempt to stimulate the fur-trapping industry of the state, but no one properly understood their propagating capabilities. They soon came to infest stream beds and lakes throughout Louisiana and adjoining states—even the Eastern Shore of Maryland! Nutria multiply with frightening speed, and their burrows undermine streams banks and cause lake dams to weaken and break; they also deplete wild vegetation. Heavy trapping for several decades controlled their numbers, but recent declines in the market for their fur have led to overpopulation. Louisiana officials have even tried, unsuccessfully, to promote nutria meat for human consumption. So far, despite the publication of recipes and attempting to label nutria "swamp rabbits," these rodents have not become a culinary favorite. In 2002 the state put a 4-dollar bounty on nutria, hoping hunters could kill as many as 400,000 annually.

Biological invasions are ongoing and within a generation or so can disperse new plant or animal organisms across the entire South. Any southerner of middle age or older who has lived in one place or visited that place regularly will be aware of very significant biological changes in his or her lifetime. Three examples indicate this trend, and the first is related to how a newly introduced bird, the cattle egret, responded to the changed southern environment as cotton fields gave way to pasture lands across the region. The cattle egret is indigenous to the Old World, both Europe and Africa, and it first appeared in Surinam about 1880. It spread northward, reaching Florida in 1942. This bird prefers grasslands and follows cattle to eat the insects that bedevil them. The cattle egret thrived and expanded its range as the development of improved breeds of grass made possible the expansion of the cattle industry in the South. By 1955, the cattle egret had spread to Texas, and now throughout the South wherever one sees cattle grazing, nearby will be cattle egret. The region's waters have been attacked by another more recent import. Southern ponds and lakes now often become clogged with hydrilla, a plant native to Africa, Asia, and Australia but introduced into Florida in 1960 by the aquarium trade. Hydrilla creates thick mats of vegetation that destroy fish and wildlife habitat and interfere with recreation. It is the most troublesome aquatic plant in the nation, and many southern states spend millions of dollars yearly trying to control it.

The most recent biological invader yet is the so-called killer bee. Originally from Africa, these honeybee look-alikes entered Texas from Mexico in 1990. Entomologists suggest that the fearsome aggressiveness of the bees—their individual stings are no more venomous than those of common (European) honeybees—reflects the number of natural enemies they had in Africa. In addition, there humans are bee hunters rather than beekeepers. In Europe, beekeepers have purposely bred (through careful selection) bees with more manageable traits such as reduced swarming, which lessens the tendency to defend their nests. Press reports in the mid-1970s coined the term "killer bees" after stories of several people in Latin America dying as a result of massive bee attacks. Then in 1978 the sensationalist movie *The Swarm* portrayed horrendous killer bees sweeping into Texas and terrorizing the city of Houston. The movie was a critical disaster, but it did fix in the public mind the image of super-deadly bee attackers. In one of those cases of history following fiction, the Africanized bees have now spread into several southwestern states and were first documented in Houston on July 27, 2001. Not quite Jurassic Park, but worrisome still.

Even several of the ornamental plants that have come to symbolize the southern landscape are the fruits of human intervention. The crape myrtle was probably introduced from China into the South by the French botanist André Michaux, who in the late eighteenth century imported various plants into his nursery near Charleston. The climbing wisteria vine, also a native of either China or Japan, came to the South by way of England. It was named after the famous Philadelphia doctor, amateur botanist, and friend of Jefferson, Dr. Caspar Wistar. The poinsettia was named after Dr. Joel Robert Poinsett, the South Carolinian who served as ambassador to the newly independent Republic of Mexico from 1825 to 1829; he brought this colorful plant, native to tropical Mexico, back to South Carolina at the end of his service.

Human intervention has also affected entire biosystems in the South. Beginning in the seventeenth century, farmers, would-be industrialists, and timber workers sought to remake portions of the landscape to increase productivity. Rice planters in the early eighteenth century began to reclaim vast portions of the swamplands lying near river mouths. By clearing the lands and building networks of levees, sluice gates, and irrigation ditches, they produced lucrative rice plantations. Entire ecosystems were transformed or destroyed in the process. Later in the eighteenth century and repeatedly thereafter there were attempts to drain, ditch, and otherwise improve what was known as the Great Dismal Swamp south of Norfolk. Canals and roads were built through the region, huge amounts of the timber (especially cedar for the making of shingles) were cut, and farms were carved out of the landscape. In the twentieth century, massive urban development in Florida has decreased by two-thirds the extent of the Everglades, a unique ecosystem, and draining, filling, and road building have had a devastating impact on the fauna of the region. In several other southern states, hundreds of thousands of acres of wetlands, so vital for animal and fish life, have been similarly destroyed by what was euphemistically called the march of progress. In the single decade of 1985 to 1995 alone, the Southeast lost a half-million acres of forested wetlands. Southern Louisiana has another problem, losing land to the Gulf of Mexico and Lake Pontchartrain at the rate of about thirty-five square miles annually, or three acres per hour. Forest lands have changed too. Hundreds of years ago the upland region of the South from Maryland to Alabama had plentiful hardwood forests—intermixed with pines—and the nut-bearing trees supported a rich population of small animals and birds. Oaks and hickories particularly thrived because their thick bark allowed them to survive naturally occurring forest fires. Over the past century humans have largely eliminated such fires, and as a result an aggressive secondary tree, the red maple, able to thrive in shadows underneath large trees, has taken over some forests, eventually crowding out oaks and hickories. The resulting forests provide much less food for squirrels, deer, birds, and even insects, similar to the way the huge pine-tree farms have impoverished plant and animal diversity in many areas of the South.

In the Everglades, as elsewhere, agricultural pollutants (pesticides, chemical fertilizers, runoff from hog and cattle feedlots) and sewage waste have destroyed much plant and animal life. In some regions, as in the Chesapeake Bay and in North Carolina's Pamlico and Albemarle Sounds, such pollutant runoff has actually created dead zones in the saltwater bays, crippling the fishing, crabbing, and oystering industries. Polluted air and water are not respecters of state boundaries. Acid rain originating in the Midwest falls on Appalachian forests, and millions of gallons of pollutants, including dioxin, dumped by a western North Carolina paper mill into the Pigeon River that flows into eastern Tennessee fouls the sources of drinking water for Knoxville. The areas most severely affected by such manmade pollutants, however, are the lower Mississippi River and parts of the Gulf of Mexico. The Mississippi River drainage basin covers 40 percent of the nation, and the chemicals associated with food crop production in the Midwest eventually flow through the mighty Father of Waters to the Gulf. There the eastward rotation of the earth sweeps a hearty mixture of pollutants westward, creating a dead zone, sometimes thirty miles wide and three hundred miles long, stretching along the Gulf Coast from just west of the mouth of the Mississippi River almost to the Texas border—otherwise a prime location for shrimp fishermen. Not all the blame belongs to the Midwest. The 150 miles of gently curving river bank from Baton Rouge to New Orleans is lined with petrochemical and fertilizer plants that dump hundreds of millions of tons of pollutants annually into the river—Louisiana leads the nation in the amount of chemicals released into surface water. Over a hundred toxic chemicals are released along this route, producing a dangerous river brew; the Mississippi River provides the drinking water for the region, including the city of New Orleans. The result is a cancer rate substantially above the national average, and the whole region between Baton Rouge and New Orleans has gained the unhappy epithet of Cancer Alley. In other cities such as Houston, airborne pollution from petrochemical plants, along with automobiles, has produced smog that sometimes rivals that of Los Angeles. Mining has also created localized ecological disasters in several Appalachian sites, such as near Ducktown, Tennessee, where the scar produced by strip mining is visible by naked eye from the orbiting space shuttle. Southern state and local governments have been slow to act to correct such problems, usually preferring the creation of industrial jobs to the preservation of the environment.

Most southern states—pushed by the federal government—have slowly come to understand that unintended ecological problems can have long-term effects. For example, the use of the chemical DDT to eradicate the mosquitoes that spread malaria had catastrophic implications for southern birds and fish that far outweighed the limited gains in malaria prevention. Malaria had been a major disease in the South for more than two centuries, and there was another serious outbreak in the early 1930s, but by the end of the decade and the early 1940s, malaria almost disappeared in the South. However, American soldiers during World War II suffered terribly from the disease, especially in the Pacific theater where hospitalization from malaria at times outnumbered that caused by battle casualties by a ratio of thirty to one. Public health authorities understandably feared that returning soldiers would re-infect the South. Because the Japanese had seized most of the world's quinine (used for treating malaria), the United States emphasized eradicating the mosquitoes that spread the disease. A Swiss chemist had discovered in 1939—while seeking a way to kill moths in clothing—the insecticidal properties of DDT. Consequently U.S. authorities made massive use of DDT to kill a whole range of insects, including lice, bedbugs, cockroaches, and mosquitoes, and DDT took on almost magical qualities, even being called the "atomic bomb of the insect world." From 1944 until the early 1950s, the Center for Disease Control spearheaded the movement to use massive amounts of DDT in the South to prevent the feared reoccurrence of malaria; southerners clamored for the spraying, seeing it as practically a panacea for a wide range of insect pests.

No malarial outbreak occurred in the South following WWII (whether as a result of the DDT campaign or for natural reasons is not known), but the DDT compound proved to have an unsuspected persistence. Its chemical nature was little affected by sunlight, soil microorganisms, or animal metabolism, and its toxicity passed through the food chain. It accumulated in the bodies of animals that ate food of any sort contaminated by the substance, and it proved especially harmful to a variety of birds and especially fish. The result was massive fish kills in the South, leading to DDT's being banned for most uses by the Environmental Protective Agency in 1972. More than twenty years later, traces of DDT were still being found in southern animal life.

Over the course of time, southerners have also sought to control the flow of rivers, limit flooding, change the contour of island cities, and create artificial waterways, all to very significant effect. From almost the earliest settlements along the lower Mississippi River, people have tried to limit the destruction from spring flooding by building levees, but one of the problems was that for levees to really work, they must stretch for hundreds of miles. Also, levees often broke, causing even worse damage because the height of the river had been artificially raised by the levees themselves. Natural flooding meant that, in effect, the river spread out over hundreds or even thousands of square miles, moving horizontally rather than vertically. Beginning in the 1850s, the U.S. Corps of Engineers commissioned studies on how best to confine the Mississippi: Should the levees be built higher and higher, or should natural overflows be simulated by constructing gates or controlled spillways? Would the riverbed silt up, lifting the river always upward? There were spirited debates about these matters, but essentially the idea of controlling the river by complete dependence on a levee system won out. The result, in addition to the cost of constructing and maintaining the levees (and, incidentally, convincing some southerners at least that the federal government did have legitimate duties and supervisory authority), was ironically producing a river system that, in the case of truly extraordinary flooding and breaks in the levees, led to ever-worse floods. The great flood of 1927, for example, forced almost a million people from their homes. The levees and river bed have today risen to such an extent that below New Orleans one looks up above tree level to see oil tankers and barges floating to their destinations. In the aftermath of the disastrous flood of 1927, a giant overflow spillway was built at Bonnet Carré thirty miles upstream from New Orleans. Now when the river level threatens the levees and hence the Crescent City, the Bonnet Carré gates are opened and 250,000 cubic feet of water per second are diverted via Lake Pontchartrain. The system has worked so far, although the fear is that some future flood of unprecedented dimensions will break through the levees farther north and carve a new route to the Gulf via the Atchafalaya River, redirecting the Mississippi River westward and leaving New Orleans bereft of a water route to the sea. The mighty Mississippi still seems poised to defy the best efforts of government and engineering.

New Orleans itself, situated as much as five feet below sea level between the Mississippi River and Lake Pontchartrain, both of whose water lever at mean elevation is substantially above sea level, is the lowest spot in the watery Louisiana universe. The levee system, by raising the water level of the river, has exacerbated the flood potential. For most of its history, the development of New Orleans was confined to the higher ridges amid the low-lying swamps. The city's twentieth-century growth was made possible by building an elaborate network of canals that gather all the rain runoff in the city; this water is moved to holding areas where 112 huge electrically driven screw pumps—invented by local engineer Albert Baldwin Wood in 1913—lift the water fifteen feet or more and dump it into Lake Pontchartrain. The pumping system can evacuate 25 billion gallons of water in a day and can in theory handle up to ten inches of rain in twenty-four hours with only minimal flooding. This means that all over the city, in the aftermath of a rainstorm, one hears the whine of pump motors as surely as in other southern cities one hears the croaking of frogs. But the swamps have been drained and filled and residential and commercial developments have been made possible in places nature never intended. Other southern cities located on flat terrain suffer from occasional flooding after heavy rains. Several areas, including much of Houston, have seen their surface elevation sink or subside by ten feet or more because underground water was pumped out for human use. Subsidence has greatly worsened the incidence of flooding in such regions.

If engineering fooled Mother Nature in New Orleans, an equally audacious attempt to secure human habitation took place on a slender, low island of sand off the coast of Texas. The city of Galveston, at the eastern end of this island, was devastated by a hurricane that struck the unaware city on September 8, 1900, killing more than six thousand persons—the nation's worst natural disaster—and destroying more than a third of the city's houses. Rather than give up on the city and relocate—as other smaller Texas coastal towns had done previously in the aftermath of hurricanes—the people of Galveston devised an elaborate plan to rebuild the city and make it immune from such devastation in the future. The result was a massive concrete seawall three miles long, later extended to ten miles, seventeen feet high and curved on the Gulf side to deflect the force of the storm surge up and back away from the coast. Then the surface of the city was raised to the top of the seawall, sloping back toward the mainland. This required jacking up every structure, constructing a spindly but temporary network of catwalks linking the elevated structures, and then over the next seven years pumping in 16,300,000 cubic yards of sand mixed with sea water to fill the surface of the island up to the bottom of the houses. This massive engineering feat, known locally as the grade raising, required that all structures had to be raised and that every tree and bush on the eastern end of the island be replaced. Women's groups promoted the replanting of the city, and today, the resort city of Galveston proudly boasts about its live oaks, its oleanders, and its azaleas. The city has survived relatively unscathed every subsequent hurricane.

Engineers have long worked to dredge and thereby improve ports in the South as elsewhere. For decades, silting had clogged the mouth of the Mississippi River, requiring ocean vessels to often wait for days before they could get past obstructive sandbars. A self-taught engineer, James Buchanan Eads, devised a plan in 1875 to construct a series of jetties that would constrict one of the mouths of the river, thereby accelerating the flow and scouring the river bed to greater depths. Despite opposition, ridicule, and incredible hardships, by 1880, Eads succeeded in producing a thirty-foot-deep channel to the Gulf, thereby unclogging the river for maritime commerce. Within several years, shipborne tonnage to New Orleans increased seventy-fold, eventually making the city one of the largest-volume ports in the world.

Even earlier maritime interests had advocated canals to move commerce coastwise. In the late eighteenth century, a canal was begun through the Great Dismal Swamp in Virginia to connect the port of Norfolk with the agriculture-rich areas surrounding Albemarle Sound in North Carolina. Over the decades, both private companies and the federal government worked piecemeal at constructing a canal to facilitate barge traffic along the eastern seaboard: To avoid the rigors of the high seas, these canals were built several miles inland in order to take advantage of natural swamps, lakes, and rivers. Finally these efforts were integrated into the idea of a continuous intracoastal canal by the River and Harbor Act of 1909 that authorized the surveying of a route for such a water highway all the way "from Boston to the Rio Grande." In fact, though a continuous Atlantic Intracoastal Waterway does sweep from Boston to Key West and the Gulf Intracoastal Waterway (completed in 1942) links Carrabelle, on the Florida panhandle, to Brownsville, Texas, there is a gap along western Florida that for environmental reasons will never be build. Nevertheless, these two manmade rivers, skirting the East Coast and the Gulf Coast for a total of 2,700 miles, have been a boon for maritime shipping. The Gulf link especially is important for commerce as well as pleasure craft, and in the 1990s, more than 100 million tons of cargo annually are shipped along that route, most of it petroleum and chemical products. In 1984, the U.S. Corps of Engineers linked the Gulf Intracoastal Waterway to the Tennessee River in northeastern Mississippi by completing the 234-mile-long, 10-lock Tennessee-Tombigbee Waterway. This massive federal project, which involved moving more cubic yards of earth than did the building of the Panama Canal, offered barge traffic on the Ohio River an alternative, shorter route to the Gulf.

In the twentieth-century South, several regions of unusual natural beauty or ecological diversity have been protected as part of our national heritage. The two most visited are the Great Smoky Mountains and the Shenandoah National Parks. Both of these, in preserving the natural environment, resulted in the displacement of farmers and small towns, as did the construction of the lakes in the Tennessee Valley project. For the displaced people who lost home places and saw their cemeteries moved, such environmental changes came at a significant sentimental cost. For many urban southerners, these national parks and similar restricted areas like the Big Thicket National Preserve, the Buffalo National River, and the Cape Hatteras National Seashore, are their only connection to an earlier, relatively unspoiled southern environment.

For almost four centuries of written history, humans have affected the environmental and biological landscape of the South, sometimes purposely, sometimes unknowingly, sometimes for good, and sometimes for ill. No history of the South, its people, its economy, its folk culture, or its self-image is complete without consideration of how the regional ecosystem has been affected as a result of both human intention and natural biological invasions. The face of the land has been changed and human history influenced by factors often forgotten but never absent. Today many southerners, historically identified with the land and characterized as a people for whom "place" is important, have lost touch with their natural environment, but much of the history of the South has been shaped in response to biological, climatological, and geological factors.

CHANGES DOWN ON THE FARM

By the decade of the 1970s, it was clear that a genuine New South was emerging. Solid industrial growth, fueled by low energy prices, low wages, and cooperative state and local governments (the southern states were rated as having "good business environments," which primarily meant low taxes, lax regulations, and weak labor unions), diversified the various state economies. Federal government funds continued to flow south, enhanced by the effort to put an American on the moon and soon further increased by the Pentagon as American involvement in Vietnam deepened. One other great barrier to the South's entering the American mainstream also began to be removed in the 1960s: legal segregation. Sit-ins, the Montgomery bus boycott, the rise of Martin Luther King, Jr., and then the Civil Rights Act of 1964 and the Voting Rights Act of 1965 slowly but surely reshaped the political, cultural, and economic landscape of the former Confederate states. That momentous story—the great story of the modern-day South—is told more amply later in this part, but the gradual process of removing the most flagrant abuses of segregation opened the South up to a welcome and positive invasion by national corporations. With investment came population growth, and both ushered in a prosperity that enhanced tax rolls. With greater tax revenues, southern states could begin to address some of their problems: poor schools, too few hospitals, and inadequate public health programs. The stage was set for the next level of southern economic growth.

The two decades following 1965 were the most prosperous in southern history. The century-long population and brain drain from the South reversed itself, and the population flow, including blacks, became positive. The South had long been a region of small towns with no really big cities. Suddenly the migration from the North, and from southern rural areas, brought unparalleled urban growth to Atlanta, Charlotte, Dallas, Houston, Jacksonville, New Orleans, and San Antonio. John Portman with his striking hotel lobbies helped make Atlanta a byword for the prosperous New South, and futuristic skyscrapers like the Pennzoil Building and Transco Tower made Houston's skyline an architectural wonder that attracted urban experts and architects from around the nation to see the new form of a spread-out, automobile city with nodes of skyscrapers scattered across hundreds of square miles. In 1971, DisneyWorld opened near Orlando, Florida; it soon became the largest tourist attraction in the world and made Orlando an instant city. As in the Progressive Era, in the recent South, cities were the loci of economic advance and political change.

Even the old mainstay of the southern economy and way of life, agriculture, was transformed during the generation following World War II. In the 1930s, fully half the region's labor force worked in agriculture—today, less than 5 percent does. Of course, the roots of this transformation went back several decades, to the arrival of the boll weevil and the beginning of acreage reduction plans during the New Deal. But changes set underway earlier came to full fruition in the postwar South. Cotton production continued to shift westward to Oklahoma, west Texas, New Mexico, Arizona, and California, in part because the boll weevil was less of a problem in the different soil and drier climate, and because the huge, level fields available there, usually irrigated, were much more conducive to the large-scale, completely mechanized agribusiness that now dominated cotton production. By the late 1970s, one could see more cotton being grown between Phoenix and Flagstaff than between New Orleans and Memphis. However, in recent years, cotton has made a resurgence in the Southeast, stimulated by the new national popularity of natural cotton fibers as opposed to synthetic fibers (hence higher cotton prices) and new developments in pesticides that have virtually eliminated the boll weevil. Between 1983 and 1990, for example, the number of acres devoted to cotton cultivation in the South more than doubled. But no longer is cotton king. Southern agriculture is now much more diversified than at any time in the past.

Tobacco cultivation remained relatively stable, in terms of both acres cultivated and production methods, until the 1970s. Higher costs for land, fertilizer, and fuels had resulted in some consolidation, and large farmers increasingly shifted to tractors for hauling and to seasonally employed extra hands for harvesting. By the early 1970s, bulk curers were introduced and began to change the old way of curing tobacco leaves practically leaf by leaf. Also, in 1970, a successful tobacco harvesting machine was finally developed by the agricultural scientists at North Carolina State University. Production per acre increased because of new fertilizers and chemicals, and the man-hours of labor required per acre decreased drastically. Luckily, by the mid-1970s, paved roads and the migration southward of light industry provided jobs for the thousands of displaced tobacco farmers. Through the political prowess of the congres-

SOUTHERN AGRICULTURAL PRODUCTION, 1995

	CORN *grain* (1,000 bu.)	COTTON *lint* (1,000 bales)	TOBACCO (1,000 lbs.)
Alabama	16,500	460	
Arkansas	9,775	1,460	
Florida	5,400	100	17,352
Georgia	31,500	1,970	84,000
Kentucky	123,120		375,150
Louisiana	23,205	1,375	
Maryland	42,000		11,475
Mississippi	26,125	1,845	
North Carolina	74,900	830	483,720
South Carolina	24,115	390	105,000
Tennessee	63,720	730	104,344
Texas	216,600	4,551	
Virginia	30,525	130	81,807
West Virginia	4,000		3,400

Source: *The American Almanac, 1996–1997: Statistical Abstract of the United States* (Austin, 1998), 661–81.

sional delegations from the tobacco-growing states, the federal government still provided subsidies for the crop even though the evidence linking tobacco to cancer—and hence tremendous personal and economic losses nationwide—was incontrovertible.

Rice cultivation continued in portions of Florida and southeast Texas and especially in southern Louisiana and the delta regions of Mississippi and Arkansas. This was highly capitalized agribusiness with a vengeance: huge, flat fields, gigantic machines, and planting and fertilization by airplanes. In fact, the daredevil flying exploits of crop dusters for both rice and cotton production often brought incredulous stares from tourists driving along the interstates in southern Louisiana as well as west Texas. Delta Airlines, the Atlanta behemoth, began as a small crop dusting outfit in 1924 in the Mississippi delta; in 1928, it changed its name from Huff Daland Dusters to Delta. Although passenger service began the following year, the company, having lost a federal mail contract, quickly returned to crop spraying exclusively. But soon the company reinstated passenger service, moved its headquarters to Atlanta in 1941, and earned sufficient profits during World War II to expand greatly after the war. Today it so dominates air travel in the Southeast that a standing joke in the region is that whether one goes to heaven or hell, one will have to transfer at Delta's hub in Atlanta.

Truck farming, the production of fresh vegetables for sale, usually in nearby urban areas, has also boomed in the postwar South, and with modern truck transport over the interstate highway system, southern vegetables now often find their way to the tables of most Americans in the eastern half of the nation. Florida and Texas lead the region in such agricultural production. Florida also emerged in the 1940s as the nation's leading producer of oranges and grape-fruit, and simultaneously a lesser center of citrus production developed in the lower Rio Grande Valley of south Texas. (The citrus industry had begun in both regions in the 1920s.) Apples (in Appalachia) and peaches (in Georgia and South Carolina) are also grown in the South, but production of such so-called deciduous fruit does not come near the value of citrus crops. And as Jimmy Carter brought home to the nation, peanuts are also a significant crop in por-tions of the South, along with, in particular areas, pecans, spinach (there is a statue of Popeye the Sailor Man in Crystal City, Texas), sugar cane, soybeans, blueberries, and sweet potatoes. Many small producers of these crops supple-ment their income with town or factory employment, made possible by the net-work of paved farm-to-market roads and the ubiquitous pickup truck.

The modern beef industry bears little resemblance to the small-scale pro-duction and scrawny cattle of years ago. From the eighteenth century until the 1930s, most southern cattle suffered from a low-grade infection caused by two parasitic blood diseases, babesiosis and anaplasmosis, spread by a species of tick whose range almost exactly matched the Confederate South. The cause of this cattle disease, often called Texas fever, became understood by the early twenti-eth century, and a government-enforced cattle dipping program—whereby cat-tle were made to walk through trench-like vats filled with an insecticide mixed with water—eventually eradicated the tick that spread the disease. This program mostly benefited larger, commercial cattle producers at first, and the associated costs in money and labor hurt small family farmers who had only a few cattle for home consumption. Ultimately, however, all farmers gained by having improved livestock. Later, a vaccine effective against anaplasmosis was developed, and southern farmers could grow healthy cattle, with a weight gain per pound of feed consumed comparable with other regions of the nation.

Beginning in the 1920s, plant scientists at a number of southern agricul-tural schools and experiment stations worked to improve southern pastures. Agronomists at the Coastal Plains Experiment Station at Tifton, Georgia, in the late 1930s developed new grasses that would thrive in the southern soils and climate. Cotton farmers had worked for a century and a half to keep the native Bermuda grass out of their cotton fields, and now experts were working at producing a hardier, faster growing Bermuda grass. The result, in 1943, was what plant geneticist Glenn W. Burton called coastal Bermuda. By the late 1940s, the new grass was being planted across the South, and this higher qual-ity of grass (and hay) made possible significant additional improvements in the southern cattle industry.

Major cattle diseases were controlled, improved grazing was available, and fencing laws that required farmers to keep their livestock confined were almost universal across the region—finally ending the open range in the South. These changes made possible selective breeding of cattle. In the late 1940s and early 1950s, farmers throughout the South began to import purebred bulls to improve their stock. A variety of Brahman bulls from Texas—a breed noted for its resistance to disease and heat—were imported, especially into Florida, which became a major cattle-producing state. Purebred Herefords, Black Angus, Charolais, and other breeds became common, along with hybrids like the Brangus, which combined the meat quality of the Black Angus with the hardiness of the Brahman. Now all the pieces were in place, and with cow pastures replacing old cotton fields, the South as a region became a leading producer of cattle.

Before 1930 or so, poultry production in the South consisted of a handful of broilers raised by the farmer for Sunday dinners and perhaps several dozen "laying hens" for eggs. Usually the farm wives were in charge of the poultry, and they would market their few surplus eggs in the nearest small town for "egg money" to supplement the family's meager income. There were also traveling "hucksters" who regularly picked up the surplus eggs to take into town for sale. This small poultry business was important both to provide school supplies and simple luxuries but also to promote the farm wives' sense of being what was called "a good manager." Even the *Progressive Farmer* magazine had a monthly column entitled "Poultry Yard" to pass on tips to farm wives. Before 1920, in the Delmarva peninsula farmers began to develop large-scale commercial broiler production for the urban markets of Washington, Baltimore, Philadelphia, and New York City. During the 1930s, when cotton production decreased, farmers in several southern states—Arkansas and Georgia, particularly—thought of broiler production as a viable source of jobs and income. A feed dealer in northern Georgia named Jessie Dixon Jewell pioneered the development of the vertically integrated broiler industry; he built a hatchery, produced feed, contracted with growers, brought the mature chickens to the processing plants, and marketed the fresh meat.

After World War II, this new kind of poultry industry, whereby the farmer himself was little more than an employee of large, completely integrated feed companies, spread rapidly across the South. No longer did chickens mean a few laying hens in a small backyard pen; fully automated chicken houses longer than a football field were found on many farms, with a farm family often raising 100,000 to 300,000 broilers at a time. Feed was now delivered in bulk, a far cry from earlier times when the cotton bags that contained the feed were widely used by farm wives to make shirts and dresses for their families. (Women would even go into the feed stores and warehouses to pick out the pattern of the bag.) The modern broiler industry seemed to thrive especially in what had been the poorest, least urbanized portions of the South, bringing a small but steady income to relatively unskilled farmers who otherwise would have fled to cities or remained poor. Of course, the growth of the broiler industry required laying farms for fertile egg production, hatcheries, feed mills, and poultry processing plants—all of which produced jobs. Improvements in breeds of chickens and their feed and medication halved the time it took to grow a marketable broiler, and the national consumption of chicken grew phenomenally. "Egg money" had become big business. To a degree that would have been unimaginable in 1930 or even 1940, cattle and chickens had replaced cotton as the quintessential southern agricultural product.

To the casual observer, it began to seem by the 1970s that the South had completely escaped its past of poverty, prejudice, and backwardness. Jimmy Carter and Andrew Young, along with Martin Luther King, Jr., and Lyndon B. Johnson, taught the nation something about racial understanding—although the journey toward justice had been long and perilous and was still not complete. Dispelling old national stereotypes about hayseed southerners living on Tobacco Road, television now portrayed oil millionaires in Dallas and the life styles of the rich and comfortable in Hilton Head. H. L. Mencken's "Sahara of the Bozart" was emphatically refuted by distinguished art museums in Richmond, Atlanta, Dallas, Fort Worth, and Houston, and internationally acclaimed ballet and opera companies and symphony orchestras were located in Atlanta, Baltimore, St. Louis, Dallas, and Houston. With urban growth and wealth came the high art whose absence Mencken had bemoaned. The South now even sported major league professional teams in baseball, basketball, and football, perhaps the ultimate American symbol of urban maturity.

EMERGENCE OF THE SUN BELT

In the early 1970s, a new sobriquet began to be applied uncritically to the South. In 1969, political strategist Kevin Phillips had argued that the Republican party should tailor its rhetoric and platform to appeal to the rapidly growing southern portion of the United States, a region he called the "sunbelt," and in 1975, journalist Kirkpatrick Sale published an acerbic analysis of the conservative political tendencies of what he termed "the southern rim" of the nation, stretching from Florida to southern California. Suddenly the label "Sun Belt" became the media buzzword for the South, although the definition was so loose that in some hands the putative region was stretched all the way to Portland, Oregon. But, by popular consensus, the Sun Belt came to mean a newly prosperous, rapidly growing (and urbanizing) South that was increasingly free of racism and gaining a disproportionate share of federal revenues through various government programs. An almost necessary corollary of the Sun Belt was the idea that the rest of the nation (or particularly the Midwest, soon tagged as the Snow Belt or Rust Belt) was losing an unfair portion of its share of government transfer payments to a politically regnant Dixie. One could hardly pick up a magazine without finding pictures of smiling whites and blacks working together in an Atlanta "too busy to hate," with the reflective-glass skyscrapers in the background, a not-so-subtle suggestion that Henry Grady's New South had finally arrived.

Southern boosters were only too glad to promote this image, and in truth there was much data to prove that the South had prospered and urbanized to a remarkable degree in the last generation. The South had narrowed the gap that separated it from the rest of the nation in most measures of economic and social well being. Neither southerners nor the press could refrain from publishing the happy statistics. In many ways, the South now seemed better and more truly integrated than most regions of the North. Southern per capita income inched toward the national average, and Texas finally went over it for several years before the oil depression of the middle 1980s. By 2000, Maryland and Virginia, fueled by burgeoning government salaries, had per capita incomes above the national average.

Even southern higher education, which had long seemed embarrassingly weak and a detriment both to regional self-esteem and economic development, had made significant strides forward. Southern universities had first benefited in a significant way from the introduction of federal research grants during World War II, and such funding, augmented during the Cold War, helped transform a number of moribund, underfunded southern universities into research centers. Within the former Confederate states, for example, most admittedly subjective rankings of American universities by 1990 had Duke University, the University of North Carolina, the University of Virginia, and Rice University in the top twenty-five, with Emory University, Vanderbilt University, and the University of Texas just behind. In terms of membership in the National Academy of Engineering and the National Academy of Sciences, the South has increased its share of members, suggesting again that the academic and research gap was being narrowed. For example, no one from the former Confederate states was a member of the National Academy of Engineering when it began in 1964; in 1970, southern members (defined by institutional affiliation) made up 8.8 percent of its membership, and this had risen to 14.1 percent in 1990. In that year (when the eleven former Confederate states had 28.5 percent of the nation's population), only 6.9 percent of the members of the National Academy of Sciences worked in the South, but that number was up from 3.99 percent in 1960 and zero percent (out of 158 members nationally) in 1917,

PER CAPITA PERSONAL INCOME FOR SOUTHERN STATES, 2000

U.S. average, $29,676

Alabama	$23,471	Missouri	$27,445
Arkansas	$22,257	North Carolina	$27,194
Florida	$28,145	Oklahoma	$23,517
Georgia	$27,940	South Carolina	$24,321
Kentucky	$24,294	Tennessee	$26,239
Louisiana	$23,334	Texas	$27,871
Maryland	$33,872	Virginia	$31,162
Mississippi	$20,993	West Virginia	$21,915

Source: *Time Almanac 2002 with Information Please* (Boston, 2001), 636.

when Mencken's famous diatribe against the South was first published. In 1996 two scientists at Rice University shared the Nobel Prize in chemistry, the first Nobels outside of those in medicine ever earned at a southern university. The average Scholastic Aptitude Test (SAT) score is an indicator of academic preparation, and students from the southern states do not perform as well as students from other sections on these examinations. But these results are difficult to interpret because a higher percentage of high-school students take the test in, for example, South Carolina than in Iowa, and the correlations for race, urban or rural, and income level vastly complicate comparative interpretations.

The South has not yet produced multipurpose research universities to compare with Harvard or Stanford, but below the world-class level, southern educational institutions are now competitive with those elsewhere in the nation. Curricula are similar, and the standards for employment and tenure are essentially the same as for universities throughout the nation. Several southern professional and medical schools also are top ranked: the law schools of Duke, Texas, and Virginia; the medical schools at the University of Alabama at Birmingham, Duke, Vanderbilt, Southwestern in Dallas, and Baylor College of Medicine located in the huge Texas Medical Center in Houston, the largest and most comprehensive assemblage of medical institutions in the world.

At several locations in the South, sophisticated high-tech industries have developed, usually in cooperation with nearby universities. The major example of this phenomenon is the Research Triangle Park in North Carolina, tapping the resources of the University of North Carolina, North Carolina State University, and Duke. Similar concentrations of Ph.D.-earning workers and electronic, computer, and biotechnology industries have been spawned on the outskirts of Washington, D.C., at Charlottesville, Virginia, and near Atlanta, Dallas, Houston, and especially Austin. Nothing quite like California's Silicon Valley or the Boston Route 128 concentration has yet arisen in the South, but such major computer firms as Texas Instruments, Compaq Computer, and Dell Computer are headquartered in the region. Texas is today second only to California in the number of high-tech workers. None of these levels of academic or technological attainment were reached before World War II. And perhaps nothing has better epitomized the nation's combination of technological success and economic prowess than the space program: to a significant degree that program has had a southern base from the early rocket research at Redstone Arsenal (now the Marshall Flight Center) in Huntsville, Alabama, to the launchings at Cape Canaveral, Florida (now the Kennedy Space Center), and the subsequent flight control at the Mission Control Center (now Johnson Space Center) near Houston. The South and the space program are virtually synonymous.

These glowing Sun Belt statistics, however, do not reveal the entire picture. Wages are still lower in the South than elsewhere, and although living costs are also lower, they do not completely make up the difference. State agencies were so eager to attract industry to the region that they figuratively gave away the store to win the factory. As a result, tax revenues have not increased as they should have, and the environment has suffered more than it needed to. One Louisiana governor openly admitted before a national television camera that the state had traded environmental purity for employment and suggested that it was the responsible course for a job-poor state. A disproportionate number of jobs have come South precisely because wages were low, regulations were few, and unions seemed nonexistent. So the workers have not benefited proportionately. And once southern wages began to catch up with the nation's in the 1980s and southern states—prodded by the national government—became more attentive to the environment, the South's comparative advantage over the North diminished.

Some southern states and cities learned too late that high quality industrial development (paying high wages and not polluting) was drawn by total quality-of-life concerns, not just low wages and taxes. Moreover, the relatively undesirable industrial employment that formerly was attracted to the South was now moving to Taiwan, South Korea, and Mexico, where wages were far lower, pollution laws practically unknown, and government officials cooperative or capable of being made so. The real Third World now competes for jobs that the nation's domestic third world—the South—previously gained. In Mexico alone in the early 1990s, some 500,000 workers were employed in "maquiladora" factories along the border. Plant equipment and new materials are shipped to Mexico, then finished products are shipped back to the United States with practically no duties paid. These maquiladora workers average from five to seven dollars per day, and they represent Mexico's second-leading source of income after oil. But much of this employment and investment south of the border comes at the expense of the U.S. South. Several American industries, for example, the manufacture of typewriters and televisions, have completely disappeared north of the border. Moreover, with the end of the Cold War, U.S. defense budgets have fallen, and a number of southern locales, heavily dependent upon military jobs, have suffered severely in the early 1990s. Future defense cuts suggest additional blows to once-favored cities. Some initial reports in the summer of 1993 projected job losses in Charleston, for instance, of 25 percent, representing a full one-third of the city's wages.

Not only has much of southern industrial development been in low-paying extractive industries or low-value-added manufacturing, such as textiles, but much of the apparent boom has been in the tourist industry. Many Americans only know the South from vacation trips to southern beaches, golf courses, Williamsburg, DisneyWorld, and like attractions, and several old cities that have preserved much of their architectural and historical heritage: Charleston (remarkably so), Savannah, New Orleans, and San Antonio. Mississippians who quote the Bible to defend prayer in the schools and attack homosexuality silently hide their Bibles when welcoming gambling casinos to their state, and today its Gulf beachfront has become a gaudy poor-man's Las Vegas. But tourist-related jobs are notoriously low-paying, and the chances for upward mobility are severely limited. Money lost in casinos also buys no food, clothing, education, or health care, and casinos leave little of their profits in the state. New Orleans, despite a thriving tourist industry, is the poorest large city in the South. Furthermore, much of the economic development has been uneven, with concentration near the largest cities or scattered along the interstates—for example, between Atlanta and Charlotte. There is a broad band of light manufacturing stretching from Virginia to northern Georgia, a tourist mecca along coastal South Carolina and portions of Georgia and the Florida peninsula, and an oil belt in Louisiana and Texas (today 49 percent of the nation's petrochemical products are made in the region stretching from Houston to Beaumont!). Low wages and special tax abatements have induced a number of high-profile corporations to locate plants in the South—Nissan in Smyrna, Tennessee; Saturn in Spring Hill, Tennessee; Toyota in Georgetown, Kentucky; BMW in Greer, South Carolina; Mercedes-Benz in Vance, Alabama—and the jobs have made significant economic impacts. But here and elsewhere, the economic incentive packages offered to attract such companies often make their coming a mixed blessing. Also spread throughout the region are still great pockets of rural poverty where Sun Belt change and prosperity seem nonexistent.

Much of the southern infrastructure was quickly and poorly built in the boom areas by local governments that made a fetish of keeping taxes (and hence services) low. Job growth has slowed, environmental costs are increasing, and roads and bridges are wearing out. The southern cities' growth came so late in the century that they tend to be automobile cities with practically no effective mass transit systems. In 1998, for example, Atlanta's traffic congestion was ranked the worst in the nation. It has been difficult to keep up with the need for new roads, water and sewerage systems, and schools in several of the region's boom cities, and after several decades, the blunders, short cuts, and bad planning are crippling sustained growth. Again in 1998 Atlanta was ranked the nation's worst case of so-called sprawl development—a ranking Houston had once been proud to hold. The South still has a disproportionate number of poor and old people, and that is one reason some analyses of government transfer payments suggested a tilt toward the South. A relatively poor region (hence below average federal tax receipts) with above-average human needs (hence above-average transfer payments) will on the screen of a computer look like a region being given an unfair advantage in the Sun Belt/Snow Belt competition. But the so-called advantage is misleading. Despite all the Sun Belt discussion, and despite undeniable southern gains over the last three decades, the South remains the poorest region in the nation. Most contemporary southerners, however, including the author, remembering (or having read about) how things were before 1940, prefer to see the glass as half-full.

No development in the postwar South has been more striking than the growth of its cities, fueled by immigration from the North, Mexico and Latin America, Asia, and especially the rural South. Many rural counties have been steadily losing population since 1940. But the rise of the cities has been more noticeable than the decline of the countryside. Excluding Baltimore, St. Louis, and Washington, D.C., New Orleans in 1940 was the largest southern city (population 494,537) even though it ranked only fifteenth in size in the nation. No other southern city was in the top twenty, although Houston was twenty-first in size and Louisville twenty-fourth. By 2000, the national and regional rankings had changed considerably. Houston had passed New Orleans during World War II to become the South's largest city, and in 2000, it was the nation's fourth largest. Joining it in the top ten cities were Dallas (seventh) and San Antonio (eighth), while Jacksonville (fourteenth), Austin (sixteenth), Baltimore (seventeenth), Memphis (eighteenth), Washington (twenty-first), Nashville (twenty-second), and El Paso (twenty-third) all were in the top twenty-five. Atlanta's city population ranked it only thirty-sixth in size, but when metropolitan population is included it moves up to the fourth position in the South (behind Dallas-Fort Worth and Houston) and reigns as the capital city of the Southeast. (It hardly makes sense after 2000 to call Washington-Baltimore a southern metropolitan area even though by census classification it is so listed.) Miami, too, in metropolitan population moves up in the ranks, and with its huge Cuban and other Hispanic population and its vast economic ties to Latin America, it currently is among the most cosmopolitan of southern cities.

Miami is also indicative of how southern cities have become far less provincial as they have become larger. All of the large southern cities have significant

THE SOUTH'S LARGEST CITIES, 1940 AND 2000

1940		2000	
Baltimore	859,100	Houston	1,953,631
St. Louis	816,048	Dallas	1,188,580
Washington	663,091	San Antonio	1,144,646
New Orleans	494,537	Jacksonville	735,617
Houston	384,514	Austin	656,562
Louisville	319,077	Baltimore	651,154
Atlanta	302,288	Memphis	650,100
Dallas	294,734	Washington, D.C.	572,059
Memphis	292,942	Nashville	569,891
Birmingham	267,583	El Paso	563,662
San Antonio	253,854	Charlotte	540,828
Richmond	193,042	Ft. Worth	534,694
Ft. Worth	177,662	Oklahoma City	506,132
Jacksonville	173,065	New Orleans	484,674
Miami	172,172	Kansas City	441,545

Sources: *The World Almanac and Book of Facts for 1941* (New York, 1941), 483; *The World Almanac and Book of Facts for 2002* (New York, 2002), 382.

THE SOUTH'S LARGEST METROPOLITAN AREAS, 2000

Washington-Baltimore	7,608,070
Dallas-Ft. Worth	5,221,801
Houston-Galveston	4,669,571
Atlanta	4,112,198
Miami-Ft. Lauderdale	3,876,380
St. Louis	2,603,607
Tampa-St. Petersburg	2,395,997
Orlando	1,644,561
San Antonio	1,592,383
Norfolk-Virginia Beach-Newport News	1,569,541
Charlotte	1,499,293
New Orleans	1,337,726

Source: *The World Almanac and Book of Facts for 2002* (New York, 2002), 381.

numbers of people from Europe, South and Central America, and Asia, and they all have benefited from migration southward of skilled workers from the northern states. Most major corporations have branch offices or branch plants in the South, and the white-collar employees that staff them are drawn from all over the nation. In the affluent sections and suburbs of Richmond, Charlotte, Atlanta, Tampa, New Orleans, Houston, and Dallas, one finds a cosmopolitan, even international, mix of peoples. The Texas cities, in particular, have large Mexican populations, Houston has a substantial Asian population as well (for example, it leads the nation in the production of egg rolls, which are distributed to restaurants nationwide), and of course, Miami's Cuban population gives that city a decidedly Latin flavor. By the middle of the first decade of the twenty-first century, Latin Americans will outnumber Anglos in Texas (and in 2002 they came to outnumber blacks in the nation). The 1990s saw significant Hispanic growth in many other southern states such as North Carolina and Alabama, and as a result Mexican-American grocery stores proliferated in the Raleigh-Durham metropolitan region. Houston, whose population is approximately 37 percent Latino, 25 percent African-American, 7 percent Asian, and 31 percent Anglo, and enjoys positive economic growth along with favorable race relations, may well be the prototype city for the increasingly multiethnic nation. The readers of *Black Enterprise* magazine in 2001 and 2002 voted Houston the best city in the nation in which to work and live, and Atlanta ranked third.

A recent analysis of U.S. cities cited a positive correlation between the existence of a so-called creative class and urban economic growth. The "creative class" that contributes to urban prosperity is attracted to cities that are open to new ideas and diverse lifestyles. According to this analysis, in 2002 four of the top ten "creative" cities were southern: Austin (ranked number 3), Raleigh-Durham (6), Houston (7), and Dallas (10). What would Mencken think of this development?

Florida and Texas receive a disproportionate percentage of the newcomers to the South, and the diversity of their immigration is noticeably differentiating these two most populous southern states from the rest of the region. But in all the cities, one finds a variety of ethnic restaurants, hears a range of foreign accents, and sees supermarket shelves stocked with herbs, peppers, and tubers that would have been rare indeed a generation ago. Ethnic foods make curious accommodations in the New South. At the New York Coffee Shop in Houston, for example, grits are offered at breakfast along with various kosher items, and even jalapeño bagels are sold. Atlanta's hosting of the 1996 Olympics enabled it to publicize globally the degree to which it had become what boosters labeled a world-class city. Certain southern romantics have been highly critical of the region's biggest cities, but few southern urban dwellers—enjoying better jobs, better schools, better health care, a wider range of cultural opportunities, and the undeniable excitement of urban life—are choosing to move back to family farms or isolated small towns. A weekend country home is nice, but not a permanent residence.

Until 1950 or so, most southern cities seemed to be peopled only by blacks and whites and had the character of overgrown towns. Now the largest cities and their school systems represent far more of the world's diversity and sustain a genuine urban ethos. The availability in the largest cities of home delivery of the *New York Times* symbolizes the degree to which the South has become economically and even culturally integrated into the national mainstream. Charlotte has become the nation's third-largest banking center, behind New York City and San Francisco. Southern-based corporations, such as Delta Airlines and Holiday Inns and Coca-Cola—and fried-chicken stands in New York City and catfish recipes in the *New York Times*—suggest that, from the national perspective, the South is now much less of a land apart. Southern institutions, musical styles, and folkways have gained currency throughout much of the nation, often in ways seldom recognized. A Memphis grocery merchant named Clarence Sanders, for example, in 1916, invented the modern supermarket with his Piggly Wiggly stores, and another southern merchant, Sam Walton, in 1962 in Rogers, Arkansas, invented another marketing concept, the Wal-Mart discount store, that by 1992, with annual sales surpassing 25 billion dollars, had become the nation's largest retailer. The secret of Wal-Mart seemed to be down-home southern folksiness and friendly service combined with high-tech communications, skilled management, efficient distribution, and everyday low prices.

In the 1930s Colonel Harland Sanders, after drifting from job to job, began experimenting with a blend of eleven herbs and spices that, when mixed into the batter for fried chicken, gave it a distinctive flavor. Soon people were flocking to his gasoline service station in Corbin, Kentucky, to eat his chicken that at first he sold on the side. He perfected his process before 1950 and in 1953 began to franchise his patented "Kentucky Fried Chicken." The product

NEW YORK TIMES CIRCULATION IN THE SOUTH, 2000

	DAILY			SUNDAY		
	Mail	Home delivery	Total including newsstand sales	Mail	Home delivery	Total including newsstand sales
Alabama	191	—	1,759	385	106	2,991
Arkansas	75	36	418	185	292	1,515
Florida	468	34,623	60,929	872	51,688	88,400
Georgia	382	7,277	14,308	620	10,987	17,560
Kentucky	163	1,375	2,363	333	2,538	4,420
Louisiana	125	—	2,494	329	841	4,965
Maryland	243	11,053	17,989	307	22,414	33,675
Mississippi	112	—	264	261	—	665
Missouri	230	5,617	5,847	458	5,981	9,680
North Carolina	650	1,896	6,414	916	6,756	14,349
Oklahoma	130	—	1,174	247	—	2,981
South Carolina	295	—	4,648	474	1,261	8,834
Tennessee	225	650	2,945	407	2,029	6,514
Texas	611	16,723	24,343	1,238	26,867	37,853
Virginia	449	7,882	13,470	639	17,095	29,108
West Virginia	138	—	372	258	—	1,653

Source: Robert Barry, Circulation Department, *New York Times*, based on Audit Bureau of Circulation data for March 24 and 26, 2000.

has been so successful that in 2002 there were almost 12,000 restaurants world-wide serving the tasty chicken.

Texas radio pioneer Gordon McLendon, self-styled "The Old Scotsman," first developed or perfected the concept of "Top 40" and beautiful music formats, the all-news station, editorials on the air, and advertising jingles based on the call letters of his radio stations. By 1950, his Liberty Broadcasting System had 458 affiliates across the nation, with listeners estimated at between 60 and 90 million. McLendon's stations—usually the most popular in each city in which they were located—had easily pronounced call letters: KILT in Houston and KEEL in Shreveport. Radio programming has evolved away from McLendon's trademark styles in the last generation, and today the most popular music format in the nation is country-western, perhaps the most southern music of all. And a southern evangelist, now headquartered in Minneapolis—Billy Graham—is the best-known and best-loved religious figure of the twentieth century. His crusades in their music, sermon style, and altar call are unmistakably Southern Baptist, and they are skillfully choreographed and nationally televised.

To a remarkable extent, the nation's popular culture has been southernized. What could be more American than hamburgers and french fries, washed down with a Coke? The hamburger was apparently invented by a cafe owner in Athens, Texas, in the 1880s: he pioneered the concept of fried beef patties served between two slices of bread and garnished with onions, pickles, and mustard. The local popularity of his new kind of sandwich led to a concession booth—Old Dave's Hamburger Stand—at the 1904 world's fair in St. Louis celebrating the centennial of the Louisiana Purchase. In response to a question from a *New York Tribune* reporter about how he learned to cook the fried potatoes that accompanied the hamburgers, Old Dave replied that he had gotten the technique from a friend in Paris—meaning Paris, Texas, about a hundred miles from Athens. The reporter thought he meant Paris, France. Hence "french fries" were publicized. The hamburger, french fries, and Coca-Cola (first concocted in Atlanta in 1886 by John S. "Doc" Pemberton) were all southern creations, and the rest is, again as the saying goes, history.

At the very beginning of the twentieth century, northern automobile enthusiasts, southern civic boosters, and automobile manufacturers and dealers began to promote automobile racing on the long, hard, flat, sand beaches first of Florida and then of Galveston. "Stock" cars, specially modified cars, even so-called Indy-style cars were employed. Large crowds attended, drivers came from across the nation and Europe, and many international speed records were set. Soon dozens of tracks were constructed throughout the region—even planked tracks made of boards—and a southern car-racing craze was begun that much later became incorporated as NASCAR. Contrary to popular myth, southern auto and "stock" car racing did not arise from good-old-boy moonshiners out-running federal revenue agents. Rather, the origins of the southern romance with racing cars lie in the promotional efforts of urban and corporate boosters.

After World War II, NASCAR officials seized on the colorful myth of whiskey-drivers and moonshiners to capitalize on antigovernment sentiment and a desire of many modern southerners to identify with free-spirited individualism even as they were increasingly tied to their jobs and mortgages. Almost like characters in a Merle Haggard song who dreamed of breaking loose from their factory jobs, many modern-day southerners wanted to believe in the NASCAR myth and identified vicariously with the devil-may-care rebels who supposedly founded the sport. That savvy but historically inaccurate marketing scheme has helped spread NASCAR's popularity across much of the nation. It is but another example of myth blending fact and fiction, harsh reality and fond wish, to transmute an aspect of the South into a more palatable history—one that conceals as much as it reveals.

But if to a significant degree the North has been southernized, in still other ways the South has been Americanized. Northern tourists traveling now on an interstate highway through the region experience a South far less distinctive than they might have expected. Everywhere they visit in the South has standardized road signs, the same chain hotels, fast food outlets, and national brand-name stores that they are familiar with, and people wear similar clothes and listen to the same music. Southerners read the same magazines, see the same movies, watch the same television shows as other Americans do. Only when these hypothetical tourists get off the interstate highway and out of the car and listen to native southerners (if one could be found in Atlanta or Houston) or taste the local food do they begin to realize that the South is not completely an undifferentiated part of the larger nation. Despite all the economic growth and urbanization, despite the standardization and cosmopolitanization of the region, something almost intangible still seems to set the region apart, especially in the small towns and rural areas.

Perhaps it is more a state of mind than anything susceptible to scientific analysis, but most southerners insist the region is still "southern" whether they love or hate what that defining label means, and most northerners, too, profess to see a region still recognizably different from the rest of the nation. The people living in the region, particularly the native-born whites and blacks, struggle with coming to terms with their region and ponder what part of their heritage should be discarded and what should be held on to. Academicians and journalists who study the region also struggle to understand the persistence of southern identity and debate its future. In the end, most discussions of the South come around to that topic.

CHAPTER 29

The Civil Rights Movement

SEGREGATION UNDER ASSAULT

The shift in the national media's stereotype of the South is represented by the difference between the sharecropper shacks and hillbillies, as portrayed in the book *Tobacco Road* and in such comic strips as "L'il Abner" and "Snuffy Smith," and the opening scenes of the popular television series "Dallas" with the skyline of that rich and powerful city towering over the surrounding plains like some giant mountain range; yet the region's most profound change in the last fifty years has occurred in race relations. One must always hasten to say that much yet remains to be done, but nowhere else in this nation has there been such a shift in basic attitudes. More than in any other aspect, in terms of race relations, a New South has indeed emerged in the last generation.

    The desegregation of American life in general, and southern life in particular, is the most significant social movement in modern American history. The movement began to chip away at the prevailing system in the 1930s, gained momentum in the 1940s, saw landmark changes in the 1950s, and by the 1960s had already begun to change forever how blacks and whites interacted in the South. The movement worked at several levels: There was the carefully constructed legal effort on the part of the National Association for the Advancement of Colored People (NAACP), the gradual but ultimately essential efforts of the federal government, and the courageous folk crusade of thousands of black men, women,

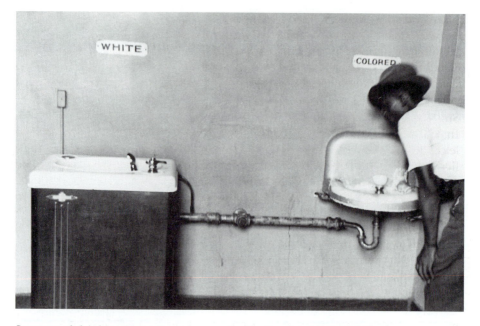

Segregated drinking fountains were seen in the South until the 1960s.
(Elliott Erwitt/Magnum Photos, Inc.)

and children (and not a few whites) in the South, with assistance from people of conscience throughout the nation. To this complex story we now turn.

It is practically impossible for anyone not old enough to have experienced it to appreciate how totally separate blacks and whites were in the South before World War II. Segregation was so complete that the football teams of the white-only universities of the major conferences of the South would not schedule northern teams that had black players and would not compete in bowl games with non-southern teams that were integrated. On some occasions by so-called gentlemen's agreements, northern coaches would bench their black players and southern teams would bench supposedly equivalent players, so that the games could go on without threatening the southern racial etiquette. Basketball and baseball teams that won conference championships routinely turned down automatic bids to participate in NCAA post-season tournaments rather than risk playing against integrated teams. Blacks had separate churches, schools, and social organizations; lived in special sections of most towns; could shop in regular department stores, but not try on clothes; could not eat in the dining rooms of restaurants; could not stay in motels unless they happened to find a rare "colored" motel; could not, in Mississippi, even go to the beaches to swim in the Gulf of Mexico. Blacks could not address a white adult by first name (unless "mister" or "miz" was prefixed), although even white children called black adults by their first names. The slightest infraction of the code of racial etiquette by a black brought down punishment by whites—often death, and even as recently as the mid-1950s. Throughout the deep South, but especially in Mississippi, blacks were routinely cheated, humiliated, abused, deprived of basic human rights, and kept in abject poverty.

The ultimate legal basis of this system of rigid segregation was the 1896 Supreme Court decision, *Plessy v. Ferguson,* based on the case of Homer Plessy. In 1892, he had sat in the whites-only car of a train traveling between New Orleans and Covington, Louisiana, only to be dragged off and arrested by policemen. The very light-complexioned Plessy argued that the Fourteenth Amendment guaranteed equal protection under the law and hence made illegal such segregated cars. However, the U.S. Supreme Court ruled in 1896 that the Civil Rights Act of 1875 required only "separate-but-equal" facilities and that a blacks-only railroad car, if it offered equal facilities, met the letter of the law. This decision governed race relations in the South until 1954, but in precious few instances were the facilities available to blacks equal to those provided for whites. By every conceivable measure, the general usage emphasized the separate in the dictum, but ignored the equal.

In the middle of the Great Depression, the NAACP finally decided to mount a full-scale legal battle against segregation in the South, where it was most pronounced. Although earlier a NAACP staff lawyer had argued that the entire principle of separate-but-equal was wrong and based on faulty legal reasoning, the organization believed that a more limited campaign would be more effective. The logic of this campaign, which was directed by Charles Hamilton Houston, dean of the Howard University School of Law and Special Counsel for the NAACP, was to highlight those instances in which southern states clearly failed to offer "equal" facilities as required by the law. Reasoning that it would be less antagonistic to the prejudices of the white South to begin by attacking inequalities in higher education, where the discrepancies were most outrageous, Houston further decided to attack the discrimination rampant in legal education. The first case concerned a young man, Donald Gaines Murray, who was not accepted at the University of Maryland Law School solely on the grounds of race. Arguing the case in the Baltimore and Maryland courts, Houston and his assistant, Thurgood Marshall, showed that sending Murray out of state for his education, which the state was prepared to do, would not be equal training because Murray wanted to practice law in Maryland. When the state court in 1935 upheld the decision in favor of Murray, the NAACP knew it had gained an important first breach in the wall of segregation. The following year, the team of Houston and Marshall made similar arguments on behalf of Lloyd Lionel Gaines, who sought to attend the University of Missouri's law school, and this case went all the way to the U.S. Supreme Court. Again the decision was in favor of admission of the black candidate to the previously all-white law school.

When Heman Sweatt, a former mailman in Houston, applied for admission to the law school at the University of Texas, the university attempted educational subterfuge. Under the guise of separate but equal, the university proposed to establish a law school for blacks in Houston in three basement rooms, staffed with part-time faculty. The NAACP took up Sweatt's cause and challenged the quality of the education offered—such a pitiful facility for educating black lawyers was in no way comparable to the strong law school in Austin, with its good library, distinguished faculty, and roster of influential alumni. This case became joined with the case of George W. McLaurin, an elderly black professor who had applied for admission to the Ph.D. program in education at the University of Oklahoma and was rejected on the basis of race. Later, the university made a compromise of sorts and allowed McLaurin to enroll, but he was required to sit at a special desk with a railing surrounding it, and there were separate tables, for his use only, in the library and cafeteria. With the NAACP's support, both the Sweatt case and the McLaurin case were heard by the Supreme Court in April 1950. This time, the NAACP was joined by the nation's Department of Justice, which filed a friendly brief in support of the cause of equal education. But when the Court ruled, on June 5, 1950, in favor of Sweatt and McLaurin, it did so in narrow, technical terms. The University of Texas Law School had to admit Sweatt, and the University of Oklahoma had to stop putting humiliating restrictions on McLaurin's attendance. The opportunity to address segregated education in general was not taken, and the ruling was confined to postgraduate education. It did require, however, genuine equality of educational effort on the part of the states at the postgraduate level. Knowing how difficult the South found it to support higher education in general, the NAACP reasoned that support of dual but truly equal systems would be financially impossible and ultimately repugnant even to diehard segregationists. Slowly but surely, Thurgood Marshall and his associates—Charles H. Houston had died—sensed that the tide of history was on their side, and they had a decade of increasing involvement by the federal government to support that optimistic assessment.

Franklin D. Roosevelt—perhaps in part because of the sensitivities of his wife Eleanor—slowly came partially to understand the situation for blacks in the South; but fearful of political retaliation by southern congressmen, he was extremely hesitant to criticize the South's Jim Crow practices. Once World War II loomed, he feared that any effort to promote the interests of blacks might jeopardize wartime production needs. But blacks were quick to realize that they were not being fairly treated as new war-related job opportunities arose. They were almost always excluded from high-skilled, high-paying jobs and were usually confined to janitorial positions. The discrepancies between national rhetoric about freedom and justice and the reality for American blacks rankled race leaders. A. Philip Randolph, more militant than many NAACP leaders who preferred to work through the court system, began to plan a mammoth March on Washington Movement to dramatize the issue. Roosevelt was worried about how such a visible protest would affect the national image abroad as he was seeking to become the leader of the Allies. When Randolph refused to cave in to Roosevelt's pressure, Roosevelt moved to create the Fair Employment Practice Committee (FEPC) to examine cases of job discrimination in the hope that publicity would discourage such practices. In return, Randolph called off the march. The FEPC proved less efficacious than Randolph would have liked, but at least the federal government had officially taken cognizance of the plight of blacks in the workplace. Conservative white southerners saw the handwriting on the wall. Many of them began to break with Roosevelt and the New Deal because in their minds "the southern way of life" was threatened by such federal interference.

One of the ways the southern white establishment had defended its position was with the white primary, which eliminated blacks from participating in the only election that made any difference in most parts of the South. As long as blacks were disfranchised, southern white politicians had no incentive to redress black complaints because to do so gained them no black votes and cost them white votes. In 1923, the NAACP began to protest legally the white primary in Texas, and Supreme Court decisions in 1927 and again in 1932 had narrowly decided against the Democratic white primary as an official state election institution. But the state had withdrawn its laws concerning the primary, declaring it to be simply the activity of a private party and hence not subject to the provisions of the Fourteenth Amendment. In fact, the Supreme Court in 1935 (*Grovey v. Townsend*) upheld the idea of the primary as a private (not state) matter. Many Texas blacks were outraged. The local NAACP set out to find a way to challenge the decision, and they found a Houston dentist, Lonnie Smith, who agreed to become part of the case after being prohibited from voting in the 1940 Democratic white primary. Almost four years later, in a landmark decision, the Supreme Court in *Smith v. Allwright* ruled that, because in fact the primary was integral to the election process, the exclusion of blacks from it violated the Fifteenth Amendment. Southern states and localities quickly devised other ruses to limit voting, including the previously instituted poll tax and various new literacy or so-called understanding requirements. But *Smith v. Allwright* was another crack in the hitherto solid wall of segregation.

When Harry S Truman from Missouri became president following Roosevelt's death in 1945, many blacks were unsure of his position on race. The significant shift of black votes away from the Republican party to the Democratic party had begun with Roosevelt, but would it continue? The massive migration of southern blacks to northern cities, where their political participation was possible, had begun to make the black vote a significant, sometimes the decisive, factor in local, congressional, even presidential politics. Whatever his previous attitudes toward segregation, Truman could count votes. But he was also frankly appalled at the racism that had continued in the South during the course of and immediately after the war. On several occasions, black soldiers, in uniform, were assaulted, discriminated against, or killed. Truman's strong sense of fairness was touched; both his conscience and his political instincts suggested that here was an issue that the nation could ill afford to ignore any longer. In 1946, he appointed a Committee on Civil Rights—with two liberal white southern members—to investigate what Truman was beginning to see as a moral crisis as well as a political opportunity. The following year, the committee issued a powerful report, *To Secure These Rights*, which called on the federal government to put its weight behind the campaign to achieve racial equality. In words that dismayed southern segregationists, this official government committee urged "the elimination of segregation based on race, color, creed, or national origin from American life."

In the midst now of a Cold War that rhetorically pitted the free world against Communist slavery, Truman and others were aware of how southern race relations made a mockery of American ideals. And his political advisers suggested to him that the growing power of black voters in northern cities lessened the national Democratic party's dependence on white southern support. Still Truman acted cautiously. Nevertheless, civil rights seemed to be an idea whose time was coming, backed as it was by the great study published in 1944 by Gunnar Myrdal and his associates, *An American Dilemma: The Negro Problem and Modern Democracy*. Black leaders were pushing hard for presidential action. Although Truman addressed Congress in early 1948 on the issue, he again hesitated to advocate a bold program in Congress for fear of alienating southern whites still further. But at the Democratic National Convention that summer, Senator Hubert Humphrey employed his moving oratory and skilled leadership to ensure that the party platform had a strong civil rights plank. Even as diehard southern segregationists abandoned their historic commitment to the Democratic party and turned instead to a new States' Rights party—the Dixiecrats—Truman rose to the occasion and issued two presidential proclamations, one aimed at desegregating the armed forces and the other providing for nondiscriminatory employment practices in the federal government. Truman won a surprise reelection campaign that fall against Thomas E. Dewey, governor of New York, but the loss of southern support contributed mightily, four years later, to the election of military hero and cautious racial moderate, Dwight David ("Ike") Eisenhower, the Republican candidate, as president. (Eisenhower had supported neither Truman's desegregation of the armed forces nor Roosevelt's creation of the FEPC in the 1940s.) On October 5, 1953, less than ten months after taking office, Ike was present when former California governor Earl Warren took the oath of office as Chief Justice of the Supreme Court, replacing the deceased Fred M. Vinson of Kentucky.

The decision makers in the NAACP's Legal Defense Fund had earlier determined in 1950 that the time had come to shift the legal strategy from demanding that the southern states meet the separate-but-equal requirement to attacking the whole legal basis of that doctrine itself. After a planning session in New York City in June 1950, the NAACP set itself the task of accumulating psychological and sociological evidence of the damaging consequences of racial segregation. And they began to search for cases involving secondary schools that lent themselves to a judicial challenge of the 1896 Plessy separate-but-equal decision. In Clarendon, South Carolina; in Topeka, Kansas; in Prince Edward County, Virginia; in the District of Columbia; and in Claymont, Delaware, cases emerged. The details of each case differed, but all spoke eloquently to the issue of shocking discrimination and outrageous inequality. With consummate legal skill, the NAACP argued and nurtured these various cases through the courts. In June 1952, the Supreme Court announced it would hear two of these cases, then in October it added a third, then, after another delay, the final two cases were added. Consolidating all five under the name of *Brown v. Board of Education of Topeka*, the Court set December 9, 1952, as the day to hear arguments.

Thurgood Marshall led the arguments on behalf of the plaintiffs, his skills honed by years of experience and given added poignancy by his evident devotion to the cause. Backed by friendly briefs filed by a who's who of historians and social scientists, and documented with the powerful though controversial evidence of psychologist Kenneth Clark—whose research on black children's attitudes toward black and white dolls gave chilling evidence of the crippling psychological effect of segregation—Marshall faced John W. Davis, a very experienced attorney noted for the vigor of his preparation and presentation. For three days, the court heard arguments before convening. Months passed and the justices sent written questions to both sides. Before the court could reach a decision in what everyone understood to be a truly momentous case, Chief Justice Vinson died. Earl Warren, the new chief justice, desperately wanted a unanimous decision in this, his first case, and the final decision was apparently delayed as he struggled to construct a consensus.

Finally on Monday, May 17, 1954—a day segregationists soon called Black Monday—Chief Justice Warren read the ruling. His words would prove to be a turning point in southern and American history: "We conclude, unanimously, that in the field of public education the doctrine of 'separate but equal' has no place. Separate educational facilities are inherently unequal." A new birth of freedom was in the making, but the making proved difficult indeed. The following May, the Supreme Court ruled to leave actual implementation of the decision up to southern federal judges and merely urged them to proceed "with all deliberate speed." The ruling meant that hasty changes would not take place in southern racial practices.

The next decade essentially brought racial war to the South, sometimes a hot war, at other times cold, and whites conducted a terrorist campaign throughout. The eleven years between the *Brown* decision in 1954 and the Voting Rights Act of 1965 seemed like a prolonged series of bloody skirmishes and irrational white intransigence, with fervent protestations that the white South would never cave in to Communist-inspired racial mongrelization. Southern whites developed a bunker mentality, tried to eliminate outside influences, and resorted to angry violence to stem the tides of change. But as the old spiritual put it, a new day was a'coming.

In retrospect, it is clear that the very outrageousness of segregationist protest not only morally armed a growing black movement, enabling them to overwhelm the forces of apartheid, but also gradually awakened most of the nation to the cancer in its midst. The behavior of southern white segregationists eventually persuaded the nation that legal segregation was wrong. Polls showed that most Americans at the time disagreed with the 1954 *Brown* decision, and President Eisenhower studiously avoided providing any forthright moral leadership on behalf of civil rights; ten years later, President Lyndon B. Johnson took up the civil rights motto, "we shall overcome," and used the phrase to win approval in Congress—and in the public opinion polls—for both the Civil Rights Act of 1964 and the Voting Rights Act of 1965. A great watershed had been passed in the nation's history.

There are some indications that the triumphs of 1964 and 1965 might have been accomplished more quickly and with less turmoil and injury had there been courageous white leadership a decade earlier. When the *Brown* decision was announced, governors of several states, including Alabama and Arkansas, expressed regret but said that the law must be obeyed. A *New York Times* poll of southern school administrators suggested that with a minimum of conflict the new ruling would be put into effect. In various communities, white political and religious leaders indicated acquiescence in the ruling—after all, the South had once before tried to go its own way, and that had brought failure. Had President Eisenhower immediately and directly used his enormous prestige and popularity, and the bully pulpit of the White House, to insist that the Supreme Court ruling was the law of the land and must be obeyed in spirit as well as in letter, then these glimmers of acceptance might have been nurtured into a groundswell of pragmatic approval. But that leadership was not forthcoming, and once again the meaner angels of the southern body politic took over and produced one tragic encounter after another in the dark and bloody ground of Dixieland.

In July 1954, meeting with a group of friends in the Mississippi Delta town of Indianola, a World War II veteran and plantation manager named Robert B. Patterson organized the White Citizen's Council, a middle- and upper-class version of the Ku Klux Klan that quickly spread across the deep South and eventually had more than a quarter-million members. Eschewing the violence of the Klan, however, the Citizen's Council used economic coercion to punish blacks who transgressed the region's strict racial etiquette. Suddenly they would lose their jobs, or have their insurance canceled, or find it impossible to get a bank loan or a home mortgage. The result was less bloody but almost as dispiriting as Klan terrorism. Another Mississippian, Judge Tom P. Brady, wrote a pamphlet vigorously attacking the logic of the *Brown* decision, and his argument soon became part of the verbal artillery of militant segregationists across the region. Prominent journalists like James J. Kilpatrick of the *Richmond News-Leader* used their pens and editorial pages to criticize the idea of integration. Kilpatrick resurrected the antebellum doctrine of interposition in an attempt to contravene the decision of the Supreme Court and the federal government. In the absence of powerful countervailing voices, these voices of hate— sometimes vicious, sometimes restrained—quickly came to dominate white public opinion in the South. An opportunity had been missed.

As southern segregationist attitudes hardened, many white southerners felt besieged, their traditional ways threatened once again by the lengthening and strengthening arm of the national government. At a time when the nation itself was caught up in Cold War hysteria, it was easy for desperate segregationists to see a Communist conspiracy behind integrationist efforts. Even otherwise good southern whites lost all sense of proportion when they felt what they called "the southern way of life" (i.e., strict racial segregation) was in the least bit endangered. Seemingly kind and decent white men and women would countenance unspeakable evil to support segregation; would lie to protect murderers; and would ignore their consciences to keep solidarity with the white community. Even the slightest acknowledgment that perhaps segregation was wrong could bring down upon the heretic the smashing fist of community authority. In fact, progressivism in any form, such as labor unionism, was crushed by charging the proponents of change with either promoting integration or Communism. The state of Mississippi in 1956 created the Mississippi State Sovereignty Commission, a Gestapo-like investigative body used to harass blacks who in any way threatened the preservation of segregation. An unforgiving iron curtain of racial conformity descended around much of the South, producing what one historian-participant called a "closed society." Not even a child was allowed to transgress.

Emmett "Bobo" Till, a fourteen-year-old boy from Chicago, was visiting his relatives in Money, Mississippi, in August 1955. Emmett attended an all-black school on the Chicago South Side but was innocent of the rigors of the racial etiquette of Mississippi. To make matters worse, he was a lively, almost swaggering youth who enjoyed impressing his country-bumpkin Mississippi relatives with his big city wiles. He even showed his Mississippi friends a wallet photo of a white girl back home whom he claimed was his girlfriend. One of the local boys doubted that Emmett was bold enough to have a white girlfriend, and taunted him by saying that there was a white girl working in the small country store nearby. Words to the effect that "I bet you won't talk to her" were said. The brash Chicago teenager then went into Bryant's Grocery and Meat Market, bought a piece of candy, and apparently said something to Carolyn Bryant, the wife of the store's owner. There is conflicting testimony over whether he called out "Bye, baby" as he left, or whether he whistled at her. (Emmett had a slight lisp and often seemed to whistle when he talked.) Whatever happened inside that store on Wednesday afternoon, August 24, 1955, the local blacks standing outside who heard the encounter immediately understood the danger.

For some reason Carolyn Bryant—a native of Indianola, Mississippi—did not tell her husband of the incident when he returned from driving a truckload of shrimp from Louisiana to Texas. But Roy Bryant was no sooner back at his store than another black, having heard of a "Chicago boy" who had spoken out of place, regaled Bryant with a probably embellished version of Till's encounter with Bryant's wife. That fateful conversation set the brutal plot unfolding, because Bryant considered his honor, and his wife's virtue, at risk. After the close of business late Saturday evening Bryant, accompanied by his brother-in-law J. W. Milam, drove in a pickup truck out to Mose Wright's house, where the Chicago visitors were staying. They asked Wright for the youngster, and Wright pleaded with them that the boy was young, that he wasn't from Mississippi and didn't know any better, but the two white men drove off with Emmett, who was probably too naive to know the danger he was in.

After a vicious beating, the teenager was shot in the head, weighted down with a heavy piece of metal tied to his body with barbed wire, and dumped in the nearby Tallahatchie River, which soon washed up the body. There was overwhelming evidence against Bryant and Milam: Mose Wright risked his life to testify against the murderers and pointed to Milam in response to a question from the prosecutor asking him to identify the kidnappers and said, in his imperfect English, "Thar he." The court, in a flagrant mockery of justice, failed to convict the murderers. (Bryant and Milam later confessed for pay to a journalist who published their unrepentant story.) Much of the nation was aghast, especially when Emmett's mother insisted on an open-casket funeral and a national publication printed a shocking photo of the child's face battered beyond recognition. Mississippi was not accepting desegregation peacefully.

The next civil rights skirmish that captured national attention occurred in Montgomery, Alabama, and it resulted in a signal victory for blacks. Montgomery, where the Confederacy had been established in 1861, was like most southern cities in that its buses were segregated. In Montgomery, whites began seating row by row at the front of the bus, working backward, while blacks began at the back and worked forward. However, if a white boarded and there were no more white seats available, then the entire next row of black riders had to relinquish their seats so that the white would have a white row in which to sit. Moreover, black riders had to enter the bus at the front to pay the driver, step back out, and walk to the back door to enter and sit. It was not unknown for white drivers to pull away from the curb before the black could reenter the bus. The result was a constant inconvenience and humiliation to the black community.

On December 1, 1955, Rosa Parks, tired after a long day's work as a seamstress at a downtown department store and tired of a lifetime of discrimination, was resting in her seat on the way home when several white men boarded the bus, more than the existing white section could hold. The bus driver then yelled to the blacks, "Niggers, move back." Rosa Parks, who had recently attended a race relations workshop at the Highlander Folk School—a pioneer institution advocating peaceful desegregation—refused to budge. The bus driver stopped the bus and called the police, who promptly arrested Mrs. Parks and took her to jail. The white authorities expected no repercussions from their unexceptional response to what was, in their terms, a black person getting out of line.

But Rosa Parks was exceptional; she had a high-school education, she had an excellent reputation, and she was an active member of Montgomery's very active NAACP. The head of the local NAACP branch, E. D. Nixon, knew Mrs. Parks well and quickly sized up the situation: She was the perfect person, and this was the right occasion, to challenge in the courts Montgomery's segregated buses. Jo Ann Robinson, a black English professor at the city's Alabama State College, was head of the Woman's Political Council and an organizer extraordinaire. Nixon, Robinson, and Fred Gray, a black lawyer, decided to put together a community-wide black boycott of the bus system. Over the following weekend, Robinson mimeographed thirty-five thousand handbills and, with a small group of students, distributed them all over the city. Monday morning only a handful of blacks rode the buses. The white officials expected the boycott to fade in a day or two, but they did not appreciate Robinson's skills or the commitment of the blacks. An incredible network of car pools, makeshift taxis, and a remarkable willingness to walk simply wore down the city authorities. For month after month, blacks walked and car pooled, regardless of the weather or the distance.

Early on in the campaign, E. D. Nixon realized that the boycott needed support from local black churches. He understood that he and Robinson had reputations for radical protest that might put off some blacks; the ministers, though, had unparalleled influence in the black community, and they were largely insulated from white economic pressure. At that moment, a new minister had just arrived at the Dexter Avenue Baptist Church—so new that he had no enemies among the other ministers. This young minister, despite personal hesitation, had leadership of the movement forced on him, and, unbeknownst to anyone at the moment, the civil rights movement found its leader. Martin Luther King, Jr., accepted the mantle of leadership, found himself invigorated with the moral power of the endeavor, and utilized his growing eloquence as a speaker to electrify the black crowds in his church. It was as if a mighty moral force had been unleashed. The black community discovered a sense of pride, purpose, and power it had not known before, and with that came a feeling of confidence that overrode the physical exhaustion of walking. "Yes, my feets is tired," said one elderly black lady in response to a query, "but my soul is rested."

The whole nation took note of what these blacks had discovered within themselves, and after almost twelve months of boycott, on November 13, 1956, the Supreme Court ruled that the city's segregated bus system was unconstitutional. Montgomery blacks had won a great victory, and the civil rights movement had found itself a great leader. Two years later, in 1958, King and others founded the Southern Christian Leadership Conference (SCLC), in effect adding the powerful influence of the black church and its ministers to a civil rights movement that had previously been led by lawyers. Perhaps even more important, black people had discovered the self-empowerment and exhilaration of meaningful political involvement. King knew about Henry David Thoreau and *Civil Disobedience* and about Mohandas Karamchand Gandhi and his philosophy of nonviolent resistance in India. King was also well read in Christian theology; consequently he could put the black movement in a universal context and articulate the desire for justice in universal language of great power.

The year 1956 proved to be explosive in Montgomery. It began with Martin Luther King, Jr.'s home being bombed in January, and it concluded in December with another bombing at the home of Fred Shuttleworth, a black minister, who survived by what he considered a miracle. There were other boycotts in other cities. After Autherine Lucy enrolled at the University of Alabama on February 3, a full-scale riot erupted, and the officials suspended her from school. When she protested, the college expelled her. Less than six weeks later, in Washington, D.C., Senator Sam Ervin of North Carolina turned his considerable legal talents to drafting a so-called Southern Manifesto attacking the constitutionality of the *Brown* decision. The overwhelming majority of southern legislators signed the document, with only Tennessee's senators Albert Gore and Estes Kefauver refusing; by prior arrangement, Texas senator Lyndon B. Johnson and Speaker of the House Sam Rayburn were not asked to sign. That fall, Eisenhower was easily reelected president.

Ike was certainly no racist, though by experience and temperament he was not very sensitive to the implications of legal segregation. (Ike never declared his support for the *Brown* decision, and he never commented on the racist murder of Emmett Till or on the University of Alabama's expelling of Autherine Lucy.) But as a military man, he was committed to the rule of law, and, whether he agreed with the Supreme Court or not, his constitutional duty was to enforce the law. He feared to push the South too fast, although from the black viewpoint, the commitment to equality had already been delayed almost a century. Ike's attorney general, Herbert Brownell, was more attuned to the black viewpoint. Moreover, he was dismayed by the continuing southern violence and total intransigence. After the Emmett Till case and in the midst of the Montgomery bus boycott, Brownell proposed a major civil rights package to Congress. Eisenhower hesitated but finally accepted Brownell's proposal, only to have it defeated by Congress.

Following the 1956 election, Ike found an unlikely ally in the Senate Majority Leader, Lyndon Johnson. Johnson had a real commitment to society's underdogs. He also wanted to assume a political posture that would make him a national figure, and he understood that, given southern congressional strength, only a moderate version of Brownell's program had a chance of being approved. The opponents of segregation had not yet learned what a master of the Senate Johnson could be, and with masterful manipulation and cajoling and calling in of chits, Johnson pushed through Congress on August 29, 1957, the nation's first civil rights bill since Reconstruction. Eisenhower quickly signed the watered-down bill, after giving assurances that it was "the mildest civil rights bill possible." Still, passage of the bill proved to be of great importance because in a profound way it made the subsequent civil rights movement possible by putting the federal government on the side of desegregation. Yet with its passage, there was no way Ike could know that his biggest civil rights crisis was just in the offing.

Little Rock was a racially progressive city in a racially progressive southern state. In fact, promptly in 1954, two school districts in the state desegregated. Within a week of the *Brown* decision, the Little Rock school board indicated its willingness to comply. On May 24, 1955, the school board approved a plan to begin integration in September 1957 by admitting black students to the city's Central High School. Affairs looked promising; after all, Arkansas governor Orval Faubus was himself a racial moderate and political progressive. But segregationist sentiment began to rise in the state, led by a young politician named James Johnson who tried to have the state constitution revised so as to prevent school integration. Faubus intended to run again for the gubernatorial office in 1956, and he feared Johnson would use race-baiting against him. As so many earlier southern demagogues had done before and later, Faubus opportunistically decided to pick up the racist banner and champion that cause—selling his soul for election victory. In early 1956, he began to say that the citizens of the state were opposed to integration, and he had no intention of going against their desires. In effect, Faubus legitimated the protest of racist fanatics, who then began to harass local NAACP leaders, such as Daisy Bates. But according to the school board's plan, Central High was scheduled to open, integrated, on September 3, 1957.

The day before integration was to take place, Faubus deployed the Arkansas National Guard to encircle Central High, ostensibly to prevent violence from breaking out but in reality to prevent nine black students from entering. Faced with the troops, the school board asked the students to stay home the next day and sought a ruling from federal judge Ronald Davies; Davies ruled that school officials should follow the integration plan. So the next day, the black students came to the school and found it surrounded by a screaming, hateful mob of white segregationists. One of the black students, Elizabeth Eckford, had missed a message to rendezvous with the others and came alone, only to find herself engulfed by an angry sea of whites. She had to turn back, rescued by two kind whites, one a *New York Times* reporter and the other a local woman. The other eight students were prevented by the National Guard from entering the school. A series of telegrams passed between Faubus and President Eisenhower, who pressed the governor to obey the law. Faubus even met with the president in Rhode Island, but Faubus refused to budge.

Judge Davies then issued an injunction ordering Faubus to remove the guardsmen; Faubus did so but replaced them with policemen. On September 23, the black students again approached the school, but the mob had grown in size and worsened in demeanor. Faubus had become a segregationist hero, and the city was nearly out of control. At that point, President Eisenhower, recognizing duty if not morality, honored the request of the mayor and sent in a thousand federal troops from the 101st Airborne Division, the first time since Reconstruction that federal military forces were employed in the South to protect the constitutional rights of its black citizens. (Eisenhower made clear that the troops were sent "to uphold the law," not enforce integration.) The Arkansas National Guard was also federalized and commanded to protect the students.

As the world watched on television, the whole force of the national government was directed to allow the matriculation of nine black students in a southern high school. Military bodyguards were assigned to each, and for the rest of the year an uneasy peace ensued. The students survived taunts and stares, but that spring the only black senior, Ernest Green, graduated (two decades later, he had a position in the Carter administration). The following year, Little Rock closed its public schools rather than have them integrated. The Supreme Court then ruled that closing illegal, and in August 1959, Little Rock began a new school year with integrated classrooms. By no means had the forces of segregation been defeated in the South. Yet Eisenhower, despite his caution and lack of passion for the cause, had made a fundamental decision: The federal government had entered the fray on the side of racial change. It was very clear that without such federal involvement, racial segregation in the South would persist far into the future.

By the late 1950s, some progress had been made in school desegregation in the southern fringe areas of Kentucky, Tennessee, Arkansas, and western Texas—at least in regions in those states where there were few blacks. But in the rest of the South, white segregationists dug in their heels. The whites of Prince Edward County, Virginia, even shut their public schools in 1959 for five years rather than integrate. In other areas, school boards experimented with various student assignment gimmicks to void the effects of desegregation. Throughout the region, parents resorted to private schools—so-called "seg" academies—rather than send their children to integrated public schools. Often these segregated private schools were associated with churches, and the parents claimed tax deductions for the tuition "contributions." (The number of such private academies mushroomed in the 1960s, and by the fall of 1970 about a half million southern white children attended private segregated schools. Ostensibly the reason was "better academics.") When New Orleans in November 1960 prepared to integrate its public schools, a crowd of angry white mothers, soon tagged "the cheerleaders," surrounded the schools and shouted their opposition: "Two, four, six, eight; we don't want to integrate!" Mob violence threatened to tear the city apart. The spectacle of hate personified was shocking; so much so that city business leaders, fearing the loss of tourist dollars, insisted on peaceful and gradual integration within several months. In more progressive southern cities like Atlanta, Tampa, Charlotte, Houston, and Dallas, that desire to protect the business climate overcame the more retrograde forces and promoted acceptance of integration in order to avoid ugly racial confrontations. By the early 1960s, many southern urban school systems, particularly in the border and western states of the South, had at least begun a gradual, grade-by-grade process of integration, and soon the rural areas followed suit. The focus of desegregation then shifted to other aspects of the Jim Crow system.

The civil rights movement took a different tack beginning in 1960, one based more upon mass participation than upon legal briefs. The shift had unpremeditated origins. Four male students at North Carolina Agricultural and Technical College in Greensboro, in a bull session on the evening of January 31, 1960, began to reflect on one of them having been refused counter service at a bus station snack bar. The conversation led to a decision that the next day they would go to a downtown Woolworth store to challenge the refusal to let black customers—who could purchase anything else in the store—sit at the counter and eat a sandwich or drink a cup of coffee. So on February 1, 1960, four polite, neatly dressed college students inadvertently started a movement that eventually shook the foundations of segregation. As expected, the waitresses would not serve them; even the white policeman who was called seemed nonplused by the event. Word spread back to the college and more students arrived to continue the sit-in; soon white students came also to protest the discriminatory policy. Within several days, a thousand students were involved, crowds surrounded the store, and hecklers began to harass the students. Many otherwise conservative whites suddenly had brought home to them one of the more ridiculous points of southern race etiquette.

The sit-in movement spread—and it spread like wildfire: Within two weeks, fifteen other cities were involved; within two months, it spread to over fifty cities throughout the South, and by the end of the year to one hundred cities. At stake were not abstract constitutional arguments and arcane legal points but rather the simple absurdity of being willing to sell a student a package of Juicy Fruit but not a glass of Coca Cola. Black students and black laypersons now had a visible way to act out their protest. Inspired by the opportunity, Ella Baker, an energetic woman who had been a pioneer in SCLC, called together some two hundred student leaders in Raleigh over the Easter week of

1960 and organized the Student Nonviolent Coordinating Committee (SNCC, pronounced Snick) to marshal student activists against segregation. The control of the civil rights movement was slipping still further away from the more conservative NAACP.

The new emphasis on demonstrating the injustice of segregation by putting live bodies at the point of contest took still another form the following year. Twenty-five years before, in 1946, the Supreme Court had ruled against segregated seating on interstate bus systems, but the law was not enforced in the South. In May 1961, thirteen brave riders, seven black and six white, boarded two buses in the nation's capital and set out to test the law. The ultimate destination was New Orleans, where they hoped to arrive on May 17, the anniversary of the *Brown* decision. The trip was uneventful through Virginia and North Carolina, and the bus terminals voluntarily desegregated as the so-called freedom riders arrived. There was a minor altercation in Rock Hill, South Carolina, but then there was clear sailing all the way to Atlanta. There the two buses split up, with the Greyhound bus routed through Anniston, Alabama, and the Trailways through Birmingham.

As the Greyhound pulled into the Anniston terminal, an angry crowd of protesters attacked the bus, slashing at its tires and pummeling it with rocks. The bus pulled away and headed down the road, only to have multiple flat tires a few miles away. When the bus stopped, the mob caught up. Someone threw a fire bomb through a window, and in seconds the bus was aflame. The freedom riders barely escaped in time and were rescued by a car caravan, headed by the Reverend Fred Shuttlesworth, that arrived from Birmingham just in time. When the Trailways bus pulled up to the Birmingham station, all seemed peaceful. In a flash, the scene changed as dozens of thugs and Klansmen came out of nowhere and proceeded to beat the bus riders with a wild vengeance. Newspaper headlines and television images spread the sickening story worldwide, embarrassing the Kennedy administration but not moving them to intervene effectively. The Congress of Racial Equality (CORE), the Chicago-based organization that had sponsored the freedom riders, could not find bus drivers willing to continue the journey, and so the original freedom riders were flown by the Justice Department to New Orleans.

SNCC, fearing the long-term effects of a defeat, found new volunteer riders who were willing to risk their lives for the cause. President Kennedy and his brother Robert, the nation's attorney general, were simultaneously moved and annoyed by the black persistence, but they used their influence to obtain a bus driver and extracted a promise from the Alabama governor, John Patterson, that the freedom riders would not be harmed as they drove from Birmingham to Montgomery. The twenty-one freedom riders noted the police protection as they drove along, but when they neared Montgomery, the protection disappeared. When the riders disembarked at the terminal, a mob crazed with anger attacked the students with frenzied violence. Hundreds of screaming people swarmed around the bus, and even John Seigenthaler, a presidential aide sent to observe, was knocked senseless by a pipe-wielding assailant.

Finally the Kennedys began to realize the gravity of the situation, and the president sent in six hundred federal marshals. When the city threatened to explode in violence the next day, Governor Patterson declared martial law and—with the eyes of the world looking on—employed the National Guard to protect the freedom riders. The Kennedys then arranged for the freedom riders to leave and be allowed to pass peacefully through Mississippi. (By prior arrangement, they were quietly arrested in Jackson, Mississippi, but not assaulted—the best compromise the Kennedys could arrange with Mississippi officials.) The freedom riders had not reached New Orleans, but they had reached the consciences of millions of Americans, and they drove home to the Kennedys the necessity of action by the federal government. By early autumn 1961, the Interstate Commerce Commission ordered the desegregation of all interstate bus facilities.

In retrospect, 1962 seems the lull before the next big storm. Martin Luther King, Jr., had been called in to Albany, Georgia, to help lead a protest, but the wily sheriff there, Laurie Pritchett, also knew about Gandhian protests and understood that police overreaction only brought publicity and helped the blacks' cause. So he devised a policy of passive counter-resistance whereby the protesters were politely treated and jailed without violence. He reserved cells for a hundred miles in each direction so that the protesters could never completely fill the available jail spaces. Pritchett essentially defeated King at his own strategy, and King began 1963 despondent and fearful that the movement was stalled and that he had lost his leadership role.

Events continued to ensnare the Kennedy administration and force it to take an increasingly active role in desegregation. On September 3, 1962, a federal judge ordered the University of Mississippi to enroll James Meredith. The state's governor, Ross Barnett, rose to the occasion to champion again the racist cause. Before a football crowd's chants of "Never, never, never, never ..." he perorated on his love of Mississippi's customs. But by now, President Kennedy was willing to play hardball with the racist demagogues of Dixie. On Sunday evening, September 29, as Meredith arrived at campus, a full-scale riot broke out. In the midst of the chaos, Governor Barnett spoke about the rights of Mississippians being trampled by federal power, but as the destruction, injuries, and then deaths increased, the federal government responded by sending in troops in the early morning hours. An uneasy order was restored, and on Monday morning, protected by federal marshals, James Meredith walked to his first class—American history. Again, the courage of blacks, reinforced however reluctantly by federal power, was successfully challenging segregation in the very heart of Dixie.

Birmingham, a muscular, tough city with the smell of its blast furnaces suggesting the racial hate that smoldered and occasionally erupted into flame, was called the most racist city in America. The Reverend Fred Shuttlesworth had been battling that reputation for years, and now, in early 1963, he was pressuring Martin Luther King, Jr., to come and lead a protest. Shuttlesworth had done the hard preparatory work; it was time for King to lend his charisma. King worried about the city and its notoriously racist police commissioner, Eugene "Bull" Connor. But after the failure in Albany, King needed a success. Bull Connor was exactly the type of arrogant policeman who could be counted on to act outrageously, so outrageously that he would, against his will, both inspire black courage and create international publicity for the cause of integration. With these considerations, King and SCLC planned Project C—*C* standing for *confrontation.*

The campaign began on April 3, as the city government was in turmoil over a recent disputed election. The city council got an injunction to halt the SCLC-sponsored protests, but King ignored the order. On Good Friday, he was arrested and jailed. With time on his hands, and in response to a group of white clergy who objected to his efforts, King sat down over the Easter weekend and penciled around the margins of a newspaper his reply to the white remonstrance. This "Letter from a Birmingham Jail" was an eloquent defense of the religious and moral necessity to work against the racial status quo—"One day the South will recognize its real heroes," King prophesied—and like the Declaration of Independence and Gettysburg Address, the brief essay spoke to the heart of the world. "There comes a time," King concluded, "when the cup of endurance runs over... I hope ... you can understand our legitimate and unavoidable impatience." King was released on bond from jail on April 20 and immediately made preparations to continue Project C. Now a bold new strategy was hatched. One of the factors that crippled mass black protest was the economic coercion the white establishment could wield against black adults. But black school-children did not hold jobs. Did the movement dare to use children as protest marchers? Would Bull Connor be so unyielding as to use violence against helpless children? Would parents consent? Would the children be willing? The answer to all these questions was yes.

The first day, May 2, the police were restrained. But the following day, Bull Connor reverted to form. His policemen tore into the defenseless black children, hitting them with clubs and siccing their vicious German shepherd dogs against the school kids. Black adults rushed to defend their children, and the police went berserk. Connor ordered firemen to turn their fire hoses, with water pressure at one hundred pounds per square inch, against the blacks. The powerful stream of water knocked people down, tore the bark off trees, rolled screaming, terrified children across the ground and over curbs. Three days later it happened again, with more black adults—enraged—participating. Finally, faced with the possibility of genuine race warfare, the city business leaders intervened. The city agreed to desegregate the downtown lunch counters, remove the hated "white" and "colored" signs, and employ more blacks. Racists fumed, but the movement had won another victory.

But the larger victory was not in Birmingham. For millions of Americans, the television images of attack dogs and high-pressure water hoses, employed against small children, became one of the defining moments of the twentieth century. Bull Connor's hateful excesses finally awakened the nation to the cancer in its midst. No longer could decent people pretend things were okay, pretend that blacks would accept their traditional place, pretend that no great moral principles were at stake. Still Alabama continued defiant. Governor George Wallace on June 11, 1963, in response to a court order that the University of Alabama integrate, sought political mileage from the state's white majority by symbolically standing in the doorway to a university building to block the entrance of black students. When faced down by the nation's attorney general, Nicholas Katzenbach, Wallace—by then out of range of the television cameras—stepped aside. Nevertheless, Wallace had solidified his position as a feisty defender of "segregation today, tomorrow, and forever." The next day in Jackson, Mississippi, in a completely unrelated incident, Medgar Evers, field secretary of the NAACP, was murdered on his front doorsteps by an assassin. President Kennedy, forced by this series of intolerable events to enlarge his commitment to civil rights, introduced a strengthened civil rights bill to Congress on June 19.

CIVIL RIGHTS AND VOTING RIGHTS

Capitalizing on the moment, and wanting to keep the pressure on the president and the Congress, A. Philip Randolph, Bayard Rustin, and other race leaders began to plan for a march on Washington to make concrete the demand that justice be done in the South. There was some dissension among various civil rights organizations; recent events had radicalized some for whom the pace of the NAACP and the SCLC seemed too slow and too mild. However, the disagreements were papered over for the sake of the march. On the appointed day, August 28, 1963, upwards of 250,000 marchers—a quarter of them white, and with blacks arriving by bus from all over the nation—came together in the nation's capital. At the biggest protest meeting in American history, thousands listened to the speakers and entertainers, and everywhere the strains of the anthem of the civil rights movement—"We Shall Overcome"—could be heard. The climax of the march, televised throughout the nation, was an extraordinarily powerful oration by Martin Luther King, Jr., at the foot of the Lincoln Memorial. With the moving cadence of the black preacher style, King captivated the audience and the world, concluding with the image of his dream of a nation undivided by race. "And when this happens and when we allow freedom to ring," he said in words that produced goose bumps on listeners, "when we let it ring from every village and every hamlet, from every state and every city, we will be able to speed up that day when all God's children, black men and white men, Jews and gentiles, Protestants and Catholics, will be able to join hands and sing in the words of the old Negro spiritual: 'Free at last. Free at last. Thank God Almighty, we are free at last.'"

Seldom had the nation been so moved by words. Opinion polls showed that a majority of Americans now desired to redress the racial problems. But the heady optimism was quickly brought up short less than three weeks later. On Sunday morning, September 15, a mighty explosion tore through the Sixteenth Street Baptist Church in Birmingham. Buried beneath the rubble were four young black girls, killed by white hate. Kennedy's proposed civil rights bill was soon bogged down in Congress, stymied by a Senate filibuster led by Strom Thurmond—the former Dixiecrat—of South Carolina and James Eastland of Mississippi, the Senate champions of racism. Then the nation was to be stunned again. On November 22, riding in a motorcade in Dallas, Texas, a citadel of right-wing politics, President Kennedy himself was killed by an assassin's bullet. Much of the nation was in mourning as Lyndon B. Johnson, newly sworn in as president, came to Washington and sought to assure a shocked Republic that stability was restored. Johnson went out of his way five days later to say to the nation at a joint session of Congress that the programs and policies of Kennedy would be continued and that nothing would so honor the slain president as the passing of the civil rights bill.

Johnson had begun his political career almost four decades earlier as a racial moderate in central Texas, and although political considerations had caused him to take a conservative detour in the late 1940s and early 1950s, events of the early 1960s recalled him to his original principles. Through the spring and early summer, his civil rights bill was tied up in Congress; despite Johnson's masterful maneuvering, progress was slow in breaking the segregationists' opposition. At a critical juncture the diehard South once again produced an outrageous act that demanded national action. Beginning in 1962 a coalition of civil rights groups—the Council of Federated Organizations (COFO)—had organized to register voters in Mississippi only to be met with unrelenting terroristic violence intended to intimidate them. To dramatize the desire of Mississippi blacks to enjoy an elemental privilege of democracy, COFO arranged a mock election in 1963 in which eighty thousand blacks cast their "Freedom Ballot."

COFO leader Bob Moses also put out a call for northern college students to come to Mississippi and do voter registration during a 1964 "Freedom Summer" campaign, recognizing that the national media would pay more attention to them than to local blacks. Almost on cue, three of the COFO workers disappeared, a local black (James Chaney) and two northern college students (Andrew Goodman and Michael Schwerner), murdered on June 21, 1964, in Neshoba County, Mississippi. An extensive FBI search led, some six weeks later, to the discovery of the bodies in an earthen pond dam near Philadelphia,

Martin Luther King, Jr. (Library of Congress)

Mississippi—the work of the local Klan in collaboration with local law enforcement officers. The abduction and murder of the three civil rights workers provided the immediate background against which, in late June, Lyndon Johnson labored hard to defeat the opponents of the civil rights bill. Finally breakthrough came, the bill passed, and Johnson signed the Civil Rights Act of 1964 on July 2, two days before the national celebration of freedom. The year ended with Martin Luther King, Jr., being awarded the Nobel Peace Prize.

The new year began with King and the SCLC planning a major voter registration drive in Alabama, centering on the notorious region near Selma in Dallas County where almost no blacks were allowed to vote. In February, a black teenager was killed in a racial incident, and King matured plans for a protest march from Selma to Montgomery, the state capital. Sheriff Jim Clark of Dallas County looked like a character from a civil right's worker's nightmare: potbellied, wearing mirrored sunglasses and a short Eisenhower jacket, and walking with a swagger while he tapped his nightstick against his open palm as if itchy to club a black head. On Sunday, March 7, as the black marchers reached the apex of the Edmund Pettus Bridge that crossed the Alabama River at the edge of town, they saw Sheriff Clark's policemen and an army of state troopers. After a momentary warning, the policemen attacked the marchers, swinging their clubs, using electric cattle prods, tear gas, and even flailing the defenseless blacks with short lengths of chains and loops of rubber hose encircled with barbed wire. As the blacks fled back down the bridge and sought refuge in their homes, the policemen followed, continuing their brutal attack. ABC news television cameras were on hand, and suddenly Sunday evening television viewers had ABC break into their feature program of the evening—ironically, the movie *Judgment at Nuremberg*—to broadcast live shots of the carnage at Selma. Again, the conscience of the nation was shocked by the violence meted out to citizens in a southern state.

Two days later, before King could reorganize a full-scale march, Lyndon Johnson worked out a compromise whereby King—much to his chagrin—would only symbolically cross the bridge and then turn around and return to Selma. But Johnson's response did not stop there. Six days later, on March 15, he made a rare presidential address to a joint session of Congress. To the members of Congress, and to a national television office, he gave the most impassioned and eloquent speech of his career. Making vivid reference to the brutality against blacks in the last ten days, Johnson in his slow Texas accent told the nation: "Their cause must be our cause too. Because it is not just Negroes, but really it is all of us who must overcome the crippling legacy of bigotry and injustice. And we shall overcome." He sent his voting rights bill to Congress two days later. Then Johnson notified Alabama governor Wallace that the state's national guard would be federalized to protect the marchers. Later, augmented by volunteers from around the nation, twenty-five thousand marchers walked across the bridge named for a Confederate general through central Alabama to the steps of the state capital, from which Jefferson Davis had taken the oath of office as president of the Confederacy on February 18, 1861. There, on March 25, 1965, joined by such heroes of the movement as Rosa Parks, Martin Luther King, Jr., addressed the crowd and the nation by television. Back in

Washington, Johnson continued his efforts and on August 6 signed the Voting Rights Act of 1965. The great ship of southern race relations had finally been slowed and turned. The South would never be the same again.

Of course, the victory was neither instantaneous nor complete. Thereafter in hundreds of different places and at a variety of paces, the dead hand of the past was gradually lifted from the South. Residential segregation and the concept of neighborhood schools eventually made total integration practically impossible in the South's cities; ironically many of the smaller towns, which could support only one school, more nearly achieved complete integration. The South's private universities, on occasion, found the transition more complicated than did state universities. One, Rice University, actually had to sue the state in 1963 to have its 1891 charter of incorporation revised to allow it to integrate. And there were occasional backwater counties (McIntosh in Georgia and the notorious Delta region of Mississippi) where integration's arrival was delayed a decade. But throughout most of the South, the changes at last came so quickly as to belie the vehemence with which they had been opposed.

Title VII of the Civil Rights Act of 1964 forbid discrimination in employment with regard to pay, hiring, or promotion, and the act created the Equal Employment Opportunity Commission (EEOC) to enforce compliance. Over the next decade or more thousands of blacks used the EEOC and the new law of the land to attack decades-old patterns of job discrimination of all sorts—including the pernicious practice of only hiring blacks for the least skilled, lowest paying jobs. One effect, for example, was a huge increase in the number of blacks working and having better jobs in the textile industry, the largest employer in the South. In some ways concerning economic discrimination, the Civil Rights Act of 1964 began the civil rights movement rather than concluded it.

The changes were more far-reaching than merely a revision of laws. Black people found a new self-respect, a sense of importance and worth, that had not always been possible in a segregated society. This feeling of respect often led them to embrace political participation. Blacks were organizing, winning political office at the local level (and higher), and serving on boards and commissions. The civil rights breakthrough of 1964 and 1965 had emboldened blacks to step forward and seize political and economic opportunities that had been nonexistent several years before. By the early 1970s, for example, Mississippi had more black elected officials than any other state. And in 1993, 69 percent of the nation's black elected officials were from the South. Throughout the South, blacks found jobs as clerks, secretaries, and in low-level management; they could sit in restaurant dining rooms and attend movies and concerts; and their children could become Boy Scouts and Girl Scouts and participate on school athletic teams. And once blacks voted in substantial numbers, white politicians—even notorious racists like George Wallace and Strom Thurmond, both of whom certainly knew how to count votes—learned to moderate their policies, address at least some black concerns, and hire black assistants. In truth, in fundamental ways, a New South had arisen from the ashes of banished legal racism.

Yet the hopes awakened in the early 1970s have been only imperfectly realized. While many remarkable successes have been achieved in integrating southern life and society, unanticipated developments have once again made the historical outcome problematic. Very significant numbers of urban whites have fled to the suburbs seeking larger homes, bigger yards, better schools, less crime, and fewer blacks. The center-city populations of most southern cities have declined (as have those of the North) along with the tax base and general economic prospects. The resulting downward spiral of weakening schools, failing infrastructure, and increasing crime has worsened living conditions for many of the region's poorest blacks, which has only further accelerated white flight, undermined majority white support of government assistance and reform programs, and contributed to the resegregation of southern cities by class as much as by race. The black ghettoes in most large cities of today are much less supportive communities than were the black ghettoes of the early twentieth century, where there were usually at least some positive middle-class role models present and job opportunities. No solutions for the plight of the black underclass seemed politically feasible in the final decade of the century.

Small southern cities and towns, not large enough for substantial suburbs and multiple high schools, have more successfully weathered the desegregation storms and emerged as the best integrated areas of the South. Yet amidst this paradox of ugly urban ghettoes and systematic resegregation, every southern city also has growing minorities of well-educated, upwardly mobile black professionals and middle-class workers who live in integrated neighborhoods, send their children to integrated public schools, and move freely and easily in the affluent, comparatively cosmopolitan world of the modern South. And yet again there are pockets of rural black poverty in the region that remind one of the Third World. The gap between prosperous and poor blacks is widening.

Most southern whites today see racism as essentially a thing of the past, but most blacks experience it as still present and something extra that blacks must strive to overcome. Subtle racism clearly still exists, and even affluent, educated blacks often find it difficult to obtain loans, rent apartments, win promotions, or receive the respect they've earned. Conservative whites increasingly think special government programs for blacks are no longer needed, while most blacks see government as the primary and still necessary benefactor of their people. Suspicions between the two races appear to be on the rise as the new century begins, in part fueled by widespread attacks (some by blacks themselves) on affirmative action programs and increasingly regressive tax policies. Many blacks fear that the gains of the past generation will be rolled back. Sadly, in 2003 southern schools are becoming increasingly segregated. These differences in perception, these conflicts, these reversals of former progress, sharpened political debate in the years following 1980 and again after the election

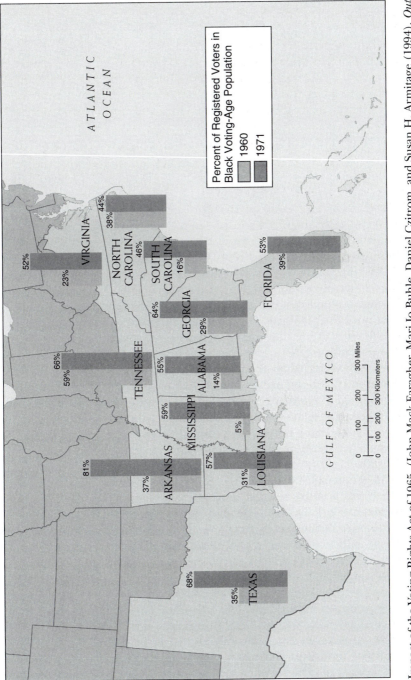

Impact of the Voting Rights Act of 1965. (John Mack Faragher, Mari Jo Buhle, Daniel Czitrom, and Susan H. Armitage (1994). *Out of Many: A History of the American People.* Upper Saddle River, New Jersey, Prentice Hall.)

of 2000. Between these two versions of reality lie the hard business of determining the domestic political agenda of the South in the future. Short of achieving a utopian New South, how does a society reconcile such incongruous understandings or cope humanely with such diversity, economic disparity, and unequal social outcomes? The nation's experiment with liberty, of which Abraham Lincoln spoke so nobly at Gettysburg in 1863, remains open-ended. But the future seems less hopeful in 2003 than it did in the 1960s.

THE SOLID DEMOCRATIC SOUTH AND SEGREGATION

The vital political role of southern blacks in the 1970s and the election in 1976 of Jimmy Carter from the deep South to the presidency suggest something of the changed nature of politics in the region since World War II, but perhaps the popularity in Louisiana of David Duke in 1991 cautions southerners from too quickly assuming that the old racial ghosts have been completely banished. The Democratic Solid South of the 1920s and 1930s was replaced with a Republican Solid South in the 1970s and 1980s, unless extraordinary events intervened—as they did in 1976 in the aftermath of the Watergate scandal and the presence on the Democratic ticket of a born-again candidate from Georgia. However, until the 1990s the Republican dominance obtained only for presidential elections; at the state and local level, a surprising degree of biracial cooperation continued the supremacy of the Democratic party—albeit a very different Democratic party from that of 1940. Along with the newfound regional prosperity and the breakdown of the worst vestiges of racial segregation, post–World War II southern politics completes the triad of change that has largely remade the recent South. As so often in American history, southern issues have had a major impact on national politics—largely causing the Republican party to reshape itself over the last generation.

To a dismayingly large degree, the primary purpose of Democratic party politics in the decades before World War II was to maintain the racial status quo. The Republican party was effectively nonexistent in most of the region, and one of the South's defenses of one-party politics was that it allowed, through the congressional seniority system, disproportionate southern power in Congress—power especially to protect regional racial mores. Even so masterful a political operator as Franklin D. Roosevelt felt constrained to acquiesce to southern racial feelings lest his programs in Congress be blocked. Likewise, through the requirement in the Democratic party that nominees at its quadrennial conventions receive a two-thirds vote for nomination, the southern Democrats normally had the power to prevent the nomination of presidential candidates whom they considered especially unfriendly.

The first indication that the national Democratic party would in the future not be so cozy with the conservative forces in Dixie came in the midst of the New Deal. The southern politicos were receiving the programmatic benefits of Roosevelt's administration and felt comfortable with their influence. They were caught unaware at the 1936 Democratic convention when, by voice vote, the delegates adopted a simple majority vote rule. Diehard southern states' rightists were alarmed, and more so in the later years of the New Deal as Roosevelt's relief programs began to threaten local control. Moreover, increasing support by northern labor unions and urban blacks made Roosevelt less beholden to the votes of southern Democrats. Southern politicians, now alert to the slightest indication that their power in national political circles was diminishing, began to be more critical of Roosevelt and his New Deal reforms. But the specter and then the reality of war delayed a significant southern revolt against the national party in 1940 and 1944.

As we have already seen, political pressure and increasing sensitivity to the nation's racial problems—magnified in the midst of a war against Nazi ideas about racial superiority—brought home not simply to American blacks but to national politicians the necessity of redressing the worst abuses of the Jim Crow system. Harry S Truman had become president in 1945 following Roosevelt's death, and the man from Missouri surprised black leaders by showing a depth of humanity and an ability to change his attitudes toward black rights. His appointment of a Committee on Civil Rights and his issuance of presidential proclamations desegregating the armed forces and providing for fair employment practices in the federal government were the last straw for many southern Democratic segregationists. After Truman had called for "effective federal action" against discrimination in his 1948 State of the Union address, southern party leaders seethed.

Truman understood that he faced a difficult election in 1948, and he momentarily hesitated to risk a break with the southerners, but when advisors—incorrectly as it turned out—told him he could push forward against segregation without losing the support of southern Democratic leaders, Truman moved ahead boldly. Pushed by the liberal Americans for Democratic Action and such senators as Hubert Humphrey from Minnesota, the Democratic party became the champion of civil rights. As angry southern delegates were outvoted time and again at the 1948 convention, a strong civil rights plank was accepted. Although Texas congressman Sam Rayburn, the presiding officer, tried to prevent a wholesale southern walkout, in the end some thirty-six southern delegates—13 percent of the southerners present—did bolt. Nevertheless, the national Democratic party and its president were on record as favoring significant action to reform the nation's racial practices.

Three days after the Democratic convention, six thousand southern white Democrats gathered in Birmingham, organized the States' Rights party (popularly known as the Dixiecrats), nominated Governor Strom Thurmond of South Carolina as its presidential candidate and Governor Fielding Wright of Mississippi as its vice-presidential candidate, and mounted a forthrightly racist campaign to preserve every last vestige of segregation against what they termed a Communist-integrationist onslaught. In the deep South states of South Carolina, Alabama, Mississippi, and Louisiana, whites cast the overwhelming majority of their votes for this party of the past, but in the South as a whole, Truman won almost eight out of ten votes and upset Thomas Dewey to win the presidency in his own right. But the future was foretold: Southern whites, especially in states where blacks were most numerous, would break with their traditional party over the race issue. In what might be called the peripheral or rim South, many whites still voted for the Democrats as much by habit as by conviction, but a crack had been made in the wall of the Solid South, and that fissure would widen until the wall collapsed in the aftermath of the civil rights advances of the 1960s. Race would be the key to the rise of the Republican party in the South.

Actually, southern Democratic committee chairmen still had inordinate power in Congress, and for that reason among other concerns that occupied him—such as the rising tensions in the Cold War—Truman did not seek a full-scale legislative attack on segregation. In fact, for a decade the major battles would take place in federal courts, and race receded somewhat as the paramount issue in presidential politics, in part also because national Republicans were not yet noticeably less supportive of civil rights than Democrats were. The saliency of the issue remained, however, as illustrated by the upset defeats of Claude Pepper of Florida and Frank Graham of North Carolina in the senatorial elections of 1950. Graham's defeat in the Democratic primary was particularly prescient of the future campaigns against liberal Democrats: a vicious racist attack, orchestrated by a staff that included a young journalist named Jesse Helms, depicted Graham (a bungling campaigner in the best of circumstances) as an ultraliberal whose values threatened the white South's way of life, which, it was argued, was already under siege by Communists whose ultimate aim was the mongrelization of the white population of Dixie.

But at the presidential level, the Republicans rejected the more conservative candidate, Senator Robert A. Taft of Ohio, who opposed federal fair employment and school desegregation efforts, and chose instead war hero Dwight D. Eisenhower. Two southern Democrats, senators Richard B. Russell of Georgia and Estes Kefauver of Tennessee, made a run for the nomination. Kefauver's personable campaign style won considerable success in several early primary states, and he entered the Democratic convention with more delegate strength than any other candidate. But the moderate from Tennessee lost on the third ballot to the more liberal and more eloquent Governor Adlai Stevenson of Illinois. Many southerners who had become increasingly disenchanted with the national Democratic party, yet bound by tradition to the Democrats, found in General Eisenhower an authentic hero who made switching parties at the presidential level palatable. He was the first Republican presidential candidate ever to campaign actively in the South. In the fall 1952 elections, Ike won 50 percent of the southern white vote and carried the peripheral states of Virginia, Florida, Texas, Oklahoma, and Tennessee. In a number of states, "Democrats for Eisenhower" movements represented a kind of political halfway house for those who were moving away from the governmental activism of the Democratic party but were not yet ready to quit the party of their fathers.

Eisenhower was a cautious leader in domestic affairs, and he firmly believed that states, not the federal government, should somehow ultimately handle social matters like school desegregation. Nevertheless, Ike believed even more strongly in his responsibility to enforce the law as defined by the Supreme Court. Because the Court had decreed in 1954 that segregated education was inherently unequal, and although he probably regretted the issue having been thus made a concern of the federal government, when the crisis came in Little Rock, the former general sent in troops to defend the law of the land. Needless to say, many southern whites felt betrayed. Still, much that Eisenhower stood for—strong defense, limited government, a modified conception of states' rights—appealed to white southerners, and most felt that, the appointment of Chief Justice Earl Warren notwithstanding, Ike was less aggressive on desegregation than any national Democratic president would be. When the national Democrats in 1956 once more put Stevenson up against Eisenhower, Ike swept to an easy victory, winning 53 percent of the South's electoral votes and adding Louisiana to the five southern states that he had carried in 1952.

Despite these Grand Old Party (GOP) victories in the presidential balloting, at the local level the South's politics remained overwhelmingly Democratic. As late as 1960 the Republicans held only forty-eight seats in the South's lower houses (out of more than thirteen hundred) and twelve seats in the upper houses (out of about 450 total). In hundreds of rural counties, there were no Republican candidates, no party tickets, no party organization. In the affluent suburbs of the larger cities, there were tiny organizations, but these were far more conservative and rabidly anticommunist than the national Republican party. Some of these southern GOP organizations were hotbeds of activity on behalf of paranoid radical-right groups, such as the Christian Anti-Communist Crusade and the John Birch Society, whose founder Robert A. Welch called even Eisenhower a dupe of the Communist conspiracy. At the local level, the Republicans were not a factor in southern politics, and most southern racists found state Democratic leaders such as Orval Faubus, John Patterson, Ross Barnett, Strom Thurmond (who had returned to the party after the failure of the Dixiecrats), and senators such as John Eastland and Herman Talmadge to be the leaders of their cause. Particularly after President Eisenhower's sending of troops to Little Rock in 1957, southern segregationists turned increasingly to homegrown Democratic racists to protect the so-called southern way of life.

CHAPTER 30

The Rise of
the Republican Party

THE PARTIES SWITCH ON THE ISSUE OF RACE

Precisely because at the national level both political parties seemed mildly progressive on racial issues, neither party had an automatic advantage in the South in 1960. Although Vice President Richard Nixon, the Republican candidate in 1960, did not possess the personal charisma that Eisenhower had, Ike had shown southerners that they could vote Republican and not have to hide their faces. But southern conservatives were still angry about the Little Rock intervention and were uncertain that a GOP vote was necessarily a defense of segregation. At the same time, the head of the Democratic ticket, Senator John F. Kennedy, a Roman Catholic from Massachusetts, raised religious issues that he only partially settled at a skillful meeting with Baptist ministers in Houston. Kennedy, wary of losing the South, had chosen Lyndon B. Johnson of Texas as his vice-presidential candidate. Still, many southern segregationists, remembering LBJ's support of the 1957 Civil Rights Act and his lack of support for the 1956 Southern Manifesto that defended states' rights principles, were lukewarm toward the colorful Texan because they felt he had betrayed the South. Nevertheless, Kennedy had telegenic charisma in abundance, and Johnson proved to be a skillful campaigner in the South. Nixon himself had long supported civil rights, and though he carefully positioned himself slightly to the right of the Democrats in 1960, such positioning did not allow him to increase the GOP share of the southern white vote. On the other hand, LBJ's residual southernness appealed to even conservative southerners, while Kennedy's telephone call to offer sympathy to Coretta Scott King when her husband, Martin Luther, was in jail, won Kennedy a substantial majority of the votes of the relatively few southern blacks who could vote (and of course it galvanized the many northern blacks in support of the Democrats). The result of these conflicting factors was a razor-thin Democratic victory in the South and in the nation. Thanks largely to the presence of LBJ on the ticket, Kennedy reversed the last two elections and won the majority of white southern voters. Together the Kennedy-Johnson ticket carried South Carolina, Georgia, Alabama, and Louisiana in the deep South, and Texas, North Carolina, and Arkansas in the peripheral South. Nixon, however, did win Virginia and Florida, two states with significant in-migration of northerners who had traditionally supported the GOP, and Tennessee, whose strong base of mountain Republicanism stretched back to the Civil War.

The popular election in the South was much closer than the Democratic tally of electoral votes indicated, and Republican strength in Virginia and Florida suggested that population growth and emergent prosperity could vastly enlarge the GOP base in southern states beyond the small group of right-wing radicals who had dominated the party in the 1950s. The concept of the Sun Belt was unknown in the early 1960s, but already in the growing suburbs of Atlanta, Charlotte, Nashville, Dallas, New Orleans, and Houston there were increasing numbers of middle-class, professional voters who identified with the national Republican party in its opposition to what was called "big government." Thousands of these new suburban southerners were recent migrants from the North, lifelong Republicans with no regional devotion to the Democratic party.

An entire constellation of values associated with the GOP had first arisen in opposition to the New Deal, and newly prosperous white southerners, no longer seeing themselves or their relatives as benefiting from government relief programs, came to identify with the conservative Republican agenda. Central to this agenda was opposition to taxes, opposition to federal government involvement in any local matters, a strong belief that the least government was the best—indeed, that government was the enemy of freedom and prosperity—and a patriotic defense of a strong military establishment. Race per se was seldom mentioned as a central issue, although calls for less government intervention indirectly attacked the only agency that seemed to advance black interests in the South. Vicious race-baiting was not a characteristic of this country-club Republicanism. The powerful rural Democratic domination of southern state politics had long thwarted the development of the suburb-based Republican party in the region by rendering urban districts politically impotent, but the Supreme Court's one man, one vote decision in *Baker v. Carr* in 1962, amplified by a series of like decisions (*Gray v. Sanders* in 1963, *Reynolds v. Sims* in 1964, and *Drum v. Seawell* in 1966), brought about a very significant reapportionment. This resulted in a redistribution of political power in the South, essentially enfranchising the cities and suburbs and providing a window of opportunity for southern Republicans. This potential for growth also meant that the Republican party in the South could move beyond advocacy of extremist policies to join the national party ideologically. Ironically this occurred at the very moment when the national party itself moved away from moderation. As its 1964 standard bearer would say, "Extremism in the defense of liberty is no vice."

The national Democratic party was more publicly identified with support for civil rights than the Republican party was, but President Kennedy had little interest in and less passion for the issue. Yet, his administration found itself preoccupied with civil rights because southern blacks had made their cause a folk movement and forced the nation to face southern segregation squarely. The sit-ins, the freedom rides, the fire hoses of Bull Connor in Birmingham, and the deaths of Medgar Evers and the four little girls in the church bombing pricked the nation's conscience. President Kennedy, Attorney General Robert Kennedy, and the administration were thereby forced to get involved. Their nemesis, Governor George C. Wallace of Alabama, became nationally prominent as a vocal opponent of integration and helped politicize the issue. Civil rights pushed Cold War concerns aside to become the defining issue of the day, and in the very midst of these troubled times, as President Kennedy traveled to Texas in part at least hoping to temper conservative Democratic opposition to his policies, Lee Harvey Oswald shot and killed the president as he rode in a motorcade through the streets of Dallas on November 22, 1963. Later that day, Vice President Lyndon B. Johnson took the oath of office in Air Force One, the presidential jet, and became the nation's president at a moment of great tragedy.

Johnson was an enormously complex man, simultaneously power hungry, crass, and egocentric, yet caring deeply for the poor and oppressed. He wanted to outdo his hero Franklin D. Roosevelt in improving the life of the average people and wanted to show the northeastern provincials—by whom he had long felt patronized—that he could push programs through a Congress that had completely bottled up Kennedy's proposals. In part, too, Johnson wanted to save the South from its most besetting sins so that it could more completely join the rest of the nation. Johnson was often vulgar and self-indulgent and occasionally corrupt, but he identified with the lowly in American society who had been denied justice, and he immediately sensed that this moment of tragedy could be in part redeemed by passing landmark legislation. The most urgent social problem was racial discrimination. Johnson took advantage of the emotional intensity and mood of national introspection following Kennedy's assassination to break the congressional logjam over civil rights legislation. With surprising eloquence and typical legislative skill, putting together a bipartisan, multisectional coalition and winning the cooperation of Republican Senator Everett Dirksen of Illinois, LBJ in the year following his abrupt ascendancy to the Oval Office pushed through not only the Civil Rights Act of 1964 but the greatest amount of progressive social legislation in the nation's history. His Great Society program represented the logical fulfillment of Roosevelt's New Deal, and from

Head Start and Medicare to the National Endowment for the Humanities, LBJ reshaped American society. The role of the national government had never been larger, its commitment to racial and economic justice had never been stronger.

Not everyone approved of the direction the national government had taken. George Wallace began campaigning in January 1964 in opposition to the expanding role of the government, particularly in the realm of civil rights, and he took his message to the North and border states with considerable success. Wallace was clear in his aims: He was running to force the national Democratic party to shift back to the right. But just before the Democratic convention, anticipating Barry Goldwater's nomination by the Republicans, Wallace withdrew from the race. Johnson automatically won renomination along with Hubert Humphrey of Minnesota as his running mate. No major party figure had a longer or more forthright identification with integration than Humphrey, who had led the fight for the civil rights plank at the 1948 convention. If the Democratic convention was unambiguously for civil rights, the Republican convention rejected the tide of racial reform. Party conservatives, increasingly from the West and the South, defeated the more moderate northeastern faction of the party and nominated the conservative movement's hero, Senator Goldwater of Arizona, for president, along with a little-known New York congressman, William E. Miller, as the vice-presidential candidate. Goldwater was honest, outspoken, suspicious of the urban Northeast, a rugged individualist, and personally not a racist, but he was a tenacious opponent of the Civil Rights Act of 1964 and a strict states' rightist. In the early part of the campaign, Strom Thurmond switched his party allegiance to the GOP and traveled throughout the South speaking on Goldwater's behalf. Goldwater also had a penchant for off-the-cuff militaristic statements, so the national Democratic campaign strategy capitalized on fears that a Goldwater victory would lead to nuclear holocaust. But in the South, the overriding issue was race.

All the southern white opposition to civil rights and federal government intervention and increasing black militancy in the South welled up in support of Barry Goldwater. Johnson had said when the Civil Rights Act had passed that "I think we just delivered the South to the Republican party for a long time to come," and as far as white voters are concerned he was correct. Nevertheless, Johnson did not back away from his support of civil rights even when campaigning in the South, and Goldwater and his supporters made the issue their cause, too, openly campaigning against government-mandated integration. Segregationist Democrats, the ones who normally supported Wallace and Thurmond, switched by the droves to Goldwater. This proved to be a transitional election for the southern GOP, and Goldwater's primary appeal was to racially conservative whites. He did best in those states and regions of states with the highest percentage of blacks, winning, for example, 91 percent of the white vote in Mississippi. Goldwater's greatest appeal was to former Democrats who had rejected their party's stand on civil rights. No longer was the Republican party strongest in the peripheral states and among affluent suburbs. In fact, Goldwater did less well in those regions where Eisenhower and Nixon had done best. The Republican party had in effect rejected the heritage of Lincoln and dismissed the aspirations of southern blacks for equal treatment. In the deep South, the new Republican ascendancy was clearly based on opposition to racial change first and on traditional GOP economic issues second. Goldwater carried only his home state of Arizona and the five deep South states: South Carolina, Georgia, Alabama, Mississippi, and Louisiana. Johnson won the election in a landslide and received practically every vote cast by a black, but in the South as a whole, Goldwater won 55 percent of the white vote. Those returns would suggest future political strategies for both parties. Cast in the mold of Goldwater rather than Lincoln, the GOP had changed and thereby redefined itself to gain the support of white southerners.

Goldwater was too inept a campaigner, and the Johnson electoral victory too overwhelming, to allow the 1964 election to be called a true realignment election that positioned the Republican party as the dominant party in the South. But the GOP was positioned to gain dominance as the party of white protest in the South. This protest was directly proportional to the national Democratic party's continuing support of civil rights, including the Voting Rights Act of 1965 and the Open Housing Act of 1968. A series of massive urban riots, beginning in the Watts section of Los Angeles in 1965 and erupting in Detroit, Baltimore, Washington, D.C., and other cities, frightened many Americans, including those who had been heartened by the civil rights advances of the early 1960s. The rise of the black power movement, the assassination of Martin Luther King, Jr., in March 1968 and then Robert Kennedy in June of that year, the increasing opposition and divisiveness of the war in Vietnam, especially after the Tet offensive by the enemy forces in early 1968 revealed that—Pentagon reports to the contrary—the war was not going well from the American point of view, all made the election year of 1968 chaotic. Senator Eugene McCarthy of Minnesota was mounting a movement against LBJ and the American presence in Vietnam, and Johnson, discouraged about criticism of his war policies and also worried about a second heart attack, announced on March 31, 1968, that he would not run for reelection. Not since the Civil War had American society been so rent by racial, political, and cultural divisions.

THE NEW POLITICS OF RACE

George Wallace, who had stepped aside for Goldwater in 1964, now mounted a national campaign against what he and many conservatives saw as military spinelessness in much of America and racial meddling in Washington. An articulate, capable campaigner with a knack for mobilizing white supporters who felt unfairly taxed by the federal government and discriminated against in favor of blacks, Wallace carried white southern opposition to civil rights to the North. He shocked liberal media commentators by his appeal in states like Illinois, Michigan, and Wisconsin. Attacking federal bureaucrats, "pointy headed intellectuals," and student antiwar demonstrators, Wallace's angry campaign proved to be the most potent third-party protest in over half a century. For years Democrats had fired up their lower- and middle-class supporters by attacking Republican plutocrats; now Wallace was mobilizing these same voters by attacking "elitist" Democratic bureaucrats. Wallace's angry diatribes against liberals, the press, student activists, black leaders, and government workers were laced with contempt and sarcasm, and Wallace found a ready audience among whites who felt that somehow life had treated them unfairly and considered themselves powerless. His success showed how fluid American public opinion was in 1968 and revealed seething economic and class tensions.

The Democratic party was itself very conflicted that year. Johnson had assumed that Vice President Humphrey would be the nominee and would continue Johnson's policies, but Vietnam now so dominated Johnson's agenda that his Great Society reforms seemed in the remote past. In 1967 and early 1968, McCarthy and then Robert Kennedy had conducted major challenges to Humphrey, and the Democratic convention in Chicago that summer turned into a bloody riot. Humphrey won the nomination, and with his running mate Senator Edmund Muskie from Maine, emerged from the convention to face a nation that seemed to be coming unraveled. Following Johnson's landslide victory only four years earlier, the Democrats had seemed invincible; now they were threatened on the right by George Wallace and his fellow racial reactionaries and on the left by uncompromising antiwar radicals. And, rising like a phoenix from the ashes of 1964 was the Republican party and, even more phoenix-like following his devastating California gubernatorial defeat in 1962, former Vice President Richard M. Nixon. Nixon adopted a "southern strategy" that made the South the GOP stronghold and the 1968 election a true watershed event in recent southern politics.

The political turmoil of the previous four years, and white southerners' identification of the Democratic party with racial change, had led to a marked increase in the vitality of the Republican party in local politics. In state after state, especially in the rapidly growing suburbs, the GOP was emerging as an effective competitor to traditional Democratic dominance, and the emerging GOP was far more mainstream than the 1950s brand of southern extremism. Republican John Tower had won a special election in Texas in 1961 to replace Johnson in the Senate, and Tower was the first Republican senator elected in the South since Reconstruction. Tower was on the right edge of the party and opposed all civil rights legislation, but he was no John Bircher. In the later 1960s, Republicans began to win scattered state and local contests in the South. Nixon and his strategists, such as Harry S. Dent, saw the potential for growth of a conservative but mainstream Republican party in Dixie.

Nixon and Dent understood that the white racial extremists would support Wallace, but more moderate whites who nevertheless wanted to slow the pace of racial change could be appealed to without losing all northern support. Carefully chosen code words substituted for blatant racism but suggested much the same sentiment. Nixon and the GOP learned to announce support for racial equality in abstract terms but oppose governmental policies aimed at achieving that result. Many whites were upset at what was called reverse discrimination and government "give-away" programs that redistributed tax revenues and government benefits downward. Policies that had begun as an attempt to address unfairness in the economic and legal spheres were now themselves under attack for being unfair. Lower- and middle-class whites often felt that the real costs of what was called "social engineering" fell on them; in their language, money was taken from those who worked and given to those who did not. Skilled politicians were quick to seize that anger and make it a potent campaign issue.

Moreover, Nixon's substantial experience in foreign affairs saved him from being compared with the reckless militarism widely associated with Goldwater. In addition, Nixon's vice-presidential years and his identification with traditional pro-business economic conservatism made him acceptable to the kinds of northern mainstream Republicans who had migrated to the increasingly prosperous South. Nixon carefully sized up his niche: appeal to affluent, suburban southerners, position himself slightly to the right of Humphrey on foreign policy issues and slightly to the left of Wallace on racial issues, and bank on the fears of social chaos in a year of rioting and assassination to win mainstream conservative support. After all, Nixon had lost in California in 1962 and, though now living in New York but clearly not representative of the moderate Republicanism represented by Governor Nelson Rockefeller of New York, Nixon had no natural political base in the Empire State. Nixon had to create one for himself among the whites of the South. In effect, the white South would shape Nixon's new version of the Republican party.

The 1968 election was extremely close, with Wallace winning 40 percent of the southern white vote overall, but less than a third in the peripheral South, where Nixon received 45 percent of the white vote. Humphrey did not lead in the white vote in a single southern state, although the growing southern black vote went almost entirely for him. In the last days of the election, northern labor and the liberal vote swung heavily for Humphrey, but he carried only Texas in the South. Wallace won Arkansas, Louisiana, Mississippi, Alabama, and Georgia. Nixon's shrewd southern strategy enabled him to win Florida, South Carolina, North Carolina, Virginia, and Tennessee, and with those southern votes, Nixon squeaked through to win the presidency with a solid electoral majority but with only a seven-tenths of 1 percent advantage in the popular vote. The Democrats had won just one southern state, Texas, partly a sentimental vote for retiring president Johnson.

As president, Nixon nurtured his southern strategy, backpedaling from his comparative racial liberalism of the 1950s and early 1960s. The result was a skillful campaign that capitalized on the racial backlash and fear of change rampant among southern whites in particular. Nixon disavowed busing to achieve school integration, slowed the Justice Department's efforts on behalf of integration, nominated three "strict construction" southern justices for the U.S. Supreme Court (only one of whom was approved by the Senate), advocated "law and order" policies, and supported traditional GOP economic issues to firm up his appeal to conservatives nationally. Seldom was explicitly racist language used; instead, a subtle new political vocabulary of code words and abstractions spoke to the old concerns, but in a way that did not embarrass better educated, more affluent southerners. Nixon consistently defended the principle of equal opportunity as he opposed so-called quotas and affirmative action. In effect, a new kind of conservative populism had emerged that, on the basis of opposition to special privileges for some, attacked government programs on behalf of minorities. With Nixon in the White House, the GOP began to replace the Democratic party as the local preserve of whites in much of the South. Republicans now regularly won elections as state legislators, governors, even congressmen and senators. Many of these were essentially mainstream national Republicans, like senators Howard Baker and W. E. Brock; others, like Jesse Helms, represented the far-right-end of the GOP's political spectrum. Much of the South in the 1970s experienced true two-party politics for the first time since before the Civil War.

The rise of local, respectable Republican party organizations in the South was not the only significant political change in the South. The southern Democratic party became more liberal and more similar to the national Democratic party partly as a result of the rise of southern Republicanism. Angry at the liberalism of the national Democrats, the most conservative southern Democrats began to leave the party of their fathers and join the GOP, which was seen now as far more supportive of what was euphemistically called "the southern way." This tendency reached floodtide in 1972 when the Democrats nominated its most liberal candidate in decades, Senator George McGovern of South Dakota, whom southern conservatives pilloried as unpatriotic, fiscally irresponsible, and pro-drugs (the drug culture was widely associated with everything bad in the late 1960s and early 1970s). The southern Democratic party was liberalized by the departure of its most conservative members and transformed by the Voting Rights Act of 1965 and a massive campaign by various civil rights groups to register black voters. The ratification of the Twenty-Fourth Amendment in 1964, prohibiting the imposition of a poll tax for presidential elections, and the extension of that prohibition to all elections by the Supreme Court in 1966 had made the fundamental democratic act of voting accessible even to the poorest of southerners. By 1972, more than 3.5 million southern blacks were registered to vote, and their vote was almost entirely Democratic.

A whole new group of southern white politicians understood the changed nature of the southern electorate and began to put together coalitions of moderate white and liberal black voters, realizing that such coalitions could often defeat the almost all-white conservative support of the southern GOP candidates. Large numbers of local black officeholders emerged too, though mainly in counties or urban precincts that were heavily black. The result was a new kind of two-party politics at the state and local levels in the South: economically and racial conservative Republicans and socially and racially liberal or moderate Democrats who still were quite conservative on fiscal issues. Nevertheless, though coalition-building could result in the election of Democrats at the state and district level, the GOP emerged as the dominant party in southern political elections. The election year of 1972 made that point emphatically.

The Republican ticket in 1972 was headed by President Nixon and his tough-talking vice president, Spiro Agnew of Maryland, who had become the bête noire of Democrats because of his spirited attacks on liberals, intellectuals, college radicals, and protesters against the Vietnam war. Republican strategy was in large part following the guidelines established by Kevin Phillips, who had written *The Emerging Republican Majority* in 1969. Phillips had argued convincingly that the GOP could replace the Democratic party as the permanent majority party by linking national economic and cultural conservatives with the racial conservatives of the South. That is, if Nixon could capture the Wallace supporters and add them to more traditional, mainstream Republican voters, then the Republicans could expect to control the presidency for a generation. Nixon and Agnew pursued policies that were intended to polarize the American public on the cutting issues of the day: school busing to achieve integration, affirmative action and set-aside programs, the Vietnam war, and amnesty for those who evaded the military draft. Also appealing to conservative voters, George Wallace ran for the presidency in 1972. He was willing to speak more bluntly than even Vice President Agnew, and Wallace had every intention of running a national campaign, less to win the presidency than to move both major parties significantly to the right. A string of stunning primary victories in early 1972 showed that Wallace, a feisty and effective politician, was not merely a regional candidate. Then the entire presidential campaign was turned upside down when Arthur Bremer, a demented would-be assassin, shot and wounded Wallace on May 15 while he was campaigning in the parking lot of a suburban Maryland shopping center. Wallace had to withdraw from the election and was left paralyzed for life. With Wallace out of the race, the conservative vote was Nixon's for the taking. The Democrats by their choice of the very liberal George McGovern as the party's nominee effectively stampeded the conservative vote to Nixon.

What happened to the Democrats in 1972 can only be understood if the historical context is kept in mind. The national Democratic party, and especially its nominating convention, had been transformed since the mid-1960s—

a transformation that severely alienated conservative southern white Democrats and caused many of them to leave the party and join the Republicans. Eight years earlier at the 1964 convention, LBJ had hoped to avoid all controversy because he was trying to maintain the broad coalition that he had put together to pass the Civil Rights Act a few weeks earlier. Johnson had other progressive legislation in the hopper and did not want to risk alienating any possible congressional supporters. But a group of black activists from Mississippi felt conditions back home were simply too offensive to be swept under the rug of political coalition-building. The Council of Federated Organizations, or COFO, had developed in 1962 a concerted plan to register black voters in Mississippi, and the violence and corruption that they fought against had emboldened, not disheartened them. In 1963, they had held a mock "Freedom Election" to demonstrate the black hunger for the franchise, and in 1964, they had created the Mississippi Freedom Democratic Party (MFDP) complete with convention delegates in part to protest Mississippi's all-white delegation to the Democratic National Convention.

The regular Democratic delegates from Mississippi of course resented this black challenge to their credentials, but when members of the MFDP presented their case to the convention, especially in a moving talk by Fannie Lou Hamer, the justice of their cause was evident. However, Johnson at this juncture wanted consensus above all else. He worked out a compromise by promising to name Hubert Humphrey as his running mate (which was probably already decided), agreed to seat two of the MFDP members as at-large delegates, required the all-white delegations from Mississippi (and Alabama) to pledge their support of the Democratic candidates, and stated that at future conventions delegations would not be accepted from states that disallowed black participation. This compromise satisfied neither the MFDP nor the regular white delegates from Mississippi, most of whom went home and voted for Goldwater. But the way was cleared for far greater black participation at subsequent Democratic conventions.

The next major reform of Democratic convention procedures followed the absolute debacle at Chicago in 1968, when Chicago's Mayor Richard Daley controlled events inside the arena with an iron fist even as chaos reigned outside. Though Hubert Humphrey, a liberal stalwart in the past, emerged as the nominee, many Democrats were offended by the convention proceedings—so offended that, in response, the convention delegates approved (against overwhelming southern opposition) the McGovern-Fraser Commission to study and recommend reforms in the entire process that produced delegates. By 1970, the party had accepted the commission's recommendations. States would have to open up the delegate selection process. Rules were adopted that guaranteed better representation of minorities, women, and younger delegates, with limitations on the number of officeholders who had seats. The resulting delegates who met in 1972 at the Democratic convention in Miami were 36 percent women and 24 percent black. Reformers, activists, and antiwar liberals had wrested control of the convention away from traditional party power brokers.

The Democratic primaries represented a broad range of candidates, with Wallace on the right, Hubert Humphrey and Edmund Muskie in the center, and George McGovern on the left. Wallace withdrew following his gunshot wound in May, and Humphrey, crippled by his association with LBJ and the increasingly unpopular war in Vietnam, never picked up momentum. Muskie began as the front-runner, but his calm, dispassionate style did not seem to fit an election year filled with passion. Senator George McGovern, the idealistic son of a Methodist minister and a history Ph.D. from Northwestern University, welded together an enthusiastic reform, antiwar campaign consisting largely of young, college-age supporters and long-time opponents of the continuing war. McGovern's liberalism appealed to the new makeup of the 1972 convention, and he won the nomination. He proved to be by far the most liberal candidate ever nominated by a major party and, along with Goldwater in 1964, the weakest candidate ever put forward by a major party.

McGovern's forthright opposition to the war, his support of amnesty for what were called draft dodgers, his strong support of civil rights and busing, and his proposals for modest income redistribution made him absolutely anathema to most southern white Democrats. Richard Nixon and the proponents of a southern strategy for a new Republican majority were handed the perfect foil for their campaign. The election was a foregone conclusion: Nixon won 79 percent of the southern white vote (86 percent in the deep South states), carried every southern state, and swept to a landslide national victory. McGovern positions allowed the Republicans to put together a powerful coalition. In contrast to the Democrats, the southernized GOP stood for fiscal conservatism, law and order, limited government, strong defense, traditional cultural values, opposition to busing to achieve integration, a sense that civil rights should not be pushed any faster or further, and opposition to affirmative action.

White liberals and blacks might interpret much of this as subtly coded, polite racism, but it was also an aggregation of attitudes and policies that perfectly matched majority white sentiment in the South and in much of the nation. Gone were the Depression-era days when the government was seen as a benefactor. Especially for middle-class, upwardly mobile white voters in Sun Belt suburbs, government primarily meant taxes and civil rights and give-away programs that both cost them and favored minorities. The GOP understood those gut-level reactions far better than did the national Democratic party. George Wallace may have lost in his presidential bids, but his visceral anger, borrowed and only slightly toned down and expressed more politely by GOP spokesmen, was key to Republican success. Modifying Wallace's message and making it their own, the Republican party has not lost the white vote in the South in a presidential election since 1968. With Nixon's resounding victory in 1972, it is possible to speak of the emergence of a Solid Republican South.

However, the Democratic party was not dead in the South; it was in the process of being transformed. The continuing departure of conservative Democrats to the triumphal Republican party meant that liberals, moderates, and blacks would control the residual Democratic party. In many southern states, the so-called independents had grown greatly, made up usually of former Democrats who still hesitated to join the GOP and regional newcomers who were not ready to join either the Republican conservatives or the Democratic liberals. The 1972 electoral victories of Barbara Jordan of Houston and Andrew Young of Atlanta, the first blacks elected to the U.S. House of Representatives from the South since Reconstruction, demonstrated the enhanced political power of black voters when augmented by liberal and moderate whites. Certainly on the state and local level, black votes could often be decisive.

CHAPTER 31

Southern Democrats and the Nation

THE NEW SOUTHERN DEMOCRATS

Southern Democratic politicians understood that carefully constructed coalitions of black and white liberal and moderate Democratic voters, with a scattering of moderate independents, could still win elections. Coming on the heels of this discovery was a group of young, attractive, and aggressive Democratic gubernatorial candidates: Reuben O. Askew in Florida, Albert Brewer in Alabama, Dale Bumpers in Arkansas (to be followed by David Pryor and Bill Clinton), Jimmy Carter in Georgia, James B. Hunt in North Carolina, and John C. West in South Carolina. Such new-style Democrats could prosper in a South whose presidential vote was overwhelmingly Republican. The region seemed to have a split mind: at the presidential level one type of candidate, at the local level another. The South did not completely reject progressive social legislation. Rather, it chose to base such political programs in the hands of politicians closer to home than the White House. Democrats could still win state legislative and gubernatorial office, congressional seats, even election to the Senate.

Could a white southern Democrat possibly win the presidency by finding an ideological middle ground between progressive local interests and conservative presidential politics? Could a southern candidate dare to be liberal enough to win northern labor voters and black voters—old New Deal Democrats—and yet conservative enough to attract moderate Democrats and independents in the

South? Perhaps so, especially after the national Republicans were severely wounded by the Watergate scandal (a break-in to the Democratic campaign headquarters, a presidential coverup, and revelations of a variety of illegal "dirty tricks" and pay-offs). Vice President Agnew was forced to resign because he had taken bribes, President Nixon was so threatened by revelations and lies that he had to resign to avoid impeachment, and then President Gerald Ford, who had been appointed vice president and became president when Nixon resigned, pardoned the previous presidential malefactor. This almost unbelievable chain of events made possible the presidential victory of southerner Jimmy Carter of Georgia in 1976, an electoral anomaly in a Republican age.

Carter's election shows both the possibilities for, and the limits to, Democratic presidential politics in the modern South. In many ways, Jimmy Carter seemed perfect for a Democratic renewal. His maternal grandfather had been a Populist politician whom family legend credited with originating the idea of Rural Free Delivery of the mail. His father became a regional director of the Rural Electrification Administration, another government program that significantly improved the lives of rural southerners. His mother was a nurse who often had to go to patients' homes and in effect substitute for a doctor. Young Jimmy had grown up in rural Georgia, where his family ran a peanut farm, with this strong family tradition of public service. Like many rural southerners, then and since, who were inspired by good school teachers, Carter absorbed a strong work and self-improvement ethic. In part because of his father's political influence, Jimmy Carter won a congressional appointment to the U.S. Naval Academy for 1943. After graduating and marrying his hometown sweetheart, Rosalynn Smith, Jimmy Carter was commissioned a naval officer and began what looked to be a traditional southern career in the armed services. Soon he was attracted to the nuclear submarine program and took additional training in nuclear engineering and propulsion, which advanced his naval career. His father died of cancer in 1953, and the felt responsibility for carrying on the family peanut business made Carter decide to leave the navy and return to the small town of Plains, Georgia.

Farming and business success soon led to involvement in local political issues. Perhaps because of the influence of his mother and his naval background, Carter was opposed to racial segregation. His refusal to join a local Citizen's Council caused him to lose business in the mid-1950s, and his comparative racial liberalism set Carter apart from many of his neighbors. Still, Carter gained the respect of the townspeople of Plains, and eventually he was appointed to the local school board, his first personal taste of politics. He liked it, and soon began to consider running for a position in the Georgia Senate. Carter had to overcome shocking political fraud to win his first race, but in so doing he was bitten by the political bug—he had long seen politics as a means of serving the people, a duty taught by his parents. In 1964, Carter was elected to the Georgia state senate. By 1966 he was considering running for the U.S. Congress but instead ran unsuccessfully for the governor's office. Lester G. Maddox, a colorfully outspoken defender of segregation, was elected governor. Carter had not even made the runoff, but he began working immediately for another run in 1970. Following his 1966 gubernatorial defeat, in a mood of depression and introspection, Carter was, in evangelical parlance, born again and became far more active in his Baptist church. This born-again, farmer-businessman who had served in the armed services, all cardinal southern virtues, threw himself into the gubernatorial campaign of 1970 with almost fanatical devotion. Carter's major opponent, Carl Sanders, campaigned as the liberal, and Carter ran as the more conservative candidate, appealing to the erstwhile Wallace and Maddox voters. Carter's opportunistic strategy worked: He won the governor's office.

In his inaugural, Carter signaled that it was time to put aside old racial issues: "I say to you quite frankly that the time for racial discrimination is over. Our people have already made this major and difficult decision, but we cannot underestimate the challenge of hundreds of minor decisions yet to be made...No poor, rural, weak, or black person should ever have to bear the additional burden of being deprived of the opportunity of an education, a job, or simple justice." In one of his first acts, Carter hung a portrait of Martin Luther King, Jr., the assassinated civil rights leader, in the Georgia capitol. Then Carter set about reorganizing the state's governmental machinery to make it more efficient and responsive in order to attract industry, to improve education, to enact environmental protections, and to establish procedures for long-range planning. Carter believed that economic growth, civil rights, equal opportunity, and efficient government would improve the lives of all Georgia's citizens. But Carter was not long content to confine his ambition for public service to the state of Georgia. In 1972, midway through his four-year term as governor, he decided to run for the presidency of the United States.

No one had ever seen a campaign like that Carter and his major strategist, Hamilton Jordan, devised, and no one had seen a presidential candidate as indefatigable as the ever-smiling Carter. Although starting with practically no national name recognition, Carter—carrying his own luggage to counteract the media image of Nixon and the imperial presidency and seemingly shaking every hand in the caucus states—racked up a series of stunning victories. First in Iowa, then New Hampshire, then a major victory over George Wallace in Florida, and the peanut farmer from Georgia was on his way. To a nation still upset by Watergate and then President Ford's pardon of Nixon, a nation upset by the lying and cursing and immorality revealed by secret tapes at the highest levels of government, Carter—the quiet-spoken Sunday School teacher from the South, the straight-arrow former naval officer, and the businessman-farmer—seemed a wholesome throwback to another age of downhome values. At the conclusion of his triumphant nomination at the Democratic convention at Madison Square Garden in New York City, and after his rousing, old-time Populist acceptance speech, Carter and other leading Democrats, black and white, including Martin Luther King, Sr., stood, raised their clasped hands in unity, and sang together the anthem of the civil rights movement, "We Shall Overcome." To many southern blacks and liberal and moderate whites, it was a poignant moment. Perhaps at last, the South's long estrangement from the nation over race—first slavery, then segregation—was ending. Carter stood as the representative of the new American South.

The election proved extremely close, for Ford had the power of the incumbency behind him, and Carter found it difficult to modulate his appeal so that he could hold on to the New Deal coalition and at the same time not lose conservative and moderate whites. When the votes were tallied, Carter had won by a nose with 51 percent of the popular vote, winning ten of eleven former Confederate states. Yet his southern vote was deceptive. Carter garnered over 90 percent of the black vote but only 46 percent of the southern white vote. The black vote enabled him to win every southern state but Virginia. Yet the loss of the white vote signaled that he had little maneuvering room in the region, little margin for political error. After all, at least some of the white vote was a kind of southern sympathy vote, not an endorsement of the national Democratic agenda. Nevertheless, most southerners took a degree of pride in the inauguration of the first deep South president in over a century. Southern cooking and country music in the White House, southern accents in the Oval Office, and members of the national press attending a fish fry in rural Georgia: It all made southerners feel that a regional albatross had been lifted from around their collective necks.

Yet President Carter found governing more difficult than running for office. Having campaigned as a political outsider, he found it difficult to bargain with Congress. Because of his training as an engineer, Carter seemed to think that the rationality of his programs would automatically recommend themselves to Congress, but of course Congress does not work that way. Though he still taught a Baptist Sunday School class whenever he was in his hometown of Plains, Georgia, Carter favored the Internal Revenue Service putting restrictions on the tax-exempt status of many private religious schools that had often begun as segregation academies. This policy alienated the Christian fundamentalist vote and contributed to its shift of support to the GOP by 1980. Manipulation of the international oil markets by the Organization of Petroleum Exporting Countries (OPEC) caused a rapid increase in world oil prices followed by double-digit inflation in all the western nations, and Carter was blamed for inflation in this country. In an absolutely unprecedented act of international terrorism, Iranian fundamentalists seized the American embassy at Tehran and held American personnel as hostages. Carter, valuing the lives of the hostages, was powerless to rescue them. Nightly television coverage made Carter seem as helplessly hostage to events as the embassy prisoners were to their captors.

Supporters might point to the number of blacks Carter appointed to government positions, or to his progressive environmental policies, or to his essential

Jimmy and Rosalynn Carter. (Jimmy Carter Museum and Library)

involvement in the Camp David accords that brought peace between Israel and Egypt, or to his willingness to brave public opposition and work for a Panama Canal agreement that all presidents since Eisenhower had supported yet hesitated to advocate, but these policy successes meant naught to the American public in the face of high inflation and Iranian highhandedness. Carter misunderstood the psyche of the nation. In the midst of the energy crisis, he warned the nation of the profligacy of consuming far more than its share of the world's energy and cautioned the people about putting self-interest above all other values. "In a nation that was proud of hard work, strong families, close knit communities and our faith in God," Carter said to the American people in a televised speech, "too many of us now tend to worship self-indulgence and consumption. Human identity is no longer defined by what one does but by what one owns." But such homilies to selflessness was not what the increasingly materialistic American public wanted to hear. They wanted lower inflation, cheaper oil, America standing tall in the world wielding, metaphorically, a big enough stick to have its way untrammeled by Third-World anti-American leaders such as the Ayatollah Khomeni, the leader of Iran. Carter seemed as wrong for the political climate of 1980 as he had seemed right in 1976. It took more than decency and intelligence to survive as president; it took political know-how and a great deal of good luck.

Events over which the United States had no control appeared to take over Carter's presidency. Russia's invasion of Afghanistan was simply another example. The Democratic establishment never warmed to the political outsider from Georgia, and now that he was falling in the polls, political sharks began to circle. Carter's presidency seemed out of control, almost in free fall. Democratic Senator Edward M. Kennedy of Massachusetts, never personally attracted to the Georgian, announced that he would challenge Carter for the nomination in 1980, a brutal battle that Carter eventually won only to find himself thoroughly bloodied. Independent John Anderson mounted a third-party challenge, attracting many liberal Democrats and independents who were mildly suspicious of Carter's southernness and disillusioned by his inability to solve intractable problems. By June 1980, Carter's approval rating in the polls had fallen to a dismal 21 percent, even lower than Nixon had ever fallen. The presidency appeared ripe for the picking by a Republican.

DEMOCRATS DISCREDITED

The Republican candidate in 1980 was not just any Republican but the ideological embodiment of the American right, Ronald Reagan. Reagan had had a modestly successful career in the movies, but it was his hosting in the 1950s of a popular television program entitled *General Electric Theater* that made him a conservative icon. For much of eight years, he toured the nation giving patriotic, pro-business talks for General Electric, perfecting a script that became known as The Speech. It was this address that he gave at the 1964 GOP convention in support of Barry Goldwater, and The Speech made Reagan, even more than Goldwater, the conservative spokesman for what media pundits in the Nixon era began calling Middle America. The Speech was antigovernment and antitax, enlivened by folksy anecdotes of federal excess. Government was the people's enemy; the free enterprise system, devoid of meddlesome government controls, was the people's truest benefactor. For comfortable, middle-class white Americans, Reagan's speech seemed a breath of fresh air. Reagan had ridden these ideas to two terms as governor of California, the nation's largest state, so he ran for the Republican nomination as an experienced politician, no mere movie star. Mediagenic and with a gift for giving even pedestrian speeches with oratorical flair, Reagan swept aside his more prosaic opponents and handily won the nomination for the presidency.

Reagan and his able strategists understood the importance of rewinning the South for the GOP, and they understood the political potency of the antigovernment, low-tax ideology of The Speech, especially when yoked to flag-waving patriotism. Reagan opened his 1980 campaign in Neshoba County, Mississippi, where the three civil rights workers had been murdered in 1964, and to an audience of ten thousand whites at the county fair he announced "I believe in states' rights." He promised to "restore to states and local governments the power that properly belongs to them." Here was Nixon's old southern strategy of muted racism with a newly honed edge. Carter opened his campaign in Alabama by denouncing the Klan and older racial animosities, but Carter's style never stood a chance against Reagan's in the changed atmosphere of 1980. Carter would give fact-filled lectures about energy and environment and America's need to recognize limits, but listeners, though impressed with his knowledge and insight, left feeling mildly depressed. Reagan spoke optimistically about unlimited potential and freedom and prosperity and America's standing strong in the world, and because it sounded like a pep rally, listeners left feeling proud and upbeat. There was no question who would win the election. Carter captured only 36 percent of the South's white vote and carried only his home state of Georgia. Nationwide, Reagan won forty-four states and 489 out of 538 electoral votes. Carter, his party, and the values he stood for were thoroughly discredited both regionally and nationally.

Exit poll interviews showed that the voters who were most opposed to taxes, government services, and civil rights programs and most favorably inclined toward increased defense expenditures were the strongest supporters of Reagan. By 1980, the antitax crusade had grown to be an almost unstoppable force in American politics. The crusade was fueled both by the decade-long white backlash against paying taxes that were felt to be unfairly transferred to blacks and to support government programs considered wasteful, intrusive, and permissive, and by a genuine rise in the tax rate paid by millions of middle-class voters as their climbing incomes over the past decades had pushed them into higher tax brackets. The antitax movement was crystallized in 1978 when California voters passed a tax limitation bill called Proposition 13. The idea swept like wildfire across the nation. The GOP, far more attuned to white attitudes than the Democrats, understood what a powerful issue lay at hand. And no one saw the issue more clearly than President Reagan. His mandate seemed clear, and so did the dilemma of the Democratic party.

Reagan proved to be a popular president, bringing the people sharply lowered taxes and increased defense budgets. His administration began with a severe recession that led to the highest unemployment since the Great Depression, but it squeezed much of the inflation out of the economy. Also, because energy prices had stabilized, so did inflation. The pump-priming effect of lowered taxes and tremendously increased government expenditures for defense led to a long, steady low-grade boom. European and Japanese investors underwrote the mushrooming national debt, keeping interest rates low. True to his promises, Reagan cut back on government regulation of business and of the environment; civil rights and affirmative action programs were slowed; and strong conservatives were appointed to government positions and the judiciary, many of whom, like James Watt as Secretary of the Interior and Anne Burford, head of the Environmental Protection Agency, were essentially opposed to the mandated mission of the government agency they now headed. Reagan had, in effect, campaigned to turn back the political clock, the majority of Americans had heartily approved, and New Deal–Great Society expansion of government programs ceased. The budget deficit ballooned as never before and the United States became the world's largest debtor nation, but with lower taxes, the average American cared little about long-term economic consequences. Iran had held the hostages till Reagan was inaugurated, then let them go instantly, as if to spite Jimmy Carter. After a generation of rule by Cold War troglodytes, Russia got a youthful, pragmatic leader in Mikhail Gorbachev who understood that Afghanistan-type adventurism and the continued Cold War arms race were bankrupting the already weak economy of his nation. Gorbachev sought domestic reforms and a relaxation of international rivalries. The result was an epochal break in the arms race and ultimately the end of the Cold War. Reagan profited from these diplomatic windfalls and the long-term though narrow-gauged prosperity of the 1980s.

During the mid-term elections of 1982, in the midst of the recessionary downturn, the Democrats won a number of state and local victories in the South, as in the nation. But with the return of prosperity in time for the 1984 presidential elections, and with Reagan's mastery of symbolic politics, the election was a foregone conclusion. Inflation was down, the recession was over, and, borrowing Reagan's campaign theme, it seemed to be morning in America once again. Reagan—ironically, not personally devout—had also succeeded in wedding the growing political support of the religious right to the GOP, a powerful political advantage in the South. Especially for white voters in the region, Reagan had put race and religion on his side. The Democratic candidate, Walter F. Mondale, who had been Jimmy Carter's vice president, was associated in the popular mind with Carter and with liberal Democratic programs. He even said that it would be necessary to raise taxes to balance the federal budget. Consequently Reagan was reelected in one of the greatest landslides in American political history, carrying every southern state, winning 72 percent of the white South's vote, and sweeping forty-nine states. Given the vocabulary of southern politics in the 1980s, Mondale with his calls for New Deal–type progressive government never had a chance against Ronald Reagan.

The dominance of the GOP in southern presidential politics now seemed complete. But Reagan's second term was marred by several scandals, including the revelation that, contrary to stated policy, arms were traded to Iran in the hopes of securing the release of American citizens held hostage by Muslim fundamentalists in the Middle East. Then it turned out that profits from such arms sales were illegally used to support the conservative Contra rebels, who opposed the Sandinista government in Nicaragua. A firestorm of opposition broke out, with the administration quickly responding more for damage control than to get to the bottom of the scandal. A congressional committee suggested that Reagan's administrative style was so relaxed that extralegal, almost freelance policies were undertaken without his knowledge. Yet the immense public reservoir of goodwill he had created left Reagan relatively untouched, and he was not as injured by this scandal as Nixon had been by Watergate even though the constitutional issues involved were far greater in what became known as the Iran–Contra Scandal. Moreover, after two terms in office, there were a number of indications that the economic miracle of the 1980s was more mirage than reality. Investment was down, job creation per annum was down from the Carter years, workers' annual income, adjusted for inflation, was down, bank failures were up, the federal debt had tripled, the trade balance had gone from positive to negative. The combined tax rate for the poorest one-fifth of Americans rose during the period from 1980 to 1985 from 8.4 percent to 10.6 percent, and it fell for the richest one-fifth from 27.3 percent to 24 percent. For the entire decade, 1980 to 1990, after-tax income for the poorest decile of the population decreased by 10.3 percent, while for the richest decile it increased by 41.1 percent. The wealthy prospered, the poor saw their relative position slip. Would this combination of foreign-policy scandal and economic bad news domestically be enough, as it had been in 1976, to allow a Democratic presidential victory?

Only the Republicans seemed aware that the South was now the nation's largest region, with one-third of the population and over one-quarter of the total electoral votes needed for presidential victory. A candidate who won the southern states could win the presidency by picking up only a third of the remainder of the nation's electoral votes. Significantly, no Democrat had ever lost the South and won the presidency. Furthermore, the GOP strategists understood the continuing efficacy of Nixon's southern strategy. The secret was to appeal to mainstreet business-conservative economic concerns and, more important, emphasize cultural-racial issues: law and order, uncritical patriotism (of the "America: Love it or leave it" variety), "family values," and conservative religion; and opposition to busing, affirmative action, welfare, and meddling government "interference." Most Americans, but especially white southerners, subscribed to this set of values. Cultural politics proved more salient than economics, in fact, they could conceal economic reality. Cobb County, Georgia, for example, a hotbed of antigovernment rhetoric in 1994 and a showcase of New South prosperity, nevertheless ranked as the third-leading county in the nation in amount of federal funds received—this was the foundation of its prosperity. (In fact, all but two southern states got more back from the federal government than they paid in federal taxes.) Conservative whites were often genuinely worried about what they perceived as the breakdown in family structure, changing sexual mores, the rise in population groups (black, Hispanic, and Asian) that had different cultural styles, and the obvious increase in crime.

Often this unease was not consciously racist at all but rather a fear of what was happening to the once-familiar America that had been depicted in such television shows as "Leave it to Beaver." That fear of loss, though, could be channeled into support of conservative politics. Reagan's vice president, George Bush, had learned from the master how to evoke these sentiments and appeal to them, and as the Republican candidate in 1988, he faced another Democratic pushover, Governor Michael Dukakis of Massachusetts. Dukakis, a bright, hardworking technocrat, believed that the election was about competence, not ideology, showing thereby how little he and his strategists had learned from the last two elections. It was as if the Democrats had set out to find a candidate and a campaign style guaranteed to fail in the South.

Early in the campaign, Dukakis let himself be painted as a candidate who let black criminals out of jail early so they could rape white women, a knee-jerk critic of America who wanted to weaken the military defenses, and a secular humanist who did not support America's religious heritage. Lee Atwater, directing Bush's campaign with a sort of diabolical brilliance, raised negative campaigning to an art form and perhaps changed forever how candidates used the media. The inept Dukakis campaign never recovered from the onslaught. Bush, smarting from liberal jibes that he was a wimp, tore into the seemingly defenseless Dukakis like a man possessed. Before an East Texas audience Connecticut-born and Yale-educated Bush called the Democrat a

FEDERAL FUNDS RECEIVED, BY STATE, PER DOLLAR OF TAX REVENUE PAID

For fiscal year 2000		For fiscal year 2000	
Alabama	1.54	Missouri	1.26
Arkansas	1.38	North Carolina	1.06
Florida	1.00	Oklahoma	1.46
Georgia	.99	South Carolina	1.27
Kentucky	1.41	Tennessee	1.20
Louisiana	1.39	Texas	.96
Maryland	1.32	Virginia	1.48
Mississippi	1.78	West Virginia	1.75

Source: *The World Almanac and Book of Facts, 2002* (New York, 2002), 154.

"'liberal Massachusetts governor' who opposes gun ownership, the Pledge of Allegiance, prayer in public schools, and is weak on crime." Bush and Atwater knew those kind of charges drew blood, so across the nation Bush repeated that "I can't understand the type of thinking that lets first-degree murderers who haven't even served enough time to be eligible for parole out on parole so they can rape and plunder again and then isn't willing to let the teachers lead the kids in the Pledge of Allegiance."

It made little difference that Dukakis's Republican predecessor had developed the parole program or that many states with conservative Republican governors, like Texas, had similar release programs. Dukakis never mounted a sufficient defense, and the Atwater-Bush attack made most white Americans—and southerners even more so—dismiss as irrelevant Iran-Contra issues and such abstractions as the astronomical federal debt. The Republicans knew what kind of cultural issues would keep them in office and solidify the GOP as the new majority party. The national Democrats often seemed stunningly obtuse about the issues the white majority was most concerned about. Hence, the Democrats failed to attempt to educate and promote social understanding, and the Republicans capitalized on the visceral emotions of the public. Bush won 67 percent of the southern white vote, all the region's electoral vote, and swept to another Republican landslide victory. Bush won in forty out of fifty states, and he led the electoral vote by 426 to 122. It was not quite Reaganesque, but a resounding victory nevertheless.

Perhaps nothing so demonstrated the political attractiveness of the basic GOP economic and cultural conservatism as the remarkable political career in Louisiana of David Duke. A handsome, suavely dressed, college-educated politician, Duke had a long history of right-wing extremism, having been a leader of the Ku Klux Klan and a neo-Nazi who publicly doubted the holocaust. Yet he shed his sheet, switched his party allegiance from Democrat to the GOP—much to the chagrin and embarrassment of national Republican leaders who quickly repudiated him—and in 1991 ran a highly publicized and surprisingly strong race in the Louisiana gubernatorial election. Duke stressed economic issues in an oil-depressed state; he attacked welfare abuse and affirmative action; he assailed taxing those who he said worked in order to give to those on welfare—a euphemism for blacks; he preached law and order; and he advocated the advancement of the white race. That a majority of white Louisianians would vote for a politician with such an unsavory background testifies to the powerful attractiveness of the set of economic and conservative values he espoused. In this case, after nationwide attention, an infusion of outside money, criticism of Duke by most national Republican leaders, and a remarkable black voter turnout, former Democratic governor Edward Edwards put together a liberal-moderate-black good-government coalition, despite his own unsavory record, and beat Duke in the runoff election. Louisiana liberals put tongue-in-cheek bumper stickers on their cars that read "Vote for the crook."

Although Louisianians, who are usually quick to claim that their state is unique, in this case claimed that the Duke phenomenon could happen practically anywhere that economic distress was high, no doubt the state's peculiar tolerance for political chicanery contributed to his near success. The larger point is that the political tables have been reversed. For the half-century preceding World War II, the white South looked to the Democratic party to preserve the region's racial status quo. Following the evolution of the two parties in the region over the past half-century, present-day white southerners turn to the Republican party to slow social change. The shift that had begun in 1948 with the Dixiecrats, then picked up steam with Goldwater in 1964 (symbolically, Strom Thurmond switched to the GOP that year), was almost fully realized as a result of Reagan's ascendency. Race, camouflaged by coded language, still dominates southern politics. Economic issues, even when evoked, are secondary. The New South has not completely escaped its heritage, for good and for bad. The past, in all its complexity, still shapes the course of southern life.

THE END OF SOUTHERN HISTORY?

At first glance, the national election of 1992 would seem to suggest that the GOP dominance of presidential politics in the South had ended. After all, the successful Democratic ticket broke with recent tradition not only by having both presidential and vice-presidential candidates, Bill Clinton and Albert Gore, Jr., from the same region, but from neighboring southern states, Arkansas and Tennessee, respectively. (George Bush had lived much of his pre-political adult life in Texas, but he was still considered a New Englander.) And Clinton and Gore carried four southern states—Arkansas, Georgia, Louisiana, and Tennessee—and four border states—Kentucky, Maryland, Missouri, and West Virginia. But these state victories notwithstanding, Bush beat Clinton in the total southern vote,

won the southern white vote easily, and in fact, Clinton only won two percentage points more in the South than Dukakis had four years earlier and trailed
Jimmy Carter's 1976 southern performance by eleven percentage points. The
GOP, despite running in 1992 against two well-financed southern whites who
had a masterful campaign strategy and despite bearing the burden of having
arguably the most dismal economic record of any administration in over half
a century, still won the South as a whole and the southern white vote handily.
Following the Congressional redistricting necessitated by the 1990 census,
Bush's Department of Justice had required states to draw up as many districts
as possible that would have majority black populations. That drained most
blacks from the remainder of the congressional districts. The result was a modest increase in the number of safe black-dominated Democratic districts and a
large increase in the number of districts with fewer blacks, hence sure Republican districts. That calculated redistricting policy meant several more black
congressmen, fewer white Democratic congressmen, and a significant net gain
in [white] Republican congressmen. This policy would pay rich GOP dividends
in 1994 and afterwards.)

Part of the explanation for the poor showing of the Democratic ticket in the
South was the surprising success of the third-party candidacy of Texas billionaire
Ross Perot, who capitalized on a national feeling of frustration with both major
political parties. Perot, with his unorthodox campaign, largely on television, won
the second highest vote total of any third-party candidate in American history, with
19 percent of the ballots cast. In the South as a whole, Perot garnered 16 percent
of the white vote, but most of those were apparently at the expense of Bush, not
Clinton. Paradoxically, the election of a southern Democratic president and vice
president did not indicate that the Democrats had finally broken the GOP conservative stranglehold on the white South.

What, if anything, did the election of a complete southern ticket for the
first time since the Andrew Jackson–John C. Calhoun victory in 1828 mean to
the region? It suggested once again that the only hope Democrats had of making headway in the region in presidential politics was to run moderate southerners. In fact, the ticket's narrow victory margin (after three sound Democratic
defeats) indicated that the national mood of conservatism was still so strong
that, even in the midst of severe economic frustration and a strong desire for
change, only moderate Democratic leadership could possibly win public approval. It does appear also that the southern-style politics of moderation, pioneered by southern governors, adept at appealing to blacks and other minorities
and simultaneously appealing to traditional values of home, place, family, the
work ethic, and patriotism, is the key to Democratic success nationally. More aggressive liberal policies in the mold of FDR or LBJ were still out of fashion and
discredited. Clinton and Gore exemplified this new kind of southern moderate politics. They were self-consciously southern, yet they symbolized progressive change; they rhapsodized the small-town South yet talked about global

competitiveness and environmentalism; but all the while they were careful to stake out a position as a new kind—less liberal—of Democrat.

Pundits were quick to call Clinton and Gore the "Bubba" ticket, but these two Ivy League graduates (Clinton a Rhodes scholar from Georgetown, Oxford, and Yale; Gore from Harvard and Vanderbilt) are hardly provincial, even though they were quick to offer a southern folk aphorism when the occasion arose. Together, they represent how much the New South has changed since World War II. Yet the mixed success in the South of Clinton and Gore also symbolizes how a progressive element in the region coexisted with orthodox forces that were still conservative on matters of race and social change. While Clinton and Gore are every inch modern Americans, they still are very recognizably southern. In that "twoness," both southern and American, they accurately reflect the modern South. The majority of demographically "typical American" cities used to market test new products are now located in the South. In so many outward ways, the region appears almost identical with the nation at large, and yet it has a style, a feel, an accent, a pinch of soul that distinguishes it even to the casual observer. Part of the apparent national appeal of Clinton and Gore was their combination of modern images of high-tech American competence with an almost intangible down-home southern folksiness. For many educated southerners who still take umbrage at the often automatic national association of their region with backwardness and racism, the academic panache Clinton and Gore possessed also brought a rare public pride last experienced during the early days of the Carter administration.

The Clinton administration is difficult to characterize. On a number of issues, the president proved that his governing instincts were more liberal than his campaign had suggested, but Clinton was too shrewd a politician generally to go beyond what seemed politically possible. Often his decisions—such as to allow gays to serve in the military or to send U.S. troops to Bosnia—suggested he put principle ahead of politics, but his rhetoric, attuned to opinion surveys, promised a scaling back of government. Not, it is true, as scaled back as many Republicans called for (Reagan in his first inaugural had even said that "government is not the solution to our problem; government is the problem." But only the most privileged Americans actually believed that, and they too were quick to seek government assistance when it suited their purposes.), but a real departure from older Democratic programs. In his first administration, Clinton, despite ferocious Republican opposition, pushed through a tax increase, and the result was continued economic expansion, a drop in the unemployment rate, and, for the first time in decades, five consecutive years of falling federal deficits. Clinton worked with Republicans to reduce tariffs on trade between the United States and Canada and Mexico, here breaking with much of his union support.

But Clinton's largest policy initiative, a debacle it turned out, was an ambitious proposal for health insurance and reform of the entire system of health care delivery. Momentarily seeming to lose his political skills, Clinton and his advisers devised complicated plans to solve complicated problems while the Republicans mounted a highly effective television assault that frightened Americans with visions of socialized medicine. Not only did this negative advertising campaign kill the Clinton administration hopes of restructuring health-care delivery; it also allowed the Republicans to raise the specter of "big government" and "higher taxes." The result was a stunning GOP victory in the 1994 midterm elections masterminded by Georgia congressman Newt Gingrich. The Republicans controlled Congress for the first time in forty years, picked up many seats in state and local elections, including governorships, and entrenched themselves as the dominant party throughout much of the South. Gingrich was elected Speaker of the House and Trent Lott of Mississippi was chosen Senate Majority Leader.

Gingrich and GOP leaders, a disproportionate number of whom were also southerners, responded with a bold "Contract with America" that called for tax cuts, the line-item veto, term limits, junking the existing welfare system, and eviscerating most government regulations of business, occupational safety, and the environment. Gingrich and his GOP colleagues talked of revolution, talked of totally remaking the federal government, talked of changes so dramatic during their first one hundred days that they would restore government to the way it was before the New Deal. The antigovernment, antitax rhetoric that had begun with Wallace and then been perfected by Nixon and Reagan came to a climax with the vaunted Republican Revolution of 1994. Then, in the characteristic way that Americans tend to flinch at radicalism on either the left or the right, the public began to back away from Gingrich's vision of the future. Public opinion polls showed him to be significantly less popular than Clinton. Rediscovering his political touch, Clinton began to portray the Republicans as extremists and himself as the caring, sensible voice of moderation trying to save Medicare, Medicaid, the environment, and education at the same time that he was working to balance the budget. Even his enemies recognized Clinton's political genius and ability to project himself via the television screen. And then two events practically insured Clinton's political resurgence, propelling him to the highest approval ratings of his administration and securing his reelection in 1996 as the first Democrat to win a second term since Franklin D. Roosevelt.

On April 19, 1995, the federal building in Oklahoma City, Oklahoma, was destroyed by a massive truck bomb, killing 168 men, women, and children. Americans were shocked by such senseless violence and angered to discover that members of a militant antigovernment hate group had planted the bomb as an act of warfare against the government. Suddenly, Americans saw firsthand what dedicated extremism could lead to, and the names and faces of the government workers killed—and those who led the rescue effort—helped the public to see that they were the government. The government was not made up of faceless bureaucrats but real people, just plain folks, who served their fellow citizens. Clinton came to Oklahoma City and in an emotional address both warned of extremism and offered words of healing. The nation responded with an outpouring of patriotism and found itself, as Clinton later said, moving "back to the vital center."

The second event that Clinton turned to his advantage was a colossal miscalculation by the Republican congressional leaders. In dispute with the administration over the budget, the GOP lawmakers brought the government to a shutdown twice in late 1995 (and the first week of 1996), thinking this would rally the public to their position. Instead, the shutdown and accompanying inconvenience reinforced to millions of voters just how useful the federal government actually was. The Republicans looked like extremists, fiscal bomb throwers, in their willingness to close down the government. Clinton masterfully responded to this GOP blunder in an unprecedentedly extensive television campaign in 1995, successfully painting the Republicans as callous extremists unconcerned about significant government programs that helped many people. Clinton had rebounded from his midterm repudiation and now looked politically invincible. Multiple charges of scandal against him had little effect, and when the Republicans chose as their standard-bearer a man old enough to be Clinton's father—Senator Robert Dole—the election was a foregone conclusion, so much so that turnout plummeted. Clinton won 49 percent of the popular vote, Dole 41 percent, and third-party candidate Ross Perot 8 percent, but Clinton had a commanding 379 to 159 electoral majority.

In his second inaugural address, Clinton announced that the era of big government was over, and in his second administration, he scaled back his expectations of what government could do, emphasized voluntarism, and used the White House as a bully pulpit more than as a dispenser of programs and funds. He worked with GOP leaders—again, most of whom were also southerners—to achieve a compromise that mandated a balanced federal budget in 2002, a far cry from the budget-busting days of the Reagan years. In actuality, with the economy booming and tax revenues high, the federal budget showed a multibillion dollar surplus in the fiscal year ending June 30, 1998. Clinton agreed to a fundamental reform in the federal welfare system, angering his more liberal supporters. Yet by pushing former welfare recipients to get jobs, Clinton helped change the perception of them from welfare cheats to workers, and with this improved political reputation he gained for them billions of dollars in earned-income tax credits, child care subsidies, and subsidies for children's health insurance. He successfully pushed to increase the minimum wage. Millions of persons were moved off the welfare roles, unemployment plummeted, and crime rates fell. Clinton also used his office to advocate racial reconciliation, he pledged to defend Medicare and Medicaid, he called for increased spending for education, and he emphasized the importance of protecting the environment. There were no dramatic new programs like the New Deal or the Great Society; rather, Clinton projected a pragmatic, moderate appreciation of government's positive role with steady but incremental gains for a progressive agenda.

Clinton was still less popular in the South than in other regions, even though he had carried Arkansas, Tennessee, Louisiana, Kentucky, Florida, Maryland, and West Virginia in 1996. He had won only 36 percent of the southern white vote but 87 percent of the black vote. The South was still a Republican stronghold, but moderate Democrats, Clinton demonstrated, could do well enough there that the South was no longer an albatross for Democratic candidates. In effect, Clinton had recentered the Democratic party and in so doing shifted the Republicans even more to the right. Clinton's stances on taxes and balancing the budget without risking Social Security had established the Democrats as the party of fiscal responsibility. No one could tell in 1996 if this forecast a new Democratic era or represented only an interlude in a Republican dynasty. Either way, clearly southerners near the end of the twentieth century were shaping the mainstream of national politics.

Suddenly Clinton's presidency, and especially his personal prestige, were threatened in late January 1998 when charges were published that he had had an improper sexual relationship in the White House with a young (but certainly not inexperienced) intern named Monica Lewinsky. Clinton quickly denied the charges, but in the media frenzy that followed, more lurid details emerged. The Republicans—many of whom already hated Clinton—pushed for and got a tough federal investigation, headed by special prosecutor Kenneth Starr, a determined opponent of everything Clinton stood for and represented. Media fascination on the all-news cable networks and radio talk shows outpaced public interest, but as evidence mounted, Clinton eventually admitted an inappropriate relationship with Lewinsky. GOP investigations of other so-called Clinton evils, some of them quite far-fetched, turned up no credible evidence. But it subsequently became obvious that Clinton had lied about his dalliance with Lewinsky to a grand jury that was investigating another matter. On the basis of that lie to cover up a private immoral act, the GOP pushed energetically for impeachment. The House brought charges, but the Senate, on February 12, 1999, failed to convict. Ironically, even after a year of extensive media coverage, fervent Republican opposition, and substantial public disgust with Clinton's personal behavior, Clinton's positive approval rating soared to 73 percent while that of the GOP Congress fell to below 40 percent. Why did Clinton's ratings remain so favorable?

A booming economy covers many sins, and the economy was certainly booming. Clinton pushed economic globalization, and his policies—whether bailing out the Mexican peso or pushing for Asian economic reforms—facilitated growth. He had learned from the health-care imbroglio to advocate piecemeal change, and through skillful politics he had pushed through or achieved via executive orders a number of small reforms that in the aggregate represented a substantial achievement. And GOP extremism—symbolized by Newt Gingrich and Kenneth Starr—allowed Clinton to portray himself as the reasonable protector of government services, the environment, women's rights, and affirmative action—on that issue, "mend it, don't end it" was Clinton's advice. The public clearly differentiated between Clinton's personal immorality and his presidential policies and achievements. Actually a series of prominent Republican legislators (Newt Gingrich, Henry Hyde, Bob Livingston), as it turned out, had similar moral failings, which tended to make the impeachment charges seem in part motivated by policy differences rather than by high principles. Nevertheless, though crippled by the impeachment proceedings and juicy grand jury leaks that the GOP made sure got maximum press exposure, Clinton tried to govern progressively and thereby earn a positive legacy. There were significant foreign policy achievements in Northern Ireland, North Korea, Haiti, Bosnia, and the Middle East. Environmental protections were strengthened and millions of acres were safeguarded as national monuments. Next to Theodore Roosevelt, Clinton proved to be the greatest presidential conservationist. But though most indicators of national well-being were up and the federal budget was balanced for the first time in decades, Clinton's personal reputation was understandably in shambles. Perhaps none were more disillusioned by his irresponsible and self-indulgent sexual immorality than his strongest supporters, who—aware of his intelligence, energy, and unrivaled political skills—had expected so much of him and a redirected Democratic party.

As the election year 2000 opened, Vice President Albert Gore was the automatic Democratic nominee, and he subsequently chose Senator Joseph Lieberman of Connecticut as his running mate. Gore had already decided to distance himself from Clinton, and Lieberman—the first orthodox Jew on a national ticket and a sharp critic of Clinton's inexcusable behavior with Lewinsky—was intended as a moral inoculation against a Clinton infection. But Gore proved to be a dull, "wooden," and arrogant campaigner, and in distancing himself from Clinton, he failed to campaign effectively on the undeniable policy achievements of the administration of which he had been a part. The GOP nominee, on the other hand, former Texas governor George W. Bush, was widely perceived as more personable if not as informed as Gore. (Bush chose the seasoned Dick Cheney as his running mate to add heft to the ticket.) Bush had served successfully as governor of Texas during prosperous times, and using family connections and immense fund-raising skills, he had accumulated such a campaign war chest that potential GOP rivals melted away during the primaries. Bush also campaigned on behalf of "compassionate conservatism," an obvious rhetorical rejection of the harsh tone of Gingrich and the Republican right wing's Contract with America. The election generated little enthusiasm, although both parties raised and spent unprecedented sums of money. No issues really caught on, with Bush running against Clinton's character and Gore running against Bush's inexperience. Polls showed a public almost evenly divided, but as election night grew late, it appeared that Gore was winning. Television analysts projected, on the basis of exit polls, that Gore had narrowly won Florida, where candidate Bush's brother Jeb was governor, and hence garnered both the national popular and the college majority. Then the analysts withdrew that projection and said

Florida was too close to call, then still later one network called the election for Bush. That confusion only foreshadowed what was to come.

At the end of election night, Florida's official election results gave Bush a 1,784-vote majority. Recounting quickly narrowed the majority to 327 votes. Both candidates then mobilized to project their interests, and the public was treated to a fiasco of irregular and inconsistent ballot counting (*chads* entered the common vocabulary), confusing ballots, and a barrage of legal challenges. The GOP clearly wanted the election more desperately than the Democrats did, and in the legal maneuvering that followed, the Republicans skillfully played hardball while the Democrats seemed indecisive. Seizing on the final (and spurious) television calling of the election a Bush victory, the GOP portrayed Gore as a sore loser. However, antiquated voting machines and poorly designed ballots had resulted in approximately 172,000 ballots being thrown out—the majority of which represented votes intended for Gore. Yet an accurate tally of the ballots that were permitted to be counted indicated a narrow Bush victory of several hundred votes. Democrats asked the Florida courts to broaden the recount. In a stunning and unprecedented decision that repudiated its recent states-rights tendencies, the U.S. Supreme Court, on December 12, 2001, by a five-to-four vote overruled the Florida lower-court decision and prevented an expanded recount, giving the Florida electoral votes to Bush. That ruling by Republican-appointed conservative justices gave Bush—who had lost the national popular election by 540,000 votes—an electoral college victory of five votes and hence the presidency (one elector from the District of Columbia, where Gore defeated Bush by a nine-to-one margin, abstained from casting a vote).

Despite the dubious validity of his election, once the Supreme Court had ruled, the American public—evidently exhausted by the controversy—decided to move on and accept Bush as the new president; even Gore accepted the authority of the court and pledged his support to the new commander-in-chief. Such was the prestige of the court that the transition in administrations went smoothly. And Bush dismissed the narrowness of the election (in which Democrats had picked up seats in both the House and the Senate, achieving a 50-50 tie in the Senate that soon became organized 51 to 49 in their favor when GOP Senator James M. Jeffords of Vermont switched to an independent and aligned with the Democrats) and set about governing with a decidedly more conservative bent than he had indicated during the campaign. Fiercely conservative Republican stalwarts disproportionately from southern states again controlled important House and Senate committees. The southernized GOP that had emerged during the 1980s and 1990s had a clear agenda. Appointments and early policy decisions revealed a determination to roll back Clinton positions on the environment, conservation, stem cell research, and abortion rights and cut taxes significantly. Internationalism was out, unilateralism was in. Even before the election the long economic boom had shown signs of faltering, and by the spring of 2001 the economy had clearly cooled. Bush had simply and boldly assumed a mandate for change where none existed, and he governed accordingly: he shifted the direction of the government in a sharp right turn, a direction that accurately reflected the majority opinion of white southerners.

How this would play nationally was rendered moot by a terrible tragedy on September 11, 2001, when Islamic terrorists attacked the World Trade Center in New York City and the Pentagon in Washington, D.C., killing approximately three thousand persons. Shocked as by no event since Pearl Harbor in 1941, the American people responded with an enormous outpouring of patriotism and a strong determination to attack the terrorists and other perceived enemies (primarily Saddam Hussein of Iraq) of the nation. Bush exemplified this patriotic anger and resolve and naturally soared in the opinion polls, a popularity that lasted through the midterm elections of 2002 and enabled the GOP to widen its lead in the House and retake control of the Senate. With international events dominating the political consciousness, it was difficult to evaluate the long-term political popularity of Bush's "more Reagan than Reagan" policies. Terrorism along with major corporate corruption and bankruptcies (exemplified by two southern-based rogue companies, Enron and WorldCom) stifled the economy. Unemployment was up (1.5 million jobs were lost in 2001–2002), the stock market was down, and there were once again large federal budget deficits long into the foreseeable future. Afghanistan had been freed from Taliban control, but Osama bin Laden, the terrorist mastermind, was still at large. Yet Bush remained personally popular even as polls showed by a two-to-one ratio that Americans doubted the wisdom of further tax cuts or a possible war with Iraq. The hawkish U.S. position on Iraq isolated the nation from world opinion as had no event in recent history. In an interesting switch from the Clinton years, when the president was personally less popular than his policies, Bush domestically was personally more popular than his policies. The European public excoriated Bush, and half-century-old alliances were threatened.

Exactly what this meant for the future was unclear at the beginning of 2003. Bush had succeeded in placing a compassionate smiley face on conservative policies, and when Senate Majority Leader Trent Lott from Mississippi in late 2002 praised retiring Senator Strom Thurmond by saying the nation would have been better off if it had followed Thurmond's racist Dixiecrat platform of 1948, Bush quickly and rightfully acted to disassociate the modern GOP from this revealing link to its not-so-subtle racist origins in the postsegregation South. With the retirement in 2002 of Thurmond and Jesse Helms from the Senate—reminders of an earlier era—and the disavowal of Lott and the sentiment he expressed, optimists hoped that the South (and the nation) was finally putting Jim Crow to rest. But that optimism was quickly dashed when the administration entered a brief against the University of Michigan's affirmative action plan and forwarded the nomination of a series of appointees who represented far-right positions on practically every issue. U.S. public opinion was more deeply divided over foreign policy as 2003 began than it had been since the domestic turmoil of the Vietnam years.

In the age of George Washington and Thomas Jefferson, the South had been the region of progressive nationalism, not defensive regionalism. New Englanders were the secessionists then. William Jefferson Clinton's decision to begin his 1993 inaugural journey to Washington with a tour of Monticello, then essentially replicate by bus caravan Thomas Jefferson's 1801 inaugural journey to Washington, suggests the symbolic connection Clinton wanted to make to that earlier age. It would be tempting to argue that to some degree with Jimmy Carter, but more completely with Clinton and Gore, the South once again represented progressive nationalism, not a defense of retrograde regional institutions and attitudes. In that sense, the South's long estrangement from national norms that at its apex led to Civil War and separate nationhood was finally finished, and the region had at last fully rejoined its rightful place in the nation. Segregation was no longer legal, the South basked in the warmth of the Sun Belt, and two-party politics thrived in the nation. Now in late 2002, Bush and most prominent Republicans had categorically repudiated racist sentiments and forthrightly condemned the past age of segregation. If the GOP proceeded to govern and campaign in this vein, could one dare imagine that, in some sense, one long and tragic phase of southern history had ended?

Blatant racist politics was no longer acceptable, but Bush's basic conservative politics of opposition to taxes and most government regulations and increased support for the military still better reflected the sentiments of the majority of southern white voters than did the more liberal policies of national Democrats. Early indications in 2003 suggested that Bush planned to use GOP control of Congress to push a very conservative social agenda that would also reflect the strong influence of the South's religious right. But international events had put normal politics on hold, and only time would tell which party, if either, would dominate the region in the coming decades. Perhaps there would never be another Solid South but rather an era of spirited if not quite equal two-party competition. One could predict that for the foreseeable future the GOP would usually be victorious in the region both in presidential and Congressional politics, as well as in local, with Republican dominance occasionally interrupted by successful campaigns skillfully conducted by moderate Democrats. Clearly the region tilted toward the GOP and among white southerners, political liberalism was dead in 2003. But blacks still overwhelmingly voted Democratic. Only the rapidly growing Latino vote appeared to be contested ground for the coming decade. At the beginning of the twenty-first century, southern politics remained in flux.

CHAPTER 32

Forever Southern

THE SEARCH FOR SOUTHERN IDENTITY

No other region of the nation has been as concerned with and as compulsive about understanding its identity as has the South, especially since the 1820s when it began to be increasingly evident that the South had an identity, or at least institutions and interests, separate from the rest of the nation. After New England won the cultural battle in the early nineteenth century to define itself as the American norm, with the nation portrayed as New England writ large, the South by definition was the other region against which American values and attributes were contrasted. The southern difference was more often simply assumed rather than explained. Jefferson, though, had early posited climate as the determining factor that explained the South's difference, and as late as 1929, so prominent an interpreter of the South as Yale historian U. B. Phillips could begin an interpretation of the South by first talking about the weather. The climatic argument continued to be heard into the 1960s, for example, in the writing of historian Clement Eaton, but after air-conditioning practically eliminated the discomfort of the South's long hot summers, the argument about climate's shaping role diminished.

Another perennial explanation of the South's distinctiveness has involved the presence in the region for more than three centuries of large numbers of blacks. This argument has taken a variety of forms, but the most common one, also based on the writings of U. B. Phillips, involves the persistent resolve of whites to dominate the blacks, whether through slavery or segregation or more subtle pressures. Variations of this persuasive view interpret much of southern politics in terms of race, particularly the recurrent desire to minimize white class differences so as to pose a united white stand against the so-called threat of the black underclass. From the aftermath of Bacon's Rebellion in late seventeenth-century Virginia to the appeal of George Wallace and David Duke in the twentieth, white leaders have tried to promote white racial solidarity, a kind of white-folks democracy, in order to maintain strict racial control. Yet the growing reality of biracial politics in the recent South, especially in the Democratic party at the state level, suggests that this feature of southern politics is less salient now. The politics of racism has not disappeared, as David Duke showed by his near success in Louisiana in 1991, but perhaps more important than his electoral prowess was the forthright opposition to him by the leaders of both the Democratic and the Republican parties. Even the southernized GOP found the starkness of Duke's racial polarizing objectionable. Blatant racism is no longer a political asset in the South, and subtle racism in recent years has seemed as evident in Boston and Detroit and Los Angeles as in Atlanta or New Orleans. Racism no longer defines the Dixie difference.

Another traditional explanation for the South's seeming uniqueness within the nation was that for much of its history, the region was more rural and its economy more dominated by agriculture than the rest of the nation. The relative absence of cities and industry was evidence of what, in effect, was an argument that, compared to the United States as a whole, the South was less modern. A variation of this explanation was the argument that the frontier experience lingered longer in the antebellum South; in fact, the southwestern portion of the Old South at the beginning of the Civil War was barely more than a generation removed from frontier days. Perhaps this explained the absence of cities, the easier acceptance of violence, the undeveloped state of social institutions. But, however valid these arguments for rurality and the frontier being responsible for the nature of the southern difference may have been in the past, their utility seemed far less evident for the South after 1960. Now the great majority of southerners live in cities, and more work in industry than in agriculture. Skyscrapers, shopping malls, suburbs, and traffic jams are as much a part of the southern landscape as they are of the northern. So comparative lack of urbanization is no longer a characteristic of the South. Still, it could be suggested that the South's large cities, newer and less dense, have a different feel than such cities as Boston and Philadelphia. But it is more a matter of degree than of kind.

Beginning about 1830, as large-scale European migration began to make more diverse the essentially English cultural and social mores of the North, the relative absence of such migration served to set the South apart. Moreover, almost all blacks lived in the southern states. As the white South remained comparatively British and Protestant, the North became ever more ethnically and religiously diverse, particularly in its growing urban areas. As much as anything else, a southern visitor to a northern city in about 1900 would have remarked on the presence of ethnic enclaves and ghettoes there, a babble of languages and cultures that often made portions of the North appear like a foreign country. In turn, the South's biracial society often seemed exotic to northern visitors, but at least southern whites and blacks usually shared the same religious faith, spoke the same language, and had similar attitudes on a range of issues. The South, despite the presence of a rigid color line that affected social relations, was probably the more culturally homogeneous society. Southerners black and white shared more ideas about faith, food, and family than did the peoples of the more urban North.

In the almost two generations following the end of World War II, however, very significant northern in-migration to the South, along with the rise of Cuban, Mexican, and Vietnamese communities, have diversified the southern population. Certainly the large southern cities—Miami, Atlanta, New Orleans, Dallas, and Houston—are far more demographically complex than they were a half-century ago. Moreover, during the first six decades of this century, millions of southern blacks migrated north, mostly to cities. Now one can find soul food almost as easily in Newark or Chicago as in Memphis. Southern cities on the whole still lack the rich panoply of ethnic neighborhoods that characterize cities in the Midwest and Northeast especially, and they tend to be far less densely peopled. Yet the urban South today seems more urban than southern, and in that sense less different from northern cities than it did two generations ago.

For many decades, the South's pathological tendencies set it apart. The South was the poorest, the least educated, the most violent, the most racist portion of the nation. Yet in all these measures of the lack of social well-being, the difference between the South and the rest of the nation has been very significantly narrowed. While the South as a whole still has the lowest per capita income of any region in the nation, it no longer has the social characteristics of a so-called Third World nation. The murder capital is no longer typically New Orleans or Houston, but Washington, D.C.; Detroit; or Oakland, California, instead. The gap between the South and the nation at large in many areas of social welfare has become small enough to have little apparent explanatory value. Poverty and homelessness and all the attendant social ills are now truly national problems, not stereotypically southern ones.

Other developments in recent years give further evidence that the destructive malignancy of racism may go into remission. In 1994, after the resounding Republican takeover of Congress, Newt Gingrich, the very conservative GOP helmsman, spoke on behalf of healing racial wounds and even praised former Democratic leadership in this area of national politics. The Southern Baptist Convention (SBC), the largest Protestant denomination in the nation, met in Atlanta in June 1995 to celebrate the 150th anniversary of its founding in nearby Augusta—the SBC was formed in response to abolitionist pressure and was explicitly proslavery. For most of those 150 years, the SBC, like all mainstream southern Protestant churches, had been conservative on social issues and focused narrowly on spiritual matters. The SBC had been charitable (founding hospitals and colleges, for example) but had never challenged regional racial mores. Many local white churches had resisted the civil rights movement. But in Atlanta, on June 20, the almost twenty thousand delegates (called messengers) voted overwhelmingly to "repent of racism" and to apologize for slavery. The resolution stated that "we lament and repudiate historic acts of evil such as slavery… and we recognize that the racism which yet plagues our culture today is inextricably tied to the past." The SBC members also apologized "to all African Americans for condoning and/or perpetuating individual and systemic racism in our lifetime.…" These were historic, hopeful, healing words, but only time will tell to what extent deep-felt attitudes are changing.

These initiatives were, however, forwarded by then-President Clinton, who on June 12, 1997, put together a seven-person board—headed by a preeminent black historian, John Hope Franklin—to advise him on racial issues. Two days later, Clinton delivered a major address defending the principle of affirmative action and calling for the nation to begin a yearlong "candid conversation on the state of race relations today." He concluded by evoking the image of "the world's first truly multiracial democracy." Achieving that goal is, said Clinton, "the unfinished work of our times, to lift the burden of race and redeem the promise of America." Perhaps on the matter of race, the South and southerners can be in the vanguard of progress.

An indication of developing black pride and a decreasing sense of alienation is the resurgence of Juneteenth celebrations. The term arises from the date, June 19, 1865, when Union general Gordon Granger in Galveston, Texas, read out the Emancipation Proclamation and issued General Order No. 3 declaring that the state's quarter of a million slaves were henceforth free. The day became an African-American holiday in Texas, but it faded in the 1960s during the civil rights movement. In the 1970s African Americans renewed their search for and celebration of their cultural identity and revived Juneteenth. It became an official Texas holiday in 1979, and by the late 1990s Juneteenth had spread across the nation—from California to Maryland—as an occasion to celebrate black freedom, becoming in effect a kind of black Independence Day.

But if air-conditioning and urban growth and regional prosperity and racial gains have so merged the South and the rest of the nation, can one still usefully speak of a distinctive South? Perhaps it is in the realm of mind and culture that we must today look for the essence of southernness. In fact, that is precisely what modern polling data indicates. Sociologist John Shelton Reed first began to analyze what he called "the enduring South" after informal polls in his University of North Carolina classrooms indicated that southern students used different words to characterize the South than they did the North, and so did northern students, and in fact, there was great similarity in the words or values associated with each region by northerners and southerners. Often the words were at best only one remove from stereotypes, but stereotypes indicate social perceptions. As one might expect, the South was described in such terms as warm, friendly, informal, traditional, slow-paced, and racist, while the North was seen as cold, rude, busy, progressive, and urban.

The results of these classroom questionnaires led Reed to examine the national Gallup poll data over many decades. The results were instructive. Northern and southern attitudes diverged widely over a broad range of issues in the 1930s, but even though both regions showed marked changes in attitudes over the years, statistically the southern divergence from the national norm was greater in the early 1970s—when Reed did his analysis—than it had been four decades earlier. In other words, across a spectrum of questions, southerners were even more different attitudinally from other Americans in the 1970s than they had been in the 1930s. Controlling for economic status, educational attainment, degree of urbanization, and other factors, people in the South were still regionally distinct. And the better educated, more urban, more widely traveled, and more affluent they were, the more different southerners seemed to be from their fellow Americans in terms of attitudes. That would suggest that as the South as a region continued to narrow the measurable income, educational, and other gaps between itself and the nation as a whole—became more like the nation—the sense of southern distinctiveness might be ironically strengthened rather than dissipated.

John Shelton Reed has made the point that a sense of distinctiveness does not exist in isolation. Rather, one must have some understanding of others who are perceived to be unlike oneself before one can develop a self-consciousness of one's own identity. That is, one defines oneself in relative terms, either positively or negatively, and those southerners who have traveled or worked in the North or abroad, who are educated and who have been exposed to a range of viewpoints, who have become urbanized and experienced in more cosmopolitan social interactions, are the very ones most able to recognize their southernness because they have seen it juxtaposed to other cultures. The least traveled, least educated, and least cosmopolitan persons in the South, on the other hand, have the least self-awareness of their culture. Hence the paradox that those southerners who by education, employment, and lack of provincialism would seem to be candidates for loss of their southern self-identity are, in fact, most aware and protective of their felt southernness. What are the origins of this resilient sense of mental southernness, and of what does it consist?

Perhaps the most helpful interpreter of the South has been historian C. Vann Woodward. In his presidential address to the Southern Historical Association in November 1952, he suggested that the South was different from the rest of the nation largely because it had had such a different historical experience. The nation as a whole had largely escaped the normal consequences of history in that, unlike most other nations, it had never been "confronted by complete frustration"—the United States had a "legend of success and victory… not shared by any other people of the civilized world." Southerners, in contrast, knew "that history has happened to our people in our part of the world." In other essays, Woodward elaborated this insight, arguing that while in its experience the nation had known mainly success, prosperity, and innocence, the South had struggled with failure, poverty, and guilt. Yet, ironically, what set the South apart from the nation gave it the potential to understand the larger world better, because the South's historical experience was more like that of the rest of the world. That could explain why Europeans, for instance, were so quick to understand and appreciate southern fiction and music.

Woodward was, of course, implicitly writing about the white South, and his analysis of the national experience predated the 1960s "war on poverty" and the 1970s experience with defeat in Vietnam and the guilt of Watergate. Still, the burden of his interpretation obtains: the South's entire historical experience—slavery, secession, Civil War, sharecropping, segregation, its variation from the national norms and expectations—is what defines its sense of separateness. The recognition of apartness has often led to a defensiveness that became transmogrified into an apotheosis of southern ways. Few southerners were probably even aware of this process; many simply assumed that southern values and habits and tastes were normative, with other ways less acceptable. Rural, defensive, and comparatively homogeneous for generations, the South's people created unawares a folk culture, an identification with place and family and religion and even gastronomic preference, whereby they understood and defined themselves without premeditation. Rural isolation and loneliness led the southern people to prize kinship, often cemented by visiting; hardship and dislocation caused them to romanticize home and place; evangelical religion offered meaning and hope (and paradoxically fatalism) amidst a life of travail; simple, spicy fried foods provided sustenance; conversation, song, and folk recreations such as hunting and quilting that combined practical results with pleasure in the process brought joy into otherwise humdrum existence. While southern ways were thus grounded in the historical reality of the region, once the mores existed, they came to have a life separate from their origins. Thus reified, these values, habits of mind, and cultural preferences have long outlived their folk roots and become an integral part of a southern consciousness that persists even in the modern urban South. Affluent, educated southern cosmopolites attend church far more frequently than do their northern cohorts; they still express a biracial hunger for so-called soul food, diets be damned; they eat junk food like Moon Pies, Krispy Kreme doughnuts, and Goo Goo Clusters as almost self-conscious statements of southernness; they often reveal an awareness and affection for kin relationships—even to second and third cousins—that leave non-southerners befuddled. Southerners still greet newcomers by asking where they are from, revealing that they expect others' identity, too, to be somehow intertwined with their home place.

SOMETHING OLD, SOMETHING NEW

Not every southerner today defends or identifies with every aspect of the region, from stock-car races to country music to fanaticism about football to fervent defenses of a favorite barbecue restaurant. Most understand that certain older characteristics of the region—racism and general close-mindedness, for example—need to be eradicated. Probably most white southerners recognize that whatever the intrinsic meaning of the so-called Confederate flag, it has been so abused by the Klan and other fringe groups that its contemporary display symbolizes hate and violence for most Americans. But even the most cautious son or daughter of the South who wants not to be stigmatized with certain aspects of the region's past identity will nevertheless defend other southernisms, such as notions about manners or respect for kin. The task of many modern, progressive southerners is discovering what from the stockpile of past southern ways ought to be discarded and what ought to be preserved and nurtured. There remains among many southerners a habit of politeness, a personalism, a patience that sometimes merges into fatalism, a respect for history, that can be very attractive. These values also turn out to be surprisingly biracial; southern whites and blacks are less different from each other in their basic attitudes than both are from other Americans.

This should not really be surprising. Blacks and whites have lived cheek by jowl together in the South for 375 mostly unhappy years, but in so doing they have been shaped by similar forces. In terms of accent, food preference, religious style, music, and attitudes toward kin and home, white and black southerners share far more than they differ. Perhaps it is this centuries-old blending of black and white ways, conscious and unconscious, ignored and denied, that is at the heart of the southern character. These matters of mind and habit, forged together in the southern past, constitute the southern way that both races today largely recognize and label good. As exemplified in the persons and values of Lamar Alexander, Jimmy Carter, Bill Clinton, Albert Gore, Jr., Martin Luther King, Jr., Andrew Young, Barbara Jordan, and many others, reformed southern values, drained of racism and violence and drenched in generations of evangelical preaching, can even be redemptive for the nation. Southerners of both races now think the South is the better region of the nation in which to live, and they value highly those aspects of the regional folk culture that they consider essential to themselves as southerners. Now that reformed southern ways are cherished, the occasional fear that their manners of the heart and mind are threatened by societal change or are unappreciated by outsiders or the larger culture only leads southerners to attempt to strengthen them by an act of the will, "Dixiefying Dixie," in the words of journalist Edwin M. Yoder, Jr. Southern identity may now be in significant part a self-conscious evocation, but so is French culture, and neither appear to be headed toward extinction.

Different groups in the South use different ways of revivifying and celebrating their folk roots. College professors attend and promote symposia on the nature of the South and such cultural icons as W. J. Cash and William Faulkner. Other southerners associate stock-car races or college football games or hunting and fishing with their sense of the South. Nostalgic forms of music, primarily country, blue grass, gospel, jazz, and blues, which remain creative but relate to earlier versions of the genre, tie many southerners to a selective portion of the past. Old-time "fiddlin' contests" and radio programs like the "Grand

Ole Opry" are self-consciously traditional. Folk crafts are still another popular way to maintain a relationship with older ways, and particularly throughout the mountain South such items as Shaker furniture and the objects made, displayed, and sold at such locations as Berea, Kentucky, and Bransom, Missouri, are almost artifactual fossils from yesteryear. Quilting, military reenactments, a fascination with genealogy, and a rich variety of family and church homecomings with dinner on the grounds, are but representative activities that offer contemporary southerners a connection to what is perceived to be a past that provides stability and meaning to their lives. Certainly many of these activities are not exclusive to the South, but in this region—perhaps more so than elsewhere—they are an important part of regional self-identity.

Fiction, autobiography, and history are also components of present-day southern regionalism. The great works of William Faulkner, Thomas Wolfe, Carson McCullers, Flannery O'Connor, Richard Wright, Zora Neale Hurston, Robert Penn Warren, and Eudora Welty are still read in the South and often constitute the fare of college literature courses, along with more recent serious authors like Truman Capote, Harper Lee, William Styron, Reynolds Price, Ralph Ellison, Ernest Gaines, and Alice Walker. A broader public reads the less serious but equally southern fiction of Bobbie Lee Mason, Fanny Flagg, Anne Rivers Siddons, Lee Smith, and especially Pat Conroy. National critics label such writers regional novelists, and their works certainly contain much local color. But a great many southerners find themselves and their world reflected in this literary outpouring. Another extremely revealing genre of southern writing has been autobiography. William Alexander Percy's *Lanterns on the Levee* (1941), William A. Owens's *This Stubborn Soil* (1966), Anne Moody's *Coming of Age in Mississippi* (1968), Maya Angelou's *I Know Why the Caged Bird Sings* (1969), and Will Campbell's *Brother to a Dragonfly* (1977) have become beloved books to many southerners wherein they discover something familiar, something new about both themselves and their region. Race is a theme in all these books, a tragic and at times triumphant motif that is central to southerners being who they are.

Movies and television have been powerful creators, propagators, and sustainers of myths about the South—the Old South, the benighted South, the good ol' boy South. In the 1920s and 1930s, many of the most popular movies—from *Birth of a Nation* (1915) to *Gone with the Wind* (1939)—continued the moonlight-and-magnolia stereotypes about the region, with a vicious pinch of racism often thrown in gratuitously. These stereotypes were reversed in later films such as *Mandingo* (1975), *Drum* (1976), and *Hurry Sundown* (1967), where white males are moral monsters. Other films, like *Thunder Road* (1958) and *Macon County Line* (1973), feature moonshiners, car races, and lawbreaking but goodhearted good ol' boys—a theme that found itself repeated in the popular though mindless 1970s television hit series, "The Dukes of Hazzard." Yet also in the 1960s, a spate of more sophisticated films began to suggest ways the South could move, and indeed was moving, beyond its racist heritage. In the *Heat of the Night*

(1967) suggested moral growth on the part of a pot-bellied southern sheriff. *Sounder* (1972), a poignant film about a black sharecropper family in depression-era Louisiana, represented a distinct advance over caricatured one-dimensional depictions of blacks—either as Sambos or rebels—in most previous movies. *To Kill a Mockingbird* (1963) showed a white lawyer willing to stand up against racism in a small southern town, and southerners who saw this powerful cinematic drama understood full well with whom they should identify. The 1960s television series named after actor Andy Griffith, who played a wise and kind country sheriff, also offered an affectionate rendering of the small-town South, seemingly all-white but never openly racist or mean-spirited.

In the 1970s, the popular television program "The Waltons" (a far cry from the 1960s "Beverly Hillbillies") portrayed a depression-era Virginia family as having wholesome, idealized all-American virtues. In fact, Jimmy Carter in 1976 in many ways seemed to have stepped out of the television screen and onto the political stage. In the 1980s and 1990s, such reformed images of the South continued, with television shows like "I'll Fly Away" and movies like *Driving Miss Daisy* (1989) and *Fried Green Tomatoes* (1991). A cultural breakthrough of sorts was achieved with the movie *Broadcast News* (1987), which had actress Holly Hunter playing a southern-accented television news producer from Atlanta who, despite being obviously southern, was simply portrayed as an immensely competent professional. Gone was the automatic identification of attractive southern women with so-called southern belles, empty-headed flirts who cared only about their next date. In real life, Rosalynn Carter was a repudiation of the silliness of such outdated and erroneous stereotypes.

The southern states had not been at the forefront of the women's movement that began in the 1960s and accelerated thereafter. Southern men had a long and deep investment in male hierarchy, and many if not most southern women accepted their dependent position or gave lip service to the concept even if they personally acted otherwise. Congressman Howard W. Smith of Virginia assumed these conventions were immutable and so obvious that he added the word "sex" to the draft of the 1964 Civil Rights Act (prohibiting discrimination on the basis of race, color, religion, sex, or national origins) because he was confident that such a patently ridiculous proscription would insure the defeat of the act. But he was wrong. In perhaps the greatest irony of recent women's history, sexual discrimination became illegal in part because of the prejudice of a southern white man. Nonetheless, the modern feminist movement had limited success in the South, with only Texas unequivocally endorsing the movement to pass the Equal Rights Amendment.

Yet urban growth, economic development, the desire to attract northern investment and in-migration, and a gradual acceptance of changing national attitudes toward equal pay and fair employment practices subtly modernized the South. The region accommodated to the evolving rights of women even if it seldom led the way. A new generation of college-educated southern women also pushed—politely but ever so firmly—to break down old barriers. After 1970, women, particularly in the cities, found enhanced professional opportunities in the region. By the 1990s, southern women had served as mayors, governors, representatives, and senators; had led corporations and universities; had indeed proven that old images and habits and prejudices no longer dictated behavior. Southern white women, as well as southern blacks, were liberated as a result of their own efforts and the efforts of the federal government in the decades after 1960.

History in a variety of forms is another strong cultural adhesive binding the evolving present to a perception of the South's past. Most southern colleges offer courses in the history of the South—as do many colleges and universities outside the region—and the academic discipline supports a scholarly journal and a large annual meeting of historians. No longer is the written history of the South defensive or hagiographic. Rather, it is analytical, often critical of the past, and completely reflects the national trends in scholarship. Every southern state also has an active state historical society and at least one historical journal. All of the southern states have concrete reminders of their past in historic buildings and sites. History in the form of museums, battlefields, restored homes, and recreated structures (such as Colonial Williamsburg) is big business throughout much of Virginia and in Charleston, Savannah, New Orleans, Natchez, and Vicksburg. There is endemic fascination with the Civil War, sometimes even still quaintly called the War Between the States. As one travels across the region, old buildings, rather like geological outcroppings, offer silent evidence of a very different age and society that is now all but vanished. For many southerners, these standing physical artifacts are the most vivid expressions of their sense of connection to a past variously and selectively remembered. Organizations such as the Sons of the Confederacy and United Daughters of the Confederacy, along with glorified plantation homes, recall a past often romanticized; while more recently organized civil rights tours in cities like Birmingham and Memphis remind tourists of a very different South that should not be forgotten. Birmingham now has an emotionally powerful Civil Rights Museum, and Atlanta has a museum and memorial celebrating the life of Martin Luther King, Jr. Black and white southerners alike share a belief that who they are is tied up with where they are from, and monuments and shrines serve as symbols that give meaning and value to place. The phenomenal publishing (1976) and television mini-series (1977) success of Alex Haley's *Roots* illustrates the biracial nature of the southern identification with kin and place.

The South as a distinct region is now mostly a state of mind, a complex reaction to a shared historical experience, as the great southern historian C. Vann Woodward eloquently explained. Myth and memory, history and fiction are essential ingredients, along with a number of folk practices that keep alive vital links to an otherwise forgotten past. The South's long history incorporates blacks and whites in a common tragedy, while the more recent past offers incentives for regional pride. The occasional scorn directed southward also strengthens a sense of regional community that nurtures southern identity. But the South is no huge living museum. While the past often seems astonishingly close at hand, no other region of the nation has experienced such transforming change during the last two generations. The greatest domestic success story in the nation since World War II has been the civil rights movement in the South. No political party and no major political leader can any longer campaign in openly racist terms. The journey yet to be traveled must not be allowed to obscure the distance already covered. We cannot afford to loose the gains of the past several decades. The promise of progressive social change should be the South's offering to the nation. The greatest irony of all would be if the states of the former Confederacy could help heal the racial wounds of the United States. Pain—and history—can be redemptive, and in the South there are grounds for hope.

A Guide to Further Reading

The literature on southern history is immense, and there is no one comprehensive guide. Three historiographical volumes are indispensable for the scholarly literature, Arthur S. Link and Rembert W. Patrick, eds., *Writing Southern History: Essays in Historiography in Honor of Fletcher M. Green* (Baton Rouge, 1966); John B. Boles and Evelyn Thomas Nolen, eds., *Interpreting Southern History: Historiographical Essays in Honor of Sanford W. Higginbotham* (Baton Rouge, 1987); and John B. Boles, ed., *A Companion to the American South* (Malden, Mass., and London, Eng., 2002). Because these three volumes provide detailed coverage of the literature on southern history, this guide to reading emphasizes books and articles published that have shaped the author's understanding and discussion of the issues. It should be recognized that what follows represents only a fraction of the important works on the South, and the author apologizes to those authors whose works have been omitted because of limitations of space. Titles are repeated when they are relevant to several sections of this book.

In addition to the three historiographical volumes just mentioned, several specialized reference books are also useful for quick information and for pointing the way toward a more extensive literature. Among the most valuable of these are David C. Roller and Robert W. Twyman, eds., *The Encyclopedia of Southern History* (Baton Rouge, 1979); Charles Reagan Wilson and William Ferris, eds., *Encyclopedia of Southern Culture* (Chapel Hill, 1989); Samuel S. Hill, ed., *Encyclopedia of Religion in the South* (Macon, Ga., 1984); Randall M. Miller and John David Smith, eds., *Dictionary of Afro-American Slavery* (New York, Westport, Conn., and London, 1988); and Louis D. Rubin, Jr. et al., eds., *The History of Southern Literature* (Baton Rouge, 1985). The book reviews in each quarterly issue of the *Journal of Southern History* are a good index of the range of scholarship in the field, and each May issue of the journal contains a detailed, topical bibliography of periodical literature on southern history published in the preceding year. Also useful is Jessica S. Brown, ed., *The American South: A Historical Bibliography* (Santa Barbara, Calif., 1986), which reprints abstracts of almost nine thousand articles in southern history selected from approximately five hundred periodicals. Also extremely valuable are Donald B. Dodd and Wynelle S. Dodd, *Historical Statistics of the South, 1790–1970* (University, Ala., 1973), and William J. Cooper, Jr., and Thomas E. Terrill, *The American South: A History, Second Edition* (New York, 1996), which concludes with a long bibliographical essay.

PART 4:
THE COLONIAL SOUTH

For reasons that are not entirely clear, the lay public has been slower to accept the conclusions of revisionist scholarship on the general topic of Reconstruction than on any other topic in southern or American history, even though the revisionist viewpoint has been overwhelmingly dominant among academic historians for almost a half-century. Two extremely effective accounts that popularized—in the best sense—the new understanding are John Hope Franklin, *Reconstruction After the Civil War* (Chicago, 1961) and Kenneth M. Stampp, *The Era of Reconstruction, 1865–1877* (New York, 1965). These two books have had a profound influence, though not as universal as one would wish. The two standard college textbook accounts, which cover the entire Civil War and Reconstruction Era, are J. G. Randall and David Donald, *The Civil War and Reconstruction* (second ed., Boston, 1961), reprinted several times, and James M. McPherson, *Ordeal By Fire: The Civil War*

and Reconstruction (New York, 1982). The most up-to-date general account, distinguished by its research in secondary and primary sources and by its vigorous interpretation, is Eric Foner, *Reconstruction: America's Unfinished Revolution, 1863–1877* (New York, 1988). The best treatment of the important legal and constitutional issues raised and sometimes resolved during the entire era are Harold M. Hyman, *A More Perfect Union: The Impact of the Civil War and Reconstruction on the Constitution* (New York, 1973) and Hyman and William M. Wiecek, *Equal Justice Under Law: Constitutional Development, 1835–1875* (New York, 1982).

For the very beginning of Reconstruction see Willie Lee Rose, *Rehearsal for Reconstruction: The Port Royal Experiment* (Indianapolis, 1964), masterfully written; LaWanda Cox, *Lincoln and Black Freedom: A Study in Presidential Leadership* (Columbia, S.C., 1981); Dan T. Carter, *When the War Was Over: The Failure of Self-Reconstruction in the South, 1865–1867* (Baton Rouge, 1985); and Michael Perman, *Reunion Without Compromise: The South and Reconstruction, 1865–1868* (Cambridge, Eng., 1973). The different positions of Abraham Lincoln, Andrew Johnson, and Congress over the method and pace of Reconstruction have been the topic of very extensive research. Among the essential books are Michael Les Benedict, *A Compromise of Principle: Congressional Republicans and Reconstruction, 1863–1869* (New York, 1974) and *The Impeachment and Trial of Andrew Johnson* (New York, 1973); David Donald, *The Politics of Reconstruction, 1863–1867* (Baton Rouge, 1965); and Eric L. McKitrick, *Andrew Johnson and Reconstruction* (Chicago, 1960).

Much of the most exciting research has focused on specialized topics rather than national or state-level politics. Books that are especially effective at demolishing old stereotypes about the Reconstruction Era are George C. Rable, *But There Was No*

Peace: The Role of Violence in the Politics of Reconstruction (Athens, Ga., 1984); Richard Nelson Current, *Those Terrible Carpetbaggers* (New York, 1988); Lawrence N. Powell, *New Masters: Northern Planters during the Civil War and Reconstruction* (New Haven, 1980); Thomas Holt, *Black over White: Negro Political Leadership in South Carolina during Reconstruction* (Urbana, Ill., 1977); Eric Foner, *Freedom's Lawmakers: A Directory of Black Officeholders During Reconstruction* (New York, 1993); Allen W. Trelease, *White Terror: The Ku Klux Klan Conspiracy and Southern Reconstruction* (New York, 1971); Joseph G. Dawson, III, *Army Generals and Reconstruction: Louisiana, 1862–1877* (Baton Rouge, 1982); William S. McFeely, *Yankee Stepfather: General O. O. Howard and the Freedmen* (New Haven, 1968); James L. Roark, *Masters Without Slaves: Southern Planters in the Civil War and Reconstruction* (New York, 1977); and Mark W. Summers, *Railroads, Reconstruction, and the Gospel of Prosperity: Aid Under the Radical Republicans, 1865–1877* (Princeton, 1984). Laura Edwards's very impressive study, *Gendered Strife and Confusion: The Political Culture of Reconstruction* (Urbana, 1997), ably demonstrates how a gendered analysis can contribute to our understanding of the past. For some of the agricultural consequences of the Civil War see G. Terry Sharrer, *A Kind of Fate: Agricultural Change in Virginia, 1861–1920* (Ames, IA, 2000).

There now exist good, modern studies of the Reconstruction process for each southern state. Representative of the new viewpoints are Stephen V. Ash, *Middle Tennessee Society Transformed, 1860–1870: War and Peace in the Upper South* (Baton Rouge, 1988); William C. Harris, *Presidential Reconstruction in Mississippi* (Baton Rouge, 1967); Ted Tunnell, *Crucible of Reconstruction: War, Radicalism, and Race in Louisiana, 1862–1877* (Baton Rouge, 1984); and Joel Williamson, *After Slavery: The Negro in South Carolina During Reconstruction, 1861–1877*

(Chapel Hill, 1965). Randolph B. Campbell has written two model studies: *A Southern Community in Crisis: Harrison County, Texas, 1850–1880* (Austin, 1983) and *Grass Roots Reconstruction in Texas, 1865–1880* (Baton Rouge, 1998).

As with slavery, the topics of emancipation and the black experience in Reconstruction have generated a huge body of literature, much of it stunningly good. One may begin with Leon F. Litwack, *Been in the Storm So Long: The Aftermath of Slavery* (New York, 1979); Peter Kolchin, *First Freedom: The Responses of Alabama's Blacks to Emancipation and Reconstruction* (Westport, Conn., 1972); C. Peter Ripley, *Slaves and Freedmen in Civil War Louisiana* (Baton Rouge, 1976); Ira Berlin et al., *Slaves No More: Three Essays on Emancipation and the Civil War* (Cambridge, Eng., 1992); Janet Sharp Hermann, *The Pursuit of a Dream* (New York, 1981); and Michael Wayne, *The Reshaping of Plantation Society: The Natchez District, 1860–1880* (Baton Rouge, 1983). Most freed persons were soon caught up in the agricultural system called sharecropping. For this process see Roger L. Ransom and Richard Sutch, *One Kind of Freedom: The Economic Consequences of Emancipation* (Cambridge, Eng., 1977); Jay R. Mandle, *Not Slave, Not Free: The African American Economic Experience Since the Civil War* (Durham, 1992); and Harold D. Woodman, "Sequel to Slavery: The New History Views the Postbellum South," *Journal of Southern History*, 43 (November 1977), 523–54. The best account of how white farmers also were pulled into the system of sharecropping is Steven Hahn, *The Roots of Southern Populism: Yeoman Farmers and the Transformation of the Georgia Upcountry, 1850–1890* (New York, 1983). See also Peter Wallenstein, *From Slave South to New South: Public Policy in Nineteenth-Century Georgia* (Chapel Hill, 1987); Gavin Wright, *Old South, New South: Revolutions in the Southern Economy since the Civil War* (New

York, 1986); and Gilbert C. Fite, *Cotton Fields No More: Southern Agriculture, 1865–1980* (Lexington, Ky., 1984).

C. Vann Woodward's great book, *Origins of the New South, 1877–1913* (Baton Rouge, 1951), has profoundly shaped how historians ever since have conceptualized the entire era. His overview should now be supplemented with Howard N. Rabinowitz's *The First New South, 1865–1920* (Arlington Heights, Ill., 1992) and Edward L. Ayers, *The Promise of the New South: Life After Reconstruction* (New York, 1992). An extremely helpful historiographical essay is James C. Cobb, "Beyond Planters and Industrialists: A New Perspective on the New South," *Journal of Southern History*, 54 (February 1988), 45–68. Among the important studies are Jonathan M. Wiener, *Social Origins of the New South, Alabama: 1860–1885* (Baton Rouge, 1978); Dwight B. Billings, Jr., *Planters and the Making of a "New South": Class, Politics, and Development in North Carolina, 1865–1900* (Chapel Hill, 1979); Paul D. Escott, *Many Excellent People: Power and Privilege in North Carolina, 1850–1900* (Chapel Hill, 1985); James Tice Moore, "Redeemers Reconsidered: Change and Continuity in the Democratic South, 1870–1900," *Journal of Southern History*, 44 (August 1978), 357–78; Lacy K. Ford, "Rednecks and Merchants: Economic Development and Social Tensions in the South Carolina Upcountry, 1865–1900," *Journal of American History*, 71 (September 1984), 294–318. Paul M. Gaston in *The New South Creed: A Study in Southern Mythmaking* (New York, 1970) shows how quickly the image of a rebuilding South changed from exhortation to myth. The lingering influence of the Confederacy is the topic of Gaines M. Foster, *Ghosts of the Confederacy: Defeat, the Lost Cause, and the Emergence of the New South, 1865–1913* (New York, 1987).

Both Ayers, *The Promise of the New South*, and Rabinowitz, *The First New South*, give ample treatment of southern urban-ization following the Civil War. The best analysis of how blacks fared in the process is Howard N. Rabinowitz, *Race Relations in the Urban South, 1865–1890* (New York, 1978). See especially Don H. Doyle, *New Men, New Cities, New South: Atlanta, Nashville, Charleston, Mobile, 1860–1910* (Chapel Hill, 1990) and Harold L. Platt, *City Building in the New South: The Growth of Public Services in Houston, Texas, 1830–1910* (Philadelphia, 1982). The best survey of southern urbanization is David R. Goldfield, *Cotton Fields and Skyscrapers: Southern City and Region, 1607–1980* (Baton Rogue, 1982). For religion see Paul Harvey, *Redeeming the South: Religious Culture and Racial Identities among Southern Baptists, 1865–1925* (Chapel Hill, 1997) and Ted Ownby, *Subduing Satan: Religion, Recreation, and Manhood in the Rural South, 1865–1920* (Chapel Hill, 1990).

Every student of Populism in the South should begin with C. Vann Woodward's *Origins of the New South* and the biography that began Woodward's distinguished career, *Tom Watson, Agrarian Rebel* (New York, 1938). An impassioned analysis of southern Populists is provided by Lawrence Goodwyn in *Democratic Promise: The Populist Moment in America* (New York, 1976); a more balanced survey is offered by Robert C. McMath, Jr., *American Populism: A Social History, 1877–1898* (New York, 1993). See also Bruce Palmer, *"Man Over Money": The Southern Populist Critique of American Capitalism* (Chapel Hill, 1980). An important interpretation of how Populism was a response to far-reaching social changes is Steven Hahn's previously cited *The Roots of Southern Populism*. A fascinating debate that arose from this book is illustrated by the exchange that takes place between Hahn and two critics, Shawn Everett Kantor and J. Morgan Kousser, in the *Journal of Southern History*, 59 (May 1993), 201–66. For the collapse of Populism see Robert F. Durden,

The Climax of Populism: The Election of 1896 (Lexington, Ky., 1965). Two important articles are William F. Holmes, "Populism: In Search of Context," *Agricultural History*, 64 (Fall 1990), 26–58, and Gregg Cantrell and D. Scott Barton, "Texas Populists and the Failure of Biracial Politics," *Journal of Southern History*, 55 (November 1989), 659–92. Cantrell has since published *Kenneth and John B. Rayner and the Limits of Southern Dissent* (Urbana, Ill., 1993) on race and political reform in North Carolina and Texas. For women's involvement see Marion K. Barthelme, ed., *Women in the Texas Populist Movement: Letters to the Southern Mercury* (College Station, Tex., 1997).

Anne Firor Scott's work is essential for understanding the life experiences of women during the post–Civil War South. See *The Southern Lady: From Pedestal to Politics, 1830–1930* (Chicago, 1970) and *Natural Allies: Women's Associations in American History* (Urbana, Ill., 1992). An illustrative diary is Margaret Jones Bolsterli, ed., *Vinegar Pie and Chicken Bread: A Woman's Diary of Life in the Rural South, 1890–1891* (Fayetteville, Ark., 1982). A model monograph is Marjorie Spruill Wheeler, *New Women of the New South: The Leaders of the Woman Suffrage Movement in the Southern States* (New York, 1993). Four exemplary works on Texas women are Angela Boswell, *Her Act and Deed: Women's Lives in a Rural Southern County, 1837–73* (College Station, Tx., 2001), Megan Seaholm, "Earnest Women: The White Woman's Club Movement in Progressive Era Texas, 1880–1920" (Ph.D. dissertation, Rice University, 1988), Elizabeth Hayes Turner, *Women, Culture, and Community: Religion and Reform in Galveston, 1880–1920* (New York, 1997), and Judith N. McArthur, *Creating the New Woman: The Rise of Southern Women's Progressive Culture in Texas, 1893–1918* (Urbana, 1998). Several recent works ably portray the lives of farm women; see Rebecca Sharpless, *Fertile*

Ground, Narrow Choices: Women on Cotton Farms of the Texas Blackland Prairie, 1900–1940 (Chapel Hill, 1999); Melissa Walker, *All We Knew Was to Farm: Rural Women in the Upcountry South, 1919–1941* (Baltimore, 2000); and Lu Ann Jones, *Moma Learned Us to Work: Farm Women in the New South* (Chapel Hill, 2002). And no one should miss the brilliant chapter, "The Sad Irons," in Robert A. Caro's *The Years of Lyndon Johnson: The Path to Power* (New York, 1982), 502–15.

The place to begin studying the Progressive movement in the South is Dewey W. Grantham's impressive survey, *Southern Progressivism: The Reconciliation of Progress and Tradition* (Knoxville, 1983), which is detailed, analytical, and well written. Sheldon Hackney minimizes the connections between Populism and Progressivism in *Populism to Progressivism in Alabama* (Princeton, 1969), but see the corrective offered by Samuel L. Webb, "From Independents to Populists to Progressive Republicans: The Case of Chilton County, Alabama, 1880–1920," *Journal of Southern History*, 59 (November 1993), 707–36. There are a number of other relevant state studies and many biographies. For representative biographies see Robert C. Cotner, *James Stephen Hogg: A Biography* (Austin, 1959) and William F. Holmes, *The White Chief: James Kimble Vardaman* (Baton Rouge, 1970). Of the many specialized, topical studies, William A. Link's *A Hard Country and a Lonely Place: Schooling, Society, and Reform in Rural Virginia, 1870–1920* (Chapel Hill, 1986) and James L. Leloudis's *Schooling the New South: Pedagogy, Self, and Society in North Carolina, 1880–1920* (Chapel Hill, 1996) are of particular interest.

Southern industrialization is a major theme of C. Vann Woodward's *Origins of the New South, 1877–1913* (Baton Rouge, 1951). An important study that supplements Woodward's interpretation is David L. Carlton, *Mill and Town in South Carolina,*

1880–1920 (Baton Rouge, 1982). Dwight B. Billings, Jr., *Planters and the Making of a "New South,"* previously cited, is a strong challenge to Woodward. The best survey of southern industrialism is James C. Cobb, *Industrialization and Southern Society, 1877– 1984* (Lexington, Ky., 1984), but do not miss his important article, "Beyond Planters and Industrialists: A New Perspective on the New South," previously cited. The essential work for Appalachia is Ronald D. Eller, *Miners, Millhands, and Mountaineers: Industrialization of the Appalachian South, 1880–1930* (Knoxville, 1982). Allen Tullos presents a sensitive analysis of how industrialization affected people in *Habits of Industry: White Culture and the Transformation of the Carolina Piedmont* (Chapel Hill, 1989).

The New Deal was an incomplete blessing for the South. A brief interpretation is offered by Frank Freidel, *F. D. R. and the South* (Baton Rouge, 1965), but more detailed studies that emphasize the farmer's plight include David Eugene Conrad, *The Forgotten Farmers: The Story of Sharecroppers in the New Deal* (Urbana, Ill., 1965); Donald H. Grubbs, *Cry from the Cotton: The Southern Tenant Farmers' Union and the New Deal* (Chapel Hill, 1971); and Paul E. Mertz, *New Deal Policy and Southern Rural Poverty* (Baton Rouge, 1978). Two unusually good histories of recent southern farming exist: Pete Daniel, *Breaking the Land: The Transformation of Cotton, Tobacco, and Rice Cultures since 1880* (Urbana, Ill., 1985) and Jack Temple Kirby, *Rural Worlds Lost: The American South, 1920–1960* (Baton Rouge, 1987). See also D. Clayton Brown, *Electricity for Rural America: The Fight for the REA* (Westport, Conn., 1980) and the discussion of New Deal agricultural policies in James C. Cobb's powerful *The Most Southern Place on Earth: The Mississippi Delta and the Roots of Regional Identity* (New York, 1992). The impact of the New Deal on the South's cities is portrayed in Roger Biles,

"The Urban South in the Great Depression," *Journal of Southern History*, 56 (February 1990), 71–100.

The shameful story of race relations in the late nineteenth- and early twentieth-century South has been the subject of a series of important books. One should still begin with Rayford W. Logan, *The Negro in American Life and Thought: The Nadir, 1877–1901* (New York, 1954), and August Meier, *Negro Thought in America, 1880– 1915: Racial Ideologies in the Age of Booker T. Washington* (Ann Arbor, Mich., 1963). Joel Williamson provides a sweeping interpretation in *The Crucible of Race: Black–White Relations in the American South Since Emancipation* (New York, 1984), and Jack Temple Kirby's useful *Darkness at the Dawning: Race and Reform in the Progressive South* (Philadelphia, 1972) is an excellent survey of developments. The most important study of black disenfranchisement is J. Morgan Kousser, *The Shaping of Southern Politics: Suffrage Restriction and the Establishment of the One-Party South, 1880–1910* (New Haven, 1974). Anyone interested in the sad history of lynching should begin with W. Fitzhugh Brundage, *Lynching in the New South: Georgia and Virginia, 1880–1930* (Urbana, 1993). Three excellent state studies are John Dittmer, *Black Georgia in the Progressive Era, 1900–1920* (Urbana, Ill., 1977), Neil R. McMillen, *Dark Journey: Black Mississippians in the Age of Jim Crow* (Urbana, Ill., 1989), and John William Graves, *Town and Country: Race Relations in an Urban-Rural Context: Arkansas, 1865–1905* (Fayetteville, Ark., 1990), but no one should miss William Ivy Hair, *Carnival of Fury: Robert Charles and the New Orleans Race Riot of 1900* (Baton Rouge, 1976). Glenda Elizabeth Gilmore's *Gender and Jim Crow: Women and the Politics of White Supremacy in North Carolina, 1896–1920* (Chapel Hill, 1996), is a pathbreaking book certain to become a classic. It forces one to reconceptualize the topic of late nineteenth- and early twentieth-century southern politics. There are many topical studies, but see especially Matthew J. Mancini, *One Dies, Get Another: Convict Leasing in the American South, 1866–1928* (Columbia, S. C., 1996), Alex Lichtenstein, *Twice the Work of Free Labor: The Political Economy of Convict Labor in the New South* (New York, 1996), Walter B. Weare, *Black Business in the New South: A Social History of the North Carolina Mutual Life Insurance Company* (Urbana, Ill., 1973), and Willard B. Gatewood, *Aristocrats of Color: The Black Elite, 1880–1920* (Bloomington, Ind., 1990). Essential biographical studies include Louis R. Harlan's *Booker T. Washington: The Making of a Black Leader, 1856–1901* (New York, 1972) and *Booker T. Washington: The Wizard of Tuskegee, 1901–1915* (New York, 1983) and Elliott M. Rudwick's *W. E. B. DuBois: A Study in Minority Group Leadership* (Philadelphia, 1960). Dan T. Carter's beautifully and powerfully written *Scottsboro: A Tragedy of the American South* (Baton Rouge, 1969) vividly demonstrates the power of racism. See also James Goodman, *Stories of Scottsboro* (New York, 1994). The most influential book in the entire history of post–Civil War race relations remains C. Vann Woodward, *The Strange Career of Jim Crow*, third revised edition (New York, 1974), a book that had an enormous influence on a generation of white southerners.

An indispensable source for southern literary history is Louis D. Rubin, Jr. et al., eds., *The History of Southern Literature* (Baton Rouge, 1985). Several important works in intellectual history are essential for putting the literary developments in context. See Daniel Joseph Singal, *The War Within: From Victorian to Modernist Thought in the South, 1919–1945* (Chapel Hill, 1982); Michael O'Brien, *The Idea of the American South, 1920–1941* (Baltimore, 1979); and Richard H. King, *A Southern Renaissance: The Cultural Awakening of the American South, 1930–1955* (New York, 1980). Paul K.

Conkin's brief *The Southern Agrarians* (Knoxville, 1988) is a cogent interpretation of that literary movement. On W. C. Brann see Charles Carver, *Brann and the Iconoclast* (Austin, 1957). For women writers in general see Anne Goodwyn Jones, *Tomorrow Is Another Day: The Woman Writer in the South, 1859–1936* (Baton Rouge, 1981), and for the creator of *Gone with the Wind*, see Darden Asbury Pyron, *Southern Daughter: The Life of Margaret Mitchell* (New York, 1991). A huge critical literature exists for William Faulkner, but historians can usefully begin with David Minter, *William Faulkner: The Writing of a Life* (Baltimore, 1980), and Joel Williamson, *William Faulkner and Southern History* (New York, 1993). W. J. Cash, *The Mind of the South* (New York, 1941), is part history, part diatribe, part artifact of the age, and it is still necessary to read, but one doing so should balance Cash against James C. Cobb, "Does *Mind* No Longer Matter? The South, the Nation, and *The Mind of the South*, 1941–1991," *Journal of Southern History*, 57 (November 1991), 681–718, and Paul D. Escott, ed., *W. J. Cash and the Minds of the South* (Baton Rouge, 1992).

The author's discussion of southern music is drawn almost entirely from the scholarship of Bill C. Malone. See his *Country Music, U. S. A.* (Austin, 1985), *Southern Music, American Music* (Lexington, Ky., 1979), and *Singing Cowboys and Musical Mountaineers: Southern Culture and the Roots of Country Music* (Athens, Ga., 1993). One should complement Malone with Eileen Southern, *The Music of Black Americans: A History* (New York, 1971); William Ferris, *Blues from the Delta* (Garden City, 1978), and Lawrence W. Levine, *Black Culture and Black Consciousness: Afro-American Folk Thought from Slavery to Freedom* (New York, 1977).

T. Harry Williams, in his book of lectures, *Romance and Realism in Southern Politics* (Athens, Ga., 1961), first argued that Huey Long pioneered a realistic attitude toward Louisiana politics, but his magisterial biography, *Huey Long* (New York, 1969), ultimately becomes a rather romanticized portrait of the Louisiana phenomenon. The author finds William Ivy Hair's recent study, *The Kingfish and His Realm: The Life and Times of Huey P. Long* (Baton Rouge, 1991), far more persuasive. See also an even more critical study, Glen Jeansonne, *Messiah of the Masses: Huey P. Long and the Great Depression* (New York, 1993). For Lyndon B. Johnson, Robert A. Caro's multivolume biography in progress is powerfully written, but Caro has so demonized Johnson that the books ultimately lose credibility. See *The Years of Lyndon Johnson: The Path to Power* (New York, 1982) and *The Years of Lyndon Johnson: Means of Ascent* (New York, 1990). Robert Dallek also has in progress a multivolume biography of Johnson, and though his writing style is plodding, his analysis is both more sympathetic and more persuasive than Caro's. See Dallek's *Lone Star Rising: Lyndon Johnson and His Times, 1908–1960* (New York, 1991). For Jimmy Carter, see his own *Why Not the Best?* (Nashville, 1975) and *Turning Point: A Candidate, a State, and a Nation Come of Age* (New York, 1992). The best biographics of Carter are Peter Bourne, *Jimmy Carter: A Comprehensive Biography from Plains to Postpresidency* (New York, 1997) and Douglas Brinkley, *The Unfinished Presidency: Jimmy Carter's Journey Beyond the White House* (New York, 1998).

PART 5:
THE AMERICAN SOUTH

Two brief works of synthesis offer good introductions to the history of the recent South. See Charles P. Roland, *The Improbable Era: The South Since World War II* (Lexington, Ky., 1975) and David R. Goldfield, *Promised Land: The South Since 1945* (Arlington Heights, Ill., 1987). The best accounts of the events leading up to the changes that came in the wake of World War II are George Brown Tindall, *The Emergence of the New South, 1913–1945* (Baton Rouge, 1967) and Dewey W. Grantham, *The South in Modern America: A Region at Odds* (New York, 1994). For southern industrialization, see James C. Cobb, *The Selling of the South: The Southern Crusade for Industrial Development, 1936–1980* (Baton Rouge, 1982) and *Industrialization and Southern Society, 1877–1984* (Lexington, Ky., 1984). There are a number of valuable essays in James C. Cobb and Michael V. Namorato, eds., *The New Deal and the South* (Jackson, Miss., 1984). The indispensable study of World War II's economic impact on the South is Bruce J. Schulman, *From Cotton Belt to Sunbelt: Federal Policy, Economic Development, and the Transformation of the South, 1938–1980* (New York, 1991). Also see Paul Alejandro Levengood, "For the Duration and Beyond: World War II and the Creation of Modern Houston, Texas" (Ph.D. dissertation, Rice University, 1999). An essay not to be missed is Raymond Arsenault, "The End of the Long Hot Summer: The Air Conditioner and Southern Culture," *Journal of Southern History*, 50 (November 1984), 597–628. The most substantial study of the postwar South is Numan V. Bartley, *The New South, 1945–1980: The Story of the South's Modernization* (Baton Rouge, 1995). On education see Clarence L. Mohr, "World War II and the Transformation of Southern Education," in Neil R. McMillen, ed., *Remaking Dixie: The Impact of World War II on the American South* (Jackson, Miss., 1996), 33–55, 166–72, and the special issue on "Southern Higher Education in the 20th Century," *History of Higher Education Annual*, 19 (1999).

The literature on environmental history is burgeoning. My discussion has been shaped by such works as Timothy Silver, *A New Face on the Countryside: Indians, Colonists, and Slaves in South Atlantic Forests, 1500–1800*

(Cambridge, 1990), Mart Stewart, *"What Nature Suffers to Groe": Life, Labor, and Landscape on the Georgia Coast, 1680–1920* (Athens, Ga., 1996), Jack Temple Kirby, *Poquosin: A Study of Rural Landscape and Society* (Chapel Hill, 1995), John M. Barry, *Rising Tide: The Great Mississippi Flood of 1927 and How It Changed America* (New York, 1997), and Margaret Humphreys, "Kicking a Dying Dog: DDT and the Demise of Malaria in the American South, 1946–1950," *Isis*, 87 (March 1996), 1–17; and material in a number of specialized reference works on plants, animals, and locations.

The transformations in southern agriculture are spelled out in three excellent books: Gilbert C. Fite, *Cotton Fields No More: Southern Agriculture, 1865–1980* (Lexington, Ky., 1984); Pete Daniel, *Breaking the Land: The Transformation of Cotton, Tobacco, and Rice Cultures since 1880* (Urbana, Ill., 1985); and Jack Temple Kirby, *Rural Worlds Lost: The American South, 1920–1960* (Baton Rouge, 1987). James C. Cobb's account in *The Most Southern Place on Earth: The Mississippi Delta and the Roots of Regional Identity* (New York, 1992) is geographically limited, but it offers a vivid analysis of the impact, for example, of tractors and cotton-picking machines. The incompleteness of the agricultural transformation is revealed by comparing a classic, first published in 1941, James Agee and Walker Evans, *Let Us Now Praise Famous Men: Three Tenant Farmers* (Boston, 1960) with Dale Maharidge and Michael Williamson, *And Their Children After Them: The Legacy of Let Us Now Praise Famous Men, James Agee, Walker Evans, and the Rise and Fall of Cotton in the South* (New York, 1989). This reading experience should be balanced with J. Wayne Flynt, *Dixie's Forgotten People: The South's Poor Whites* (Bloomington, Ind., 1979) and *Poor But Proud: Alabama's Poor Whites* (Tuscaloosa, Ala., 1989).

David Goldfield and Charles P. Roland in their surveys of the post–World War II South provide a good description of the rise of the so-called Sun Belt. But one should also see Kirkpatrick Sale's angry analysis, *Power Shift: The Rise of the Southern Rim and Its Challenge to the Eastern Establishment* (New York, 1975). A more temperate interpretation is offered by Bernard L. Weinstein and Robert E. Firestine, *Regional Growth and Decline in the United States: The Rise of the Sunbelt and the Decline of the Northeast* (New York, 1978) and Neil R. McMillen, ed., *Remaking Dixie: The Impact of World War II on the American South* (Jackson, Miss., 1997). See also the relevant essays in John B. Boles, ed., *Dixie Dateline: A Journalistic Portrait of the Contemporary South* (Houston, 1983). George Brown Tindall, "The Sunbelt Snow Job," *Houston Review*, 1 (Spring 1979), 3–13, debunks exaggerated accounts of Sun Belt prosperity. For Sun Belt urbanization see David C. Perry and Alfred J. Watkins, eds., *The Rise of the Sunbelt Cities* (Beverly Hills, Calif., 1977); Richard M. Bernard and Bradley R. Rice, eds., *Sunbelt Cities: Politics and Growth Since World War II* (Austin, 1983); and Randall M. Miller and George E. Pozzetta, eds., *Shades of the Sunbelt: Essays on Ethnicity, Race, and the Urban South* (New York, 1988). On "creative cities" see Richard Florida, *The Rise of the Creative Class: And How It's Transforming Work, Leisure, Community, and Everyday Life* (New York, 2002).

The great story of the modern South concerns the improvements in race relations. The result has been a great outpouring of scholarship. The most useful introductions to the subject are Juan Williams, *Eyes on the Prize: America's Civil Rights Years, 1954–1965* (New York, 1987), intended to accompany the wonderful Public Broadcast System television series of the same name; Harvard Sitkoff, *The Struggle for Black Equality, 1954–1980* (New York, 1981); David R. Goldfield, *Black, White, and Southern: Race Relations and Southern Culture,*

1940 to the Present (Baton Rouge, 1990); and Steven F. Lawson, *Running for Freedom: Civil Rights and Black Politics in America Since 1941* (Philadelphia, 1991).

Two massive works fully repay reading: Richard Kluger, *Simple Justice: The History of Brown v. Board of Education and Black America's Struggle for Equality* (2 vols., New York, 1975) and Taylor Branch, *Parting the Waters: America in the King Years, 1954–1963* (New York, 1988). Among the many monographs, the author has found the following most helpful: Morton Sosna, *In Search of the Silent South: Southern Liberals and the Race Issue* (New York, 1977); Jacquelyn Dowd Hall, *Revolt Against Chivalry: Jessie Daniel Ames and the Women's Campaign Against Lynching* (New York, 1979); William H. Chafe, *Civilities and Civil Rights: Greensboro, North Carolina, and the Black Struggle for Freedom* (New York, 1980); Numan V. Bartley, *The Rise of Massive Resistance: Race and Politics in the South During the 1950s* (Baton Rouge, 1969); Jack Bass, *Unlikely Heroes* (New York, 1981); Howell Raines, *My Soul Is Rested: Movement Days in the Deep South Remembered* (New York, 1977); Adam Fairclough, *Race and Democracy: The Civil Rights Struggle in Louisiana, 1915–1972* (Athens, Ga., 1995); John Dittmer, *Local People: The Struggle for Civil Rights in Mississippi* (Urbana, 1994); Clayborne Carson, *In Struggle: SNCC and the Black Awakening of the 1960s* (Cambridge, Mass., 1981); Charles W. Eagles, *Outside Agitator: Jon Daniels and the Civil Rights Movement in Alabama* (Chapel Hill, 1993); Hugh Davis Graham, *The Civil Rights Era: Origins and Development of National Policy, 1960–1972* (New York, 1990); and Stephen J. Whitfield, *A Death in the Delta: The Story of Emmett Till* (New York, 1988). The story of the Montgomery bus boycott is best told by J. Mills Thornton, III, in "Challenge and Response in the Montgomery Boycott of 1955–1956," *Alabama Review*, 33 (July 1980), 163–235.

All discussion of southern politics begins with V. O. Key, Jr., *Southern Politics in State and Nation* (New York, 1949), and the following recent accounts test his interpretations: William C. Havard, ed., *The Changing Politics of the South* (Baton Rouge, 1972); Numan V. Bartley and Hugh D. Graham, *Southern Politics and the Second Reconstruction* (Baltimore, 1975); Jack Bass and Walter De Vries, *The Transformation of Southern Politics: Social Change and Political Consequence Since 1945* (New York, 1976); and Earl Black and Merle Black, *Politics and Society in the South* (Cambridge, Mass., 1987). See also the Blacks' *The Vital South: How Presidents Are Elected* (Cambridge, Mass., 1992), which is indispensable. Also very useful is Alexander P. Lamis, *The Two-Party South*, expanded edition (New York, 1988). Any evaluation of Jimmy Carter's presidency should include the insights of W. Carl Bliven, *Jimmy Carter's Economy: Policy in an Age of Limits* (Chapel Hill, 2002).

Two of the best state-level studies are Numan V. Bartley, *The Creation of Modern Georgia* (Athens, Ga., 1983) and Chandler Davidson, *Race and Class in Texas Politics* (Princeton, 1990); see also Davidson's earlier *Biracial Politics: Conflict and Coalition in the Metropolitan South* (Baton Rouge, 1972). Steven F. Lawson has written two books that are essential for understanding how the Voting Rights Act revolutionized black political participation; see *Black Ballots: Voting Rights in the South, 1944–1969* (New York, 1976) and *In Pursuit of Power: Southern Blacks and Electoral Politics, 1965–1982* (New York, 1985). Anyone interested in women's role in politics should see Pamela Tyler, *Silk Stockings and Ballot Boxes: Women and Politics in New Orleans, 1920–1963* (Athens, Ga., 1996). Another indispensable study is Earl Black, *Southern Governors and Civil Rights: Racial Segregation as a Campaign Issue in the Second Reconstruction* (Cambridge, Mass., 1976). For the conservative white reaction, see Neil R.

McMillen, *The Citizens' Council: Organized Resistance to the Second Reconstruction, 1954–1964* (Urbana, Ill., 1971). For the pivotal election year of 1968, the author has relied upon Lewis Chester, Godfrey Hodgson, and Bruce Page, *An American Melodrama: The Presidential Campaign of 1968* (New York, 1969).

The capitulation of the Republican party to racial politics is analyzed in Earl Black and Merle Black, *The Vital South*, previously cited, the Blacks' newest book, *The Rise of Southern Republicans* (Cambridge, 2002), and even more explicitly in Thomas Byrne Edsall and Mary D. Edsall, *Chain Reaction: The Impact of Race, Rights, and Taxes on American Politics* (New York, 1991). See also Mary Brennan, *Turning Right in the Sixties: The Conservative Capture of the GOP* (Chapel Hill, 1995) and Matthew J. Streb, *The New Electoral Politics of Race* (Tuscaloosa, 2002). The southern strategy of the Republican party was spelled out by Kevin P. Phillips, *The Emerging Republican Majority* (New Rochelle, N.Y., 1969). The essential interpretation of George Wallace is Dan T. Carter, *The Politics of Rage: George Wallace, the Origins of the New Conservatism, and the Transformation of American Politics* (New York, 1995), which focuses on Wallace's national impact. For a unique Louisiana example of racial politics, see Douglas D. Rose, *The Emergence of David Duke and the Politics of Race* (Chapel Hill, 1992). Two excellent newspaper series offer a perceptive description and analysis of the contemporary South. See the four-part series, "New South and Old," *New York Times,* July 31–August 3, 1994, and the six-part series, "In Search of the South," *Washington Post,* July 14–19, 1996. The best account of the increasing Latino influence in the South is Roberto Suro, *Strangers Among Us: How Latino Immigration Is Transforming America* (New York, 1998).

A perennial topic in southern history has been the search to define the South.

Pioneering articles whose influence has been immense include Ulrich B. Phillips, "The Central Theme of Southern History," *American Historical Review,* 34 (October 1928), 30–43; David M. Potter, "The Enigma of the South," *Yale Review,* 51 (Autumn 1961), 142–51; and George B. Tindall, "The Benighted South: Origins of a Modern Image," *Virginia Quarterly Review,* 40 (Spring 1964), 281–94. William R. Taylor, *Cavalier and Yankee: The Old South and American National Character* (New York, 1961) shows how both North and South often defined themselves in relation to the other.

C. Vann Woodward has been the most influential interpreter of the southern identity; the various essays reprinted in the most recent edition of his *The Burden of Southern History* (Baton Rouge, 1993) are required reading for anyone who wants to understand the South. See, in relation to these essays, Woodward's retrospective of his career and writing, *Thinking Back: The Perils of Writing History* (Baton Rouge, 1986). Among the books that explore the defining nature of the South are Twelve Southerners, *I'll Take My Stand: The South and the Agrarian Tradition* (New York, 1930); Louis D. Rubin, Jr., and James Jackson Kilpatrick, eds., *The Lasting South: Fourteen Southerners Look at Their Home* (Chicago, 1957); Harry S. Ashmore, *An Epitaph for Dixie* (New York, 1958); Charles Grier Sellers, Jr., ed., *The Southerner as American* (Chapel Hill, 1960); Francis Butler Simkins, *The Everlasting South* (Baton Rouge, 1963); Frank E. Vandiver, ed., *The Idea of the South* (Chicago, 1964); Howard Zinn, *The Southern Mystique* (New York, 1964); John Egerton, *The Americanization of Dixie: The Southernization of America* (New York, 1974); George Brown Tindall, *The Ethnic Southerners* (Baton Rouge, 1976); Carl N. Degler, *Place Over Time: The Continuity of Southern Distinctiveness* (Baton Rouge, 1977); Fifteen Southerners, *Why the South Will Survive* (Athens, Ga., 1981);

and John B. Boles, ed., *Dixie Dateline: A Journalistic Portrait of the Contemporary South* (Houston, 1983), particularly the introduction and the essay by Edwin M. Yoder, Jr. Richard Gray, *Writing the South: Ideas of an American Region* (Cambridge, Eng., 1986), is an interpretation of southerners' long attempt to understand and explicate their region. Peter Applebome explores the influence of the modern South on the rest of the nation in *Dixie Rising: How the South Is Shaping American Values, Politics, and Culture* (New York, 1996). The most persuasive account of the southern fascination with automobile racing is Randal L. Hall, "Before NASCAR: The Corporate and Civic Promotion of Automobile Racing in the American South, 1903–1927," *Journal of Southern History*, 68 (August 2002), 629–68.

The national media has long been fascinated with the South. The one essential study is Jack Temple Kirby, *Media-Made Dixie: The South in the American Imagination* (revised ed., Athens, Ga., 1986), but three other very useful books are Edward D. C. Campbell, Jr., *The Celluloid South: Hollywood and the Southern Myth* (Knoxville, 1981); Stephen A. Smith, *Myth, Media, and the Southern Mind* (Fayetteville, Ark., 1985); and Karl G. Heider, ed., *Images of the South: Constructing a Regional Culture on Film and Video* (Athens, Ga., 1993). In recent years, the most often quoted, and the most quotable, interpreter of the South has been the historical sociologist John Shelton Reed. His several books are necessary for anyone interested in the question of the continuity of southern distinctiveness. See *The Enduring South: Subcultural Persistence in Mass Society* (Lexington, Mass., 1972); *One South: An Ethnic Approach to Regional Culture* (Baton Rouge, 1982); *Southerners: The Social Psychology of Sectionalism* (Chapel Hill, 1983); *Southern Folk, Plain and Fancy: Native White Social Types* (Athens, Ga., 1986); and *Whistling Dixie: Dispatches from the South* (Columbia, Mo., 1990). Anyone interested in the South should also become familiar with the fiction of such literary giants as William Faulkner, Richard Wright, Eudora Welty, and Flannery O'Connor, as well as such autobiographies as those of William Alexander Percy, Anne Moody, Maya Angelou, and Will D. Campbell. The South is a topic of everlasting interest, and there is no indication that the tide of writing about it is about to subside.

Index

African-American, *see* black and blacks
Affirmative action, 594–95, 597
Agee, James, 462
Agnew, Spiro, 574, 579
Agrarians, 481–83
Agriculture
  backward, 458–59,
  change in twentieth century, 521–26
  effect of New Deal, 460–61, 465, 466
  overproduction, 459–60
  reform of, 446–47, 458
Agricultural Adjustment Act, 460–61, 465, 466
Agricultural discontent, 434
Agricultural pollutants, 516–17
Agricultural production, 523
Agricultural reform movements, 432
Air conditioning, 509–10
Alabama, 384, 397
Albany, Ga., 553
Allen, O. K., 495
Alvord, J. W., 472
Amendments, Constitutional
  Eighteenth, 447
  Fifteenth, 384, 398, 541
  Fourteenth, 381–83, 389, 398, 541
  Thirteenth, 376–77, 398–99
  Twenty-fourth, 573
Ames, Jessie Daniel, 475
Amnesty, 374, 377
American Dilemma: The Negro Problem and Modern Democracy, 542
Anderson, Joseph R., 418
"Andy Griffith Show," 511
Angelou, Maya, 606
Antisemitism, 468
Antitax sentiment, 584–85
Appalachia, 452–53
Apples, 524
Arkansas, 375, 377, 384, 397, 473
Arkansas National Guard, 549–50
Arkansas Wheel, 432
Armadillo, 513
Armstrong, Louis, 488
Art museums, 526
Asian population, 532
Askew, Reuben O., 578
Association of Southern Women for the Prevention of Lynching, 475
Astrodome, 510
Atlanta, 424, 426, 427, 501, 522, 523, 526, 528, 530–33, 551
  race riot, 469–70

Atlanta University, 428
Atomic Energy Commission, 508
Austin, Tex., 528, 531
Autry, Gene, 489–90
Aviation fuel, 505–6

Baines, Rebekah, 497
Baker, Ella, 551–52
Baker, Howard, 573
Baker v Carr, 567
Balance Agriculture with Industry Act, 504
Baltimore, 526, 531
Baptists, 566
Barnett, Ross, 553, 565
Barrow plantation, 408–9
Bassett, John Spencer, 479
Barter economy, 413, 415, 431
Baton Rouge, 517
Baylor University, 479
Baylor College of Medicine, 528
Beamont, Tex., 455
Bellamy, Edward, 430
Berea, Ky., 606
Big Thicket National Preserve, 521
Bilbo, Theodore G., 450–51
Biracialism, 605
Birmingham, 421–22, 424, 426–27, 608
  church bombing, 556
  desegregation struggle, 553–55
  freedom riders, 552
Birth of a Nation, 469–70, 486, 606
Black and blacks
  antebellum occupations, 428
  business leaders, 472
  churches, 473
  civil rights movement, 537–65
  desire for education, 410–11
  de-skilling of, 428
  disenfranchisement, 437–38, 468
  elite, 428–29
  economic advancement, 472–73
  elected officials, 392–93, 395, 501, 524, 559–60
  enfranchisement, 391–92
  folktales, 478
  Juneteenth, 602
  labor of, 411–12
  lynchings, 468–69
  middle class, 560
  military service, 401, 402–3, 473
  musical traditions, 486–88
  out-migration, 466, 470, 475–76

  professional class, 429
  Populism, 432, 435–36, 437–38
  Progressivism, 473
  Reconstruction politics, 392
  Reconstruction race relations, 405–6
  segregated South, 537–65
  self-help tradition, 471–72
  sharecroppers, 406–13
  violence against, 396
  urban transportation, 427–28
  voting, 392–93, 577
  writers, 483–84
  World War II, 507–8
"Black Monday," 543
Black codes, 375, 379–81, 389, 404–5
Blake, Eubie, 487
Blease, Coleman, 451
Blues, 487–88
Bolden, Charles "Buddy," 488
Bonnet Carré spillway, 518
Booth, John Wilkes, 376
Brady, Tom P., 545
Brann, W. C., 479
Brann's Iconoclast, 479
Bransom, Mo., 606
Brewer, Albert, 578
Britain, 402
Broadcast News, 607
Brock, W. E., 573
Broiler industry, 525; *see also* poultry industry
Brown, Charlotte Hawkins, 473
Brown, George, 506
Brown, Herman, 506
Brown v Board of Education of Topeka, 543–44, 552
Brownell, Herbert, 548–49
Brownlow, W. G., 382
Brumley, Albert E., 491
Bryan, William Jennings, 425, 436, 480–81
Bryant, Carolyn, 545–46
Bryant, Roy, 546
Buffalo, 513
Buffalo National River, 521
Bumpers, Dale, 578
Burton, Glenn W., 524
Bus, and freedom riders, 552–53
Bus boycott, Montgomery, 546–48
Bush, George H., 587–89
Bush, George W., 595–99
Bush, Jeb, 595

Butler, Benjamin F., 401–2
Butler, Rhett, 484–85

Cabell, James Branch, 483
Cable, George Washington, 478
Cable News Network, 501
Caldwell, Erskine, 460, 483, 512
Campbell, Will, 606
Camp David accords, 583
Cape Canaveral, 506, 528
Cape Hatteras National Seashore, 521
Carpetbaggers, 390–91
Carrier, Willis, 509
Carter, James Earl, 494, 500, 526, 562,
    578–80, 586, 590, 598, 605, 607
  election of 1976, 580–81
  election of 1980, 584–85
  Middle East, 583
  president, 581–83
Carter, Jimmy, *see* Carter, James Earl
Carter, Rosalynn, 579
Carter family musicians, 489
Cash economy, 415
Cash, Wilbur J., 476, 605
Casinos, 529–30
Catholics, 473
Cattle egret, 514–15
Cattle industry, 524–25
Central High School, 549–50
Chain gangs, 470
Chaney, James, 556
Charleston, 505, 508, 529, 567, 608
Charlotte, 502, 522, 532, 551
Cheney, Richard, 595
Chicago, 575–76
Cholera, 426
Chopin, Kate, 478
Cities, 423–28, 526–27, 530–32; *see also*
    urban and urbanization
Citrus crops, 465, 524
Civilian Conservation Corps, 465
Civil Rights Act of 1866, 380–81
Civil Rights Act of 1875, 539
Civil Rights Act of 1957, 548–49, 566
Civil Rights Acts of 1964, 521, 544,
    558–59, 568–69, 607
Civil rights movement, 537–65, 609
  cold war, 542, 545, 564
  heritage travel, 608
  Lyndon B. Johnson, 544
Civil War destruction, 386
Clansman, 392, 469
Clark, Jim, 558
Clark, Kenneth, 543
Cleveland, Grover B., 435–36
Clinton, Bill. *See* William J. Clinton
Clinton, William J., 500, 578, 589, 605
  election of 1992, 590
  election of 1996, 592
  impeachment trial, 594
  incremental reformer, 593–94
  Lewinski scandal, 594–95
  political progressivism, 591, 598
  political skills, 591–93, 595
  presidential administration, 591–95
  southern racism, 602
"Closed society" of Mississippi, 545
Clubs, black, 429
Coal, 452–53
Coastal Bermuda grass, 524
Coca-Cola, 533, 535

Cockroach, 512
Cold War, 508, 529, 542, 544–45,
    564–65, 568
Colleges and universities, 428, 506–7,
    527–28
Colored National Farmers' Alliance,
    432
Columbus, Ga., 508
Comer, Braxton B., 449
Command of the Army Act, 383
Committee on Civil Rights (1946), 542
Committee on Civil Rights (1957), 563
Communism, 545
"Compassionate conservatism," 595
Compaq Computer, 528
Confederate disfranchisement,
    376–77, 382–83, 395–96
Confederate flag, 605
Confiscation Act, 401–2
Congress of Racial Equality, 552
Congressional Reconstruction, 382–85
Connor, Eugene "Bull," 554–55, 568
Conservation, 595
Contraband (slaves as), 400–401
"Contract with America," 592
Corps of Engineers, 518, 520
Corruption, 392–93, 395, 420
Corsicana, Tex., 455
Cotton, 406, 411, 415–17, 424, 457,
    459, 465–66, 522
Cotton mills, 452
Couch, W. T., 482–83
Council of Federated Organizations,
    556, 575
Country music, 488–90, 604
Country stores, 411–12, 415
Convict leasing, 470
Cowley, Malcolm, 483
Crape myrtle, 515
"Creative cities," 532
Creoles, 478
Credit, 407–8, 410–13
Crittenden Resolution, 373–74, 401
Crop lien, 412
Crop limitation, 460–61, 476
Crop rotation, 462
Cullinan, J. S., 455
Culture, biracial, 605
Curfews (of freedpersons), 470

Dairy industry, 458–59
Daley, Richard, 575
Dallas, 424, 522, 526, 528, 531–32, 551,
    556, 567
Darrow, Clarence, 480
Davidson, Donald, 481
Davies, Ronald, 549, 550
Davis, Henry Winter, 375
Davis, Jeff (of Ark.), 451
Davis, Jefferson, 404
Davis, John W., 543
Davis, Joseph, 404
Dawson, Francis W., 422
Dayton, Tenn., 479–81
DDT, 517–18
De Bardeleben, Henry, 427
De Bow, J. D. B., 419
Debt, Confederate, 374, 376
Dell Computer, 528
Delta Airlines, 523, 533

Demagogues, southern, 450–51,
    493–94
Democratic convention of 1972,
    575–76
Democratic Party:
  Dixiecrat bolters, 563
  election of 1876, 398
  moderates in, 578, 590–91
  Populists, 434–38
  reform, 448–49
  segregation, 562–65
  southern and New Deal, 563–64
Democratic primary, 445
Dent, Harry S., 571–72
Department of Agriculture, 458
Desegregation, 521, 537–65
  Brown decision, 543–44
Dewey, Thomas, 542, 564
Dirksen, Everett, 568
Discontent, farmer, 431
Disfranchisement, of blacks, 437–38,
    444–45
Disfranchisement, of whites, 382,
    444–45
Dismal Swamp, 512, 516
DisneyWorld, 529
Dissenter movements, 430
Dixiecrats, 542, 563–64, 589
Dixieland jazz, 488
Dixon, Thomas W., 392
Dixon, Thomas W. Jr., 469
Dole, Robert, 593
Dorsey, Thomas A., 491
Drought, of 1929–30, 460, 465
Du Bois, William E. B., 472–73
Dukakis, Michael, 587–88, 590
Duke, David, 562, 588–89, 600
"Dukes of Hazzard," 606
Duke University, 527, 528

Eads, James Buchanan, 520
Eastland, James, 556
Eastland, John, 565
Eaton, Clement, 599
Eaton, John, Jr., 403
Eckford, Elizabeth, 549–50
Ecological change, 512–21
Economic growth, in southern
    agriculture, 521–26
Edmonds, Richard H., 422
Education, 410–11, 447
"Egg money," 525–26
Eighteenth amendment, 447
Eisenhower, Dwight D., 509, 570
  Brown decision, 544
  civil rights, 542
  Civil Rights Act of 1957, 548–49
  election, 542, 548–49, 565–65
  Little Rock crisis, 549–50, 566
Elected officials, black, 501–2,
    559–60, 574
Election dispute (1876), 398–99
Election dispute (2000), 595–96
Election fraud (1896), 437, 596
Election of 1896, 436–37
Election of 1960, 566–67
Election of 1968, 570–72
Election of 1972, 576
Election of 1980, 584–85
Election of 1984, 585–86
Election of 1988, 587–88

Election of 1992, 589–90
Election of 1996, 593
Election of 2000, 595–96
Electricity, on farms, 511
El Paso, 531
Emancipation, 386, 388, 399, 401–3, 406, 439–40
Emancipation Proclamation, 371, 373–74, 399, 402
Emerging Republican Majority, 574
Emory University, 527
Enforcement Acts (1870–71), 396
Environmental change, 512–21
Equal Employment Opportunity Commission, 559
Equal Rights Amendment, 607
Ervin, Sam, 548
Ethnic diversity, 533, 601
Evans, Walker, 462
Everglades, 516
Evers, Medgar, 555, 568
Extractive industry, 457

Fair Employment Practice Committee, 541
Fairhope, 430–31
Farmers, economic distress of, 431–32, 446
    protests, 431–32, 434
    small, 458
    white, lose land, 416–17
    women, 441–42, 525
Farmers' Alliance, 432
Farm-to-market roads, 465
Farms, 458, 459, 521–26
Faubus, Orval, 549–50, 565
Faulkner, William, 483–84, 486, 605–6
Federal Emergency Relief Administration, 461, 465
Federal Highway Act, 463
Felton, Rebecca Latimer, 469
Fertilizer, 459
Fifteenth amendment, 384, 398, 541
Fire ants, 513
Fisk University, 428
Fitzgerald, Robert G., 405, 411
Flood, Mississippi River (1927), 465
Flood control, 518–19
Florida, and disputed election of 1876, 398–99
    Reconstruction, 384, 397
    2000 election scandal, 595–96
Folktales, 478
Football, 604
Foreign investment, 530
Ford, Gerald, 579–81
Force Bill, 435
Fort Hood, 508
Fort Monroe, 400
Fort Pillow, 402–3
Fort Worth, 505, 508, 526, 531
Fourteenth amendment, 381–83, 389, 398, 541
Frank, Leo, 468
Franklin, John Hope, 602
Fraternal organizations, black, 429
Freedmen's Bureau, 380–81, 404–5, 407, 423, 472
Freedpeople, 371, 404
    autonomy of, 399–400
    cash wages, 406–7
    education, 410–11

enfranchised, 383
    farm laborers, 419–20
    labor contracts, 406–7
    marriage of, 405
    Reconstruction, during, 399–406
    restrictions against, 379–80
    rights of, 375, 407
    under Fourteenth amendment, 381
Freedom riders, 552–53
Frémont, John C., 401
"French fries," 535
Fugitive, The, 481
Fugitives (literary movement), 481–82
Fundamentalism, Christian, 480–81
Furnishing merchant, 415
Fusion, among Populists, 437

Gaines, Lloyd Lionel, 475, 539
Galveston, grade raising, 519
    hurricane of 1900, 444, 456, 519
    women, 444
Gambling industry, 529–30
Gandhi, Mohandas K., 548
Gaston, Ernest B., 430
George, Henry, 430
Georgia, 384, 397
Gershwin, George, 488
Ghettoes, urban black, 560
G. I. Bill, 507
Gilley, Mickey, 491
Gingrich, Newt, 592, 595, 601
Glasgow, Ellen, 483
Goldwater, Barry, 568–70, 572, 584, 589
Gold standard, 436
Goo goo clusters, 604
Good Roads Movement, 463, 465
Goodman, Andrew, 556
Gone With the Wind, 392, 484–85, 606
Gorbachev, Mikhail, 585
Gordon, Caroline, 482
Gore, Albert, Jr., 500, 589, 591, 595–96, 605
Gore, Albert, Sr., 548
Government expenditures, 394
Graceland, 491
Grady, Henry W., 422–23, 485, 526
Graham, Frank, 564
Grand Old Opry, 489, 605–6
Grand Old Party (GOP), 385
Grandfather clause, 444
Grange, 430, 434, 442
Grant, Ulysses S., 383, 385, 396–97, 403
Grapes of Wrath, 466
Great Dismal Swamp, 516, 520
Great Smoky Mountains, 520
Great Society, 568–69
Green, Ernest, 550
Greenbackism, 430, 434
Greensboro, NC, 551
Gregg, William, 418–19
Grovey v. Townsend, 541
Griffith, Andy, 607

Haggard, Merle, 536
Haley, Alex, 608
Halleck, Henry W., 401
Hamburgers, 535
Hamer, Fannie Lou, 575
Hampton Institute, 428, 471
Handy, William C., 487
Harlan County, Ky., 453
Harris, Joel Chandler, 422, 478

Hayes, Rutherford B., 397–98
Heat of the Night, 606–7
Head Start, 569
Helms, Jesse, 564, 573, 597
Heritage travel, 529
Herty, Charles H., 454
Hessian fly, 512
Hickory trees, 516
Higgins, Andrew Jackson, 506
High culture, in southern cities, 526
High-tech industry, 528
Higher education, 527–28;
    desegregation of, 539–40, 559
Hispanics, growth of, 532
Hogg, James S., 438
Holiday Inns, 533
Hookworm, 447
Hope, John, 473
Hope, Lugenia, 473
Hose, Sam, 468–69
Hostages, US, in Iran, 581, 583
Houston, Charles Hamilton, 539–40
Houston, Tex., 424, 426, 456, 498, 501, 505, 510, 515, 517, 519, 522, 526, 528, 530, 532–33, 551, 566–67, 601
Howard University, 428
Humphrey, Hubert, 542, 563, 569, 571–72, 575–76
Hunt, James B., 578
Hunter, David, 401–2
Hunter, Holly, 607
Hurt, John, 487
Hurston, Zora Neale, 483–84, 606
Hyde, Henry, 595
Hydrilla, 515

Identity, search for southern, 599–609
I'll Take My Stand, 482
Immigration, 533, 600–601
Impeachment, and Andrew Johnson, 384–85
    Richard Nixon, 579
    William J. Clinton, 594–95
Industry, 421–22, 424–25, 451–56, 457
    boom in twentieth century, 504–9, 529–30
    Civil War, during, 419
    extractive, 452
    lumber, 453–55
    Old South, 418
Intercoastal waterway, 520
Investment, sought by South, 504
Iran, hostages in, 581, 583
Iran-Contra scandal, 586
Iraq, policies toward, 597

Jacksonville, Fla., 522
Jazz, 488
Jeffords, James M., 596
Jefferson, Blind Lemon, 487
Jefferson, Thomas, 431, 599
Job discrimination, 540–41
Johnson, Andrew, 371, 387, 419
    impeachment, 384–85
    Reconstruction, 376–85
    Whig party, 390
Johnson, James, 549
Johnson, Lyndon B. 465, 494, 496, 497–500, 503, 506, 526, 575
    civil rights, 544, 556, 566–67
    Civil Rights Act (1957), 549
    Civil Rights Act (1964), 556–59

congressman, 498–99
election of 1960, 566–67
election of 1964, 569–70
National Youth Administration, 499
president, 556, 568, 570
senator, 499–500
southern manifesto, 548
Johnson, Sam, 497
Johnson Space Center, 506, 528
Johnsonian Reconstruction, 376–82
Joint Committee of Fifteen, 380–81
Joplin, Scott, 486–87
Jordan, Barbara, 577, 605
Jordan, Hamilton, 580
Journal of Social Forces, 482
Juneteenth, 602

Kansas, Populists in, 434
Katzenbach, Nicholas, 555
Kefauver, Estes, 548, 564
Kennedy, Edward M., 583
Kennedy, John F.,
   assassination, 556, 568
   Catholicism, 566
   civil rights, 552–53, 555–56
   election of 1960, 566–67
Kennedy, Robert F., 552–53, 568,
   570–71
Kennedy Space Center, 528
"Kentucky Fried Chicken," 533–34
Khomeni, Ayatollah, 583
Killer bees, 515
Kilpatrick, James J., 545
King, Coretta Scott, 567
King, Martin Luther, Jr., 500, 521, 526,
   554, 567, 580, 605, 608
   Albany, Ga., 553
   assassination, 570
   Birmingham, 553–55
   emerges as leader, 547–48
   March on Washington, 555–56
   Montgomery, 548
   Nobel Peace Prize, 558
   non-violent strategy, 548
   Selma, 558
King, Martin Luther, Sr., 581
Kleburg, Richard, 498
Knapp, Seaman H., 458
Knights of Labor, 430
Knights of the White Camellia, 396
Krispy Kreme doughnuts, 604
Kudzu, 514
Ku Klux Klan, 396, 473, 544, 552, 557,
   584, 588–89, 605
Kurth, Ernest, 454

Labor, in textile mills, 420
Labor movements, 430
Labor unions, 529
Land-grant universities, 458
Lee, Harper, 606
Lee, Robert E., 419
Legal Defense Fund (NAACP), 542–43
Leopard's Spots, 469
"Letter from a Birmingham Jail," 554
Levees, and Mississippi River, 518
Lewinski, Monica, 594
Lewis, Jerry Lee, 491
Lieberman, Joseph, 595
Literature, southern, 477–85
Lincoln, Abraham, 387
   assassination, 371
   emancipation, 401

freedpeople, 402
Reconstruction, 371–76, 78
war aims, 373–74
Whig Party, 390
Liquefied petroleum gas, 510–11
Little Rock, 549–50, 565–66
Livestock, 458–59, 462, 524–25,
Livestock epidemics, 387
Livingston, Bob, 595
Local color fiction, 478
Long, Huey, 460, 494–96
Longism, in Louisiana politics, 495–96
Longstreet, James G., 390
Lost Cause movement, 441
Lott, Trent, 597
Louisiana
   black elected officials, 395
   Huey P. Long, 494–96
   lumber industry, 453–54
   oil industry, 456
   Reconstruction, 374–75, 377, 384,
      397
Louisiana Farmers' Union, 432
"Louisiana Hayride," 489
Lousiana-Texas lumber war, 453
Low-wage economy, 503–4, 528–29
Lucas, A. F., 455
Lucy, Autherine, 548
Lumber industry, 453–55
Lynching, 468–69, 475
Lytle, Andrew, 481

Macune, Charles, 432–33, 435
Maddox, Lester G., 580
Mahone, William, 430
Malaria, 517–18
Manned Space Center, 506
Manufacturer's Record, 422
Manufacturing, 424
   Civil War, 419
   Old South, 418–19
"March on Washington," 555–56
Mardi Gras, 491
Marietta, Ga., 505, 508
Marriage, in Civil War, 387
Marshall, Thurgood, 475, 539–40, 543
Marshall Flight Center, 528
McCarthy, Eugene, 570–71
McCullers, Carson, 606
McGovern, George, 573, 576
McKinley, William, 436
McLaurin, George W., 540
McLendon, Gordon, 535
Mechanical cotton picker, 466
Medicare, 569
Meharry Medical College, 428
Melanie (Hamilton), 484–85
Memphis, 381, 426, 522, 531
Mencken, H. L., 480–83, 491, 501, 512,
   526, 532
Merrick, John, 473
Meredith, James, 553
Metropolitan areas, 532
Miami, 531–32
Michoud plant, 506
Migration, 390–91, 470, 475–76
Milam, J. W., 546
Military, and black servicemen, 473
Military construction, 505–6
Military governors, 374
Military Reconstruction Act, 383–84, 389
Mill workers, 452

Miller, William E., 569
Mims, Edwin, 485
Mind of the South, 476
Mississippi, elected black officials, 395
   political demagogues, 450–51
   Reconstruction, 384, 397
   recruitment of industry, 504
Mississippi Freedom Democratic Party,
   575
Mississippi River, levees, 518
Mississippi State Sovereignty
   Commission, 545
Mitchell, Margaret, 484–86
Mobile, Ala., 513
Mobile homes, 511
Moderate Republicans
   (in Reconstruction era), 375
Mondale, Walter, 586
Montague, Andrew J., 449
Montgomery, bombings, 548
   bus boycott, 521, 546–48
   freedom riders, 552–53
Moody, Anne, 606
Moon pies, 604
Moses, Bob, 556
Movies, and South, 469–70, 486, 606–7
Mules, 461
Murray, Donald Gaines, 475, 539
Music, 441–42
   blues, 487–88
   country/country western, 488–90
   gospel, 490–91
   hillbilly, 488–90
   honky tonk, 489
   impact of radion 488–90
   jazz, 488–89
   ragtime, 486–87
   recordings, 488–89
   southern, 486–91, 605–6
   western swing, 489
Muskie, Edmund, 571, 576
Myrdal, Gunnar, 542

NASCAR, 535–36
Nashville, Tenn., 424, 531, 567
Natchez, 608
National Academy of Engineering, 527
National Academy of Sciences, 527
National Aeronautics and Space
   Administration, 506
National Association for the
   Advancement of Color People,
   470, 475, 508, 537–43, 547, 549,
   552, 555
National culture, 536
National Economist, 433
National Endowment for the
   Humanities, 569
National Farmers' Alliance, 432
National Negro Business League, 473
National parks, 520
National Youth Administration, 465,
   499
Native Son, 484
Neighborhood League, 473
Neshoba, Miss., 556–57, 584
New Criticism (literary movement),
   481
New Deal, 457–66, 503, 562–63
New Orleans, 423–24, 426, 491, 502, 505,
   517, 522, 529–32, 567, 601, 608
   anti-desegregation riot, 551

New Orleans *(cont.)*
  jazz, 488
  pumping stations, 519
  race riot (1866), 382
  race riot (1900), 470
  World War II industry, 506
New South movement, 418–23, 446
New York Times, 533–34
Newport News, Va., 505
Noblesse oblige, and reform, 449
Norfolk, Va., 381
North, southernization of, 536
North Carolina, 374, 384, 393, 397
North Carolina A & T College, 551
North Carolina Farmers' Alliance, 432
North Carolina State University, 522, 528
Nixon, E. D., 547
Nixon, H.C., 481
Nixon, Richard, 566, 570–77, 579
Nutria, 514

Oak Ridge, 508
Oak trees, 516
O'Connor, Flannery, 606
Odom, Howard W., 482, 485
O'Hara, Scarlett, 421, 484–85
Oil, 455–57
"Okies," 466
Oklahoma City, 592–93
Oklahoma race riots, 473
Oliver, Joseph "King," 488
Olympics (1996), 533
Open Housing Act (1964), 570
Oswald, Lee Harvey, 568
Owens, William A., 606
Owsley, Frank L., 481

Page, Thomas Nelson, 478
Page, Walter Hines, 467, 476, 478–79, 492
Parks, Rosa, 547, 558
Parker, John M., 451
Parris Island, 505
Pascagoula, 505
Passenger pigeons, 513
Patterson, John, 552, 565
Patterson, Robert B., 544
Peaches, 524
Peanut, 512
Pease, Elisha Marshall, 378
Pellagra, 447
Pentagon, 597
Pentecostalism, 431
People's Party, 435–36
Pepper, Claude, 564
Per capita income, 527
Percy, William Alexander, 450, 606
Perot, Ross, 590, 593
Personal income, and WWII, 508
Petrochemical industry, 505–6, 509, 517, 530
Phagan, Mary, 468
Philadelphia, Miss., 556–57
Phillips, Kevin, 526, 574
Phillips, Ulrich B., 477, 599, 600
Piggly Wiggly, 533
Pinchback, P. B. S., 392
Pipelines, 456, 506
Plains, Ga., 579
Plant relocations, 530
Planter capitalists, 420–21
Plessy, Homer, 539

Plessy v. Ferguson, 539, 543
Poe, Clarence H., 458
Poinsett, John Robert, 515
Poinsettia, 515
Polk, Leonidas L., 432, 435
Political conservatism, 587–88
Political leaders, in Reconstruction, 388
Politicians, and national influence, 492
Politics, 492–509
  crippled by racism, 492–93
  freedmen, 392–93
  modern, 497–500
  provincial nature of, 492–93
  women, 442
Poll tax, 444
Pollution, environmental, 516–18
Populism, 429–38, 448, 467
  crushed, 437–38
  disenfranchisement, 445
  political fusion, 437
  origins of Progressivism, 445–46
  reform policies, 433–34
  women, 442
Portman, John, 522
Ports, dredging of, 520
Poultry, 458, 465, 525–26
Poverty, rural, 466–67
  sharecroppers, 420
  southern, 457–58, 493
Presley, Elvis, 490–91, 511
Prince Edward County, Va., 550
Pritchett, Laurie, 553
Proclamation of Amnesty and
  Reconciliation, 374, 377
Producerism, 431, 434
Progressive Farmer, 432, 458, 525
Progressivism, 444–51
  blacks, 473
  boards and commissions, 449
  leaders of, 449
  origins of, 446, 448
  Prohibition, 447–48
  regulatory legislation, 449
  styles of political leadership, 449–50
  women, 443
Prohibition, 447–48
Project C, 554
Pryor, David, 578
Public schools, 394
Pulp wood, 454–55
Purebred cattle, 524–25

Race, and politics, 492–93, 566–77, 589
Race, and religion, 601–2
Race card, 467
Race relations, 466–76
Race riots, 470, 473
Racism, 467
  central theme of southern history, 600
  Great Depression, 475
  lynching, 469
  political reform, 435–36, 450–51
  Reconstruction, 388
  rise of Republican party, 572
  southern economy, 503
  virulent, 469
Radical Reconstruction, *see*
  Congressional Reconstruction
Radical Republicans, 375, 380, 382, 384–85

Radical right, 565
  rise of Republican party, 569, 571
  Ronald Reagan, 584–85
Radio, and southern music, 488–90
Ragtime, 486–87
Railroads, 415, 420–21, 425–27, 431, 446
Raleigh-Durham, 532
Randolph, A. Philip, 540–41, 555
Ransom, John Crowe, 481
Rape hysteria, 467–69
Rawlings, Marjorie Kinnan, 483
Rayburn, Sam, 499, 548, 563
Rayner, John B., 535–36
Readjusters, 430
Reagan, Ronald
  Cold War, 585
  conservative politics, 584–85
  economic policies, 586
  election of 1980, 584–85
  election of 1984, 585–86
  Iran-Contra scandal, 586
  political background, 583–84
  race card, 584–85
  religious right, 586
  rolls back regulation, 585
Reconstruction, 371–417
  alleged corruption, 393–96
  Congressional, 380–85
  ends, 396–98
  Lincolnian, 373–76
  economic problems, 386
  racist depiction of, 469–70
  white anger, 388–89
Red Shirts, 396
Reed, John Shelton, 602–3
Refugees, black, 403
Regionalism, as movement, 482–83
Religion, 442, 444, 448, 480, 529
Religious right, 581, 586
Renascence, southern, 483–84
Republican party, 390–91, 420
  conservative agenda, 567
  election of 1876, 398
  growth in South, 567–68
  Populists, 434–38
  pursues Clinton scandals, 594–95
  race, 566–77
  racist appeal, 569–70, 572–73, 584–85, 587, 589–90
  radical conservatism, 592, 596–97
  radical right, 565
  shuts down government, 593
  social conservatism, 587
  taxation, 395
  white racial protest, 570
Research Triangle Park, 528
Resettlement Administration, 461
Resort industry, 529–30
Rice, 457, 465–66, 516, 527
Rice University, 559
Richmond, 532, 608
Right-wing extremists, 492–93
Riots (1969s), 570
River and Harbor Act of 1909, 520
Robinson, Jo Ann, 547
Rockefeller, Nelson, 572
Rodgers, Jimmie, 489
Roosevelt, Eleanor, 475, 540
Roosevelt, Franklin Delano, 457, 460, 475, 495–96, 499, 503, 540, 562, 568

Roots, 608
Rural Electrification Administration, 463, 500
Rural Free Delivery, 463, 500
Rural poverty, 493
Russell, Richard B., 564
Rustin, Bayard, 555

"Sahara of the Bozart," 481, 483, 491, 526
"St. Louis Blues," 487
Sale, Kirkpatrick, 526
San Antonio, 424, 508, 522, 529, 531
Sanders, Carl, 580
Sanders, Clarence, 533
Sanders, Colonel Harland, 533
Savannah, 508, 529, 608
Saxton, Rufus, 402
"Scalawags," 389–90
Schwerner, Michael, 480–81, 483
Seawall, in Galveston, 519
Segregation, 429, 470, 537–65
    attacked by Booker T. Washington, 472
    attacked by NAACP, 475
    jobs, 428
    origins of urban, 427–28
    racial etiquette of, 538–39
    South resegregating, 560–61
    sports, 538
Segregation academies, 550–51
Segregationists, militant, 544–45
Self-analysis, weak tradition in South, 477
Self-sufficiency, 413, 415
Selma, Ala., 558
Selma to Montgomery march, 558
Selznick, David O., 484–85
Sewall, Arthur, 436
Sewanee Review, 479
Seymour, Horatio, 385
Sharecroppers, 458, 461, 493, 501
    black, 406–13
    family choices about labor, 410–11
    freedwomen, 440
    furnishing merchants, 411–12
    poverty of, 429
    white, 413–17
Shenandoah National Parkway, 520
Sherman, Thomas W., 401
Sherman, William Tecumseh, 387, 423
Shuttlesworth, Fred, 548, 552, 554
Silver, monetization, 434, 436
Simmons, Funifold, 468
Simms, William Gilmore, 479
Single tax movement, 430–31
Sit-ins, 551
Sixteenth Street Baptist Church, 556
Slave, contraband, 400–401
Slaves
    escape to Union army, 388–89
    "faithful," 400
    marry after emancipation, 405
    massacred, 402
Slave trade, international, 402
Smith v. Allwright, 475, 541
Smith, Bessie, 487
Smith, Hoke, 449
Smith, Howard W., 607
Smith, Lonnie, 541
Smith, Mamie, 487
Smokey Mountains, Great, 520

Social conservatism, and Republican party, 587
Social Gospel, 446, 477
Soil Conservation Service, 462–63, 503
Soil Erosion Service, 462
Soldiers, in World War II, 506–8
Solid Republican South, 576
Solid South, 598
Sons of the Confederacy, 608
Souls of Black Folk, 472
Sounder, 607
South
    agricultural advantages, 418
    Americanization of, 536
    Civil War devastation, 386–87, 394
    distinctive region, 536
    electricity, result of availability of, 463
    environmental changes, 512–21
    high culture, 491
    impact of technology, 509–12
    literature of, 477–85, 606–7
    low-wage industry, 528–29
    military construction, WWII, 505–6
    movie depictions, 486, 606–7
    music of, 486–91, 605–6
    presidential politics, 586–87
    recruitment of industry, 504
    so-called intellectual aridity, 481
    soldiers in WWII, 506–7
    urban growth, 423–29
    World War II, impact of, 503–9
South Atlantic Quarterly, 479
South Carolina, 374, 384, 395, 397
Southern Alliance, 432–34, 442
Southern Baptist Convention, 601–2
Southern Christian Leadership Committee, 548, 551, 554–55
Southern Farmer's Alliance, *see* Southern Alliance
Southern identity, 602–9
Southern Manifesto, 548, 566
Southern Renascence, 483–84
Southern strategy, of Richard M. Nixon, 571–73, 576
Southland Paper Mill, 454
Southwestern Medical School, 528
Space program, 501
Spindletop gusher, 455–56
Sports, and segregation, 538
Stanton, Edwin M., 383–84
Starr, Kenneth, 594
States' Rights party, *see* Dixiecrats
Steel, 427
Stephens, Alexander H., 379
Stevens, Thaddeus, 404
Stevenson, Adlai, 564–65
St. Louis, 526
Stock-car racing, 535–36, 604
Stores, segregated, 538
Student Nonviolent Coordinating Committee, 552
Subtreasury system, 433
Suez Canal, 416
Sun Belt, 526–36
Sun Belt politics, 567
Supreme Court
    desegregation, 475, 539–41, 543–44, 548, 552, 565, 567
    election of 2000, 596
Sweatt, Heman, 540
Synthetic rubber, 505

"Talented tenth," 472
Talmadge, Herman, 565
Tampa, 532, 551
Tate, Allen, 481
Tax policies, 504, 529
Taxation, 394–95, 413, 415
Technology, impact on South, 509–12
Telephones, 426–27
Television, 511–12
10 percent plan, 377
Tennessee
    Andrew Johnson, 377
    Fourteenth amendment, 382
    race riots, 473
    Reconstruction, 374–75, 377
Tennessee Valley Authority, 463–64, 503, 508
Tenure of Office Act, 383, 384
Terrorism, against US, 597
    Reconstruction era, 396–97
Texas, black elected officials, 393
    high-tech industry, 528
    lumber industry, 454
    Juneteenth, 602
    Lyndon B. Johnson, 497–99
    oil industry, 455–56
    race riots, 473
    Reconstruction, 378, 384, 397
Texas Farmers' Alliance, 432
Texas Instruments, 528
Texas Medical Center, 528
Tex-Mex music, 489
Textile mills, 420, 451–52
Third World, 529
Thirteenth amendment, 376-77, 398-99
Thoreau, Henry David, 548
Thurmond, Strom, 556, 559, 563–65, 569, 589, 597
Tick fever, 524
Tilden, Samuel J., 397–98
Till, Emmett, 545–46, 548
Tillman, Ben, 451
Title VII, of Civil Rights Act of 1964, 559
TNT, 505
Tobacco, 457, 459, 465, 522–23
Tobacco Road, 460, 526, 537
Tobacco trust, 446
To Kill a Mockingbird, 607
"Top 40" format, 535
To Secure These Rights, 542
Tourism heritage, 608
Tourist industry, 529–30
Tower, John, 571
Transportation, and blacks, 427–28
Tree Army, 465
Treemonisha, 486–87
Trent, William P., 479
Truck crops, 465, 523–24
Truman, Harry S, 541–42, 563–64
Turner, Harry M., 393
Tuskegee Institute, 471
Tweed ring, 394
Twenty-fourth amendment, 533

Up From Slavery, 472
Uncle Remus, 422, 478
Underclass, black, 560
Union, position of South within, 375
Union, Andrew Johnson's concept of, 377
Unionism, 378

Unionists, 389
Unions, labor, 453
United Daughters of the Confederacy, 608
U. S. Army, desegregation of, 542
Universities, 506–7, 527–28
University of Alabama at Birmingham, 528
University of Alabama, 548
University of Maryland, 475, 539
University of Mississippi, 553
University of Missouri, 475, 539
University of North Carolina, 482, 527, 528
University of Oklahoma, 540
University of Texas, 527, 528, 540
University of Virginia, 527, 528
Urban infrastructure, 530
Urban population growth, 531–32
Urban riots, 570
Urbanization, 423–29, 522, 600; *see also* cities
Utopian movements, 431

V-12 programs, 507
Vance, Rupert B., 482
Vanderbilt University, 481–82, 527, 528
Vagrancy laws, 379
Vardaman, James K., 450–51
Vegetables, 523–24
Vicksburg, 608
Vinson, Carl, 499
Vinson, Fred M., 542–43
Violence, 392, 396, 420
Virginia, 377, 384, 397, 430
Vote, counting scandal in Florida (2000), 596
Voting Rights Act (1965), 521, 543–44, 559, 570, 573

Wade, Benjamin F., 375
Wade-Davis bill, 375–76
Wage laborers, 411
Wallace, George, 555, 558–59, 568, 576, 600

assassination attempt on, 574
campaign for president, 1964, 569
election of 1968, 574
election of 1972, 574
election of 1976, 580
Nixon, 572
politics of race, 570–71, 572, 574, 576
Wal-Mart, 533
Walton, Sam, 533
"Waltons, The," 511, 607
Warmouth, Henry C., 392
Warren, Earl, 542–43, 565
Warren, Robert Penn, 481, 606
Washington, Booker T., 471–72
Washington, D. C., 531
Watergate, 579–80
Watson, Thomas E., 436–37, 451, 468
Watt, James, 585
Watterson, Henry, 422
Waxahachie, Tex., 425
Weaver, James B., 435
Weiss, Carl Austin, 496
Welty, Eudora, 606
West, John C., 578
Wetlands, 516
Whig party, 374, 378, 389–90
White Citizen's Council, 544, 579
White farmers, loss of land, 413
White, Hugh L., 504
White primary, 444–45, 448–49, 541
White southerners, and Reconstruction, 378–80
White, Walter, 475
Why Not the Best? 500
Wilkes, Ashley, 484–85
Williamsburg, Colonial, 529, 608
Wills, Bob, 489
Wilmington race riot, 470
Wilson, Augusta Evans, 478
Wilson, Woodrow, 448, 451, 456, 470, 492, 500
Wisteria, 515
Wolfe, Thomas, 483–84, 606

Woman's Christian Temperance Union (WCTU), 442–44
Women, black
  civic leadership, 473
  politics, 447
  reform, 448
  sharecropping, 440
Women, white
  cities, 442
  civic leadership, 442–44
  clubs, 443
  egg money, 525–26
  emancipation, 439–40
  farm, 441–42, 458, 525
  gas stoves, 510–11
  glorified by males, 440–41
  politics, 442
  post–Civil War occupations, 440
  post–Civil War poverty, 440–41
  post–Civil War South, 439–44
  Prohibition, 448
  Progressive reform, 442–44
  Reconstruction, 387
  religion, 442
  separate culture, 441–42
Women's rights, 607–8
Wood, Albert Baldwin, 519
Woodward, C. Vann, 603–4, 608–9
Workers, biracial, 453
Works Progress Administration, 465, 501
World Trade Center, 597
World War I, 510
World War II, 475, 503–10, 527
Wormley House, 398
Wright, Fielding, 563
Wright, Mose, 546
Wright, Richard, 484, 606
Writers, black, 483–84

Yellow fever, 426
"Yoknapatawpha," 483
Yoder, Edwin M., Jr., 605
Young, Andrew, 526, 577, 605
Young, Stark, 483